The Culture of Literacy

The Culture of Literacy

Wlad Godzich

Harvard University Press
Cambridge, Massachusetts
London, England
1994

Library of Congress Cataloging-in-Publication Data
Godzich, Wlad.
    The culture of literacy / Wlad Godzich.
        p.   cm.
    Includes index.
    ISBN 0-674-17954-4 (alk. paper). — ISBN 0-674-17955-2 (pbk.: alk. paper)
    1. Criticism. 2. Literature—Philosophy. 3. Literacy. I. Title
PN85.G58 1994
801'.95—dc20
93-5810
    CIP

To Myrna
who is honor,
good memory and faith in life,
trust in love and friendship

Contents

The Culture of Literacy

Introduction: Literacy and the Struggle for Theory

The nineteen-eighties were a confusing and quarrelsome decade in American culture and literary criticism. On the one hand, they witnessed the spread of theory from its earlier beachheads in departments of French and Comparative Literature to English, where its arrival, and the controversies that ensued, caused the breakup of the hegemony enjoyed for so long by the New Criticism. On the other hand, the economic recession of the seventies and the period of high inflation that concluded that decade pushed many students, and even more university administrators, toward what became known then as the "New Vocationalism," a utilitarian conception of the university which foreshadowed its current transformation into a production site for the new force of production in postindustrial society: knowledge. The first phenomenon certainly seemed to take precedence; it occupied the pages of many learned journals and even spilled over into the editorial pages of the *Wall Street Journal* and other publications not known for their attention to literary matters. The second, less overt, ran deeper. Fed by the concern over declining scores on national tests such as the SATs and the GREs, it was interpreted as a crisis of literacy that would weaken American competitiveness in an increasingly demanding world economic environment, and it set into motion the ongoing process of redistribution of money and personnel away from the teaching of literature and criticism and toward the teaching of writing and composition.

The two phenomena unfolded in curious ignorance of each other, though sometimes in tacit alliance against the "traditionalist" teaching of literature. For the most part, though, they ignored each other, not least because they occupied different habitats: theory, the elite research institutions which continued to recruit their students from milieux for the most part unaffected by the new illiteracy; composition, the rest, including the large land-grant universities. This division was itself an important development of the eighties: it marked the reversal of the direction taken by higher education in the United States in the sixties toward greater democratization. That this reversal coincided with the coming to power in Washington of an administration ideologically committed to restoring the *status quo ante* the sixties is not a coincidence, and both the tenor and the style of what has since been termed our "cultural wars" have been very much determined by the confrontational stance adopted by this administration on cultural matters. Though less openly avowed than the loudly proclaimed aim to return the United States to the values of the fifties (work ethic, family, religion, and so on), the implied restoration of social stratification was no secret (though its inevitable concomitant, racial stratification, was), and the Reagan administration used so-called supply-side economics as a justification to let those who had profited from the run-up of inflation in the late seventies escape the capital gains taxes that were going to be owed on their certificates of deposit upon maturation in the mid and late eighties, thus digging deeper and broader the divide between those who suffered from the vagaries of the market and those who profited mightily from it without having to fear any more the redistributive policies of government.

Much of the confusion that prevailed during the decade stems from this state of affairs: an administration committed to the redrawing of boundaries between elites and the popular masses (the notorious "silent majority") trained its guns on the theoretical pursuits harbored by the elite institutions, as if these were its target, while directing the institutions it controlled, such as the Fund for the Improvement of Post-Secondary Education (FIPSE) to support the teaching of literacy, thereby giving the impression of conducting a populist, anti-elitist educational and cultural policy. The mapping of the distinction between the two tendencies, theory and literacy, onto the opposition elitism versus populism was never made explicit as such, but it determined the mutual perceptions of both movements. Theory was a speculative, effete pursuit; literacy, a crassly utilitarian one. One thing was clear: they could not have anything to do with each other, and *that*, in retrospect, *may very well have been the object of the exercise.* Now, in the nineties, as theory appears to be on the wane and as a new recession visits its devastation upon universities, the support for literacy is vanishing, and this in spite of the fact that an "educational lag" of the same magnitude as the "missile lag" of the early sixties has been consensually diagnosed. Before universities are further "rationalized" and made into more "efficient" loci of cultural reproduction and of the production of marketable knowledge, the links between the debates on literacy and those on theory must be examined.

The "Crisis of Literacy"

Given the extremely decentralized organizational structure of primary and secondary education in the United States, where responsibility for curriculum, promotion and graduation standards, and even significant portions of funding rests with elected or appointed school boards at municipal levels, American higher education has had to rely to a considerable degree on standardized tests in the evaluation of students for university admission. The most famous of these tests (for here too there is no single standard), those devised and administered by the Educational Testing Service (ETS) of Princeton, New Jersey, have been taken as a sort of index of the level of academic preparation and achievement of the university entry-level population. The median scores of annual test results are widely reported in the media and compared with the scores of previous years. With the notable exception of 1981, when a slight melioration was observed, a significant decline in the median scores on the verbal part of the exams has been reported for each year since the mid-sixties, leading to editorial questioning of the state of education in general, and to the formulation of many schemes for the remedying of this situation.

The decline in the scores on the verbal test has inevitably drawn university departments of English into these discussions. American students, it was argued, do not possess the necessary verbal skills to perform well in their studies, and they must receive remedial training in the universities if they are to be successful in their field of study, whether it be in the business, engineering, pre-medicine, pre-law, social sciences, or humanities areas of the university curriculum. Many English department faculty members have argued in return that the situation, deplorable as it may be, is certainly not of their making; they have pointed out that the blame lies with the vast expansion of higher education to racial and ethnic minorities originating from poor neighborhoods or localities where there was inadequate elementary and secondary schooling, as a result of either insufficient financial means or discrimination. Nonetheless, it has been argued in return, primarily by university administrators and those in the liberal sectors of the political spectrum, that if universities are to remain open to these new students, it is incumbent upon them to provide the required corrective training in this area. In the changed economic, political, and fiscal environment of the seventies and eighties, marked by cutbacks in the allocations for higher education, a significant diversion of monies had to take place in order to expand or to establish programs in composition, rhetoric, or writing, as they are variously known around the country. Of course, this diversion has taken place at the expense of the regular English curriculum, which has had to stagnate at best, if not suffer an outright reduction in the money allocated to it. The resulting animosity between the traditional purveyors of literature and the new teachers of composition has been, in many instances, so considerable that it has become necessary to grant budgetary and organizational autonomy to the new academic units that teach writing. I recount this in some detail because the cultural significance of this development is seldom fully appreciated. The liberal motivation for the initial establishment of these programs, recently allied with the more conservative determination to impose a core curriculum stressing so-called "basics," has, with some notable exceptions, screened them from critical examination, and has had the further effect of polarizing those who question them in any way into an undifferentiated bloc, alternatively called permissive or reactionary. What has particularly escaped examination is the nature of the concept of literacy at stake here.

Given the near-universal opposition of traditional English faculties to the new writing programs, an opposition generally perceived in territorial terms, and formulated as a defense of standard humanistic values, the writing programs have asserted their autonomy by focusing upon what they perceive as societal demand or the requirements of their clientele. The professional schools that are part of American universities (schools of engineering, business, medicine, law, forestry, agriculture, hotel management, and so forth), which were the beneficiaries of a major student enrollment shift away from the humanities and the social sciences as a result of the "New Vocationalism" of the seventies and early eighties, have played a determining role in this situation: what they want are students who can write in *their* fields, and thus, not surprisingly, the writing programs have set up different tracks for students on the basis of their future vocational orientation: writing for business, for law, for science, for medicine, for technology, and so on. The notion of literacy operative in the programs that have evolved in this way—the vast bulk of them—is very much that of a restricted literacy: it provides for competence in a specific code, with little, if any but the most rudimentary, awareness of the general problematics of codes and codification in language. To put it even more bluntly: whereas one would have expected that a crisis of literacy would have called for a greater appreciation of the multiplicity of functions that language performs, the foremost of which is the ability to code and to transcode experience and to provide cultural directions for its interpretation, handling, and elaboration, one finds a further instrumentalization of language, where the latter is shattered into a multiplicity of autonomous, unrelated languages, with the competence to be acquired restricted to just one of them. It should be noted that, in this process, any pretense of addressing the needs of so-called disadvantaged student populations has quietly evaporated.

It is not an exaggeration to state that the effect of the new writing programs, given their orientation, is not to solve a "crisis of literacy" but to promote a new differentiated culture in which the student is trained to use language for the reception and conveyance of information in only one sphere of human activity: that of his or her future field of employment. The fact that the professional schools and the advocates of vocationalism have been among the backers of this movement is a clear indication that there are powerful societal forces at work here, and it should be equally clear that the old line of defense based on traditional humanistic values, mounted by the English faculties in the seventies, is ineffectual against these forces. The question as to whether an effective defense *can* be mounted must await the examination of these societal forces and of their action upon language and literacy, or, to put it in the terminology favored during these years, it will require an analysis of the present market of language.

The Present Market of Language

We must begin by acknowledging that language and literacy are two distinct entities, and specifically that the second term is a shorthand description for a determinate set of relations that we have to language, relations that arose under, and were conditioned by, concrete historical circumstances. The historical character of literacy should suggest, at the very least, that it is neither eternal—or "natural" as we are wont to say—nor immutable. But, just as important, it should also remind us that all of our thinking about language in the epoch of literacy has been dominated by the relations of literacy that we have to it. To put it more plainly: our present constructs of language, in spite of their mutual differences, are constructs of, and for, literacy, and we cannot therefore preclude a priori the possibility of other constructs.

Only a detailed historical account of the emergence of the current constructs of language and of their eventual vicissitudes would have probative value. In spite of some distinguished efforts, no such comprehensive account is available to us, and the argument must thus proceed in somewhat more speculative fashion than it ought to; nonetheless the broad features of these developments are discernible, and it is their exact dating that remains uncertain.

The medieval polity presents the paradoxical situation of a society capable of both extreme linguistic unity and extreme linguistic diversity. Latin as the universal language of the clerical class, a class defined by its literacy, served for all cognitive and interactive purposes, and, in the high Middle Ages especially, as the instrument of both church and state bureaucracies. By contrast to this Latin universalism, which knew no other boundaries than those of the Christian faith of Roman obedience, the particularism of the medieval polity, that is, its subdivision into entities of considerable political, social, economic, and legal autonomy, bound up with each other by bonds of feudal allegiance, was accompanied by considerable linguistic diversity that did not define its territorial extension with the borders of these entities through dialectal variation, but wove itself even through their very tissue by means of specific jargons or trade languages associated with the various crafts and guilds. This latter, illiterate, sphere of linguistic praxis, about which we know very little owing to our own, literate, dependence on written documentation, represented the bulk of the population's experience of language. It was a sphere of immediate contact and transactions within a community of shared values and social orientations, however hierarchically differentiated. The variability of the languages represented the variability of social interactions: full knowledge of the language of a craft or a guild was a mark of one's participation in it and of one's rights to its privileges, just as speech inflected differently from the local one undoubtedly marked one for the levying of special excise taxes on goods imported from outside the city limits in the local marketplace. For the market already played an important role here: its size determined the scope and compass of the dominant language spoken in it.

In this respect there is little difference in nature between Latin and the vernaculars: each is treated as proper to its function, that is, as universal within its own sphere—a fact that may help explain why Latin was not retained for the role of truly universal language. Rather, one of the dialects emerged to assume this position, and it displaced Latin as well as the other vernaculars, treating them equally as rivals.

We are all familiar with this process, which we associate with the major upheavals of early modern times: the so-called revival of learning known as the Renaissance; the emergence of the modern European nations; the advent of the modern form of the state; the development of humanistic ideology; and certainly not least, the vast expansion of markets on regional, national, and even transcontinental scales. The introduction of print technology ensured that the ideological commitment of humanism to linguistic universalism would receive the purport of literacy, itself a requirement of the vast expansion of the state and of the economic sphere.

Under these conditions of expansion, the experience necessary for effective praxis in society exceeded the capacities of direct individual acquisition and thus had to be increasingly mediated by language, as in, for example, learning from books and, more generally, through (literate) education. Language in turn had to be treated as universal so that the experiences that were repertoried, coded, transmitted, and interpreted in it could be assumed by its users regardless of their degree of immediacy to these experiences. Thus, in opposition to the prior linguistic heterogeneity that was intended to acknowledge, if not produce, social differentiation and local autonomy, the new linguistic universalism of the epoch of literacy required assertions of human dignity, the co-valence of individuals, and centralism.

From the outset, however, this emergent culture of literacy was beset with ambiguity and contradictions, the most notable of which is to be found in the fact that, on the one hand, the ideology of linguistic universalism and its secondary elaboration into the values of what we know as humanism presupposes more direct and unimpeded access to all the spheres of the polity for all the members of the (presumably universal) linguistic community, while, on the other hand, its very advent is due to the impossibility of such an access and to the need for linguistic mediation. Literature as we know it, and more generally the aesthetic function of art, have come to occupy the space left gaping by this contradictory pull upon language in this epoch, universalizing according to strict humanistic principles the particular instances of mediation necessitated by further extension of the imperative toward expansion and absorption of what had remained heterogeneous and particular.

But alongside such conquests of what could be described as archaic instances of heterogeneity and particularism—vestiges of older cultures of illiteracy—there has progressively emerged the more vexing problem of the production of new heterogeneity, one that is not amenable to reduction by the culture of literacy since it is its product, and therefore one that poses a direct challenge to this culture. If, in its initial stages, the culture of literacy relied upon language as universal mediator in order to bring into communicative interaction realms of practice that had arisen and evolved autonomously, this very same culture began to produce increasingly self-standing spheres of practice that did not need to communicate with each other through the universal mediator but merely through a specialized subset of it, operating somewhat analogously to the Latin of the medieval period, and destined to evolve in the direction of greater autonomy. The increasing specialization of the production of the goods traded in the market inevitably served to promote the elaboration of certain specific linguistic codes, marked by their functionality within the restricted sphere of their application. The codes are analogous to the jargons and trade languages of medieval crafts and guilds, and, in addition to their functionalism, they serve to identify their users as members of determinate professional and status groups, a feature of social life well exploited in satirical literature in its depiction of physicians and lawyers, and, more recently, of politicians and literary critics.

The fact that the two latter groups are now legitimate objects of such mockery should, however, give us pause, for, whereas the special linguistic elaborations of medicine and law are understandable in, and consonant with, the culture of literacy insofar as they constitute realms of specialized practice, the emergence of special languages for politics and for the discourse of reflection upon linguistic practice contravenes that culture because it is in direct conflict with its foundational notion that language is universal and that it is in the polity that its role as universal mediator is in evidence. In other words, the very existence of spheres of practice marked by special languages is legitimate in accordance with the basic tenets of the ideology of literacy only if these specialized languages can be translated into a universal language and if the resulting translation is universally understandable, so that it permits the functioning of a polity based upon humanistic universalism and articulated in it. If these conditions fail and belief in their prevalence cannot be sustained, then the various spheres of practice, and those engaged in them, become literally incommunicable to each other, and the cohesion of the social realm begins to grow precarious unless it is ensured by other means. This is particularly the case if it is political language itself that becomes specialized and therefore understandable only to those initiated in it. The growing reliance upon expert advice on the part of the ruling spheres is acceptable only if the tenor of this advice can be rendered intelligible to all the citizens of the polity. The situation grows even more precarious if those who discourse upon language (linguists, literary critics, and theorists) do so in impenetrable fashion: their recourse to professional or technical jargon is taken to be an abandonment of their function of warrants of the belief in the possibility of universal linguistic mediation. It is taken to be a *trahison des clercs* with respect to the foundations of the culture of literacy, for, at this point, the values of humanism, and especially those that have to do with the universality of human experience, the co-valence of individuals, and their right of access to all spheres of human activity, are suspended; social cohesion is more likely then to be ensured by coercive authoritarian or manipulatory means than through participatory ones. The citizen, though a competent wielder of the codes in effect in the sphere of production to which he or she is attached, becomes linguistically incompetent in the political sphere, as many technical experts have demonstrated, and must defer to those who are, or are said to be, competent, for belief is now displaced from the values to the presumption of competence in some individuals. But, in the culture of literacy, the political sphere was defined precisely by its linguistic status as a sphere of universal access. For it to become specialized and autonomous is tantamount to emptying out the meaning of citizenship and to reducing the exercise of its rights and privileges to an increasingly meaningless formalism, such as a form of voting or poll-taking characteristic of plebiscites rather than the democratic determination of policy.

We seem to have returned to our point of departure: the outgrowth of the specialized languages is already contained *in nuce* in the very project of a culture of literacy, but we must also acknowledge that even though such a possibility existed from the outset, it was also neutralized with considerable success until quite recently when the equilibrium seems to have shifted toward the heterogenizing forces. The logic of literacy alone cannot account for this development.

The impulse toward literacy came from the rapid expansion of markets, as we have seen. It was rendered necessary by the fact that the traditional way of acquiring experience for effective praxis in one's society—that is, through long individual apprenticeship with master practitioners—was too slow and carried out on too restricted a scale to permit the growth of the market. Literate culture is based on mediated as opposed to direct experience, and as such it holds the potential for a gain in efficiency: much more relevant experience, offered in the guise of the kind of knowledge we call know-how, can be acquired in a much shorter time by much larger numbers of people, thus multiplying the learned experience of the master: the textbook or the manual, early prototypes of expert-systems, take the place of personal apprenticeship with a master, and present the advantage of containing the distillate of the experience of several masters. In addition, just as in the industrial production of which it is the enabling cultural condition, the culture of literacy fostered greater uniformity and control over output. Certain masters and their programs could be promoted to the detriment of others. In all such calculations, the market is ruled by the law of efficiency, for it is this law that enables it to maximize profits and further the expansion of capital while holding costs down. Training people through the mediation of the written word is much more efficient than doing so through personal contact. Once that lesson was absorbed, it was inevitable that we would see additional investment in mediation.

I have discussed the development of literacy primarily in reference to training and the acquisition of know-how, but, of course, these activities, important as they are, represent only a portion of what goes on in the culture of literacy. At least equally important in this context are all those transactional and productive activities that are mediated by the written word: contracts, sales, capital movements, instructions for production, and the like. And here we have had major changes taking place. Increasingly, these transactions are conducted through the mediation of electronic media: transfers of funds from one account to another done over the telephone, for example, where, typically, neither the money, the sender, nor the recipient are face to face. The efficiency of this operation—one that has permitted banks like Citicorp to quadruple their assets, from 25 billion dollars to 130 billion between 1970 and 1982—depends in great measure on the elimination of the now needless presence of the participants and of the face-to-face encounter in which language as universal mediator was used. Indirect and mediated forms of communication are becoming more and more common, and increasingly they involve the use of icons or images rather than language in this process. As the designers of the Macintosh and Windows interfaces have discovered, images have a greater efficiency in imparting information than language does. What is important for our present purposes is that all these developments entail a diminution in the role played by the type of language that the culture of literacy is built upon: the so-called natural language as universal mediator.

In addition, we need to take into account the fact that the claim to universalism for language has suffered setbacks with the expansion of the market to a global scale, whereas mediated images and electronic messages, backlit by the aura of advancing technology, have overcome local cultural resistances far more efficiently. Moreover, since the development of quantum mechanics at least, it has become impossible to assert that language *is* a universal mediator: it can offer only rather gross, and misleading, approximations of what the physicist knows through mathematical formulas. Yet the praxis of physicists and the technology built upon their findings show no sign of debilitation as a result of their lessened reliance upon language.

These developments, combined with the impulse toward ever greater efficiency mandated by the competitiveness of the marketplace and the need to maximize profits, have made it inevitable that the position occupied by language in our culture undergo radical change. This is tantamount to saying that the culture of literacy has been faced with transformations that it cannot control, if not with extinction altogether. The "crisis of literacy" deplored by the media and public figures of every political persuasion is but the symptom of this larger epochal shift, and the remedies offered by the new writing programs are nothing but a blind groping with the nature of this problem. But, as is frequently the case with such blindness, it contains a fundamental insight into the nature of the historical process that is unfolding.

The Postliterate State

The emergence of the new writing programs was initially presented as a remedial measure, intended to facilitate the accession to higher education of segments of the American population that had been denied such access for reasons of race and class. The fact that the setting up of these remedial programs was, in its very early stages, encouraged and assisted by traditional English department faculties suggested that the structure and the orientation of the study of literature could be carried out as it had been, and that the students who needed the remedial work would be "mainstreamed" as soon as it proved feasible for them. In retrospect, this widely prevalent belief must be acknowledged to have been a delusion resulting from an inadequate understanding of the context in which the crisis of literacy was taking place. As far as faculty and administrators were concerned, the roots of the problem were sociological and the immediate cause was the larger access to university education. But we have just seen that the crisis of literacy has much deeper roots; it is caused by the breaking out of contradictions inherent to the culture of literacy when the market forces that impel this culture advance further toward globalization.

The new writing programs, lacking either tradition or intellectual legitimation, sought to gain acceptance, and thus a legitimacy of sorts, by becoming responsive to what their practitioners saw as societal needs, and what were in fact the impulses provided by these market forces. In the spirit of the "New Vocationalism," these programs took to defining literacy as the mastery of specific codes of linguistic usage defined by the career objectives of the students. Their ascendancy, even though presented as remedial, was an indication that the traditional programs in English and in the other literatures had somehow failed, or, at the very least, could no longer be relied upon to ensure the literacy of the students. Insofar as the curricula of these traditional programs were animated by the humanistic values of the classical culture of literacy described earlier, it is these very values that were being challenged.

In effect, the teaching of New Vocationalist literacy meant that the educational system was turning its back upon the values of classical literacy, that it renounced the ideal of a sphere of communicative interaction where all the able wielders of the language, in their capacity as citizens, would overcome the heterogeneity of specialized linguistic practices in order to inquire into, and determine, their collective destiny. The teaching of specialized literacies, to the detriment of the all-encompassing one presupposed by the culture of literacy, implies the existence of a social structure that limits the participation of citizens to the carrying out of their functional tasks, and excludes them from inquiry into the nature and purpose of these tasks. One might have expected such a development in a totalitarian or, at the very least, in an authoritarian social environment, for it certainly seems to be inimical to fundamental democratic principles. Yet not only did it occur in a largely democratic environment without raising any protests, except of the kind that were immediately classified as elitist and thus counter-democratic, but it was saluted as extending democracy and even leaning toward populism. To be sure, some of the advocates of the new literacy, most notably E. D. Hirsch, Jr., did grow concerned over the disappearance of the commonality presupposed by the culture of literacy, but their solution only confirmed the demise of this culture since all they offered was a commodification of this commonality in the form of a shared content, whereas the culture of literacy implied shared processes. How could this turning away from the values of democracy have taken place without causing any upheaval?

The answer would elude many of us for quite some time, owing to the peculiar blindness that we share with respect to the nature of the historical process we inhabit, or indeed to the very notion that we inhabit a historical process. For this latter notion is typically Hegelian, and all American intellectuals have been brought up to believe that the specter of Hegelianism was successfully repulsed by William James shouting "Damn the Absolute!" to Josiah Royce, a moment preserved in a famous Harvard photograph. The interpretation given to James's ejaculation may be one of the greater misprisions of our times, for it is more likely to have been a cry of despair than that of a successful exorcism. The recent essay on the "End of History" by Francis Fukuyama, a RAND Corporation researcher and an official of the U.S. State Department, and the ensuing brouhaha, have shown that the Hegelian conception of the historical process is far from dead; nor is it inappropriate to an understanding of the American situation.

It will be recalled that Hegel sought to describe the relation of knowledge to the material world as a process whereby what he called the Spirit progressively invested itself in the material world, making it increasingly conscious of itself until such a time when all of matter would be so invested and the distinction between matter and Spirit would no longer obtain. This process of investment unfolds over time and traces the delineation of a history during the course of which there arise different figures that represent epochal moments in the relation of Spirit to matter. The final moment is marked by the advent of Absolute Knowledge, in which the intermediate figure of the State withers away to be replaced by self-regulating and autonomous institutions of knowledge that no longer need to communicate with each other, for they all partake of the Spirit and do nothing more than manage its day-to-day investment in the world. This moment corresponds to the posthistorical state. Absolute Knowledge is operative in this world under a myriad of specialized guises that ensure that whatever problems arise, they are immediately referred to and "solved" by the appropriate instance of Knowledge. In such a world, Knowledge is no longer surprised by anything since the Spirit is coextensive with all there is to be known, and the only problems that remain are problems of local management. There are no longer any discoveries to be made, and neither the nature nor the direction of the historical process is worthy of speculation, for both have become manifest.

It is readily apparent that the new literacy, though advocated by persons ignorant of Hegel's grand design, not only conforms to it but seeks to implement it. Blindly, it has put forward a notion of linguistic competence consonant with a state of affairs where the concerns of a democratic state, that is, a state still concerned with its own direction, purpose, and the adequation of its means to its goals, are superseded by an all-encompassing concern with efficiency and competence that takes the form of exclusive specialized practice and rejects as inefficient any broader concerns. Fukuyama's original essay and subsequent writings have made clear that the vaunted anti-statism of the Reagan administration was directed at the historical figure of the state and sought to hasten the advent of the posthistorical state whose fate, it bears recalling, is to wither away and let its space be occupied by the managerial forces of globalization.

These forces are clearly in the ascendancy at present, and the Hegelian view of the posthistorical state is closer to realization than ever, especially since the collapse of its Marxist alternative still rooted in the paramount function of the state. The literacy programs that already exist evince a profound distrust of interpretation and other critical functions in relation to language, and proclaim mastery and competence as their goals. They are likely to gain ground in the universities as the frenzy over competitiveness with foreign powers increases and the economic situation justifies doing away with the "frills" of interpretation and other forms of literary study. As I observed earlier, their growing hegemony has only found literary theory in its path. It is my contention that theory has arisen out of the same ground as the new literacy, but whereas the latter has sought to accommodate, or even further, the emergence of the posthistorical state, theory has sought to oppose this emergence, frequently as blindly as literacy on its side of the divide.

The Struggle for Theory

For a generation now students of literature in the United States have been arguing about matters of theory, indeed about theory itself. In spite of the constant barrage of denunciations of its ephemeral faddishness and predictions of its imminent demise, theory has managed to occupy an inordinate amount of our attention and has imposed itself as the defining characteristic of an entire generation of scholarship. I propose to inquire into the causes of this state of affairs. My approach to the matter is both historical and theoretical, and its ultimate aim is to assess the present situation of the theoretical project. My emphasis is on the situation in the United States, for that is where the battle over theory has been waged longest. One cannot take the American situation as paradigmatic of the overall situation of theory, however, even though it shares features with those of other countries; we will have to await other case studies before formulating general hypotheses concerning this period.

It is always perilous to generalize, especially when it comes to cultural matters in a country as vast and as regionally diverse as the United States. Nonetheless, some observations regarding the study of literature can be made with a degree of general validity. Until World War II, anyone who wanted to become actively engaged with his or her own culture, becoming either a writer or a critic, pursued an undergraduate degree in English. The study of English was focused on issues of style and thematic appreciation, as befitted individuals who came from the upper echelons of American society and had the benefits of private schooling or even tutoring. American literary scholarship followed British scholarship for the most part and differed from the latter only in its concern with the establishment of a distinct American identity. This concern with identity led Americans to be more attentive to factors of history and sociocultural development than their British counterparts, who viewed all such concern with identity as an admission of weakness and uncertainty, and tended to think of it as denoting a particularly Germanic turn of mind. Since the American university was largely patterned upon the German university, British scholars were not surprised to see it evince such a concern.

The Great Depression had a profound impact upon literary studies in the United States. Whereas the study of literature had been regarded as an effete pursuit prior to World War I, or a turning away from what was taken to be a Philistine materialism characteristic of the society of the twenties, the social suffering of the Depression, and the assuaging and compensatory role of culture in the mass media of the thirties (radio and cinema), led many intellectuals to seek broader ways of promoting a form of what we would call today critical cultural literacy among their compatriots. This was the ground upon which the New Criticism was born: its practitioners recognized that the transmission of literary values to a large new audience of lower-class origin could not proceed on the assumption of a shared cultural heritage, which did not obtain in any case; nor could it take the form of instilling that heritage, since the result would be to privilege even more those who had had prior access to it by virtue of their social origin. The New Critics came to the conclusion that the proper approach to this dilemma was through methodology: it should be possible to teach individuals to read poems by bringing nothing more than a knowledge of their language to the undertaking. Historical references, cultural allusions, authorial biographies could all be bracketed away without major loss of intelligence of the text if one pursued its analysis rigorously enough. In fact, the New Critics were quick to see that, if one proceeded in this fashion, one would rapidly produce a large body of analyses that would force a reexamination of the prevalent views of the history of literature: the older history, having been fashioned under conditions of privileged class domination, reflected the values of this class, whereas the new literary history would be more objective, more democratic, arising out of the objectively determined alterations in the language of poetry. Such, at least, was the hope and the theory of this group of individuals, who were quite blind to the elitism implied in the assumption of their own guiding role for the masses, or rather in their adoption of the then-current notion of vanguard found equally in cultural and left-political circles, a notion that was far from incompatible, in spite of its political origins, with their own generally patrician, agrarian, and Southern roots.

The New Critics had elaborated their basic doctrines in the thirties but did not have a chance to apply them during that decade since access to higher education was, if anything, even more restricted than usual. Their doctrines were often decried then as nothing more than ventures into theoretical activity meant to compensate for their own privileged position. The situation changed dramatically after World War II with the famous G.I. Bill of Rights, which gave access to higher education to a large number of Americans who otherwise would not have obtained it. New Criticism spread like wildfire throughout academia, playing indeed the integrative role that its initiators had envisaged for it, but at a certain cost that took the form of an institutional split. Even though it was an American movement, the New Criticism was decidedly British if not English in orientation. Its rejection of history, biography, and of all social, religious, economic, and political contexts was antithetical to the research orientation of those students who dealt primarily with American literature. Throughout the forties and fifties English departments were beset with internal conflicts between the adherents of New Criticism and the upholders of a concern with things American, conflicts that were institutionally resolved by the creation of independent programs or departments of American Studies alongside existing departments of English. The earliest and often strongest departments of American Studies were thus created in the institutions where the English department was most strongly oriented toward New Criticism, the University of Minnesota and Yale being cases in point.

The result of this far from peaceful evolution was that English departments were effectively depoliticized, and practiced a form of cultural formalism that was very safe during the McCarthy era but became more troublesome during the civil rights and anti-war struggles of the sixties and seventies. American Studies departments, for their part, found themselves strangely unbalanced: the literature scholars in them were perceived as methodologically backward by other students of literature and had to cede leadership to historians and sociologists. Many of them turned to the study of so-called popular literature and were further scorned for dealing with such a low object of inquiry, which had no legitimacy in academia at the time. Since the focus of American Studies remained firmly fixed upon issues of a distinct collective identity, research in this area was not very attentive to the differentiations that existed in American society. One need only recall the genuine sense of shock produced by the Swedish sociologist Gunnar Myrdal's study of racism in America in the forties to gauge the commitment of American students of American culture to hegemonic and unified views of the latter. All of this was translated into a state of confusion and intellectual disarray when the civil rights movement erupted onto the scene. This confusion that was further compounded by the growing anti-war sentiment of the population and the forms that it began to take, forms that were believed by scholars of American studies to be alien to the United States and incompatible with the ethos of the country.

It was thus inescapable that in the late sixties and early seventies young Americans concerned with active engagement in their own culture would have the sense that something had gone terribly wrong in the organization of knowledge. Some subscribed to the conspiracy theory of a vast and directed industrial-military-academic complex; others sought refuge in the New Left or even in the old one; still others looked to foreign countries such as Germany and France where far-reaching critiques of society, culture, and academia were being carried out, often under similar conditions of confusion. Some finally attempted to find a place in the United States where a new approach to these matters was being tried. They found the comparative literature departments at Johns Hopkins and at Yale, departments that were dealing with theory, to be such a place.

What was it about theory that seemed to address their concerns? What the new engagement with theory offered was, to put it bluntly, a comprehensive and far-reaching critique of the existing organization of knowledge and of the Enlightenment ideology upon which it was based, and thus it ushered in the poststructuralism characteristic of our postmodernity. This critique centered on language, an area in which scholars of literature are expected to have special competence. Language is indeed central to Western modernity, as the following brief example should make clear.

In the Middle Ages most learning took place through apprenticeship, that is, by having the student actively share in the experience of his teacher (this was a process reserved for men then) over the course of many years. As we have seen, such an approach proved unworkable under conditions of expanded markets, and the textbook was invented. A textbook originally was a compilation of the very best tricks of the trade drawn from the experience of the best masters. The *idea* of the textbook rests upon the assumption that the experience of one human being can be conveyed to another by means of language, and this assumption further presupposes that human beings are similarly constituted and are substitutable for each other. These are the underlying assumptions of modernity, and they lead to notions such as the progress of learning and of humankind. The critique of language, practiced by the likes of Paul de Man, focused on the fact that the very social success of this approach had elevated language to the role of universal mediator and equivalent, that is, to a situation where there is universal reliance on language without any reflection upon the price we pay for such a reliance. The research strategy of literary theorists has been to establish that language is indeed universally relied upon in modernity, leading some of the opponents of theory to accuse its practitioners of being language-obsessed. The second step in the strategy has been to draw attention to those aspects of human experience that existing discourses and languages were unable to convey, such as gender and race.

I now want to retrace these concerns of theory in some detail, and yet I want to do so globally. In other words, I do not want to go over every single argument that has been made in the course of our theoretical preoccupation, a task far beyond the scope of this chapter, but rather I want to draw up a comprehensive understanding of these preoccupations. This will lead me to regroup together individuals and groups who have been frequently at odds with each other, such as Derrida, Foucault, Lyotard, Deleuze, and the Yale School. All of these have delimited our understanding of theory, however, and I think it is not inappropriate to regroup them in this way.

The fundamental concern of theory has been difference. In this it immediately separated itself from both the New Criticism, which focused on organic determinations of unity, and from the dominant mode of doing American Studies, which pursued the German project of establishing a national collective identity. The search for such an identity is part and parcel of a logic of identity that relies upon a basic narrative schema running roughly as follows: originally there was a pure identity; for various reasons it has been lost or diluted or sullied; in the future it will be recovered. This logic assigns to the future the redemption of the present by a return to the past. The claim of difference, on the other hand, is always made in context, in reference to a specific situation. It acknowledges the existence of a process of identity lamination that aims to achieve either a reduction of all individual identities to sameness or their congealing in an alterity for consumption, of the sort to be found in tourist art where distinct or differential identity becomes a consumer good to be cashed in on. The claim of difference is not made in the name of identity, in spite of the confusion that has attended, and sometimes still attends, this point, but in the name of the right to determine oneself, to change, to evolve, to borrow, and to refuse; it is a claim made in the name of sovereignty, whether individual or collective. It is a practice of resistance.

The opposition identity/difference, which will structure my presentation, is of course the fundamental opposition structuring Hegelian thought, and it is precisely Hegel's goal to show how the dialectic overcomes this opposition. Theory, as we have known it, can be readily characterized by the fact that it rejects Hegel's solution while acknowledging his mode of posing the problem. In this sense it is anti-dialectic. I wish to stress that theory has not sought to avoid the Hegelian formulation, for, as Paul de Man was wont to say, one is never as Hegelian as when one claims that one is not, and this problem has been compounded by the fact that North Americans, not especially well read in Continental philosophy, are Hegelians in spite of themselves like Molière's *bourgeois gentilhomme.*

Difference-oriented theory saw in the Hegelian system its chief opponent, an opponent armed with a language that colonizes and that generates victims while channeling greater power to the master of the system. Against the system, theory invoked a practice of writing that seeks to draw attention to and correct the damage incurred by the victims; it seeks to articulate a resistance to the Hegelian inheritance. Theory seeks to invent a non-dialectical language that can escape the Hegelian System of Knowledge and its pretensions to foresee and enclose all possibilities in favor of a new form of infinity conceived as a ceaselessly repeated multiplicity free of any overcoming. Writing is used as a strategy of displacement and avoidance to prevent language from falling under the domination of master-words, and thus as a way of enabling the multiple and the heterogeneous to deploy themselves. This strategy of rapid and unforeseeable movement, we will discover, seeks to perturb the operations of Absolute Knowledge, for this knowledge is determined by the optical constraints of observable truth, and writing will interfere with the serene exercise of the masterful gaze that this notion of knowledge presupposes. It seeks to bring about a crisis of vision, and indeed of sight.

Theory has thus sought to exacerbate the oppositions to be found in Hegel, and to render impossible their sublation. In this respect my presentation will have to emphasize the binary oppositions that theory put into question in order to show that the refusal to have them dialectically sublated leads to the valorizing of the terms or poles that are negated in the dialectic. For instance, whereas the master-slave dialectic is meant to mark the advent of a mode of language that resolves all contradictions in Hegel, theory will emphasize the existence of two distinct linguistic modes: the language of the master, which follows the path of argumentation and silences all of the figures that are alien to it in the movement of its fulfillment, and the language of the victims, which is forced to go through detours, abrupt connections, and brief moments of lightning-like illuminations. Such a language, the language of the victims, as practiced by theory, must avoid all the generic boundaries and indeed all the accepted modes of segmentation of texts, for all these delimitations and classifications already belong to the organization of the knowledge in the service of the master. The language of the victims must weave itself through the texts and ignore the generic boundaries, but it cannot pretend that they do not exist. It cannot pretend that one could overthrow the whole system, for that is the ultimate ruse of the system: it seeks nothing so much as an opposition, for it can then absorb it within itself. Instead, theory seeks to trace new ways of navigating the system, to mark it with new and uncontrolled paths.

What this abstract formulation revolves about is the opposition of Writing to the Concept, but it is an opposition that is itself not of a conceptual but of a practical nature. The term "Concept," as I shall use it, has come to designate in theory a notional complex that recognizes that there exists a set of reciprocal implications between the notions of State, Unity, Totality, and Eternal Presence, and that these notions can never be invoked singly without drawing upon the power of the others. The Concept is thus a major force of the Hegelian system as theory has identified it, and it has focused its own counterforce against it.

One major conclusion should be readily apparent: theories of difference, which have analyzed texts as networks of words and societies as networks of differences, have also counter-established an equation of operational equivalence between the notion of System in philosophy and that of the State in the social sphere. This equation gives theory its political dimension, and it accounts for the fact that the political concerns of difference-theory do not need to be explicitly stated or thematized and yet are continuously dealt with. It is also this equation that accounts for the fact that difference-theories are modes of thinking resistance. In other words, it should be apparent that difference-oriented theory has taken on the form of a Critique of Political Reason, and this is the major reason why it has attracted so many students and scholars. Whether they have followed the paths of Foucauldian Archaeology or Genealogy, of Derridean or de Manian Deconstruction, of Deleuzian Repetition or Lyotard's Différend, these students have challenged the prevailing Hegelian conception of the organization of knowledge. In doing so they have not sought to play the Hegelian game of opposition or contradiction but rather to bring out the hidden if not repressed side of the Hegelian master concepts. Thus writing has been invoked against the language of dialectics, difference against the clocklike workings of contradiction, rhizomatic networks against the totalizations of the system, and alteration against the leveling effects of negation.

What is it about the Hegelian system that is so objectionable? It may be recalled that shortly before both the civil-rights and the antiwar movements broke out upon the American scene, the distinguished liberal sociologist Daniel Bell had proclaimed the End of Ideology, the late-fifties version of the more recent proclamation of the End of History. Bell did so in the name of a technocratism that, according to his thesis, was more interested in the concrete dimensions of problem-solving than in the imposition or the verification of a whole set of beliefs. In his famous farewell address of 1960, President Eisenhower gave the pessimistic version of this same conclusion: the United States, he claimed, was falling into the hands of a military-industrial complex that was taking over the direction of scientific research and converting universities into its own subsidiaries. In effect, both Bell and Eisenhower were proclaiming the advent of the posthistorical state as Hegel had described it, that is, as a state that was becoming selfsame with an organization of knowledge so pervasive that it had developed procedures for handling any and every problem that might arise. Theory, in the wake of history, would seek to challenge this premature conclusion.

It would begin by trying to describe this Hegelian system so that we would learn to recognize it. As I indicated earlier, the chief instrument of the system is the Concept, which reduces the meaning of knowing to a form of seizing, of capturing (*begreifen* → *Begriff*), that is, to an act of appropriation where what is appropriated is reduced to an already known sameness. Knowing is equated with conquest. The Concept is a living movement, but it is in the service of an imperious if not imperial will to domination. The exercise of this will to know, a will to absolute meaning and truth, and the invention of a radical power to homogenize, are able to seize an object only on condition that they can inscribe it within a logic of accommodation, that is, within the horizon of an already prescribed intelligibility. This is the task of negation.

Negation in Hegel had traditionally been read, and not least by Marxists, as a positive resource for the scansion of history, permitting, among other things, a positive view of revolutions, as accomplishing a historical process. Difference-oriented theory will read it as the sign of a reassuring collaboration in the service of a particular metaphysics. The Hegelian Concept is meant to allow thought not only to embrace all of the real but to annihilate it in its very alterity, that is, to appropriate the real to thought as a form of organized knowledge. That is why negation is the instrument that arrests the dynamics of the contraries and moves them toward a reconciling synthesis. In other words, negation always tolls the ending of the movement of the Concept, and for this reason it resembles a simple trial to go through before embarking back upon the journey to a unity momentarily lost. It carries within itself forebodings of the end, of the accomplishment of the process, of closure. Hegelian negation is condemned to servitude by speculative dialectics. It plays a key role in the minimal plot of this dialectic by announcing early on that everything always works out in the end.

Any critique of negation is a critique of Hegelian dialectic, and so much of theory has been devoted to this topic that I shall not belabor it. But I do want to point out that the Yale School, and Bloom and de Man in particular, devoted a considerable amount of their energies to showing how the reading of the New Criticism and other schools relied upon the dialectic for their own movement. By contrast, theory is oriented more toward the study of antinomies rather than the dialectic: in a dialectic the terms in opposition are distributed along an axis that is always already hierarchically oriented so that the outcome of the opposition is decided as soon as the opposition is identified, whereas in an antinomy no such axis exists and the effort of thought is directed to the determination of the possible relations between the terms of the antinomy.

To say that the dialectical opposition is organized around a hierarchical axis is to recognize that the dialectic is articulated around an essence and that it is linked to an eschatological teleology: it promises a final beatitude, of the type that Bell called the End of Ideology, and that Fukuyama, following Hegel, has been calling the End of History, an end that has recently been enforced as a New World Order by the force of arms. Theory's objection to the dialectic is that, since it is teleological and totalizing, it accomplishes a task of plenitude and of eternization that progressively exhausts any Otherness that presents itself in the immanence of the Concept. The dialectic underlies Hegel's double requirement of a history of reconciliation to take place at the end of the Spirit's deployment, and of the realization of transparent society, a society in which nothing will be opaque to the Spirit or Mind, at the end of its deployment; this society will be fully regulated by the apparatus of knowledge where every object, every behavior, will be the object of some discipline well equipped methodologically to render an account of it.

When theory turned to an examination of history, it challenged this Hegelian construct by showing that a dialectical conception of history and of society blinds itself to all the variegated forms of social force and power. It regards power as something that one has, that one takes, and thus it is committed to thinking the end of history. It seeks to submit events to the evidence of meaning, to describe sociopolitical developments in the linear form of a rational itinerary. Such a conception of history leads one to submit all the activities of a society to a totalizing perspective that forces one to look for correlations that may not have any common measure, to explain everything by the workings of the last instance, whether it be the spirit or the economy. Hence the Foucauldian call for the desacralization of this fetish, and his recommendation for the placing of events within specific discontinuities and modalities that are irreducible to any teleology. His archaeology has sought to deal with monuments and events that it does not reinscribe within the course of a development or of a unique process. It has sought to analyze them in the depth of the historical conditions that have made them possible, and it has described them within their dispersion without forcing them into the Procrustean bed of a common measure. The rejection of the dialectical philosophy of history has necessitated the elaboration of a new and distinct conception and knowledge of society that can lead in turn to new political practices. This knowledge must proceed from the idea that society is not a totality unified by a state.

To sum up, theory has sought to differentiate itself from, and indeed subvert, an organization of knowledge ruled by a Hegelian inheritance. At the heart of this organization one finds the Concept, which gathers to itself all of the metaphorics of light, enlightenment, sight, and vision that have constituted the Western notion of knowledge. The Concept defines the conditions under which one may have knowledge of beings. It carries within itself the project of an exhaustive ordering of things and of practices. The work of the Concept is accomplished by negation, for it is through negation that identity can recover its fullness, its unity. Finally, Hegel treated history and society in the way in which space had been treated in philosophy earlier: as a totalization within which the dialectic is charged with the task of gathering.

It is not difficult to see that this critique of Hegel is actually Kantian in origin; it amounts to relegating the Hegelian dialectic to a transcendental illusion. All of the major theorists have remarked, in their writings, upon this return to Kant, for it has provided them also with a basis for their interest in issues of epistemology and of aesthetics, but this return should not hide from us the fact that it is not a matter of recovering Kant against Hegel, but rather, as I suggested earlier, of extending his task by writing collectively and dialogically the Critique that Kant never thought of writing: a Critique of Political Reason.

Before I turn to the content of this Critique, a remark on the discursive stakes of theory is in order. One of the most common attacks upon theory has criticized its esoteric terminology, its jargon as it has become known. It should now be apparent that a philosophical debate is also a struggle to impose discursive modes, procedures of argumentation and demonstration, rhetorical and pedagogical techniques and strategies. Every philosophical battle has been carried out by questioning the philosophical authenticity of the discourse of one's opponent. Theorists have followed this venerable path, but they have had to be especially wary and thus particularly innovative in their own discourse since their opponent was nothing less than the present organization of knowledge: their challenge could not be stated in the language sanctified by this organization but had to systematically subvert it.

Turning now to the content of this Critique of Political Reason, I must begin by reiterating that I am not trying to impose upon the very diverse views of all those who have become engaged in theory some adventitious unity of purpose or intention that would not stand up to examination. It is not a matter of reducing all theory to one school, of imposing a seamless sameness upon thinkers of difference. It is simply a matter of recognizing that the common reference to Hegel has to do with the Other that has not allowed herself or himself to be fully colonized, or that has been produced as Other by a system that could not stomach her or him. Before identifying this Other with an actual group of people, the theorists of this period have sought to describe it as difference itself, the very difference that calls upon our thought from the vantage point of that which has escaped Hegel.

Thinking difference is a way of listening to the movement, not of the concept but of that which is emerging, to what Nietzsche called "the innocence of becoming." It is a way of committing oneself to the destruction of the presumption of unity, of meaning, by accepting that transformations in the social sphere and in the organization of knowledge must affect philosophical discourse and indeed all discourses of legitimation. The thought of difference posits a radically different relationship between knowledge and action, between theory and praxis, than the one posited by Hegelian thinking. It takes difference to be irreducible to the interplay of analysis and synthesis and to the operations of power. It designates gaps, excesses, remains, radical alterities.

I want to suggest that difference-sensitive theory has recognized and thematized something that had escaped earlier thought: the cry. It is a philosophy of the cry, a cry constituted by difference in all of its avatars. Theory has taken upon itself to give a body of language to this cry, a cry that is linguistically disembodied, that has no access to language in the closed systems of knowledge, where it cannot state itself but can only sound and resound. The thought of difference tries to make audible all discourses rendered inaudible by Hegelianism, statism, patriarchism, hegemonism, totalitarianism, and so on. It attempts to render visible all the language that has been erased by the imperatives of transparency, thus becoming a labor of opacification, of restoring opacity where it has been glossed over. It has not been a matter of bringing into the light that which had remained in pools of shadows at the edges of the system. The primary concern of theory has been more with the well-lit and dangerous zones where absolute knowledge is at its strongest under the species of unity and transparency. To this extent, theory has been radically opposed to the central metaphor of enlightenment, as Habermas has well recognized, for it sees in the very claim of enlightening, of shedding light by means of the concept, the imposition of domination. It opposes the opacity of writing to the enlightenment of transparent expression.

Writing suspends all the familiar ways of organizing thought and experience: the genres of discourse, the distinctions between disciplinary and disciplining modes of thinking, such as that between literature and philosophy. It opposes principles of classification and is against normative rules upheld by so many institutions that live off them without any qualms. It proceeds from another center of gravity than that of meaning or of vision. It does not contain what it says: there always takes place a spill-over that it does not control. We all know, after Derrida, that writing does not translate a spoken word; it does not work instrumentally as a different mode of expressing the unity and the integrity of a thought that can be expressed in a variety of ways without being affected by any of these ways. On the contrary, writing designates a work space; it delimits and affects regions of knowledge and their political effects. It struggles against the privilege accorded to pure thought, to presence and truth. It does not have a pole and does not proceed from truth. As an operator of destabilization, it liberates a space within which the separation between the sensible and the intelligible which has been mapped upon the distinction and the association of language to thought can no longer function. It breaks up closure by producing signs of the effect of closure. It produces an immanence of its own, which excludes that of a meaning prior or exterior to the process of writing itself. It is a form of autonomy, to be sure, but one that protests against the concept, for it both represents and is difference.

In his study of Greek tragedy, Nietzsche examines the relationship of the cry to the concept and sees writing as crying on the surface of the text, the coercion of which it feels itself to be the victim. Writing as usually practiced excludes difference, Nietzsche recognizes, but such a writing cries out this exclusion; it cannot do more than cry it out, for it must submit to the ways of that which excludes its difference if it is to be heard at all. To understand writing requires then that one apprehend the cry and the difference, to apprehend difference as cry, a cry of life against the death that is propagated by the system.

Difference, then, is not a word and certainly not a concept; it is a cry. And one must inquire into the nature of this cry, into its force of resistance and the violence that surrounds it. The cry that theory has become attentive to is not the cry that Rousseau speaks about. For him it is a cry in the language of nature that proclaims the possibility of arriving at a universal agreement between all human beings; it is a shout of agreement, of recognition. Nor is the cry of difference the cry of the prophet in the desert meant to awaken or summon forth a community. It is rather, as Lévinas puts it, the cry let out by a injured person even if there is no one to hear it. Such a cry is a difference that cannot be contained in the unity that is presupposed by immediacy. It is beyond absorption.

Theory recognizes that the cry cannot expose itself otherwise than as cry, for the ways of dialectical language occult it and bar it from presentation. In fact dialectics seeks to provide such a cry with a representation, a spokesperson, that will replace the crying voice with a disciplined and policed voice that will know how to respect the required decorum of properly organized intercourse. When I said that theory sought to give a linguistic body to this cry, I did not mean that it wished to speak for it. The cry is neither a Kantian synthesis nor a Hegelian dialectic; it escapes all discursivity, all the classical types of intelligibility, forcing thought to abandon the ground of a purely theoretical reason. The cry is excess and excessive in order that something may happen, that something be pro-duced.

One must be tempted at this point to say: but who is this crying victim? The question does not make any sense, for it presupposes an ontological answer. The victim cannot be designated by a being, but by an activity, by its efficacy. Theory could be taken as a way of coming to terms with the proposition that the concept generates victims. The term "victim" is meant to bring to mind registers of suffering, of enduring, of coercion, and the work of theory must begin with the victim—how to pay attention to the victim when dealing with a system that knows how to make it disappear. One cannot proceed by means of juridical thought, which originates in the system. From the perspective of the law, a victim is someone who has suffered a prejudice or a damage and demands reparation. But for the law it is essential that both victim and guilty party, the executioner as Lyotard says, recognize themselves in the experience of legality and acknowledge this experience as is presupposed by any trial (one thinks of Kafka, or the Mohawks). This type of victim is a victim of the law, a victim in law, and it is the law's function to ensure its disappearance as victim.

This is not the victim that theory has been concerned with. As Foucault recognizes at the end of *Discipline and Punish*, "the notions of institutions of repression, rejection, exclusion, marginalization, are not adequate to describe, at the very center of the carceral city, the formation of the insidious leniencies, unavowable petty cruelties, small acts of cunning, calculated methods, techniques, 'sciences' that permit the fabrication of the disciplinary individual." The problem of the victim must be dealt with outside of the law, for it is not a matter of dealing with the victim *of* something but with a pure victim as the figure of irreversible difference.

The result is that our conceptual landscape is radically altered: on the one hand, we find the law and its agents, the judge and the executioner, and other derivatives of the system, which include the scholarly study of notions of repression, of rejection, of marginalization, all coming together to form a complete and coherent definition of the victim that can be readily stated in a set of norms. Facing this side there is the victim whose cry fissures the system, this all-too-coherent system, in a cry that reveals its monstrosity. To listen to this cry is to get under way a Critique of Political Reason; it is to vivify the cry of the victim by tracing the arrangement of potential solidarities.

As Lyotard has pointed out in regard to the legal category of damage, a différend is translated within the legal system as a simple legal quarrel that a judge can resolve in the name of a rule which is applicable to the arguments of the plaintiffs. It stems from a procedure in which both parties agree that they can and will speak in identical terms, and accept a common ground of analysis in which both the complaint and the proof are marked by mutual receivability. A "tort" in the sense that Lyotard gives to this term, on the other hand, deprives the plaintiff of the very means of argumentation and transfers the conflict from the legal to the political sphere: it pushes the plaintiff out of the legal system into an unstable state. Litigiousness contributes to the stifling of the différend and creates situations that ensure that homogeneity is reinforced and respected, whereas the différend signals a cry, marked by the kind of silence that descends when one cannot even find the words to utter one's anguish. Lyotard does not merely complete the configuration of difference by a juridico-political argumentation. By bringing out the contrast between plaintiff and victim, where the plaintiff can be processed, like Velveeta, by the legal system, while the victim has to be shunted aside, Lyotard reinforces the thought of difference as a thought of the victim by giving us an affirmative conception of the victim. Whereas the plaintiff is a legally determinable victim and is thus locked into the mechanisms of negativity, the victim does not enter into the ways of the dialectic; it even escapes the ways of negotiation, for the latter all too often masks the rapport of forces that concern it. There is, as Lyotard acknowledges, a form of autism of the victim.

And it is in this that the victim is different from the Hegelian slave, who, as we know, becomes the object of a method. The victim is not; there is no unique and repetitive method to apprehend the cry, for the cry is not, and cannot be turned into, an object of knowledge. A cry is absolute diversity, it forces thought into singularity, and to apprehend it is to have to move to the very edges of the system, toward that which the concept cannot dissipate or resorb. Theory must thus operate on the very divide that separates the system from the victim, upon its margins but without any lyricism of marginality or marginalization.

Theory has thus come to distinguish between delinquency as a temporary straying from the common law and defined in relation to this law, and the *margin,* the radically other, the excess that practices its cunning from the outside against repression, a margin that is called resistance.

This resistance is not determined by a negation. It results from a calculated distanciation from identity. It is a force and not an operation that insists within discourses that refuse to receive it and are blind to all that exceeds the common features gathered in the concept. It is a No, to be sure, but a No that originates in an affirmation. The cry is affirmation, and since it is always repeated, it begins to generate a space not governed by identity.

The repetition of the cry produces an echo within this space, and theory, I wish to suggest, has become an echoing practice of the cry. This is far from the claim to mastery that attended the rise of some theoretical work in the sixties. In a culture that confers value on individualism, on the distinction and authenticity of voice and being, echo is a term of derogation. Connoting what is imitative, derivative, secondary, echo disowns originality. As a mythical figure—rather a voice than a figure—Echo survives as an ever-fading admonition, warning us not of the fate of unrequited love but of the course of love when there is confusion of identity, when the margins between self and other are wavering and indistinct. If echo disowns originality, disclaims the presence of being within voice, it does so the better to measure and negotiate distances. Recognizing however that there are no original voices, echo is not a mere negative, a perpetual symptom of loss; like a sign, an echo refers elsewhere (and difference-oriented theory cannot, for this very reason, be narcissistic and merely self-absorbed). Echo is to language what sign is to things. If we have nothing but signs and echoes we may come to see all quest as repetition, and repetition as futility. But, as the Kierkegaard of *Repetition* recognized, that which indicates loss and absence carries within it not just a trace or echo but the very presence of that which is absent. Echo can thus be transformed from a symptom of loss into the force of recuperation— but always on the understanding that recuperation does not look backward but advances cumulatively.

The cry is an utterance that is uttered without any concern for communication, for finding an addressee. If we take theory to be an ethics of echo, we can begin to understand why it has been so appealing to an entire generation of young people. As an ethics, it is not deduced from a prior concept of the good, nor does it originate in some putative will for community. It is responsive and responsible in both Buber's and Bakhtin's sense. To understand it better, we may wish to contrast it briefly at the level of practice with theories of *engagement*, which had also defined for a whole generation the terms of political commitment. *Engagement*, as Sartre made clear both before and after his Marxist turn, is always linked to principles of universal legitimacy, and it proceeds through identification with someone or with a group that one believes to be downtrodden. By contrast, the practice of theory is more akin to that of the refusenik, of the dissident, who rebels and resists but in a very subjective form of rebellion. A dissident is someone who denounces, and bears witness to, the abyss that separates reality from its official version. A dissident's stance draws attention to and inhabits this difference, letting it progressively inscribe itself in the dissident's very body.

Theory as a practice of dissidence and of echoing the cry thus situates itself at the intersection of the cry and of the System, and its practice consists in inventing gestures that are, at one and the same time, dedicated to the cry and a demand for an accounting from the System. This uncomfortable position is that of theory marginalizing itself, for such a practice of theory could not seek to occupy the center. It leads to the figure of the specific intellectual.

The specific intellectual begins by recognizing that to ground one's work in the universal, whether it be Reason or History, is to reinforce the domination of the System. It is a way of ensuring that the echo drowns out the cries of resistance. Instead, the specific intellectual seeks to ground his or her approach in such a way as to be able to discern any enterprise of normalization that presents itself under the auspices of truth while serving the various regimes of coercion, be they linguistic, political, social, or aesthetic. Such a practice requires patient and very rigorous work, frequently of a highly technical nature.

In contrast to previous generations of intellectuals, the specific intellectual does not give lessons or dispense advice, and even less does s/he issue directives, for this intellectual is not in the business of universalizing his or her position but in that of figuring out how to echo the cry in the fissures of a system of which s/he is very much a part. This may strike some as excessively pessimistic, and we know that even pessimism may take on tinges of glory, or at least of vainglory. Theory is not pessimistic, however, for it does not labor within a horizon of the end of history.

Nor must theory fall within a practice of mere echoing. Echo it must, but it must not limit itself to a respect for the Otherness whose cry it echoes, for then it would turn out to be in the service of the system by effacing this Otherness, obliterating its cry. It would serve immobilism and conservatism. Instead theory must show how it has become affected by its practice of echoing; it must display the contamination that is its own, and, just as important, it must ensure that this process is reciprocal, that the Otherness is contaminated as well. This aspect is especially in evidence in the writings of those intellectuals who originate, by virtue of their socially ascribed location, in the margins of the system (whether because of race, gender, geopolitical or economic origin, sexual orientation, or a combination of some or all of these) and who have had to move beyond the cry as a result of their institutionalization within universities and other centers in the organization of knowledge. They function as dissidents, to be sure, but also as living examples of the fissures within the system. Their practice is that of the asyndeton: they break up the grammaticality of the system that draws attention to, but cannot give a representation of, their own agrammaticality and the imperial violence of grammar as the criterion of rational discourse. The asyndeton, as Longinus established a long time ago, is the very figuration of the sublime: the inscription of a disruptive enunciating subject within the apparent seamlessness of representation. At the same time, these intellectuals must also challenge the grammaticality of other grammars and not merely glorify them or take refuge in them.

Such, it seems to me, has been the content of what I have called the Critique of Political Reason as the dominant drive of theory. It should be apparent that this practice, for it is a practice rather than a program, remains as urgent today as it was when first undertaken in the sixties. Sadly, though, it must be acknowledged that a substantial part of this practice has been ambushed along the way, and some of it has joined the ranks of the enemy. I mentioned earlier that in the ascetic and deliberate absence of a set of transformative goals, theory had to cultivate criteria of rigor and patience, of technicity and precision, in order to ensure that this practice not become the pure play of emotion and of subjectivity. Unfortunately, there have been those who have seized upon these criteria to foster a new ideology of professionalism for theory and theoreticians. Unbeknown to themselves, or perhaps blinded by a desire for such power as is available to intellectuals in our society, they have failed to see that this professionalization has, in effect, removed theory from the margin where cry and system intersect, to reposition it squarely at the center (if not in Centers). The center is not a very good place from which to hear the cry of the suppressed, and it is therefore not surprising that the very competent theorist, armored by his professional identity (this is something that tends to befall men more than women, although the latter are not immune), gives up on listening and begins to see himself as the source of his own political program. The practice of echo, always situated, always contextual, gives way to the mouthing of the political pieties which we have lately taken to calling political correctness.

It seems to me that this is the gravest menace to theory today: its professionalized simulacrum, well ensconced in the system of knowledge, usurping the voice of the Other while silencing it and the practice of resistance that is genuine theory. The appearance of a professionalized conception of theory would mark the advent of a total culture of literacy, in which theory, far from challenging the system of the posthistorical state, would be content to flourish in the sphere that was assigned to it.

The essays gathered in this volume were written in the 1980s, most of them in connection with the series "Theory and History of Literature" at the University of Minnesota Press that I co-edited with Jochen Schulte-Sasse. The project of this series, as originated in conversations between the two series editors and Lindsay Waters, who was then an editor at the Press, was precisely to intervene in the nascent American theoretical scene by enriching it with the work of mostly European theorists so that native strands of theory would develop. We did not expect the series to grow to the hundred volumes that it will eventually include. Our decision to give the series the name it has was meant to signal from the outset that theory should not be divorced from history—that is, that theory, as we meant it, should not be practiced as if it were a component of the posthistorical state. This is not the place for sketching an account, however brief and inevitably one-sided, of that series, but I mention this fact to explain why the texts gathered here evince such a recurrent concern with Hegelian conceptions. They seemed to me at the outset of the project, as they still do today, to require discussion on the American scene.

The reader will not fail to observe, among the many shortcomings of this collection, an enormous gap in a volume that purports to deal with theory in the past decade and that defines theory as an echoing of the cry of the victims: there is no engagement with feminism. Actually, there is little echoing of cries in general, since most of the focus is on epistemological issues. One quick and easy answer is that such echoing and engagement are to be found in forthcoming publications dedicated to what the final essay calls "emergent literature," but the reader is entitled to a fuller answer, and it is one that will take a less theoretical and more autobiographical form, as befits the current drift of feminist-inspired theory.

I came to the United States as a student and an immigrant just as the civil rights movement was gaining in national strength, leaving behind me a France that was on the verge of concluding two decades of colonial wars, but had not yet done so. My reaction to the civil rights movement was immediate and undoubtedly at variance with my American contemporaries, typical of the misprisions that Europeans visit upon the United States: it represented to me the authentic historical voice of the United States as the beacon of democracy. The importance of that voice to someone whose parents had spent long years in Nazi camps and who were forced into permanent exile by the imposition of Soviet rule upon their lands cannot be easily overestimated. I was not unaware of the irony of locating that voice in the cries of the oppressed, but I was unaware of the fact that by perceiving the civil rights movement in this fashion I was instrumentalizing it, seeing it as a means of redemption of "America" rather than as the specific struggle of Negroes, to retain the terminology of the times. In other words, I wanted the civil rights struggle to succeed not out of any genuine concern for the plight of Negroes, or because of an abstract dedication to justice, but because of a sentimental attachment to the idea of America. As I gravitated closer to the movement, and as the movement itself evolved toward the affirmation of Black Power, I observed something that shattered this illusion.

There was taking place in the middle to late sixties in New York, where I lived then, a curious forging of relations and alliances within and around the civil rights movement that I can only describe as the marginalization of the black women in the movement in relation to black men and their being supplanted by white women. I found this development, which appeared to propagate unchecked for a while, extremely disturbing, owing to my previous idyllic perception of the entire process. The appearance of race and gender politics within the movement, the net effect of which was to silence black women and to convert them into the oppressed among the oppressed, with the connivance of white women, forced me to reexamine my view of the civil rights struggle and of "America" as well. Because many of the white women involved in this process were describing themselves as "women's liberationists," I developed a suspicion of any feminism that did not address the issue of race in its own midst. At the same time, I recognized that I was subjecting feminists to a standard that I was perhaps not always invoking when dealing with other fields of theory. These are not easy matters for a white male to handle. I have preferred not to be overtly judgmental while watching and following the developments within feminism, hoping that the injustice that presided at its foundation will be recognized and reversed, and I have been gratified by evidence that some of it is. In the meantime, I have decided to hold my peace. In future publications, I won't.

1   Reading for Culture

"Literature, its history and its study, have, in recent times, fallen into greater and greater discredit," wrote Hans Robert Jauss some two decades ago in the preface to *Literaturgeschichte als Provokation,* where he set forth his program for the revival of literary studies.[1] It should be noted at the outset that, between literature and its study, Jauss inserts history, a point made not only syntactically but with considerable theoretical vigor and erudition in the key chapter of the book, the justly famous "Literary History as a Challenge to Literary Theory," originally delivered as the inaugural lecture of his seminar at the University of Constance in 1967.[2] Yet during the ten years that elapsed between that day and the original publication of *Ästhetische Erfahrung: Literatur und Hermeneutik,* history did not stand still but rather, as it is wont to do, problematized even further its relationship to literature and its study. Some may have felt discomfited by such a development, but not Jauss, who had just argued for a dynamic view of history that would govern the reception of texts. From the perspective of his own theory, he found himself in the highly enviable position of studying the reception of his own pronouncements and of responding to that reception, thereby giving concrete evidence, in his own procedures and writings, of the very processes that he had theoretically elaborated and then described in the works of others. Although too modest and too mindful of scholarly decorum to admit it, Jauss must have reflected upon this dialectic more than once in the writing of *Aesthetic Experience and Literary Hermeneutics.* Since the English-language reader may not be familiar with this history, I shall sketch it out briefly.

I

It is not easy to characterize Jauss's place in the German critical scene, for in many ways it is eccentric to the dominant centers of his day.

Although he worked for some twenty years within the framework of
a group of scholars united by similar methodological concerns, his
original thinking developed almost idiosyncratically and did not follow any previously traced paths until it burst upon the national scene
with Jauss's appointment to the new interdisciplinary university at
Constance, whereupon it contributed to a major transformation of
the German critical landscape.

Literary criticism in Germany, in the immediate post–World War II
period, was dominated by approaches derived from American New
Criticism. There was ample justification for the adoption of techniques of close reading against the prevailing tradition of positivism,
which treated texts as either biographical or historical documents or
as the sum total of the influences that had determined them. But there
was also the advantage to the *Werkimmanente* approach that it permitted the bracketing of all historical questions of recent political allegiance. This became the dominant methodological practice among the
students of German literature, but Jauss remained largely unaffected
by it because he was a scholar of romance literatures, and in this discipline the situation was different. As Harald Weinrich, himself a Ro-
manist of note as well as an early theoretician of reader's response,
noted in a personal memoir, many young Germans were struck by the
publication of Ernst Robert Curtius's *European Literature and the
Latin Middle Ages* in 1948, for it provided them with "the unsuspected chance to be all at once reintegrated, together with [their] nation, into the good old family of civilized and cultivated mankind."[3]
Although descriptions of Curtius as a Cold War humanist, and of his
version of humanism as "a strategic ideology with the aim of covering
the restoration of capitalism in the Western world"[4] may strike the
English reader as far-fetched and extreme (even though they are increasingly documented), it is nevertheless true that Curtius's influence
upon the Germany of Adenauer—of whose brain trust he was a member—coincided with the avoidance of any sociological reflection and
the construct of history as handed-down tradition. But again Jauss
was eccentric to the movement. Having studied under Hans-Georg
Gadamer, who was then reexamining the structure and function of
hermeneutics, he saw the inescapability of a problematic relationship
between the past and the present, and therefore the necessity of con-
fronting the question of history; further, he understood that confron-
tation as taking place within a framework of communication, and
therefore requiring consideration of both the individual and the social

dimensions of that encounter. He began to address the first, the historical, in his writings on medieval French literature and in a brilliant book with, so far, a very restricted readership, on the relationship of time and remembrance to the structure of the novel in Proust's *A la Recherche du Temps Perdu.*[5] The occasion for the second, the examination of the psychosocial dimensions of communication, was provided by the rapid transformation of German society in the early sixties, and especially the rise of mass media and the ensuing crisis of education. Since this is a hotly debated topic in Germany upon which agreement is not likely to be reached in the near future, no more than a brief sketch of Jauss's stand on this matter can be offered here.

The traditional methods and aims of humanistic education, whether drawn along the lines of Curtius's ideal of Romania or the stylistic formalism of the *Werkimmanente* approach, proved vulnerable and incapable of resistance to the new media. Conceived for the leisurely and considered study and transmission of masterpieces, they offered no guidance for dealing with the sophisticated, and frequently aesthetically subtle, messages of the media, which, by their sheer mass and accelerated reception-time, overwhelmed high literature. Jauss took this as a sign of the failure of literary education to perform a "critical social function." It should be the function of a literary education, he argued, to endow the individual with sufficient discrimination and moral power of judgment to protect himself or herself against the influence of the "hidden persuaders." It is clear that Jauss conceived of the development of such a critical social function within the framework of existing society. He was, and continues to be, prepared to argue that literature, especially past literature, has a formative social function. Politically, his attitude could be characterized as liberal-reformist.

What such a project required was the reformulation of the way in which we conceive of our relationship to literature, past and present. Curtius's model, already disqualified by its failure to resist the trivialization of culture, is far too reverential and makes no provision for us except as celebrant of a past richness. The formalism of close reading is found wanting on two scores: (1) it aims at an ascesis of the reader who must, in her or his own encounter with the text, bracket all personal interests and predilections so that the text may deploy its intentional structure unhindered; (2) by stressing the autonomy of each text, this methodological approach is incapable of reintegrating the text into a history. At this juncture, Jauss did something quite bold for a West German student of literature of his day: he decided to look at the model of history provided by Marxism. Although he rejected it because of its dependence upon economic determinism, he opened up a debate among literary scholars on the value of the Marxist view of history, taking at times what were seen as highly ambiguous positions, such as his claim that Marxist literary critics had not replaced the Romantic model of literary history with a conceptualization adequate to Marx's view of history. Similarly, he noted that Lukács's focus on the way in which literature reflects reality (but is not a constituent factor in the shaping of reality) resulted in studies of literary creation but not in any awareness of the effect of literature upon the reader. Jauss then turned to the newly translated work of the Russian Formalists, and especially the notion of literary evolution advanced by Jakobson and Tynjanov.[6] Although he approved of their description, derived from phenomenology but couched in a more linguistic terminology, of the processes whereby individual works set themselves off from their predecessors, absorbed and automatized some of their features, or sought to react against them by the conscious alteration of some devices, he rejected their overall view, for it claimed that works of literature evolve in their own autonomous series without reference to extra-literary history.

Coming back to his point of departure, Jauss reexamined the specific communicational situation that we call reading. If the reader is considered a part of the reading operation, the function of a reading cannot be the establishment of some objective, forever valid, meaning of the text. Rather any conception of reading must start with the recognition that the reader is already fully awash in the tradition that has given rise to the object of his or her reading, and, indeed, that the text is itself an articulation in its mode of reception. No reader of Keats, for instance, approaches a poem of his without some sense of what it is to read a high Romantic poem. But once we begin to think in this manner, a whole host of questions descends upon us: What happens when we read? Do we bring ourselves to the work or do we get something from it? What sort of prejudgments do we bring to our readings? Do we expect certain things in certain genres? Are we intimidated by certain works, certain authors, certain reputations? What is the nature of such intimidations? What is the image of the author that we bring to a reading? Do we, as the reading audience, exercise some influence upon the author as s/he writes for us? Do we have immediate access to literature or not, and if not, what mediations can we bring into play? To what extent can we be manipulated so that we respond in an expected manner? How can it be determined that we will respond aesthetically to something that may not have been intended that way? All these questions and more, especially those having to do with value, emerge in the forefront of attention as soon as a reader- or a recipient-centered approach to literature is attempted.

Jauss drew upon the teachings of Gadamer in order to establish the foundational categories of his *Rezeptionsästhetik*.[7] Gadamer is concerned with the nature of understanding, ostensibly philosophical, although he begins by conflating the distinction between philosophical and everyday understanding. For him, understanding is an event in which we are implicated but which we do not dominate; it is something that happens to us. We never come to cognitive situations empty but carry with us a whole world of familiar beliefs and expectations. The hermeneutic phenomenon encompasses both the alien world we suddenly encounter and the familiar one we carry. Whereas most philosophical conceptions of the hermeneutic phenomenon require that we overcome our own boundedness (historical, psychological, social, and so forth), Gadamer argues that this is impossible and that what matters is to use the hermeneutic phenomenon to recognize what we brought into it, so that we gain knowledge of ourselves by discovering our own unsuspected preformed judgments *(Vorverständnis)*, as well as gaining knowledge of the alien by extending our horizons until they meet with its own so that a fusion of horizons takes place.

Gadamer's best-known model for this encounter is that of question and answer. The relationship of interpreter to text must be conceived as a dialogue in which both participate on an equal footing. Such a dialogue presupposes that its participants share a common concern and are not merely intent upon each other. As a result, the interpreter must not concentrate on the text but rather must adopt an orientation toward the problem that concerns the text. In this way, the interpreter does not identify with the author—a delusion in any case—but explores the text's concern and finds himself/herself interrogated further in the direction that the text's initial question traces. A horizon of interrogation emerges, but not in the guise of a new objectivity; rather it is a way of rendering the text actual to me existentially, for I am now concerned with its questions and have brought my concerns to bear upon it.

Jauss takes over the notion of horizon, which he names "horizon of expectation" and means by it the sum total of reactions, prejudgments, and verbal and other behavior that greet a work upon its appearance. A work may fulfill such a horizon by confirming the expectations vested in it, or it may disappoint the expectations by creating a distance between itself and them. This Jauss labels "aesthetic distance." Aesthetic distance becomes an important factor in the constitution of literary history, for it may result in one of two major processes: either the public alters its horizon so that the work is now accepted—and a stage in the aesthetics of reception is set—or it rejects a work, which may then lie dormant until it is accepted, that is, until a horizon for it is forged (such was the case of medieval literature, which had to await Romanticism to find a horizon in which it could be received again). In some instances, particularly in Modernism, the public splits into groups of willing recipients and adamant refuseniks. From the perspective of a social critical function for literature, Jauss sees in this ability of literary texts to alter horizons of expectation a strong liberating force that works both upon the recipient, for it frees her or him of the views s/he held without necessarily being aware of them, and upon literature, and especially classical literature, for it permits us to recover its initial impact, which has been eroded by centuries of veneration and monumentalization.

Such a conception of the interaction of reader and text restores the historical dimension, Jauss claims, for the public of recipients, past and present, is fully involved as the mediator of the texts. The pitfall that the Russian Formalists could not avoid, namely the separation of literature and life, is thus overcome, for it is in their daily lives that readers build up their horizons of expectations, and it is in the same lives that any work-induced changes will have to take place. The public also serves as the mediator between an older work and a more recent one, and thus provides the basis for understanding the formation of the literary sequences which historiography will record. A history of literature undertaken according to these principles would appear to be eminently empirical and value-free, for it would not obey some foreordained logic but would merely record what it notes without succumbing to the totalizing news of positivism because it needs to recognize its own historical inscription. Thus, for all practical purposes, each generation of readers must rewrite history. This is not a defect of the theory but its most liberating feature, for it ensures that no fixed view ever prevails and that each generation must read the texts anew, interrogate them from its own perspective, and find itself concerned, in its own fashion, by the work's questions.

Because they stress the need to overcome the excessive mediatization of cultural life, it is ironic that Jauss's pronouncements should have emerged against a horizon that ensured their misinterpretation. The very misgivings that had led Jauss to formulate a research program for the renewal of the pedagogy of literary studies had by then become a major social and political force in the unrest of German universities and indeed in the society at large. This is a history that remains to be written, and its complexities are certainly beyond the scope of a sketch such as this one; it suffices to note here that Jauss's ideas, with their emphasis on a reauthentification of the experience of reception in literature, the legitimation of an active role for the reader, hitherto conceived of as passive recipient, the critique of the media, the call for the reorganization of humanistic studies, and the advocacy of a social-critical role for literary education, presented superficial analogies with the calls for educational and social transformation emanating from far more radical quarters. Or rather, Jauss was perceived by conservatives within the university and without, as not only legitimizing the oppositional forces of the S.D.S. and the A.P.O. (Ausserparlamentarische Opposition: extraparliamentary opposition), but as serving as their Trojan horse, for, unlike the famous Frankfurt Institute for Social Research, whose critique of the existing order was well known, Jauss appeared to be in the mold of the traditional German scholar. For the Right, then, this senior professor (an ordinarius, a member of the ultimate hierarchy in the German university system) was a traitor in its midst. But the excoriation from the Right did not differ in degree from the denunciations of the Left, which recognized readily that Jauss's project was reformist and not revolutionary in orientation and which tended to see in his enterprise an attempt at cooptation by the dominant group. How virulent these passions could become was shown when students occupied Adorno's seminar in Frankfurt and eventually had to be removed by police.[8] Jauss's position thus became quite difficult. The Right, as is its wont, used its power against him, or more precisely against his junior associates, so that on several occasions he had to threaten resignation—a threat made more credible by his acceptance of visiting professorships in the United States. The attacks from the Left he dealt with in his own writings, so that, rather paradoxically and misleadingly, Jauss's publications after 1970 give the impression of one intent upon combating the Left only, and therefore of an ally of the Right, whereas Jauss's response was more nuanced and addressed criticism from both sides with the weapons each would recognize: ideas against the Left; such power as he had against the Right.

Aesthetic Experience and Literary Hermeneutics is therefore a polemical work, an aspect which is at times quite apparent, at others less so. It polemicizes most of all against what Jauss perceives as the dominant left view of art: Adorno's aesthetics of negativity and the Ideologiekritik movement which accompanied it. Adorno is explicitly mentioned in the book a number of times and a full-fledged critique of his views is presented, but even when there is no direct reference to him, he is very much present. For example, Jauss reserves some of his severest criticism of contemporary writers for Samuel Beckett, who happens to be the author to whom Adorno intended to dedicate his *Ästhetische Theorie* had he been able to complete it prior to his death. Similarly, one may well wonder at Jauss's selection of the theme *Douceur du foyer* for his discussion of the lyric in the mid-nineteenth century, for the strongly affirmative value he places on this theme is in direct contradiction to Adorno's construct of the role played by a variant of the same theme, namely that of *intérieur* (also expressed in French) in the writings of Kierkegaard.[9]

The difference between Jauss's and Adorno's views is substantial, even though both share a concern for the current state of culture. Adorno's thinking, always dialectical in the extreme, is equally concerned with the manipulation of art, but it immediately extends into a critique of the ideological means that are invoked to justify that manipulation. For him, aesthetic theory, as indeed any philosophical activity, must be not only theoretical but critical, for only a critical theory can have an impact in the social sphere. With respect to art, the task—but we shall see that it is a utopian one—is to restore its rightful existence, which can happen, if at all, in a liberated society. Since Adorno did not address the question of the concrete means of such a liberation, all that is left is the critical moment, which of necessity is impregnated with the pessimism caused by the present.

Art, then, is for Adorno at the inscription of social conflicts, unfree and subject to ideological control, so that, for all practical purposes, art takes on the aspect of an element of the superstructure. On the basis of his previous studies of advanced capitalism, Adorno wants to bring out how, in its very form, art is compelled to embody social conflicts. A denunciation of the present treatment of art must therefore be formulated from the perspective which does not exist, which, as utopian thought, would lay the ground for a conception of art in a world in which conflicts would be sublated. But the situation of art today is, in Adorno's own term, "aporetic." For if, in the past, art had been in the service of rituals or other religious beliefs and practices, its achievement of autonomy in the age of the Enlightenment was but the prelude to a new enslavement. Our society, which Adorno sees as ruled by instrumental reason, whose institutional hallmark is the bureaucracy, is totally, and structurally, unwilling to let art have its autonomy to give it the motility of a commodity, which becomes subject to the operations of a market, and thus functions as the vehicle of dominant ideology. The market itself is the object of controls, among which is the scholarly study of art, which serves to establish hierarchies of (marketable) values and thus provides the ground for market strategies.

Turning art into a commodity leads to a valorization of concepts that insists on its form as closed, on its aspect as finished or polished product. Such closure is achievable, under present socioeconomic circumstances, only by doing violence to the form of the art object, which otherwise necessarily reproduces the conflicts and contradictions of society. True art resists commodification by refusing this closure. It insists on its unfinished character, and on its overall uselessness, its incapacity to serve any end, for, in the radical affirmation of its uselessness, it calls into question the claims to harmonious totalization that our society advances ideologically. In practice, this signifies that the study of art, and *a fortiori* of literature, should not take the form of a traditional aesthetics but rather that of an analytics which, in the immediate study of individual art objects, would elicit the mode of their apprehension of history, that is, the way in which they reproduce the social agonistics of their moment. This requires a strong denunciation of all approaches to art that wish to reestablish an ideal and separate position for it. What matters most, in Adorno's view, is that each individual analysis bring out the fundamentally critical moment in the artefact, whereby it stands in opposition to, and negates, the order and ideology of its society. For only in this manner can we recover the truth of art, which is that art is the inscription of history and therefore contains the promise of a future liberation.

What is at play in Adorno's aesthetic theory or indeed in his thought at large is negativity, a concept which he endowed with special richness, first in the formulation of the cognitive principle of nonidentity which then served as the basis of his philosophy of "negative dialectics," against which Jauss's entire critique is directed. In Hegelian dialectics, negativity is the movement of the concept toward its "other," and a necessary stage in the passage to *Aufhebung,* the overcoming or sublation of the initial concept. But for Adorno the Hegelian synthesis was, in its ideality, impossible. Reason is incapable of capturing reality, not so much because of its own finitude but because reality, always social in nature, is, in its very objective conditions, far too contradictory to be encompassed by reason without imparting contradictions to it. Thus, for Adorno, a concept and reality exist differentially with respect to each other, rather than having the concept mirror the reality, as is the case in all idealistic epistemologies. Adorno has the concept refer to the reality by virtue of its nonidentity to it; the process may be envisaged, with the same results, with reality as the starting point. The cognitive force of art is, then, but an instantiation of the operation of a general principle of nonidentity, that is, negativity.

Jauss's critique of Adorno's views is cogently and forcefully expressed in section A2 of *Aesthetic Experience and Literary Hermeneutics* and needs no extended discussion here. Yet it appeals to a notion, which is then elevated to a major analytic concept in the book, whose logical emergence in this context may not be apparent to an English-language reader, namely *identification.* It happens that German uses two words to designate what we refer to by the simple term "experience," and it becomes possible to signal an important conceptual difference by preferring one term over the other. In the context of aesthetics, and specifically within the framework of *Lebensphilosophie,* the term *Erlebnis* was the object of the subject's quest for understanding. Adorno, by contrast, has recourse to the word *Erfahrung,* by which he means to signal that reflection itself is lived experience and that it concerns the entire individual, not merely his or her capacity as knowing subject. The distinction here could be most readily apprehended through a reference to Kant. Adorno's rejection of the *Aufhebung* of Hegelian dialectics rested to a great extent on his extreme valorization of the individual, whose singularity he wished to protect against Hegel's conflation in the collective subjectivity that is Absolute spirit. To do this, he returned to Kant's phenomenology and its notion of autonomous subject. But Adorno criticized Kant's conception of the relation of subject to object, for it seemed to him to lead to the kind of postulate of identity that his own principle of nonidentity was meant to displace. In effect, he argued, Kant's notion of the individual was too formal and abstract, and therefore easily subsumable in reified thought; this is apparent in the master category of the transcendental subject, from the perspective of which every individual subject is, like a commodity, exchangeable for another, and thus not an individual, in the sense of specific, at all. If reflection is conceived of as *Erfahrung,* it will not stand in an abstract relation to lived experience and will not become the locus of reification. At the same time, this implies that cognition is not merely an intellectual matter but one that involves the entire person, including the body. Thus, it is the whole human person, as an empirically existing individual, that is engaged in *Erfahrung,* whereas *Erlebnis* is but the fodder of reflection. Jauss retains the term *Erfahrung* to designate aesthetic experience and thus gains for his discussion the reference to the somatic aspects of aesthesis, which permits the masterful discussion of pleasure.

But against Adorno, Jauss returns to another aspect of Kant's conception of the individual and his or her cognitive power. For Kant, the fact that the individual could not experience the object as it was in itself required the postulation of another dimension among individuals: intersubjectivity. This was retained by both Hegel and Marx in their respective concepts of the master-slave dialectic and the class struggle. But Adorno's insistence on the radical and never subsumable individuality of each subject prevented any solution to what appears to be a monadic existence for the individual. Against this notion, Jauss restores the intersubjective dimension of Kant's concept of the subject and grounds it in a communicational framework within which it becomes possible for individuals to share experience. The effect is that of recapturing the hermeneutic dimension of Dilthey's *Erlebnis,* without surrendering, at least ostensibly, the coprimacy of reflection implied by *Erfahrung.* The intersubjective dimension of *Erlebnis* is to be found in mechanisms of *identification* which thus come to replace Dilthey's *Einfühlung,* or empathy. In sum, Jauss replaces the Negation/Affirmation polarity of Adorno by stressing that the negativity of the work of art is mediated by identification, which thus emerges as the key counterconcept of the aesthetics of reception.

II

Some of the controversies that I have attempted to summarize here by somewhat forcedly, yet nonetheless exemplarily, pitting Jauss against Adorno may strike us as lacking a counterpart on our critical scene. Jauss's reception among us has taken place in the general space that we have taken to calling "theory," and, within it, the subdivision

known as "reader's response theory" that has been cultivated in varying degree and orientation by the likes of Norman Holland, Stanley
Fish, and David Bleich, who have already prepared for Jauss's arrival
by the earlier welcome accorded to his Constance colleague and fel-
low-*Rezeptionsästhetiker* Wolfgang Iser. But it would be a pity, in my
view, if Jauss were to be read only by such groups, for he is a thinker
whose scope of vision extends beyond the boundaries of a specific
research question. Rather, he is good for those treks that step off the
trodden paths and set out into the wilderness, the present roaming
ground of criticism, as Geoffrey Hartman reminds us.[10] Since reader's-
response theoreticians and practitioners will approach Jauss from
their special vantage point and with their own interests, they need no
guidance, whereas Jauss's qualifications for a walk through the desert
require a few comments.

Jauss's critical endeavors arose, I suggested, out of the sense of crisis
that had befallen German higher education in the 1960s, especially
the humanities and social sciences. That the United States is itself presently in a state of crisis in the same areas is too much of a commonplace to bear reiterating, although it is far from clear that we have a
sense of the transformation that we are undergoing. In many ways our
crisis is unlike the German one: theirs was one of growth, ours one of
retrenchment; theirs had to do with the rapid development of the mass
media, ours does not; theirs took place in a heavily politicized milieu,
whereas our campuses are perceived as more apolitical than ever. Such
comparisons are not particularly enlightening. What is perhaps more
important is to trace the shifts that are occurring in the organization
of knowledge. If we take the discipline of English as an example, the
dimensions of the crisis become clearer and Jauss's concerns more pertinent.

As I have said in the Introduction, we have been told, within the
universities and without, that there is a "literacy" crisis abroad in the
land, that students can neither read nor write, that they no longer
comprehend what they read, and that employers view our graduates
with distaste, or at least apprehension. Since we live in a society that
demands rapid solutions to newly discovered problems, we have invested a tremendous amount of resources, financial and human, over
the past ten years in writing programs, whether they are called that
or rhetoric, composition, or communication. This is not the place to
undertake an evaluation or a critique of such efforts, nor even to wonder at the wisdom, let alone the efficacy, of implementing on a massive

scale the results of one of the least researched areas in our field. Suffice it to consider the effect upon the department of English: in nearly all instances, faculty have been reassigned to the teaching of writing; more important, the bulk if not the totality of new appointments are made in this area at the expense of more established parts of the curriculum. Since the teaching of writing has traditionally been held in low esteem and generally delegated to junior faculty and teaching assistants, the present shift in resource allocation has begun to produce resentment among senior faculty, who see their traditional departmental strengths and disciplinary profile erode. As a result, at a large number of universities an adversary relationship has begun to develop between the central administrators, who, feeling that they are responding to societal pressure, want more writing programs, and the senior faculty in English, who fear that whenever one of their ranks retires or leaves for another position, a traditional appointment in, let us say, the eighteenth-century novel will give way to an assistant professorship in composition. The senior faculty becomes more possessive of those positions which it values and is generally prepared to argue for them on the basis of their importance as specialty fields. Slowly English departments take on a rather new configuration: a service component teaching writing and employing large numbers of graduate assistants, and a specialist component offering pregraduate and graduate training for those who intend to enter the profession, however bleak the prospects of employment might appear. In this respect, English departments are rapidly becoming like foreign language departments, which have traditionally kept their language-teaching function quite separate from their graduate training and research. But English as a discipline was never meant to be like French or German in English-speaking universities: whereas those departments rely upon exotica or special interests for their appeal, English has been the department of choice for all those who have wanted to study, and reflect upon, their own culture. The aspiring writer, the future critic, the student generally desirous of acquiring a well-rounded education that would prepare him or her for a broad array of professional endeavors, all came to English, for if it was not quite F. R. Leavis's "discipline of thought"[11] it came closer to that ideal than any other segment of the curriculum. But today, the student is faced instead with an English department that is in the business of basic or remedial literacy at one end and intent upon reproducing itself—training future practitioners of its specialty—at the other. To literate students the choice appears to be purely professional, and, not surprisingly, they opt for those preprofessional programs that hold a greater promise of gainful employment. Should the current realignment of English departments along the structural model of foreign language departments continue, the broad sphere of cultural concerns will progressively diminish and disappear, first from the university and then from public life as well. This is at once the real nature of our crisis and the dimension of our wilderness. The risk is that we will be left with the increasingly strident cries of traditionalists nostalgic for a unity that never was and confident of the universality of their own pursuits, and an array of fragmentary discourses locked away in their specialized concerns and technical terminologies.

The work of Jauss may help us to recover this lost space of cultural criticism, but it is not an enterprise free of dangers. Since my exposition has proceeded through exemplary figures (Jauss, Adorno, English), let me invoke one last one: Lionel Trilling. It is at once obvious that Trilling occupied eminently the space whose parceling we are presently observing. It would indeed be tempting to date the beginning of this process from his death, but I fear that would make better narrative than judgment, for some of the roots of our predicament are already in Trilling.

It is striking to note that Jauss's masterful discussion of aesthetic pleasure contained in *Aesthetic Experience and Literary Hermeneutics* has no recent antecedent in English unless we return to a text Trilling published in 1963 in *Partisan Review,* "The Fate of Pleasure."[12] This essay, whose translation into European languages would dispel the widely held view on the Continent that there is no aesthetic thought in English, examines a paradigmatic shift in the nature of pleasure and its consequences for our conception of art that occurred between the Enlightenment and Romanticism. Trilling begins with the puzzling statement in Wordsworth's Preface to *Lyrical Ballads* that "the grand elementary principle of pleasure" constitutes "the naked and native dignity of man." From its inception, then, Trilling's reflection upon pleasure is framed by the question of human nature: the dignity of man and the role played by pleasure in its achievement. Wordsworth's notion of pleasure is austere, to be sure, but it is not unrelated to certain historical considerations, especially the eudaemonic thrust of Enlightenment political theory, best exemplified in the French Revolution's promise of universal happiness. Trilling shows very carefully that the notion of dignity derived from a certain level of material well-being, characterized by the possession of luxurious goods. In contrast to Wordsworth, who is made to play, rather aptly, the role of a *moraliste des Lumières,* Keats is ambivalent about pleasure, or more precisely, discovers the specific dialectic of pleasure. Not content with the confinement of pleasure to the higher intellectual pursuits, though constantly mindful, in Wordsworth's sillion, of its cognitive power, Keats proceeded to affirm the principle of pleasure most boldly, discovering in this manner that it required the greatest scrutiny. As Trilling reminds us, in the "country of La Belle Dame sans Merci, the scene of erotic pleasure . . . leads to devastation" (p. 58). Keats does something that Wordsworth did not consider: he separates the experience of pleasure, which continues to be described in the most approving terms, from its effects, which are incalculable and therefore most unreliable. In "Sleep and Poetry," Keats draws upon this distinction in order to show that poetry, through the pleasure that it procures, can "soothe the cares, and lift the thoughts of man," thereby articulating what Trilling calls the "essence of Philistinism" (p. 60). Trilling takes Keats's distinction and sees it at the root of the dichotomy of politics and art today, where the first seeks to satisfy the principle of pleasure by increasing material influence, whereas the latter looks at such a goal with considerable disdain.

Since it is already apparent in Keats that aesthetic pleasure, just as much as erotic pleasure, may serve illusion as easily as cognition—that, in other words, pleasure is cognitively unreliable—modern art is forced to seek a firmer cognitive ground by abandoning the pleasure principle and cultivating what Trilling calls "the negative transcendence of the human, a condition which is to be achieved by freeing the self from its thralldom to pleasure" (p. 71). Trilling's best examples come from Dostoevsky's *Notes from the Underground* and its theme of the search for a greater intensity of life, and from Augustine's wonderment in the *Confessions* at his own perversity in stealing pears that he neither needed nor desired. The juxtaposition of the two examples results in a curious conflation of the historical dimension in the essay. Until the invocation of Augustine's sin, the phenomenon described had firm historical boundaries, corresponding to the emergence and hegemony of the bourgeoisie, which is in the business of purveying reified experience, "specious good" (p. 66). But a historical inquiry of this sort leads, in Trilling's mind, to an impasse: if his analysis is correct, the modern tilt toward a negativity of pleasure must be seen in its historical relativity, and modernity abandoned. But for what? Will it have to be "an idiot literature, [with] 'positive heroes' who know how to get the good out of life and who have 'affirmative' emotions about their success in doing so?" (p. 69). Trilling has already precluded social change ("the impulse to destroy specious good would be as readily directed against the most benign socialist society, which by modern definition, serves the principle of pleasure" (p. 67), and is left therefore with a strategy that will greatly alter the status of history in his inquiry. By showing that the negativity characteristic of modernity already obtains in Augustine, and is therefore prebourgeois, he can argue that it is a permanent feature of the human psyche, a solution already foreseeable in the decision to frame the analysis within the question of human nature. Not unexpectedly, Freud is invoked to give the stamp of scientific approval to the notion that negativity is part and parcel of humanity. The only historical question left is that of the changing equilibria between the pleasure principle and its beyond. This final gesture of Trilling's neatly removes the historical phenomenon of negativity from its contingency and relativizes history itself. Appropriately enough, the essay is collected in a volume entitled *Beyond Culture,* a space which is meant to be that of unchanging human nature and therefore "not within the purview of ordinary democratic progressivism" (p. 74).

Once historical considerations are removed, the realm of cultural criticism is set adrift, for it no longer has a function. Either the critic can argue from the perspective of an atemporal human nature and denounce the present or the past dogmatically, that is, uncritically with respect to her or his own position, or s/he can cultivate specialized subfields which by virtue of their technicity appear to be beyond the judgment of value. It would be easy to speculate upon the historical coincidence of such a choice with the political upheavals of the sixties and early seventies, but it is more to the point here to observe that for all the similarities of concern, Jauss's problematic is diametrically opposed to Trilling's: it seeks to restore the historical consciousness of criticism after a period of painful repression, and even the presumed universality of aesthetic response is shown to fluctuate historically. The very vigor of Jauss's historical inquiry ought to help us to return from Trilling's "beyond," to a realm of culture. It is for this long march through the wilderness that Jauss can be our guide.

III

The reopening of the cultural realm for criticism will not represent an advance, though, as long as the possibility of Trilling's solution remains. We must recognize that his notion of culture rested upon an anthropology that is derived from Freudian ego-psychology. Jauss's notion of culture oscillates between a historically attentive view and one derived from the Kantian model of intersubjectivity, which ultimately relies upon the consciousness of the assembled community for its reality principle, that is, its locus of cognitive determinacy. The recourse to anthropological models always carries with it the question of human nature with the consequences we have seen in Trilling and in English departments. In "The Fate of Pleasure" Trilling had come close to seeing another possibility, but by then he was already committed to the concept of "beyond culture." When Trilling first sets out to find evidence of negativity, even before Dostoevsky's *Notes from the Underground,* he comes upon Keats's "On Sitting Down to Read *King Lear* Once Again." Here, Trilling writes, Keats "dismisses all thought of pleasure and prepares himself for the pain he is duty bound to undergo" (p. 62). It is of course in connection with Shakespeare that Keats had developed the notion of Negative Capability, so it is logical to seek evidence of negativity in this poem which considers the very act of reading with its anticipations, reflecting on past readerly experience of *King Lear.*

There is little here of the Aristotelian expectation that a regenerating cleansing will occur. The experience will be painful, of that Keats is certain, but even more gravely, it may well not, through any catharsis, lead to the kind of emotional balance that would make him productive; rather, it may leave him to "wander in a barren dream." That is, it may threaten his very creative powers by closing him off from any principle of reality (wandering in a dream), so that his only recourse is to pray that he can be saved from the experience. This experience, derived from past reading, is entirely caught in the metaphor of consumption by fire:

> Adieu! for, once again, the fierce dispute
> > Betwixt damnation and impassioned clay
> > Must I burn through . . .
> >
> > > > (lines 5–7)

and

> > Let me not wander in a barren dream
> But, when I am consumèd in the fire,
> Give me new Phoenix wings to fly at my desire.
> > > (lines 12–14)

The inital choice is not very appealing: the eternal fire of damnation, by definition, concludes history and is on the far side of any possible redemption; "impassioned clay," that is, clay fixed by passion, achieves the solidity of brick, or a form already fixed once and for all. To leave romance for Shakespeare, then, is to risk either the permanent loss of the self or its imprisonment in a form that admits of no further modification. Cognitively, both possibilities are distressing, and so Keats launches an appeal to Shakespeare, rather surprisingly since he seems to be the cause of the present difficulty, and to the "clouds of Albion," a vague addressee to say the least. But the very recourse to apostrophe is here to indicate that the move about to be made is more rhetorical than cognitive, so that the invocation of the clouds and of Shakespeare participates more in a textual economy than in a semantic one. For the poem does offer a solution: in the code of fires there is always a third possibility, that of the phoenix who, though consumed by the fire, does not lose himself in it as do the damned, nor change state, as does the clay, but is reborn as a newer and better version of the self.

This solution, though, is wholly linguistic and textual. To the predicament posed by the reading of *King Lear,* and against two phenomenologically based possibilities, the poem opposes but another text, that of the legend of the phoenix, which it must temporarily treat as if it were unproblematic in its own reading. The reading of *King Lear* is framed by romance at one end and by the myth of the phoenix at the other. It remains quite obscure why the phoenix legend should prove cognitively more satisfactory than *King Lear* or indeed than romance, especially since it figures in classical romances and is in fact part of the universe of classical texts which had also been discussed with the injunction in lines 2–4:

> Fair Plumèd Syren, queen of far-away!
> Leave melodizing on this wintry day,
> Shut up thine olden pages, and be mute:

In her "melodizing" guise, we tend to think of the siren as a mermaid, and of her habitat as aquatic, but here she is explicitly qualified as "Fair-plumèd" and must therefore be the teratological version of half woman/half flying snake who hails from Arabia, which just happens to be the phoenix's original home. The reception of *King Lear,* itself traversed by negativity, is mediated by the sublation of a prior negativity: the rejection of the classical legend is itself negated, and, in its return, the classical text relieves the negativity of the Shakespearean text.

Here culture is not an intersubjective paradigm, a structure which could be abstracted, formulated, and offered up for reading itself. It is rather a set of textual operations which must be read, which inscribe our historicity in relation to its own. At their best, Jauss's readings of the meandering of our aesthetic experience recognize this dimension of culture and guide us through its discovery. Against the reaffirmation of sameness and against the New Vocationalism, Jauss proposes the ideal of a critical literacy.

2   The Changing Face of History

with Nicholas Spadaccini

Once upon a time, it was possible to make an audience chuckle by saying that history is no longer what it used to be. Everyone understood this amphibological use of the term *history*, which was called upon to mean both the representation of past events and the actual course of these events; and, whereas it was generally accepted that differing and multiple representations are possible, perhaps even desirable, the actual course of past events could only be singular and have the immutability of a fate accomplished. Today, the same statement would no longer elicit similar mirth. Not only are we all too aware of the constant manipulation and rewriting of history that is one of the hallmarks of our age, whether for reasons that we may find as abhorrent as Orwell did, or, on the contrary, for reasons that we may approve of, as in the new histories that no longer omit the fate and the feats of women; but we are also becoming more conscious of the determinant role played by the discourse of the historian in the representation of history that results from this discourse. Among historians, the work of Hayden White is preeminently concerned with this problem, while among literary scholars, the poststructuralists have used it to challenge the very possibility of historical cognition.

History, as an academic enterprise, is being haunted with something that it thought it had exorcised at its very beginnings. For, as Arnaldo Momigliano has reminded us, the oldest chairs of history in Europe were created in the sixteenth century when the chairs of letters at the universities of Göttingen and Leiden were split into two different chairs, reflecting and instituting the perceived difference between letters and history.[1] There is thus an irony, even a historical irony, in our present situation; but as with most ironies, what is at stake is not merely the discomfiture of some assertory discourse, in this instance the historical one, nor even the very setting of the distinction, which is the present institutional organization of knowledge as exemplified in the disciplinary structure of our universities, but rather our conception of what constitutes historical representation.

The discourse of the historian—to designate in the abstract singular what has been a plurality of concrete practices—has grown more remote from its original ground in letters, and it has done so by concentrating on one aspect of its formal communicational apparatus—the referent, or what historians have traditionally called the facts—at the expense of the others, and most notably of the addressee, who is the reader. History used to be read by cultured individuals almost as much, if not more, than fiction. That is the case much less today, though some forms of it, especially biography and so-called narrative history, seem to fare somewhat better. Some historians have come to believe that history must return to this traditional form of narrative to recapture its past audience or, more precisely, to move beyond the narrow readership of specialized historians. Such a conclusion is overly hasty inasmuch as it grants features exclusively to narrative that the latter shares with other forms of discourse: closure and finality. These features also happen to be the most vulnerable to an epistemological critique of a poststructuralist type, which has no difficulty in pointing out that the well-attested seductiveness of narrative is as operative in historical narratives as it is in fictional ones; but although the latter make no claim to veracity, the former do and thus may well find their claims to truthfulness to be at odds with the requirements of narrative tale-telling.

The dependence of the discourse of the historian upon narrative deserves some consideration in its own right. It may well appear quasinatural to us that historical discourse should take narrative as its privileged mode, but there is no inherent necessity for it to do so. The frequently invoked lack of distinction between the words for *story* and *history* in a number of languages has further served to obfuscate the fact that the link between history and narrative is itself historical, that history developed as a discipline in the shadow of a system of signification that placed special value upon teleological explanations couched in emplotted forms. Salvational discourse in Christianity is narrative in nature, as is its messianic predecessor in Judaism. In both instances, events in the world result from divine intention or from mostly contrary human willfulness; in any case, however, they are part of a discourse of actions, as Aristotle calls it, or plot. And plot becomes significant if the actions it repertories achieve closure, for only within such a closure does their end become clear.

This dominant Western mode of historical discourse is understood more easily if one contrasts it with the descriptive imperative of, let us say, Ibn Khaldun's reflection upon history, which places greater importance upon a structural representation than upon a cause-and-effect account.[2] The model is still one of closure and finality, but both of these are conceived in relation to a structure rather than a historical movement. The specificity of the Western mode of historical discourse lies in the fact that it is concerned with the dimension of becoming as manifested in the past—that is, with the very movement of history, where the latter is conceived as a force or as a set of forces capable of effecting movement. Under such a conception, the paramount question is *why*, whereas in Ibn Khaldun's view it is *how*.

These two questions form the articulatory axes around which revolve the various practices of history at present, but, as the debate about the new narrative history demonstrates, their role is unequal. The older interrogation into causality may appear less sophisticated in its use of quantitative techniques, for example, but it does have the seductive power of narrative at its disposal and puts itself forward as a form of explanation. It benefits from the still-powerful presence in our thought of the Enlightenment model of nature conceived as a system of ends, a model that was the successor to the sacred models of the world that dominated not only the Middle Ages but even early modern times. In the latter, time was conceived *sub specie aeternitatis;* thus, the end of human actions—their finality—was known beforehand, or at least there was in place a hermeneutics that permitted their rational calculation. The Enlightenment changed this conception of time, of course, but it reinscribed the closure of signification into nature. Nowhere is this clearer than in Kant's opuscula on history, in which he argues that the highest of human values, namely freedom, is first realized in a society governed under the best constitution, and that such a society is the means whereby nature itself accomplishes its own goals, fulfills its own ends.[3] For nature here is conceived as a system of ends, and it is the task of the philosopher to determine speculatively what these goals are so that individual and specific human actions may be evaluated according to whether they contribute to the fulfillment of these ends or contravene them.

If the goals are known, then we are back within a structural approach of the Ibn Khaldun type, but we lose the sense of historical movement. This is one of the reasons why Kant's conception was critiqued by Hegel. Modern thought is characterized by the fact that humankind no longer thinks of itself as the emanation or creature of a superior being or as a part of an external nature, but rather as a becoming. In his *Philosophy of History*, Hegel emphatically rejects Rousseau's distinction between a state of nature and a social state, a distinction that presupposes that some form of human essence, pure, absolute, and immediate, is somehow apprehensible, and then that customs and social behaviors somehow graft themselves onto it. For Hegel, human beings have only historical existence and meaning, and one does not attain some ethereal dimension of the human by stripping away the layers of the historical, that is, by abstracting humankind from its historical heritage; rather, one defines the human by uncovering the law of historical constitution that makes humankind progressively what it is. The *why* has regained its preeminence.

But Hegel's conception of the law of historical constitution presupposes not only the prior acceptance of a law of historical progression, but also that all of humankind be conceived of as a totality—and a homogeneous one at that—undergoing the very same processes in the course of historical developments. Since the historian, even a Hegelian one, cannot ignore the empirical fact of difference among human society, the postulate of homogeneity requires that, in practical terms, differences among human societies be explained as differences of temporality: an early nineteenth-century German Protestant industrialist and his contemporary Indian Hindu peasant farmer may well occupy the same chronological frame, but they represent different levels of accomplishment in the development of the spirit. Hegel's well-known distinction of the various stages of development of the spirit constitutes the privileged chronology against which all human achievements are measured, and their application serves to redistribute contemporaries and predecessors alike according to the logic of that chronology, with the paradoxical effect that people who live at the same time are no longer thought of as true contemporaries. This view has become so prevalent among us today that we are no longer conscious of its extraordinary mode of apportioning time. And, of course, the potential for the imposition of ethnocentric assumptions inherent in such a view hardly needs remarking.

Marxism has retained the Hegelian notion of stages of development, though no longer describing them as degrees in the disclosure *(Offenbarung)* of the spirit, but rather as steps in the complexity of modes of production. It has also attempted to address the question of "noncontemporaneous contemporaries" by describing the relations between two societies in terms of domination, though, of course, such an explanation is acceptable only in those instances where a direct relation between the societies in question can be established. Otherwise, the Hegelian formulation remains in effect, as, for instance, in the vexed problem of the so-called Asiatic mode of production.

The specific problematic that has drawn us into this discussion is the question of how historical representation will account for change and for difference among human societies. Faithful to the Enlightenment belief in the continuity and homogeneity of humankind, Hegelians and Marxists dealt with the problem of difference by rupturing time and supposing that one chronology accommodates itself to multiple temporalities. Those who rejected this view did so on the basis of a belief in inherent human differences, or racism. Racial characteristics would thus account for the differences in development between human societies. Under this conception, perhaps most logically carried out in the universities of Nazi Germany, and specifically in their departments of *Rassenwissenschaft,* it became necessary to distinguish as many racial types as one would distinguish levels of development. But what would be the criteria by which one would determine the different levels of development? Neither the Hegelian nor the Marxist ones would do. Instead, anthropological notions were used: first, physical anthropology to distinguish human beings on the basis of physical features (ranging from apparent ones to invisible ones, such as blood types), and then culture, which was reinterpreted in nationalistic terms so that it served to distinguish not only societies (as it commonly does among anthropologists) but also levels of development among them by reference to one ideal type of culture, which, without any bashful ethnocentrism, was affirmed to be the Germanic one.

Against these versions of history, and their specific mode of conceptualizing change and difference, there have arisen some notable expressions of dissent—though, in all fairness, the bulk of historians, especially Anglo-American ones, have continued to work in their more specialized fields (diplomatic history, intellectual history, military history, ecclesiastical history, and so on) without paying much attention to these more theoretical issues of historiography, preferring a form of theoretical agnosticism to the pitfalls of these certitudes. Such a characterization is no doubt unfair to a number of historical endeavors, especially in social, economic, and cultural history, but in its very exaggeration it seeks to draw attention to the fact that the conception of change and difference that is presently dominant, even in these areas, is that of the Hegelian-Marxist type and that the generally perceived alternative has been a fundamentally racist one. The chief dissenters have been the French schools of historians of the *Annales* persuasion or those known as historians of mentalities.

The former, gathered around the publication that has served as a useful label for their movement, have abandoned the forms of history that were mostly attentive to the narration of those events that impressed themselves upon the consciousness of the individuals who lived through them or that relied upon the memoirs of great personages, or even those who were concerned with the fate of nations. These are the very areas in which the inquiry into the *why* has been the most intense and yet least assured of the validity of its results. The Annalists are concerned with change and difference, but they believe that these result from a vast myriad of small-scale occurrences and developments, many of a highly technical nature, that generally escape the attention of those who live through them. There are no decisive events here, but an infinitesimal movement whose orientation can only be detected over the "long haul" *(la longue durée).* The historian does not tell a narrative because the actual movement of the action tends to be banal and the determination of the dramatis personae in the plot nearly impossible. The descriptive mode is favored, and the reader is presented with tableaux or *fresques,* forms of representation characterized by stasis; hence the malaise that many readers feel in relation to this form of historiography: it seems to have lost history somewhere along the way. Change and difference are not abandoned, to be sure, but they are relegated to a dimension that is hardly explored, or rather in which they are hardly detectable.

The structure of this essay may be read as a narrative itself, one that has withheld until now the historian of mentalities, in order to allow that person to make a heroic entrance and dispose of the problems that have been erected as so many straw men to be triumphantly knocked down. That may make for better narrative and its concomitant pleasures than for cognition, for the historian of mentalities, far from striking a heroic figure, may perhaps more accurately be seen as embodying some of the predicaments of historical discourse.

The very term *mentalities*—a not altogether felicitous rendition of the French *mentalités* (chiefly in the plural)—is, in many ways, a fuzzy notion. Its use in a land in which reference to the mind as a locus of cognitive operations is decried as the most used up of philosophical ideologemes is, in itself, curious. But even more significant is the relationship of the term to the two other dominant schools of French historiography: the Annalist and the Marxist. With respect to the first, the historians of mentalities seem to represent a form of attention that is almost explicitly rejected from view by the practitioners of that school. It deals with how people live, think, and (to use the term that distinguishes the school) form mental representations of their own living conditions. One could almost say that the historian of mentalities seeks to endow the Annalist representation of material life and social organization with its mental counterpart. But to say this is to run into some difficulty with respect to the distinction of the historian of mentalities from the Marxist, for such a way of describing the project of the historian of mentalities is conceived of in the Marxist framework as the study of ideology. This has led some to suspect that the historian of mentalities is really a Marxist student of ideologies who no longer acknowledges his or her Marxism, or, more precisely, who has abandoned all features and tenets of Marxism save the one that constitutes the field of inquiry, which is then renamed for the convenience of distinction. Such a conclusion is not entirely wrong, inasmuch as it recognizes—or at least permits an acknowledgment of— the difficult predicament of some historians who have wanted to make use of the intellectual heritage of Marxism without having to find themselves obliged to defend policies pursued in the name of Marxism. The term *mentalité* has been useful in this regard. But one should be aware of the fact that its content has not been a stable one.

As with similar endeavors, one may think of precursors. Huizinga's classic *The Waning of the Middle Ages* is frequently pointed to as perhaps the oldest example of this sort of approach, although one ought to recognize its continuity with the philological approaches of a Vossler, for example. But it is generally with the publication in the sixties of the works of Robert Mandrou on popular culture and on sorcery,[4] and those of Georges Duby on various aspects of the Middle Ages,[5] that the *histoire des mentalités* is felt to have come into its own. The term *mentalité* was used then without being defined except very vaguely: Mandrou equates it with *Weltanschauungen*, for example. But it is clear that the early forms of this historical approach were concerned with areas that could be described as cultural history or even history of ideas. Later developments were to take it into the areas of lived experience and everyday reality and to attempt accounts of attitudes, behaviors, and unconscious as well as conscious collective representations. Here one need recall only the work of Philippe Ariès or Michel Vovelle.[6] With a Carlo Ginzburg,[7] it becomes obvious that one is no longer concerned with the decision making of elites or even the mind-set of these elites but with the mental universe of individuals generally neglected by other forms of history since they were thought not to have contributed in any way to the "victorious march of mankind." These are the people whose sole historical accomplishment seems to have been that they lived. Until now, they have been without history. Some of the French historians, notably Emmanuel LeRoy Ladurie, have been determined to integrate them within history, though most of these studies do treat them in isolation. In this respect, José Antonio Maravall represents an advanced stage because he seeks to describe the complex interplays between mentalities, institutions, aggregate interests, and the exercise of power.

Historians of mentalities, in other words, do not believe that principles of explanation in historical development are to be found in psychic phenomena. In this they differ from psychohistorians. Rather, trained as most of them have been in a social history attentive to the quantifiable aspects of social structure and interaction, they have begun to ask themselves what are the mediations, the dialectical relationships, between these "objective" features of reality and how people live them, how they account for them to themselves. In other words, they are concerned with how people live their historicity, not as a set of momentous decisions but as the framework of lived experience.

What is interesting about this approach is that the historical pursuit is no longer the exclusive appanage of the professional historian. The historian is but the specialist who seeks to make explicit the nature of lived historical experience as all of us, and at all times, of necessity do, though mostly unconsciously and certainly not in categories that history has generally acknowledged as its own. This kind of historical activity is not that distant from the fiction making that was, and continues to be, the concern of the student of letters, a fiction making that has no fewer cognitive goals and ambitions than the disciplined activity of the historian. Here questions of *why* and *how* intertwine in an attempt to weave a representation of something that we do not directly and immediately apprehend but that we experience: what for lack of a better term we can only call the changing face of history. The historian is the specialized wielder of a discourse who seeks to give us a figural representation of that face. His or her mode is that of the prosopopoeia, the rhetorical figure that consists in giving a face to that which does not have one. Prosopopoeia is a difficult art: it does not seek to achieve closure or finality as narrative does; it does not labor under the rule of verisimilar adequacy as description does; it seeks to represent not that which is absent, but that whose presence is so intense that we can only feel it and not see it from a safe distance. It is a presence which we never doubt but of which we have no knowledge unless we represent it to ourselves. The historian seeks to give us this knowledge.

Any national history will encounter this prosopopoeic problem to the extent that it seeks to account for the lived historical experience of the people whose past it interrogates. But some national histories clearly thematize this problem: one readily thinks of Russian history and the problem of the Russian soul, Polish history and the question of Polish destiny, and, perhaps more clearly, Spanish history and the matter of Spanish character. The work of José Antonio Maravall inscribes itself within this latter tradition, though its author is quite conscious of the limitations that the tradition has imposed upon Spanish historical thought. It may be useful, in this regard, to review some of the features of that thought and how Spanish historiography has been affected by them. The distinctive character of Maravall's contribution will then become more readily apparent: Spanish specificity will not only be preserved but made apprehensible against a wider background that includes more global forms of historical understanding.

It does seem to be characteristic of Spanish historiography, and of the Spanish sense of history more generally, to think of Spain as a distinctive historical entity, one to which historical laws, as the German historians of the nineteenth century liked to call their generalizations, would not apply. It is beyond the scope of this essay to inquire into the causes of such a belief, though there is little doubt that two factors played a predominant role: the *Reconquista*, which necessitated a very early emergence of a sense that Spain had a special historical mission; and the hegemony that Castile established over the varieties of social experiences that prevailed over the territory of the Iberian peninsula. With respect to the first, one can find already in Saint Isidore of Seville the notion of a messianic Spain—a notion that will progressively find itself embodied as a specific sort of ideology throughout Spanish history in the idea that the distinctive character of Spain, its face as it were, emerged in the struggle of the early Gothic kingdoms against the Moors. It is this very ideology that one finds reproduced from age to age, and it appears even in the works of otherwise acerbic critics such as Quevedo.[8] The second in effect rides piggyback upon the first. Under the pen of its propagandists, Castile was depicted as the bearer of this messianic mission, and its progressive absorption of the other Spanish kingdoms[9] was no less than a necessary step in the realization of the broader mission, which was the divinely ordained task of the Spanish nation to establish a strong Catholic central government over the disparateness of the peninsula. One will readily recognize here the official ideology of the Franco era, which justified its repression of any desire for any sort of local autonomy by direct reference to this mission. But it is also a very powerful strand within Spanish historiography, as is evidenced by the work of Claudio Sánchez-Albornoz, one of the most widely published historians of the post–Civil War period.[10]

It is against this nationalistic and obviously simplistic view that one of the great Spanish historians of our century erected his own vision of Spanish history, a vision that precipitated a great debate in the fifties and sixties and that finds itself widely institutionalized in Hispanic studies in the United States: *The Structure of Spanish History* by Américo Castro.[11] Castro was not really a historian, but rather a *litteratus* who, from exile, sought to change the dominant view of Spanish history by focusing on what appeared to him to be the greatest distortion perpetrated by the holders of the messianic view, namely the nature of lived reality during the long centuries of the Reconquest. This period, after all, spans much more than half of the history of Spain, and it can be labeled as the *Reconquista* only from a particular retrospective view that seeks to present the varieties of phenomena that constituted the historical experience of medieval Spain as one monolithic movement. Castro attempted to show that, far from pitting the Goths against the Moors, this reality brought together in forms of productive tension—what he calls *convivencia*—the three confessional communities: the Jews, the Moslems, and the Christians. While Castro's argument meandered into questionable attempts to determine whether given figures of the Spanish past were of Jewish or Islamic origin—thus fueling much rather nasty polemic[12]—it challenged the idea of the inevitability of the historical fate of Spain and proposed an alternative vision of its past as a project for the future.

Castro's approach, concerned as it was with the correction of what appeared to him to be gross distortions, was inevitably more speculative than probative, however; it was particularly blind to the fact that the messianic ideology had become the vehicle of particular dynastic ambitions—the Castilian ones—and eventually of the centralist conception of the Spanish state. Castro's aim was reconciliatory rather than analytical and, as a result, it stands as a sort of countermyth to the myth that it opposed. It is clear that this is the sort of position that Maravall wanted to avoid for his work from the very outset. While he would eschew the nominalism of a Meinecke, he would have sufficient respect for the task of the historian as a producer of an important body of social knowledge to avoid the realm of mythmaking as a strategy of myth debunking. Having come into contact with Braudel, and by his own acknowledgment having been influenced by his work, Maravall was nonetheless more drawn toward a more properly *mentalités* approach,[13] especially since the latter is not altogether alien to the Spanish historical consciousness.

The French or the British rarely ask themselves about the meaning of British or of French history, perhaps because both nations have lived through revolutions that have shown that such meaning as history may possess results from the activity of those who live it. Spain has not really known such a moment of historical consciousness, and, to the extent that it was beholden to the messianic vision of its historical mission, it was likely that any change in the fortunes of Spain would be interpreted as somehow representing a secular equivalent of the Fall. This seems to have happened in the period that follows what the Spaniards like to call their Golden Age (and to repeat itself in significant segments of the society after the formal collapse of the empire in 1898). Although contemporary historical research has raised serious questions about the validity of any decline in the age of Philip IV, the perception the Spaniards have had of this period is that it marks a regression with respect to their previous greatness and a retreat before their appointed mission. Such a Fall had to have causes, and these have been sought in the Spanish character. Thus, as early as the eighteenth century, the prosopopoeic problem was thematized in Spain as Spaniards sought to divine the meaning of their history. The interesting thing about this enterprise is that it led to the application of a viewpoint that bears some distant resemblance to the history of mentalities and that was an original use of anthropological perspective in history: what is known as *costumbrismo*. This movement, which flourished in the early nineteenth century, sought to explore the nature of the Spanish character by investigating the lived experience of contemporary Spaniards. Its significance lies in its agnosticism with respect to any divinely ordained mission for Spain and in the fact that it brought to the fore so many of the lasting themes and motifs of subsequent discussion of Spanish distinctiveness.

Maravall is, of course, no latter-day *costumbrista,* but he seeks to reinscribe this properly Spanish mode of interrogating history within a broader framework. Unlike Castro, he recognizes immediately the key role that the hegemonic aspirations of Castile have played in Spanish history, and he focuses on the instrument that was used for the realization of these aspirations: the state. This is no doubt a controversial point that is best left to the debates of competent historians, but it is apparent that Spain did achieve relatively early in the modern period a form of state power and organization that may well constitute the distinctive feature of its past. Maravall thus can show that Castro's mythical *convivencia,* to the extent that it had any reality at all, was the result of deliberately conducted state policies, as far as the period of the Catholic kings and its aftermath are concerned. But he does not limit himself to the kind of broader institutional history that an attention to the emergence of a more modern form of the state could result in; rather, his focus has been on the specific ways in which the emergence of this entity has radically changed the mentalities of the people who have lived this change.

José Antonio Maravall's *Culture of the Baroque* is, perhaps, the work that sums up best an intellectual journey that began several decades earlier with the publication of his doctoral thesis—*La teoria española del estado en el siglo XVII* (Madrid, 1944)—in which the author was to connect the baroque, for the first time, with the political circumstances of the absolutist monarchy and thus set out on a field of research that has continued to preoccupy him to this very day. Maravall's work on the modern state and social mentality has become his trademark as a historian. Some of the key assumptions of his most important book on that subject, *Estado moderno y mentalidad social,* have since been incorporated in his studies on baroque culture and in more recent writings dealing with honor, power, and the elite in seventeenth-century Spain.[14] A central claim underlying these inquiries is that absolutist power, realizing Castilian hegemonic aspirations, began in the fifteenth century by controlling and disciplining the nobles; eventually, however, it turned into a defender of the nobility around 1600 as significant realignments took place in the body politic, especially as Castile brought within its sway areas in which other social groups had achieved significant power and autonomy. Similarly, many of the changes that took place toward the end of the 1500s are attributed to the social tensions experienced throughout most of the century as a result of widespread presumptions of social mobility (geographic, professional, and social). The political program of the baroque is, then, the formal answer of the monarchical-seigneurial segments of society to the assaults ("real" and imagined) that are launched against the traditional estatist structure.[15]

Here Maravall finds himself involved in a polemic with Castro, who shunned reference to broader period concepts as part of his global strategy of rejection against the then-predominant view of Spanish history. Castro wrote: "There is no such thing as a gothic, a renaissance, a baroque, or a neoclassicism that, from an unreal space, conditions the flow of history as the moon intervenes in the tides."[16] This negation of the baroque as a historical concept was to be reiterated in a letter to Maravall, where Castro referred to the baroque as an inoperative concept, arguing that it was not "an agent of change." He was also to intimate that, because of the particularity of Spain's past, it could not be understood on the same assumptions as the pasts of England, France, Italy, and Germany. Ironically, Castro had come to defend a form of Spanish uniqueness, whereas his life's effort had been to put into question the constitution of that form of uniqueness into a messianic version. Once again, though, his failure had been to attribute to an abstract entity—which is what he took the baroque to be—the operativity that Maravall was attempting to uncover through painstaking analysis. Castro had taken Maravall's use of the term *baroque* to be some sort of Hegelian concept, whereas Maravall was engaging in the prosopopoeic effort to understand what the culture of crisis of seventeenth-century Spain had been all about.

It may be useful to recall that the baroque was first introduced as a period concept in art history and that it became hopelessly vague when there were attempts to extend it beyond the boundaries of that field, notably toward literature. Maravall's merit lies precisely in the reaffirmation of the baroque as a period concept and not just the sort of vague style-denomination that it had become, thus giving it operative value both for the historian and for the student of literature. From the outset of this study, Maravall makes clear that he does not focus on the morphological aspects of baroque art (Wölfflin) or on the supposed connection between the baroque and the movement of religious reform known as the Counter-Reformation (Weisbach). Similarly, he does not propose to deal with, or differentiate between, rhetorical and conceptual versions of baroque literature (Warnke).[17]

For Maravall, the baroque is a historical concept belonging to, and therefore affecting, the sphere of social history. While allowing for "national" nuances, he argues, with abundant references—and along lines opposite to those of Castro—that its general traits are applicable not only to Spain but also to other countries of western Europe. He goes on to define the baroque as a culture provoked by a social crisis of major proportions, one that was felt in all of Europe and, perhaps, most intensely in Spain during the greater part of the seventeenth century.

With his accustomed precision, he makes clear that he does not speak with the voice of an economic historian, and he states that in no instance does his "interpretative construction exceed the limits of the social history of mentalities."[18] Thus when he speaks of the baroque as a culture crisis, he distinguishes between the social and economic dimensions of that crisis, arguing that whereas the latter is of an intermittent character, displaying alternating periods of growth and recession (as Spanish historians Gonzalo Anes and F. Ruiz Martín have shown), the former, which has to do with the reinscription of the entire social sphere under the new authority of the state, is clearly of *longue durée*.

The precision with which the baroque is used as a period concept also obtains with reference to his definition of culture, which is viewed as the weaving of values, aspirations, beliefs, myths, and ways of living and acting as they articulate themselves on the level of a mentality.[19] This anthropological definition of culture, with its clear *costumbrista* resonances, allows Maravall not to limit the notion of crisis to the realm of pure economic history, inserting it instead in a much broader set of considerations that encompass the changing character of culture, history, and social life. Similarly, he never forgets that the concept of crisis is essential to historical understanding, going to great lengths, especially in some of his later writings, to remind us of the attempts that have been made over time to theorize on this very subject. To back up his claims, he cites thinkers of such different orientation as Marx, F. Simiand (an economic historian), and Jacob Burckhardt, the historian of culture who also happened to be one of the first to take seriously the study of the baroque.[20]

For Maravall, then, it is the perception of crisis and instability found among the groups in power and among the individuals in the middle strata of society *(gente intermedia)* who identified with them that brings about the political program of the baroque around 1600. In Spain, it is a culture contrived and manipulated for the benefit of the monarchical-seigneurial sectors of society for the purpose of facing up to a world in which changes had seemed to turn things upside down. In this sense, it is a culture of reaction against the mobility and change that, for much of the sixteenth century, had threatened to erode the "hierarchical construction of estates."[21] Maravall would argue that, ultimately, it is the perception of change that counts. For whether change is perceived as progress or as retraction, as liberation or as repression, it implies a degree of transformation in the system of social mentality that, in turn, brings with it the potential for a displacement of values, rank, and authority. It was precisely to meet these challenges that the baroque world of seventeenth-century Spain organized its resources along lines that were either openly repressive or more subtly propagandistic. Thus, for example, in addition to the use of various agents and means of terror—particularly the Inquisition and the private armies of the nobles—or the state's attempt to mold the Church into an *instrumentum regni* directed toward the repression of individual consciences, there was the massive propaganda campaign staged by those who possessed the instruments of culture or by their surrogates. The idea was to captivate minds through the use of theater, sermons, emblematic literature, and so forth, and to cause admiration and suspense through these and other, more overt, displays of power: fireworks, fountains, fiestas. It was a culture directed especially toward the multitude of anonymous and, therefore, potentially disruptive individuals concentrated in the cities, with a message suggesting the desirability of integration within the confines of an estatist structure.[22]

The dimensions and reaches of baroque culture among the urban publics of the 1600s have been examined by Maravall in *Poder, honor y élites en el siglo XVII* and other works, including *Teatro y literatura en la sociedad barroca.* These studies have had a significant impact in a number of areas, most especially on the study of the Spanish "national theater"—the comedia of the 1600s. Perhaps the best example of the use of the theater for political and social propaganda is the work of Lope de Vega, the great playwright of the establishment in the early 1600s. The stage productions of these plays were meant to give a new, undiscriminating public—*el vulgo*—what it supposedly wanted: lots of action, a variety of verses and other forms, and, above all, the dramatic structuring of concepts with which most spectators learned to identify. These concepts were the defense of the monarchy, the safeguard of honor as the raison d'être of individual and social life, and the constant reaffirmation of love as universal justification. The large theatergoing public of the comedia thus possessed a code, a horizon or system of expectations that Lope and other playwrights of the time learned to accommodate and nurture. (An important exception is Cervantes, who in the early 1600s circumvented the public stage and addressed his plays directly to readers.)[23] One of the key characteristics of that mass, socially heterogeneous public was a large degree of homogeneity along ideological lines. That is, from the lowest social classes to merchants, artisans, bureaucrats, and others, the public that frequented the theater identified with the values or paradigms of the nobility.

With reference to the use of the honor theme in the theater (and to a lesser extent in the novel, especially the picaresque), Maravall argues that it is presented as a mirror for effecting and ensuring the integration of certain groups, whereas for others it functions almost exclusively as an instrument of marginalization. Among the latter groups he specifically lists manual laborers and, to a lesser extent, converts from Judaism or Islam. This, of course, is in line with Maravall's contention that the baroque promoted an estatist society under a powerful state rather than a caste system.

We mention this issue not only because Maravall was to go back to it in a substantive way in his *Poder, honor y élites en el siglo XVII,* but also because here as well major differences oppose him to Américo Castro. Given the wide currency that the latter's views enjoy in the United States, Maravall's theories are likely to prove controversial. In this context it is important to recall that for Maravall, the historian of social mentalities, the occurrence of a way of life founded on honor is not particular to Spain but is common to the estatist societies of western Europe. Against the absolute importance given to blood statutes by Castro and his disciples, Maravall would argue that these cannot be taken out of the orbit of an estatist structure. The centrality of the honor theme to the very structure of traditional society is a topic that also interested Lucien Febvre, who announced but never published a study on the subject.[24]

Although it is outside of the scope of this essay to discuss all of Maravall's writings—some thirty books and scores of articles that cover the span of the Middle Ages, the Renaissance, the baroque, the

Enlightenment, and contemporary culture—we should at least mention a few of his other important works, especially *el pensamiento de Velázquez, El mundo social de la "Celestina," Antiguos y modernos,* and *La Picaresca vista desde la historia social.* All of these studies have a common thread: they are written by a liberal historian of social mentalities who has struggled for forty years, not from exile but from within Spain, to give Spanish history a new face.

3　Popular Culture and Spanish Literary History

with Nicholas Spadaccini

In recent years some historians have shown an interest in popular culture. The paradigmatic statement in this area is provided by the distinguished Renaissance scholar Peter Burke in his "Oblique Approaches to the History of Popular Culture."[1] In this article Burke argues that the practice of history has generally followed one of two models: that of Ranke, who was preoccupied with the actions of ruling elites, or that of Burckhardt, who described the culture of that elite, that is, the attitudes and values of the elite as they are embodied in symbolic forms such as paintings and plays. The Rankian political historian followed, or reconstructed, the deeds of kings and statesmen; the Burckhardtian cultural historian, those of artists and intellectuals. In both instances, the lives, perceptions, attitudes, and values of the bulk of the population fell through the cracks of the historian's apparatus. Burke proceeds then to describe a variety of ways through which this "lost" element can be recovered.

In its desire to provide a more complete vision of the past, and in "rehabilitating" as it were the culture of "shopkeepers, craftsmen, beggars, and thieves," Burke's project is most laudable; yet there is about it a touching naïveté which perhaps can be maintained by the historian but which is entirely untenable to the literary scholar. It assumes that the enterprise of history itself need not be questioned, that it can go on with only some filling of lacunae, regrettable omissions to be sure, but certainly not fatal to the project. How different the project may look to the literary scholar will become readily apparent.

The past thirty years or so have demonstrated to literary scholars that they need not conceive of their activity in terms of literary history: the New Criticism in the United States, the *Werkimmanente* approach that was its counterpart in Germany, structuralism and its aftermath in France and in the United States have, for better or worse, managed to produce a sizable body of work without explicit relation to the project of literary history. Thus, unlike his historian counterpart, a literary scholar who presently would wish to return to literary history cannot simply resume where things were left and assume that project without at least inquiring into its validity. What is laudable in Burke may be laudable in literature, but that proposition needs to be demonstrated, whereas the historian must gloss it over altogether if s/he is to preserve his or her professional identity.

It may not be useless, therefore, to recall to mind some basic givens. Literary history, born of Romanticism, constitutes, together with generic studies—themselves born of the contemporaneous taxonomic impulse—the privileged mode of study of literature in the institutional settings of the universities from the latter part of the nineteenth century onward. Given our own institutional setting in the United States and its genealogy, it is exceedingly difficult for us to apprehend the fact that it is this setting and this genealogy that have constructed not only our object of study but ourselves as the subjects of that inquiry. (The resistance that projects of reexamination encounter is clearly due to the challenge they pose to our identity.) By opposition to the pre-Romantic period—a deliberately vague appellation—the verbal, in its privileged written form, is elevated by Romanticism to an autonomous object, constituting a separate sphere within the realm of culture. Literary history, from its inception, accepts this Romantic model of the "literary" boundaries of the verbal, but it reaches elsewhere for its methodological inspiration: German *Geistesgeschichte*. The latter, whose links to emergent German nationalist consciousness are too well known to be recounted here, formulated its object of study as the national spirit, to be distinguished from that of other European nations. For literary history, this spirit manifests itself in an unbroken chain of masterpieces in verse, prose, and drama, and the latter are the proper object of the literary historian.

Literature as a separate object in the sphere of culture, and the national spirit as its internal animator, constitute thus the boundaries of literary history. While such boundaries may have some validity for the epoch and the countries in which they were formulated, their retroactive importation into other cultures could not be accomplished without some violence. Yet this violence was inflicted in such a manner that it was not perceived, at least not as violence.

It has been increasingly recognized that a major mutation in the status of fiction writers occurred in the eighteenth century. Dependent until then, for the most part, upon the graces and financial support of the courtly nobility or, in somewhat fewer instances, upon the patronage of the Church, writers found themselves suddenly thrust in a rather novel environment: the first of the Moderns to have the product of their labors mechanically reproduced on a large scale by the printing press, they were, perhaps even more important, the first to experience a disjunction between the product of that labor and its eventual consumption. In the France and Germany of the eighteenth century, as with England a century earlier, the written work of fiction was no longer limited, in its distribution, to an audience of which the writer was a member, or indeed whose characteristics s/he knew. Unlike the situation of courtly patronage, in which the horizon of expectation, to borrow Jauss's useful characterization, was ascertained through direct, immediate, daily, and dialectical contact, the writer writing for the abstract reader who would purchase that writer's work in a city unknown to him or her was no longer as certain of the expectation s/he was supposed to either fulfill or contravene. Whereas in England there arose remarkably early a consensus on the nature of that "common reader," as it became known—a consensus that is only now beginning to be shattered—the situation in France, and especially in Germany, was quite different. The political, and seeming cultural, fragmentation could not provide the assurance of any common readership. Worse, such a common readership could only be constructed, that is, formulated, as a project for the future. In other words, the writer of fiction who, for reasons far too complex to be inquired into here, was among the earliest of the cultural workers to see the product of his/her labor achieve a certain degree of autonomy from the previously implicit mode of production, communication, and circulation of his/her activity, was faced with two immediate problems: the autonomization of this production had to be recognized and then legitimized.

The emergence of the notion of "literature" as a designator for the autonomous area of the sphere of culture was a response to the first problem. This is not the place to recall that the term "literature" initially applied to all that was written, and that, far from being reduced in scope during the Renaissance, the term, usually in the form of *res literaria* or *litterae humaniores,* included not only all written matter, from legal and medical treatises to poetry, including scientific writing, but also works of oratory, whether sacred or profane. Today the term "literature" is used in a far more restricted way, preserving for itself some of the legitimacy of its prior usage (by not surrendering its claim to all that is previously encompassed) but constituting itself as a separate entity in the realm of culture, an entity that would seek its institutionalization in a rather different way from its previous existence: no longer defined by the material basis of its existence (writing: literature), it would henceforth depend upon its mode of consumption (the aesthetic, the realm of art). The autonomization of art is indeed the great cultural phenomenon of eighteenth-century cultural life, and one can but allude to it here. Yet it must be recognized that, for legitimation purposes, this autonomization must present itself not as a novelty, a new development, but as the recovery of an originary reality, an essence. Such will be the task of philosophical inquiry upon the aesthetic.

Yet the problem of legitimation persists, especially in the contingency of its emergence: what is this new autonomous realm of literature for, now that it is defined as the aesthetic? The artisanal writer working at court did not have this problem: he wrote occasional pieces, for holidays, celebrations, and so on. In addition, the *litterae humaniores,* the *res literaria* made a cognitive claim: they were a form of erudition, in the most positive sense of the term, an erudition of the fundamental texts of wisdom and knowledge in the culture, inherited from antiquity. They required a critical form of cognition. No such claim is made on behalf of what comes increasingly to be known as *belles-lettres,* a notion still dominated by the concept of Eloquence and the exemplary figure of the Orator,[2] and certainly even less in the case of *literature.*

It is here that the link with *Geistesgeschichte* is made. Faced with the only certitude in his or her possession, namely language, the writer will assume a responsibility and a mission vis-à-vis the collectivity that speaks that language: the nation. Yet in the case of the German Romantics this leads to a problem: the German nation is more of a project than a reality, and although the assertion that one's activity contributed to the emergence and constitution of the German nation does provide a most powerful alibi—the social legitimation that was sought—this assertion needs to be bolstered, for, on the face of it, it appears rather improbable. Literary history, or, more precisely, the history of literature as it becomes known, is the instrumentality of that legitimation.

The problem at issue could be presented as follows: if one writes for a German nation yet to be, there is a disjunction between the present of the writing and the future of the reading. Only in the future will there be a reader adequate to what is written, yet such a reader will arise only as a result of what is being written. One has no difficulty in recognizing here the structure of what anthropologists call "magic thought." But magic thought does require some evidence that it is operational, that is, some evidence of success. The latter can be sought only in the past, and, most important for our concerns, it must be so sought outside Germany. To be sure, one can claim that one's own national awareness is the direct result of a past writer's writing, but such a claim can only legitimate an individual consciousness, not a national one. What is required is an example in which a writing can be asserted to be the full *expression (Ausdruck)* of its people, in other words, a writing whose presentness will be total, uniting its moment of writing and its moment of reading, and thus providing a fullness of presence.

It is remarkable that the German Romantics, especially Schlegel, located this moment in Spanish literature. At first, the choice is surprising: one would have expected antiquity, preferably Greek antiquity, but a careful study of the early pronouncements in this area shows that Greece, and to a lesser extent, Rome, are unavailable since they have been co-opted for the purpose of arguing for a *universality* of values and experiences and not for a national base for them. We have here one of the most interesting paradoxes of literary history: the earliest histories of Spanish literature were written by non-Spaniards and as such seem to escape the nationalistic underpinnings of literary history, be they French, German, English, or eventually Italian or Russian. Yet at the same time and precisely for that reason, Spain is the alibi for the nationalistic orientation of all subsequent literary history, and not just any Spain but that which goes from the *Reyes Católicos* to the seventeenth century.

The reasons for that choice are obvious and have not been questioned. This is the period in which Spain achieved, through the completion of the *Reconquista* and the expulsion of Moors and Jews, its territorial, ethnic, and religious identity under the aegis of the first modern state, a state capable of forging a powerful modern cultural apparatus, as J. A. Maravall has shown in his extraordinary *Cultura del Barroco*,[3] at the same time that it launched itself in imperialistic ventures within and without Europe. For the German Romantics, as well as for literary historians since, the figure of Calderón in particular, especially in his auto-sacramentales, achieves exemplary status here, so much so that even Walter Benjamin in his *Ursprung der deutschen Trauerspiels*[4] sees him as the last writer of the plenitude of meaning and its presence in our tradition.

Spanish literary history has inherited, though not always understood, the privileging of its own early modern times. It has especially failed to appreciate the fact that this privileging, whose consequences for the remainder of Spanish cultural development would condemn it to a representation of decline and backwardness and a deprivation of inner dynamics, was an alibi for someone else's project: the literary history of the Germans. But literary historians themselves have failed to appreciate the consequences of this decision: all literary histories would henceforth be in search of a classical moment, a moment defined not in literary terms but as the congruence of a cultural development with the emergence of the figure of the modern state. Unbeknown to them, literary historians, blind to the determinant role played for their endeavor by the German Romantic view of the Spanish Golden Age, are fated to write a narrative that leads to the progressive emergence of a moment in which the national spirit will be seen to actualize itself in the manner in which the Spanish one is asserted to have done, and to describe subsequent developments in the rhetoric of decline, with episodes of inevitable renewal and further downfall as its major peripeteia. It should be clear, then, that the culture of Spain's early modern times constitutes a strategic point of departure for any attempt to rethink the project of literary history on a basis other than the Romantic one. Such is the violence that has been perpetrated.

To attempt this rethinking by a consideration of popular literature is immediately fraught with dangers, for the construct "popular literature" is as much of a Romantic construct as literary history, and thus to engage in an operation of recovery of the "genuine" popular cultural expression of this period would contribute to the reinscription of the model we have been discussing. It would, after all, only repeat the gesture of a distinction between *Naturpoesie* and *Kunstpoesie*, believed to be the product of a pure and uncorrupted people, where the first was supposed to embody the soul of the nation. It may be useful to recall in this context that, just as the *Kunstpoesie* of the Spaniards was to provide the grounding of literary history, albeit as alibi, the *Naturpoesie* of the Spaniards, located this time in the national theater and in the ballads, was collected with equal fervor by the German Romantics (Jacob Grimm, *Silva de romances viejos* [Vienna, 1815];

Diez [1818, 1821]; Depping [1817]; Pandin [1823]; Wolf [1841, 1846]; and Huber [1844], leading eventually to the collections of Menéndez y Pelayo), as part of their project of validating the notion of a *pueblo poeta: das Volk dichtet,* in Grimm's phrase.[5] Nor should this be surprising: if the claim that Spain represents the perfect embodiment of a culture present to itself is to stand, that presence must be equally realized in both *Naturpoesie* and *Kunstpoesie.* Thus any attempt to "revise" our understanding of the Golden Age that would ground itself on the popular literature of the period without reexamining the mode of inscription of that sphere of culture would only confirm the prevailing model.

An examination of these Romantic texts on what is variously described as popular literature of folklore rapidly shows that the definition of their object is articulated around the following opposition: oral versus written. Discussions in literary theory of the terms of that opposition have shown us, in recent years, that there is nothing obvious about them and that the opposition itself articulates far more than a temporal ordering within the history of culture. Yet at the purely empirical level, there is little doubt that the period we are interested in witnessed a massive development of the written, thanks mostly to the development of print technology, and that such a development had to take place at the expense of the previously dominant oral.[6]

A closer examination, however, reveals a fallacy in this reasoning. The terms "oral" and "written" are not symmetrical, and our bias in favor of the written has led us to construct the written in ways that are quite excessive. The term "written culture" in the opposition "written versus oral" refers to both the mode of production and the mode of reception of texts in that culture. We do not distinguish between the writing and the reading part, primarily because, in the age of mechanical reproducibility, to anticipate Benjamin's phrase somewhat, the reception of texts is determined by their (print) status, and their production (writing) represents a limited experiential area in the culture: most people are readers, consumers, of printed texts; few are writers. Yet the terms of the opposition "written versus oral" would lead us to believe that, by contrast, in "oral culture" most people were text producers, and it is precisely upon such a notion that the Romantic idea of a *pueblo poeta* rests. If that were the case, then indeed that mutation from a fully collective and participatory, cocreative culture, as it has been described in the case of the oral, to a privatized, individual consumption and passive reception in the written one would truly represent a major cultural mutation. The reality is somewhat less dramatic: the indiscriminate use of the term "oral" occults the fact that the vast majority of the population participated in the culture as auditors—recipients and consumers—of verbal artifacts produced by relatively few. To be sure, such an auditive reception does differ significantly from a readerly one, and one should be careful not to fall here into the other extreme of collapsing the difference between the two states of culture.

What we need to consider is the coexistence of the oral and the written in a culture that is primarily auditive, where, in other words, even the written is received for the most part in an aural form. Such a culture, as Luiz Costa Lima has shown in a different context, differs from the more purely oral by no longer relying upon a shared thesaurus of formulas and motifs in the construction of its narratives or upon the collective memory for the composition of other materials; it also differs from the more purely written, that is, from the state of culture dominated by texts written for private reading consumption, but not constructing its texts around logical argumentative structures.[7] Rather, an auditive culture valorizes novelty in contrast to the attachment to the traditional found in oral culture, and it strives for emotional impact as opposed to the more deliberative mode of more purely written culture. In other words, its products will be characterized by a high level of rhetorical fabrication. Although orally delivered, such a text does not seek to establish a dialogical relation with the audience but instead to leave the audience dumbfounded: *boca abierta*. The audience does not participate, nor does it internalize the arguments: it is conquered, subjugated, carried by the persuasive flow of the rhetoric. Such a culture is a culture of persuasion, but, as Costa Lima reminds us, of persuasion without understanding (p. 16); in other words, it is a culture of seductive persuasion, given to theatricality. It lends itself eminently to manipulation.

Such a nonparticipatory (by contrast with the oral) and nondemonstrative (by contrast with the written) culture develops different styles of culture consumption. This is an area that is so little studied (the exception here is Michel de Certeau: see *Arts de faire*)[8] that only very rudimentary indications can be given. If one grants that a majority of the population receives the artifacts of such a culture in the way that they are intended, one must see this majority as being essentially manipulated (we shall see later what are some of the instrumentalities of this manipulation, such as the *literatura de cordel*). In other words, one must presuppose a certain amount of uncritical reception, a reception inattentive to the logical discontinuities of what is being propounded and unaware of the passivity enforced upon its subjects. Such a reception could, by analogy with the more recent phenomena of television advertising, be ascribed to mass culture, and we shall refer to it as mass reception.

But alongside such an uncritical reception, one has to posit the possibility of a critical one, that is, a reception by those who do sense the manipulation. However, as soon as one posits such a critical reception, one must immediately proceed to a further differentiation: a critical reception of what is perceived as manipulatory implies either agreement with, or opposition to, the ends of the manipulation. In other words, one can realize that, let us say, a speech, a sermon, or a play is relying on a structure of emotional, rhetorical, persuasion, and one can agree with the goals of that persuasion, yet by being aware of the fact that it is manipulatory persuasion, one excludes oneself from the intended audience. The constitution of a mass-oriented auditive culture permits thus, by virtue of the structure of its operation, what we shall call an elite reception, in which the receiver, perceiving the manipulation, subtracts himself or herself from it, in order to identify with the goals of the manipulators. Such a receiver need not belong to the class or group doing the manipulation, but culturally s/he seeks to join them. In such a mechanism of ideological identification lie the roots of high culture, which, in our view, should not be constructed as merely the culture of the actual manipulating elite. Almost by definition, such an elite will be quite small and its genuine internal culture quite limited. It should be observed that this mechanism of identification with the goals of the manipulators obviously lends itself to manipulation as well, a fact that should not be overly surprising, for once manipulation enters, it well extend its reach. It should also explain why so-called high culture becomes such a strong ideological vehicle as well, but one that relies on mechanisms of identification to a greater extent than the mechanisms of outright and unreflected absorption of the mass.

There is also the further structural possibility of perceiving the manipulation for oneself and refusing its goals. This is a difficult position to describe because, clearly, it is politically and ideologically the one most fraught with dangers. It is based upon the perception of the attempted subjugation and its refusal, usually in the defense of an alternative, older, cultural order, with the possibility of a strong utopian component as well. Such a process need not be fully conscious or deliberately subversive—it may be even grounded in submission to the dominant sociopolitical order—but it represents a step beyond passive consumption of the artifacts of mass culture. The latter are then reappropriated and recirculated in ways unanticipated by the purveyors of the mass culture. These artifacts are then blended with or combined with more archaic elements from the older strata of culture. Such a consumption, and further elaboration, we shall consider to be properly popular.

In other words, the distinction between mass, elite, and popular that we are proposing is not based on the inherent formal properties of cultural artifacts but on patterns of reception and usage of these artifacts. This implies that the very same artifact may be subject to at least three different usages according to our differentiation, certainly a complication that most literary historians fail to envisage.

Let us now proceed to somewhat more concrete considerations for the period that interests us. We shall begin with the new print technology.

The emergence of a print culture has definite consequences for the nascent notion of literature, both in terms of its societal status, with the assignment of literary properties, and in terms of its internal self-definition, with the introduction of criteria of propriety and decorum. It must be appreciated to what extent the severance of a text from its immediate framework of communication (that is, from the framework of oral performance) imposes restrictions on the text: considerations of decorum and property arise in order to prevent certain kinds of reception and to preempt some of the dangers associated with the uncertainty surrounding the identity, age, gender, social status, and ideological orientation of the reader. In other words, they are attempts at constraining reception and, if not entirely homogenizing it, at least defining its parameters. These considerations also represent a form of prior self-censorship by the text producers, and they lead to discussions on the effects produced by texts, discussions that are a foreshadowing, and the birthing ground, of literary criticism and of the eventual institutionalization of literature. But before such a birth can be recorded, the consequences of the emergence of literary property must be examined.

It is known that the right to publish a given text gave rise to competition and introduced issues related to monopoly and piracy

(Eisenstein, I, 120). Thus not only did printing force legal definitions of what belonged in the public domain, but it also changed the attitudes of writers to their work. Although the concepts of plagiarism and copyright did not exist in the communal culture of the minstrel, the new mode of production initiated by printing instigated the institutionalization of those concepts. Printers, in fact, may have been largely responsible "for forcing definitions of literary property rights, for shaping new concepts of authorship, for exploiting bestsellers, for tapping new markets" (Eisenstein, I, 122).

By the early 1500s there began a veritable "communications revolution" as printers' workshops were finding their way into the major municipal centers and contributing to the reshaping of urban culture. In Spain no fewer than twenty-nine towns had seen presses set up by 1521,[9] some of them by foreign printers—especially German—who contributed immensely to the propagation of old traditional ballads in *pliegos sueltos.*[10]

With the proliferation of printed texts, divergent traditions became more difficult to reconcile and contradictions became more visible. The result was that "the transmission of received opinion could not proceed smoothly" (Eisenstein, I, 74–75). The state's attempt at controlling this new technology was swift but only partially successful, especially during the first quarter of the sixteenth century. The first laws governing the printing and publication of books in Spain appeared as early as 1502, when the Catholic Kings prescribed a system whereby prelates were charged to prevent the printing of "cosas vanas, y sin provecho."[11] Yet in 1525 the scholar-printer Miguel Eguía hinted at the ineffectiveness of such laws and at the lack of self-discipline in the Spanish printing houses, for they were producing "vulgar and even obscene ballads, doggerel and books even more profitless than these" (Bataillon, *Erasmo . . .*, cited in Cruickshank, p. 806).

After the convening of the Council of Trent (1545–1563), the Catholic Church was to be especially attuned to heterodox propaganda, so that by the mid-sixteenth century, Spain saw its first official *Index* (1559) and became the battleground of the reaction against the publication of the Bible and commentaries of it in the vernacular. Thus at the trial of Fray Bartolomé Carranza (1559–1576), whose *Catechism* (1558) had incorporated no less than two thousand citations from the Bible, the Dominican theologian Fray Domingo de Soto questioned such practices on grounds that they divulged information about heresies. At the same time he went on to reject the very notion of a published Bible in the vernacular because "a work once printed becomes accessible to all people." [12] A few years later, in the "Dedication" to *De los nombres de Cristo* (1583), Fray Luís de León bemoaned the fate that had befallen the *Sacred Scriptures,* "for God—says Fray Luís—had intended the use of the scriptures for all people." [13]

The impact of the new technology of production on the acquisition of culture by different socioeconomic groups was also alluded to by the Spanish humanist Thamara in a Preface to the *Libro de Polidoro Virgilio que tractaba de la invención y principio de todas las cosas* (Antwerp, 1550). Thamara's Preface—published, ironically, on the eve of what was to be the beginning of a long process of censorship of printed texts[14]—talks about

> . . . esta nueva manera de escribir que en nuestro tiempo avemos visto y alcançado. Por la qual *un día se imprime y estampa por un solo hombre quantos apenas en* un año muchos podrían escrevir, por causa de lo cual tanta abundancia de libros ha salido y se ha derramado por todo el mundo que *ninguna obra que quiera pueda faltar a ningún hombre por más pobre que sea.*

> . . . this new way of writing that we have seen and achieved in our time. By means of which a single person can print in a single day what many could barely transcribe in a whole year. As a result, so many books have been published and scattered throughout the world that, no matter how poor a person might be, no work is outside his reach if he desires it. (our translation)

Literacy is seen here as a form of technological competence that is not limited to a particular class.

It is clear, therefore, that disjunctions have occurred between the new mode of production and the old modes of consumption. The traditional sense of community, which entailed gatherings to receive a message, was undercut by the new technology, which made possible the fragmentation of directions. The reading public was now more dispersed, atomistic, and fragmented than the readers of script had been. This movement toward a heterogeneity of audiences led to a diversity of discourses which, in turn, allowed for the manipulation of culture. Ultimately the very consolidation of the modern state was bound up with this new technology (Eisenstein), and the problem of culture became increasingly a project of the state.

While the accessibility to, and the acquisition of, literary culture began to expand significantly through printed texts in the early 1500s, it is important to keep in mind that the culture of the great majority of the population in early modern Spain was oral, aural, and visual and that life was informed by a body of beliefs that was shaped to a large extent by catechism, confessions, religious feasts, and religious art, that is, the various *retablos* and *pasos* depicting episodes of the Old and New Testaments.[15]

The interactions of learned culture and traditional oral culture were made easier by chapbooks, an early form of what Dwight Macdonald calls "mid-cult," a form that "is situated between the great and little traditions and drawing on both."[16] This fact is practically overlooked by traditional literary histories and has been all but forgotten by recent social histories of literature. Despite the fact that, on the diachronic level, a social history of literature must take into account the physical means of transmission and transform itself at some point into a social history of writing and reading, "no history of literature has as yet taken into account the means of transmission of texts, nor offered statistics, where possible, of the diffusion of works, as if the life of a work were not strongly conditioned by such extra-literary factors."[17]

One of the first Hispanists to call attention to this situation was Don Antonio Rodríguez Moñino, who in 1968 lamented the fact that virtually all histories of Spanish lyric poetry provided a chronological evolution of that genre, a neat classification by schools, a biography of the principal poets, and an assessment of the authors' interdependence.[18] His reservations about such histories rested on two grounds: for assuming that the Spanish public of the sixteenth and seventeenth centuries possessed a "horizon of information" regarding poetry that is similar to what we possess today; and for not taking into account the circulation of an important body of printed materials and manuscripts (p. 17). To underscore the seriousness of the situation, he pointed out that between 1588 and 1621, of some forty-five major poets writing in Spain, only a dozen—most of them minor writers— had books of poetry published (pp. 19–23).

Thanks to the empirical work of A. Rodríguez Moñino, E. M. Wilson, María Cruz García de Enterría, and others,[19] we have become more fully aware that, in addition to isolated poems which circulated freely in manuscript form and often found their way into anthologies *(Poesías varias o Rimas de varios ingenios),* thousands of poems became available to the public through poetical chapbooks, that is, through single quarto gatherings, generally consisting of a single sheet folded twice, known in Spanish as *pliegos sueltos* (Moñino, p. 45; Wilson, p. 15; Norton/Wilson, p. 5). It is estimated that in the sixteenth century more than a million and a half copies of those *pliegos* were printed and distributed in Spain (for a population of less than eight million). On the basis of these findings one might reasonably assume that, especially in the sixteenth century, at least part of the answer to the problem of transmission of literary culture lies in the chapbooks.

In the greater part of the sixteenth century, chapbooks served as digests of medieval and early Renaissance traditional culture. Those early *pliegos* contained a variety of materials besides ballad texts and were directed to a public that, while not yet differentiated into *vulgos* and *discretos* (that is, on the basis of whether or not one could exercise judgment in terms of literary criteria), was nevertheless heterogeneous in terms of its expectations. This may explain the fact that in the early sixteenth century it was not uncommon to find within the circuit of the *pliego suelto* learned as well as popular materials. This fact is attested to by a list of some five hundred chapbooks ("obrezillas pequeñas") that Ferdinand Columbus, the son of the admiral, was supposed to have had in his library upon his death in 1549.[20] E. M. Wilson provides a useful overview of the content of the body of chapbooks published from the early 1500s until the last quarter of the sixteenth century. Those texts included

> poems, chiefly amorous, from the *Cancionero general of 1511*, religious poems by Fray Antonio Montesinos, love poems by Juan del Encina . . . diatribes against women by Cristóbal de Castillejo, bawdy poems by Rodrigo de Reinosa, and even the . . . coplas of Jorge Manrique on his father's death. From the start poems by famous poets filtered down into these humble prints, where they occur alongside lives of criminals, burlesque testaments of asses, cocks, and foxes, narratives of captivity among the Moors such as the She-Renegade of Valladolid, survivals from the Middle Ages like Diego de San Pedro's poem of the Passion, dialogues between the body and the soul or between man and his purse, or Spanish versifications of the Creed, the Lord's Prayer, the Ave, or the Salve Regina. (Wilson, p. 16)

One cannot overestimate the role played by printers in the decisions to include or to exclude materials for public consumption. Thus while they were instrumental for the accessibility of poets such as Juan del

Encina, Fray Antonio de Montesinos, Cristóbal de Castillejo, and Rodrigo de Reinosa, they may also have been responsible for the exclusion of "champions of the new Italian metrics: Garcilaso, Cetina or the Divine Herrera" (Wilson, p. 16). One can argue, of course, that the people were attuned to listening to ballads so that the *romance,* which consists of a vowel assonance in every alternate octosyllabic verse, may have "enabled the uneducated in Spain to accept the lyrics and narrative of the cultivated" (Wilson, p. 16). Yet the question remains as to the status of what those early *pliegos* chose not to transmit. If one were to venture an educated guess, one could come to the conclusion that for practical reasons the printers of *pliegos* were for a time in the camp of the proponents of traditional metrics, whose champion, Cristóbal de Castillejo, had fueled the controversy with his famous *Represión contra los poetas españoles que escriben en verso italiano.*[21] In his *Represión* Castillejo calls on eminent poets from the past to speak in favor of tradition. Among the latter is Jorge Manrique:

> Don Jorge dixo: No veo
> Nescesidad ni razón
> De vestir nuevo deseo
> De coplas que por *rodeo*
> Van diciendo su intención.
>
> (our italics)

> Don Jorge said: I see
> Neither necessity nor reason
> To cater to this new desire
> For verses that, in a *roundabout* way,
> Express this intention.
>
> (our translation)

Apparently the printers and editors of chapbooks knew their markets well and used the new technology in the service of old cultural products, which, as opposed to the "rodeos" of italianate poetry, spoke with less aesthetic pretension and therefore appealed to a wider public.[22]

Thanks to the new technology of production which changed the text-addressee relations, those materials became accessible to different publics and, for that reason, had the potential of serving two different functions: the high and the low. For unlike the situation in many tribal societies, where everyone has the same culture,[23] or the model of medieval society, where "man . . . counts socially in that he is a part of a group and as such also has the function of representing that group, of serving as its sign" (Lotman, quoted in Corti, p. 17), in early modern Europe (in our case, Spain) there was "cultural as well as social stratification. There was a minority who could read and write as well as a majority who could not, and some of the literate minority knew Latin, the language of the Learned" (Burke, p. 23). Thus the *pliegos* were accessible to "readers" no matter where they were located within the cultural and social spheres. All readers, literate and semi-literate, as well as illiterate listeners who were tuned into the voices of blindmen who sang and graphically advertised their poems in the streets of the cities and at fairs, were familiar with the poems' general content and story line. A case in point is a chapbook of c. 1514–1519 that includes in the traditional Spanish ballad meter, the *romance,* the general plot summary of *Amadís de Gaula.* The books of *Amadís* had been published in 1508 in a version composed by Garci Rodríguez de Montalvo and had been aimed essentially at the learned, aristocratic urban gentry *(caballeros).* The printer of the chapbook—probably Juan de Burgos, Fadrique de Basilea, or Alonso de Melgar (Norton/Wilson, p. 13–14)—seized upon the success and popularity of the extended prose fiction and decided to turn a quick profit by trivializing the story of Amadís's deeds while de-emphasizing its high usage: the effects of those deeds on the knight errant's winning of his lady's love. The aristocratic public of the early sixteenth century could, of course, enjoy the *pliego* version, and might have been entertained by its oral performance at the hands of a lowly blindman. But a *caballero* could only identify with another text: the books of *Amadís de Gaula;* the text that brought before his eyes the phantasmagoric world of the knight errant, a world that did not acknowledge the existence of the city, that is, the space where financial transactions took place and where the economic activities of merchants and other progressive groups were perceived as undermining the universal values with which those aristocrats sought to identify: honor, beauty, and so on.[24] The *caballero's* expectations differ considerably from those of the semi-literate readers of the chapbook and from the expectations of an illiterate audience that hears the same poem as it is narrated or recited in song.

In a culture that is no longer signlike or communal, messages become fragmented because the addressee is no longer homogeneous. A century later Cervantes focused on the multiplicity of receptions that could be accorded printed texts. Ironically, the type of book that he chose as the centerpiece of that discussion is the romance of chivalry, the line of prose fiction that was set in vogue in Spain by *Amadís de Gaula*. That type of literature, we are told, had so caught the fancy of a poor rural hidalgo (Alonso Quijano) that he went mad and, in his madness, assumed the identity of a knight errant (Don Quijote). Now it is precisely the purported consequences of those readings that precipitate a variety of reactions in the text. Those reactions, in turn, illustrate the degree of fragmentation that exists among the consumers of culture.

The debate over the multiplicity of receptions given to books of chivalry takes place, significantly, in a rural inn and is prompted by a learned priest's remark that the readings of those books "had turned Don Quijote's brain" (I, 32). The first to react to that statement is the innkeeper, Juan Palomeque, who defends those readings quite passionately on grounds that they had put life into him as well as into plenty of others: "For at harvest time—he says—a lot of reapers come in here in the mid-day heat. There is always one of them who can read, and he takes up one of these books. Then as many as thirty of us sit round him, and we enjoy listening so much that it saves us countless gray hairs." The innkeeper admits that he looks for a particular trait in those stories; he is especially captivated by the blows and is so immersed in the fictions of battles that—he says—"I get the fancy to strike a few [blows] myself. And I could go on listening night and day." The innkeeper's wife does not listen to those stories, yet she also finds their recital useful. The reason given is a practical one: when her husband is occupied listening to someone read them, he forgets about nagging and scolding her. A fourth commentator is a prostitute named Maritornes. She also gets pleasure listening to those readings, but her attention focuses on those "parts when some lady or other is lying in her knight's embraces." A fifth viewpoint is offered by the innkeeper's daughter in response to a query by the priest: "I listen too—she says—and, really, though I don't understand it, I do enjoy it. But I don't like the fighting that pleases my father so much. I prefer the complaints the knights make when they're away from their ladies. Sometimes they actually *make me cry*. I pity them so much."

In essence one might say that, in 1605, the subject of Cervantes's discussion of the books of chivalry is how different fictions from within the same type of story have become imprinted on the consciousness of "readers" and "listeners" who bring their expectations (personal as well as collective) to the act of reception. What emerges is that all those listeners are oblivious to the totality of the work. As opposed to the priest, they are not concerned with questions that go beyond certain aspects of plot. They do not understand that "blows," "embraces," "sighs," and so forth are interdependent. Unlike the learned priest, the illiterate consumers of romances of chivalry cannot be concerned with aesthetic and moral issues; they are not preoccupied, as were the learned moralists, with questions of "truthfulness" and "responsibility." What emerges from the discussion in *Don Quijote* (I, 32) is that a largely illiterate, lower-class audience has at least partial access to books that a century earlier had been the pastime of aristocratic readers. For the occasional lower-class consumers, listening to stories of knights errant had a practical function: to find solace from the trials of daily life. For them, listening to stories that expressed aristocratic values was not a way of consecrating idleness; it was merely a respite from labor and toil.

In a sense one might conclude that we are faced with an example of the "sinking theory," which holds that "the culture of the lower classes *(Unterschicht)* is an out-of-date imitation of the culture of the upper classes *(Oberschicht)*" (Burke, p. 58). One must also keep in mind, however, that popular culture is not simply a body of texts but a way of using them (see de Certeau), that is, we must understand problems of transmission and horizons of expectation.

We have taken this apparent detour from the chapbooks because, ultimately, it is the novel that establishes popular-culture practice in the realm of high culture; it is the novel that incorporates the fictions of literature (high and low), the fictions of daily life, and the fictions of ideological discourses at a time when private readers become fully differentiated into *vulgos* and *discretos*. At the same time that the novel began to take into account a multiplicity of addressees, chapbook literature began to aim at a class reader, thus reversing the process that had characterized it throughout most of the sixteenth century, when it did not take into account only a "particular class of reader but a public that was still homogeneous and undifferentiated."[25] The changing patterns in the production and consumption of chapbooks can be said to have been tied to a number of factors. Among them, one can highlight the changing conditions of the printing industry around 1600; an ever-increasing resistance of the writers of the establishment to that medium; and, ultimately, the marginalization of the consumers of chapbooks by the same writers, along social and intellectual lines.

The crisis of the printing industry in Spain dates back to the late sixteenth century. It seems that as capital investment declined, and as printers came to rely more and more on jobbing to survive, they turned increasingly to the production of chapbooks. Since chapbooks could be produced inexpensively and the modest investments required could be recovered in a matter of days, printers viewed an expanded market in chapbooks as a way of overcoming their economic difficulties. In order to expand their markets, printers were forced to cater to an "increasingly less 'literary' (and less literate) public" (Cruickshank, p. 809). In effect, the chapbooks were to be directed to a particular class of reader.

The content of chapbooks changed substantially after 1600, when the shorter traditional ballads disappeared from circulation. In their place there appeared "learned historical ballads, derived from chronicles, collected by Lucas Rodríguez and Lorenzo Sepúlveda; . . . selections from the art-ballads of the *Romancero general* of 1600 and its sequels; isolated poems by Lope de Vega, José de Valdivielso and even verse satires of Don Francisco de Quevedo. The old plebeian pieces (the She-Renegade, the verse testament of animals, the narratives of captivity) remained popular. Jácaras, new poems in thieves' cant, had considerable vogue; some were by Quevedo, others by less talented imitators" (Wilson, p. 16). But despite the availability of new cultural products—especially the new-art ballads that were often marketed in the form of mini-anthologies of four- and eight-page octavo (Wilson, p. 16)—the new pattern of *pliego* production pointed toward a more identifiable consumer: the lower classes or the so-called *classi subalterne* (Di Stefano, p. 92; cf. Gramsci). While the interaction between works of high usage and those of low usage continued in some ways (we are thinking here of the *pliegos de cordel*), their content became increasingly more vulgar and less literary. That is, in the first quarter of the sixteenth century the *pliegos* showed a marked de-emphasis of high usage from the earlier period.

To the proliferation of the trivial *romances de ciegos* throughout the seventeenth century (García de Enterría, p. 144), one can add the significant increases in accounts of events published or "relaciones de sucesos,"[26] so that the chapbook clearly became the mass-oriented vehicle that, despite its increasing lack of prestige among the intellectual establishment, was to perform an important function as a vehicle of entertainment and as a tool of political and social propaganda. While it is clear that in the early 1600s print was not the dominant form of ideological control, it is equally evident that print media were being used increasingly for manipulative purposes. Thus the subjects covered by chapbooks in the early 1600s included religious festivals, canonizations of saints, the nativity and passion of Christ, poems dedicated to the Virgin's Immaculate Conception, and versified catechisms (with questions and answers and acts of contrition). There were also poems directed against marginalized groups such as Jews, Moors, Blacks, and Gypsies—the very groups that were the objects of many *Autos de Fe,* those official spectacles of institutional repression against all perceived deviations from the dominant values. Then there were pieces on *bandoleros,* whose freedom from social conventions and obligations generally landed them on the gallows. There were sensationalized accounts of urban crimes, the kind condemned by Lope de Vega in his *Memorial* (1615) to the king: "hombres que en las ciudades de España fuerçan sus hijas, matan sus madres" ("men who violate their daughters and kill their mothers in the cities of Spain") (cf. "Que no se vendan coplas por las calles").[27] In addition, there were substantial numbers of chapbooks that included propaganda pieces dealing with current political events: the expulsion of the Moriscos by Philip III between 1609 and 1614; the rebellion of Catalonia (1640); the successful campaigns of the Spanish armies at various moments of the Thirty Years War. In virtually all instances the chapbooks related the official version of those events: the Moriscos are thrown out of Spain for being enemy traitors ("El Rey los echa de españa / por traydores enemigos"); the Kingdoms of Spain are loyal and united against the rebels in Catalonia ("Echan bandos generales. / A cuyos Regios preceptos / todos los Reynos de España / leales obedecieron"); the Spanish armies are fighting mercilessly against the enemies of Spain and of Catholicism (García de Enterría, *Sociedad,* p. 298). And so on.

In the early 1600s print media were no less suspect than they had been in the previous century. Yet some aspects of them were incorporated into the state's plan to manipulate culture. That is, no less than the *comedia* (which used the simplicity of rural life and, with it, the songs and lyrics of the people for recuperative purposes) or the *autos-sacramentales* (which were, after all, sermons meant to dramatize on stage and at religious festivals the central teachings of the Church) or other manifestations of audio-visual culture (see Maravall, *La Cultura del Barroco*), the printed chapbooks became one more instrument in the propaganda campaign that was undertaken to consolidate the monarchic-seigneurial interests at a time when the world was deemed to be topsy-turvy and the perception of crisis and decline was commonplace among the groups in power and the intelligentsia who served them.

It is significant, for example, that the official ban on the printing of novels and plays which took place on March 6, 1625, did not extend to the chapbooks. Thus, if there was an attempt to marginalize a literature that was viewed as being increasingly vulgar and banal, that attempt came at the hands of professional writers such as Lope de Vega, who, while continuing to argue for greater official control of the *pliegos* on aesthetic, social, and moral grounds, were ultimately aiming at safeguarding property rights and at maintaining powers of monopoly over the production of literary culture (see Lope de Vega, "Memorial").

The emergence of the novel raises a number of important issues, many of which have been adequately studied. There is one issue that has not received sufficient attention, and yet it is of crucial importance to our notion of use in culture: who is the reader of the novel, or, more properly, who is the reading subject of the novel? The latter formulation should indicate that a theoretical answer must be sought before an empirical one can be searched for. It also implies that the appearance of the novel signals a mutation in the reception of texts and that a different subject must emerge. The question, then, is: who or what is this subject for the novel?

It will be recalled from the earlier discussion of the different readings that the *Amadís* receives in the episode of the *Quijote* that the reception of the *Amadís* is fragmented, representing different modes of appropriation, or different modes of using the *Amadís*. A hundred years after the publication of the original, Cervantes shows that the *Amadís* is no longer read as a totality. But one can turn the question to Cervantes's text as well: who can read it? In other words, who can read the fragmentation in such a way that it will be perceived in its fragmentary reception and yet somehow be added up, totalized? An answer to this question requires a more precise characterization of the interaction in that scene. Each of the participants (the priest, the innkeeper, his wife, the prostitute, and the daughter) represent not only a reader with a different horizon of expectation, but also a different discursive circuit. If we take the text of the original *Amadís* as discursively homogeneous, in that its diction, themes, subject matter, and allusive structure constitute a describable system of implication, the breakup of that system, and the appropriation of its diverse parts into other discursive circuits, can be taken as emblematic of a larger cultural process that occurs in the period of transition from the Middle Ages to the beginnings of our modernity.

This issue can be illuminated by extending somewhat Bakhtin's pioneering work in this area. The medieval discursive system was based on the existence of relatively autonomous linguistic entities. Beside the great opposition between Latin and the vulgar tongues, various professional groups, such as the guilds, had their own discourses, the apprenticeship of which was part and parcel of initiation into the profession. Each such discourse was self-sufficient and auto-regulated. The latter feature is important because it ensured a high degree of functionality for the discourse and made it answerable only to its own functional demands. Discourses existed for interaction with other groups, and in those instances where this was not the case, the discourses in presence negotiated from positions of equality. Their coexistence in the discursive system was not hierarchized in the sense that it did not involve passage through a mediator. In somewhat parallel fashion, though at a different level of the society, the relative sedentariness characteristic of the Middle Ages, owing to the agricultural economic base, ensured the development of differentiable local dialects, that is, once again, of immediately functional linguistic constructs. In the realm of what we call literature, and making allowances for the anachronism of the appellation, it is clear that with its reliance upon verse forms, which, by definition, are oriented toward closure (rhyme, rhythm, length), the medieval differentiation of genres is based upon the mutual separability of these, with no single genre containing or absorbing the others.

In early modern times, major changes take place: urbanization brings together speakers from different linguistic areas, either to transact commercial exchanges or in its patterns of residential settlement. The various professional groups become increasingly regulated by the state apparatus and thus become answerable to it. The emergent state bureaucracy, having abandoned Latin, favors one sociolect, and, within it, one discourse (or style, as it is known at the time), and makes all others answerable to it. Henceforth all dealings that involve interdiscursive crossing must be mediated by the dominant discourse. The state, in other words, has arrogated unto itself the capacity of containing all the discourses used on its territory, and is making them all answerable to itself, in its own preferred discourse, imposing the

latter for all interdiscursive activity. The individual discourses lose
their autonomy and, as a result of being integrated into the state's
totalization, their self-sufficiency as well. They are now fragments of
a much larger whole, patches of a great quilt. Their speakers also
lose autonomy and self-sufficiency, and must recognize that they are
speakers of fragmentary discourses which can never be totalized. Only
the state can achieve this totalization—at least such is the claim.

There is a striking similarity between this claim and what the novel
does. *Don Quijote* is paradigmatic in this respect. Its famous dialogical structure represents an attempt to inscribe as many discourses as
possible within its frame. The question is: who can read them? In a
sense, the answer is: the state. Only the totalizing state can claim to
be the adequate subject for reading a novel like the *Quijote,* for only
the state has attempted to inventory and totalize all these discourses.
In practice this means that such a novel serves to provide its readers
with an experience of what it is to look at things from the perspective
of the state, that is, to perceive the limitations of each of the individual
discourses and the configuration of their addition. At the same time,
it demonstrates powerfully the inordinateness of the state's claim and
the impossibility of its realization. Yet it is an impossibility that both
the state and the novel would attempt to overcome, the first through
increased regulative structures, the latter through a search for the perfect style, a search that would dominate the development of the novel
well into our century.

The view of Spanish culture in the years 1500–1700 that we have been
advancing is a dynamic one, based upon the recognition that this is a
transitional phase from the more static medieval culture to the more
consolidated and rigid culture of Neoclassicism.

The major transformation is the entry of the state upon the stage of
culture as its major force. Henceforth one must distinguish between
official, or state-sanctioned, culture and unofficial, or barely tolerated
and potentially oppositional or subversive, culture. Official culture itself consists of two distinct realms: an elite culture that is ideologically
consonant with the goals of the state's ruling groups and dedicated to
their promotion and realization, and a mass culture that is manipulated and purveyed on behalf of the state to a broad audience.
Whereas elite culture presupposes a critical awareness but a conscious
espousal of the state's programmatic views, mass culture rests on
uncritical reception. The content of both these realms consists of re-

cyclable elements of a fragmented and progressively disappearing medieval culture, as well as original creations and contemporary foreign imports adapted for local consumption.

Unofficial culture consists, first of all, of the excluded materials: medieval material, or remnants of even more archaic cultural strata, that cannot be integrated and reused in official culture; materials associated with banished populations (Moors, Jews, heretics). But it consists as well of the reinscribing and nonstate-serving practices that we labeled as the proper realm of popular culture: the mode of consumption of the products of official culture that detaches the latter from the goals of their purveyors and thus establishes a realm, however fleeting its extent, of autonomous and alternative cultural production.

In this respect, it must be noted how complex the position of the novel is: inconceivable without the kind of cultural fragmentation that occurs in this period, it is at once the most adequate expression of the ideological role of the state and its most obvious challenger. In fact, whereas the state can assert its hegemony over the realm of culture through gestures of exclusion from that realm of those elements it wishes to proscribe, the novel, by including all the elements of official culture (both the elite and the mass) as well as the excluded elements of unofficial culture, almost by definition engages in the practices we have called popular. The state's claim to totalization proceeded on the basis of exclusion, whereas the novel's relied upon inclusion, for unlike the state, the novel was not endangered by inner tensions and contradictions. Yet the search for a homogenizing style, which has dominated the subsequent history of the novel, shows that the novel itself was not immune to these forces and that as its practitioners came to identify themselves more with the goals of the ruling elites, the novel became increasingly part of the elite official culture and abandoned its popular grounds.

4   After the Storyteller . . .

Narratology arose from the seemingly commonsensical observation that stories are told in a variety of media: in verbal narratives, myths, cartoons, dance, mime, film, in the kind of music we call programmatic, and even in stained-glass windows. If such is the case, it has been argued,[1] then stories, or more properly their narrative component, should be studied in their own right, without reference to the medium in which they are cast. This approach, dealing with the universe presented in the stories rather than with the mode of that presentation, was quickly labeled "grammatical" by its practitioners since it did not consider the more semantic dimension of the stories' signification. Historically, it is associated with the international movement we call French Structuralism (Todorov, Barthes, Lévi-Strauss, Gerald Prince, A.-J. Greimas, Thomas Pavel). It is characterized by a search for the invariant components of all narratives and their mode of articulation; specific kinds of articulatory configurations then permit the establishment of a taxonomy of narratives. We owe to this approach the elaboration of an important body of analytical terms and procedures that have given the study of narrative a certain technical veneer and considerable descriptive power. As a result, this field of research seems to have taken on more of a scientific standing in accordance with the hypothetico-deductive protocols of the linguistics upon which it has modeled itself. In this respect, the narratological structuralists have drawn upon the fundamental work of the folklorist Vladimir Propp[2] as well as that of the morphologist André Jolles.[3]

But as soon as the very real accomplishments of this approach are brought to bear upon literary studies, in the study of verbal narratives, a new set of problems arises, and it is in the process of addressing these problems that narratology as a branch of literary studies has come into being, gathering under its label works, such as Henry James's Prefaces and Wayne Booth's *Rhetoric of Fiction,* that, in the aftermath of its emergence, appear to be its forerunners. For, uninformed as such works may be of the properly structural properties of narrative, they are nonetheless concerned with a story's mode of being in language. The structuralists, if they did not know it already, rapidly discovered that their initial methodological decision to bracket away the medium and the mode of presentation of narrative could at best serve as a delaying tactic. Eventually the scientific precision and elegance of their descriptions not only failed to clear up or dispel some of the traditional problems of narrative analysis, it actually recast them into more puzzling ones. While such a problematization may have represented a tangible gain in the appreciation of the complexity of the problems at hand, it was still somewhat of an embarrassment, if not outright discomfiture, to its formulators, who saw themselves suddenly facing such old standbys of narrative analysis as point of view. To their credit, the narratologists did not give up their project but rather expanded its scope to include these new problems, thus giving narratology its present compass and place in literary studies.

The articulation of the first set of problems—those of narrative structure—with the second—those that arise in conjunction with a study of the mode of presentation—has been effected by means of a distinction, originally drawn by the Russian Formalists, between *fabula* and *sjuzhet:* the story as a series of events and the story as it is told in narrative.[4] In English this distinction is generally rendered as *story* and *discourse,* which have been conveniently defined by Jonathan Culler as, respectively, "a sequence of actions or events, conceived as independent of their manifestation," and "the discursive presentation or narration of events."[5] But, as Culler goes on to show in his important article, this articulation is far from constituting a happy resolution. Rather, insofar as it can be called an articulation at all, it is one of necessary non-conjunction, and, frequently, of outright incompatibility. On the one hand, the analysis of the story, in Culler's sense of the term, proceeds on the commonsensical assumption of a logical and temporal priority of events over their rendition in the discourse, while, on the other, it is the empirically verifiable lot of narratological analysis to constantly come upon events in narratives that, far from being prior givens that the discourse of the narrative is merely relating, are the products of discursive forces or constructs fulfilling discursive requirements. Such an inversion in the relation of story and discourse does not merely violate what both common sense and theory require as their logical ordering but condemns narratology to a permanently cleaved state: the analyses of story and of discourse cannot be free-standing; yet, as soon as their mutual dependence is acknowledged and, in the concrete carrying out of analytic work, the absent one is brought forth—regardless of whether one started with story or discourse—it proves to be a perturbatory element rather than a resolving one, and the totalization one hoped for is irremediably gone. As Culler puts it:

> Neither perspective, then, is likely to offer a satisfactory narratology, nor can the two fit together in harmonious synthesis; they stand in irreconcilable opposition, a conflict between two logics which puts in question the possibility of a coherent, non-contradictory science of narrative.[6]

This manner of bringing to bear upon each other two components or aspects of what until then was presumed to be a single entity, in order to show that they are incompatible and yet are bound to each other, is generally associated with the procedures of poststructuralism. The latter has been quite hard not only on narratology, reducing it, as Culler does in his discussions, to a tragic critical practice—tragic because at once inescapable and doomed to alternate, without the possibility of totalization, between its dependent constituents—but on narrative as well, especially that part that is called story.

The best example of this is the one that could be said to be foundational of deconstructive practice. It is the well-known fragment of *The Will to Power* in which Nietzsche shows that causation is not a state of affairs in the world but the rhetorical figure called metonymy.[7] Again Culler's summary and discussion are to the point:

> Causation involves a narrative structure in which we posit first the presence of a cause and then the production of an effect. Indeed, the very notion of plot, as E. M. Forster taught us, is based on causation: "the king died, then the queen died" is not a narrative, although "the king died, then the queen died of grief" is . . . First, there is cause; then, there is effect; first a mosquito bites one's arm, then one feels pain. But, says Nietzsche, this sequence is not given; it is constructed by a rhetorical operation. What happens may be, for example, that we feel a pain and then look around for some factor we can treat as the cause. The "real" causal sequence may be: first pain, then mosquito. It is the effect that causes us to produce a cause; a tropological operation then reorders the sequence pain-mosquito as mosquito-

pain. This latter sequence is the product of discursive forces, but we treat it as a given, as the true order.[8]

Clearly, what is at stake here is no longer the relatively parochial issue of whether a science of narrative can be erected, but the very question of the cognitive value of narratives. If tropological operations and discursive forces order the sequence of events in stories, and do not do so in any predictable manner but only *may* do so, then we can never know from a narrative what the actual sequence of events in a given instance may have been, or what caused what. Such a narrative may give us pleasure or hold our interest, but it is useless from the point of view of cognition: it offers no reliable knowledge about that which it purports to relate.

As long as the narrative is a self-proclaimed fiction, such as a short story or a novel, there is not much harm. But we rely upon narratives in many other areas than the fictional one, and foremost in history, which we take to be the very opposite of fiction. Yet, if it is true that narratives give us no reliable knowledge of what they purport to relate, then they are all fictions, including those of history. At that point, I can no longer evaluate two differing historical accounts on the basis of their veracity, that is of their accuracy with respect to the events they relate, but on some other criteria, perhaps even aesthetic ones such as style or internal coherence. Moreover, since what is being asserted about narratives' fictionality here must clearly be taken to apply to all narratives, past and present, then it follows that reliance on some historical accounts or on explanations of a historical, that is narrative, character, could have been determined by considerations other than those of truthfulness, perhaps even by aesthetic ones such as pleasure. What I have taken to be the regularities, continuities, and discontinuities of history are perhaps, since the latter has been known to me through narratives, no more than the products of tropological operations or discursive forces, and their reassuring recurrence from historical narrative to historical narrative may just be a testimony to their power, their status as master narratives, or, even more simply, the result of ideological manipulation. But the large explanatory systems, the ideologies of liberalism, Marxism, nationalism, and so forth, the self-foundational narratives of religions—what Jean-François Lyotard calls the "grands récits" in his account of their present recession[9]— are constructed in the form of narrative themselves. From a poststructuralist perspective, explanatory regresses built upon narratives can no longer lay any claim to knowledge; although they certainly need not vanish as a result, they can no longer command the authority that once was theirs.

There is a stinging irony here: once upon a time it was claimed, under Marxian auspices, that "men made history," that human beings were the subjects of history. Now, with the equation of history and narrative,[10] that claim becomes the derisory one that "men make stories," that human beings are the subjects of stories. Yet, while this scaled-down claim has little of the sweep of its prototype, it does have the advantage of any truism: it gains assent. We do tell stories. It also shifts the focus away from *what* stories are about, from what they recount, to *who* is telling the story to *whom,* or as Ross Chambers puts it in *Story and Situation:*[11] stories *relate* speakers and listeners in an act of communication they constitute. The question of *what* is recounted will not, however, be so easily dismissed. Even when the focus is shifted onto the communicative act, it persists, but in a new guise: by virtue of what does the speaker, the storyteller, spin the tale?

II

This, of course, is the very question that Walter Benjamin addresses in his essay "The Storyteller."[12] His inquiry proceeds on the assumption that the storyteller and his function are in a state of decline. Though the immediate historical reference is to the aftermath of the Great War, the process must have started earlier since the references to the period in which the storytellers flourished clearly establish that they preceded our modernity: peasants told the stories of the land where they toiled and thus endowed it with a dimension of temporal continuity; seamen related tales of the lands to which they had sailed and thus extended (made continuous) the space of human experience; and the artisans, who in the years of their apprenticeship had to roam the land as journeymen but then settled to practice their craft, achieved a conjunction of both the temporal and spatial dimensions, earning their class the title of the storytelling university (p. 85).

In all three instances of storytelling, the enabling condition of the storyteller is experience, and it is clear that, for Benjamin, the ability to exchange experiences, to pass them from mouth to mouth, is the fundamental function of stories and their telling. He considers it an "inalienable" right, the "securest among our possessions" (p. 83). Yet, as I noted earlier, his essay begins with the observation that we are losing this possession presently, and that we are losing it because experience is falling in value.

Benjamin does not go into the causes of this devaluation here, although he does give some hints. As I have argued elsewhere,[13] the rapid expansion of markets in the fifteenth and sixteenth centuries necessitated an equally rapid acquisition of the types of knowledge we call information and know-how. The traditional mode of lengthy individual apprenticeship with several master practitioners in different locations proved inefficient under such circumstances and had to be replaced by a form of learning no longer based on experience but on mediation. Instead of acquiring experience directly or through the stories the master would have told them, the students (no longer apprentices) increasingly learned their trade from the systematic expositions of the most efficient practices in the profession presented in the forms of models and not as records of actual activity. This was even truer for those forms of economic and sociopolitical activity that require knowledge of vastly different sectors of the market and the society. Book learning thus came to replace direct acquisition of experience, and, as Benjamin observes, it gave rise to a desire for a form of knowledge that would no longer be guaranteed by the life experience of its propounder—the master—but that would instead be "understandable in itself" and subject to "prompt verifiability" (p. 89), namely information. At the same time, information is not so much stored in order to be reflected upon and to serve as a guide for one's future practice as it is consumed. Instead of contributing to the growing awareness of the individual's continuity with others in space and time, that is, to what has been traditionally called wisdom, information fragments time and space even further, isolates the individual even more from others, and indeed by its news-like obsolescence, its incompleteness and inherent recalcitrance to totalization, it unmoors the individual from such values as he or she may have acquired, especially since the latter are no longer determined by the inherited wisdom of the collectivity or the precepts of relation but by the momentary needs of the market. Although it was meant to supplement experience, and not supplant it, mediated knowledge destabilized it and, in the process, produced the condition characteristic of our modernity, in which we find ourselves caught in the gap between the lessons of acquired experience and the values fostered upon us in the various apparatuses of mediation.

This is where literature, and art in general, came in. Already previously, the storyteller not only recounted personal experience but, in the narrative in which he or she couched it, endowed that experience with meaningfulness. While the lived experience of the storyteller was, as Benjamin saw, the condition of his or her authority, the efficacy of the telling lay in the fact that it articulated learnable modes of endowing experience with meaningfulness. Literature would increasingly rely upon this capacity of narrative. We may observe, for example, that the large-scale explosion of narrative literature in the eighteenth and nineteenth centuries was preceded by several decades of memoir writing in which the writer, like the storyteller earlier, appealed to the authority of lived experience in the recounting of his or her life. Similarly, the epistolary novel provides the means for reflecting upon experience and thus serves as a guide to it. Its future was to be the novel of manners. The aesthetic function of art, in other words, was, paradoxically, to become a mediator itself, but a mediator that would deliberately play the role of a supplement to a fragmentalized and unmoored experience, and thus hold open the possibility of totalization. Narrative form was particularly well suited to such a task because of its special mode of articulating temporality: what was fragment today could be completed tomorrow.

We may wish to pause and consider the movement of our reflection so far: on the one hand, we have seen that the attempt to develop a science of narrative as a branch of literary studies was thwarted, but in a curiously undebilitating fashion, by the inescapable necessity of maintaining at once two incompatible approaches, the analyses of story and discourse, and that moreover the only apparent achievement of narratology—outside of the development of its technical apparatus and the production of some illuminating textual exegeses—is to have provided the means for a devastating attack upon narrative, an attack that has resulted in the invalidation of the claims made on behalf of all explanatory regresses that are narrative in form. On the other hand, we have seen that the increasing mediation of daily life has resulted in the fragmentation of experience and the dethroning of the storyteller but, at the same time, in the granting of greater power to the aesthetic function of art, and to narrative art-forms in particular. Our own movement does not escape the process it describes: the analysis of the fragmentation of the study and status of narrative propelled us into narrative form ourselves. Such a happenstance is too curious not to deserve some attention. And this is where a reading of Ross Chambers's *Story and Situation* proves necessary.

III

To reiterate: Ross Chambers is a scholar of modest pretensions. He knows better than to write either a systematic treatise on narrative or a history of its development. Rather, he focuses on that element of lived experience that we have in relation to all stories when we ask: What's the point? He starts then with what seems like the derisory conclusion that human beings are the subjects of stories, but instead of reading in it the truism that we do tell stories, he subjects it to the same kind of analysis that recognized in the Marxian quotation that "men make history" not a statement of fact but an admonition, a call to revolutionary action, the expression of a desire. That human beings are the subjects of stories means then that the communicative act in which a story is told is constitutive of its participants, that it is an experience itself, and not merely a way of talking about experience, though it is that as well. But whereas the experience told in the story is, as Benjamin saw, dependent on the authority of the teller, the experience of the telling, lived equally by teller and audience, writer and reader, narrator and narratee, is a function of the authority of the story.

Chambers readily accepts Benjamin's observation of the decline of the authority of the storyteller, but he sees it as leading to the necessity for the story to take on more authority itself. Forced to function more autonomously and without the claim to respect and attention that the storyteller could put forward, the story, functioning like a commodity in the market, must take on the aura of art in order to maintain itself. Divorced from the lived experience of the teller, who previously stood as its guarantor, it must become part of ours. Since in the mediated universe that is ours we are no longer engaged in processes of intersubjective communication—that is, we no longer conceive of knowledge as consisting in the acquisition of personal experience and the sharing of that experience with others, but rather we model our concept of knowledge upon the acquisition of information about an object so that our subjecthood is defined in the cognition of objects, be they things, ideas, or other human beings—the story, commodified as it has become, will take on the guise of an object rather than being a process between human beings. In this way, we will indeed become its subjects, just as students of narrative become narratologists as their object dissolves in their cognitive undertaking.

But, as Chambers is quick to observe, when stories assume the status of objects, they do not do so with the passivity of reified entities, things. They begin to exert powers of their own, and foremost among them, those of seduction. Chambers has written a very detailed account of the ways in which seduction becomes the only recourse of entities reduced to objecthood under our present model of cognition.[14] Since the latter is a model known to us, if at all, from the perspective of the subject, Chambers's account provides a wholly new outlook on something we thought we knew. It permits him to retrace ground covered by others, but by doing so from his special vantage point, he makes us aware of how different the configuration of that ground is from the impression we had formed. It becomes clear as one proceeds that in the communicative act in which a story is told in the age of its commodification, the subject, whether as teller or narratee, is in the weak position; yet that is the position from which we had judged the entire encounter. Chambers's modesty was thus the recognition of a necessity, a coming to terms with the existing state of affairs. It also represents an attempt to practice criticism from a position other than that of a pre-formed subjecthood coming to invest an object given to it readymade, inert and powerless. For Chambers, the object to be known knows that it is such an object, and that it is an object of desire. What is the critic then to do?

IV

In a fine example of *mise-en-abyme* in his own text, Chambers gives us a model of his practice in his seventh chapter, where he subjects Henry James's *The Figure in the Carpet* to close scrutiny. This tale, which so fascinates critics because it depicts our lot, stages the desire of the critic to achieve subjecthood, not only cognitively but socially, by penetrating the secret of the author. Chambers shows that the narrator-critic conceives of the penetration of this secret as the appropriation of what Vereker, the author, calls "the particular thing I've written my books for."[15] In other words, the critic conceives of his task in accordance with the model of subject-object cognition. But the text, represented in *The Figure in the Carpet* by the figure of the author who, in a crucial scene, stands *on* the rug of the narrator-critic's bedroom,[16] refuses to submit in such a fashion and begins to play what Chambers calls a cat-and-mouse game, in which its powers of seduction and its mastery of the communicative situation give it the upper hand. As Chambers puts it, the text's "true superiority over the critic does not lie in [its] possession of a secret so much as it results from [its] successful deployment of discursive strategies for which the younger man is not a match."

We recognize here our point of departure: the attempt to elicit from the text its narrative structure, its secret, runs into the text's discursive forces or tropological operations that render the task impossible. The critic is stymied, but not undone. What is undone is the critic's reliance upon the model of subject-object cognition that presupposes that the path to knowledge for a subject requires the appropriation and "thesaurization" of the object. But this model is deconstructed in the text as it is by poststructuralism in relation to the claims made for narrative. James's text shows that this need not be the end of the story, in either instance. Chambers observes that the figure of Vereker recedes from this point onward in the tale, and the focus shifts to the relation of the narrator to other critics. In the painstaking analysis that follows, Chambers leads us to the scene of the revelation of the narrator-critic's practice, which occurs when the narrator tells Drayton Deane his story, that is, the very story the reader is reading: "I told him in a word just what I've written out here." In other words, once the critic abandons the framework of a subject-object cognition, with its scientific pretensions, and focuses on his or her relations to others, s/he will produce a story that will indeed relate him or her to others, and in this manner the critic will indeed lay the secret bare.

Chambers, as I have written, has no scientific pretensions. His rigorous analyses of nineteenth-century art-tales[17] bring to light the variety of modes in which they play the cat-and-mouse game of communication. In the process, as by now we should expect, Chambers tells us a story, or rather at least two stories: one is that of the art-tale from Poe to Joyce, passing through Balzac, Flaubert, Nerval, and James; the other we are less quick to notice until we observe that the texts that Chambers has chosen to reread could be said to constitute the canon of narratology: "The Purloined Letter," "Sarrasine," "Un Cœur simple," and so on. This is also then the story of narratology from Barthes, Lacan, Derrida, to J. Hillis Miller, Shoshana Felman, and Wolfgang Iser. But these are stories the reader will have to read by him- or herself; otherwise, what's the point?

. . . comes the storyteller.

5   Where the Action Is

In his introduction to *The Poetics of Plot*,[1] Thomas Pavel characterizes his study as a quantitative contribution to the field of formal narrative analysis. Quite rightly he observes that "more often than not, recent plot analysis has operated on relatively simple literary artifacts, such as folktales, short stories, or small poems." By contrast, his study "attempts to demonstrate the fruitfulness of formal analysis when applied to more sophisticated literary products," namely, several well-known English Renaissance plays. The claim is quantitative because it suggests that there is only a difference in degree of sophistication between a Russian wonder-tale of the type analyzed by Vladimir Propp and *King Lear,* the object of Pavel's last chapter; and speaking strictly from the perspective of formal narrative analysis, there is merit to this view. But, as happens whenever a well-delimited subject is studied with rigor and thoroughness, Pavel's results, implicit and explicit, go well beyond quantitative considerations to address and inform such broad concerns of literary theory and cultural criticism as the role of linguistics in literary studies, the nature and function of agency in plot advancement and in history, and the relation of plot patterns to dominant epistemes. Pavel's clarity of style and lucidity of exposition are such as to require no paraphrase, but the issues that he raises deserve attention.

I

Disciplinary specialization has become so common among us that we accept readily the present division of labor among those who deal with language. In this respect, Thomas Pavel is an anomaly: he is a trained linguist with a background in the philosophy of language; he has written fiction in the form of the philosophical tale,[2] as well as that of modernistic écriture;[3] and he is the author of several studies in the field of literature.[4] Such a broad spectrum of activities leads him to cast a different glance upon what many of us take as a given in the present organization of knowledge, and this perspective is reflected in his critical practice, which implies a new set of relations between linguistics and literary studies.

Although interest in matters of language and of verbal art is as old as civilization itself, the institutionalized forms of this interest, which we call linguistics and literary studies, emerged more or less contemporaneously in the second half of the eighteenth century. They did not emerge in a vacuum, however, but against the backdrop of another institutional practice that was directly concerned with language: rhetoric. It would seem that a modus vivendi could have been arrived at among the three disciplines. Linguistics was but a fledgling endeavor then, and it was specifically concerned with the historical aspect of language.[5] Rhetoric was concerned with the social force of language: the study of the effects it could achieve and the means by which it could accomplish them.[6] Literary studies, primarily focused on matters of taste and literary history, were less concerned with the questions of power that rhetoric inevitably encounters than with the constitution of a distinct cultural tradition conceived of as the historical heritage of a nation. Given the historical nature of their respective concerns and the fact that both were more interested in integrative community functions than in polemical tactics, there developed an affinity between literary studies and linguistics, perhaps most evident in ancient and medieval studies, but actually inherent to the great philological project of the nineteenth century. Such a project could be carried out as long as inquiry into language, on the part of linguistics, was primarily concerned with the expressive qualities of specific languages and the determination of hierarchies between them by means of historical deviation and kinship. It also required that literary studies be focused upon the elaboration of so-called national traits and that such traits be shown to be evident in the work of the "great geniuses" of the literature, as well as in the almost unconscious folk productions of the speakers of the language,[7] although, in both instances, these traits would be offset by other features, of "universal" dimension. Both of these concerns were quite alien to rhetoric, and the latter found itself increasingly isolated and eventually eliminated from the school curricula in which it had prominently figured since the establishment of a Greek presence in Sicily. However, linguistics and literary studies cannot be said to have shared the spoils of rhetoric, since their relation to the older practice had been one of studied indifference. Their respective social functions had been different and did not require them to compete directly with rhetoric, whose social function was clearly in decline. Yet rhetoric's passing created a vacuum—the study of the social sphere of language—that would prove to be a pitfall to both linguistics and literary studies, and it would come to haunt the relationship of the two younger disciplines.

The positivistic movement in literary studies, when it took hold in the nineteenth century, did so against the background assumption of a broadly shared general culture that did not need to make explicit many of the mechanisms of the actual functioning of literary works and was therefore much more at home examining the role played by individuals in the manipulation of linguistic resources and other cultural codes of the time. When the process of cultural production and reproduction functions optimally for a given social aggregate, considerations of style and individual expression will prevail over considerations of coding and code formation within this aggregate. The aesthetics of genius that is concomitant to positivism did not prevail because of some putative philosophical superiority, but because there obtained a social base for such an aesthetics that was precisely the broad sharing of those cultural codes. The crisis would come when those codes could no longer enjoy widespread social recognition, and it would require that a linguistic type of attention be paid to the functioning of literary writing.

Societies such as those of Spain and even France, in which social stratification was well established and deeply entrenched, would remain positivistic in their literary studies until modernism would begin to affect them, something that did not happen until the late 1950s and early 1960s in France, which saw then the advent of structuralism, and in Spain only in the late 1970s. But the very same process struck Germany, Russia, England, and the United States much earlier, and in each instance, it led to the emergence of linguistic approaches to literature: the so-called morphological school in Wilhelmine and Weimar Germany, the Formalists in revolutionary Russia, and New Criticism in the English-speaking countries.

The case of the Formalists is perhaps the most telling one. The very identification of defamiliarization as the fundamental mechanism of literary writing signifies two things of a rather different order: (1) such a mechanism or device can be effective only if there are shared cultural communicative codes between author and audience; (2) something puzzling must have been emerging, inasmuch as the focus of the inquiry was no longer on the individual's manipulation of the codes but on the actual mechanical functioning of the device. This suggests that the process of literary constitution had become at once very obvious and yet very mysterious. It was obvious in its actual workings: it may be unorthodox to say so, but anyone who has read a great deal of Formalist analysis cannot fail to be struck by how commonsensical and easy it really is. It was mysterious because it was beyond the powers of understanding and elucidation of many readers. Why? One reason is that many readers did not have the cultural background and training necessary to understand what they were reading. Accounts of Russian Formalism are written for students of literary theory; they therefore tend to focus on the issues debated between the Formalists and their opponents, all of them part of the intelligentsia, and they generally neglect to remind us of the fact that the Formalists, no less than their opponents, on the Left, elaborated their concepts and analytical tools at the time of a vast increase in the literate population of Russia and the Soviet Union. Many of these newly literate individuals were the first in their families to achieve literacy, and they clearly had but vague knowledge at best of the codes of literary constitution that had been elaborated for a social class quite distinct from their own. They were in need of analytical approaches to the actual functioning of literary texts, much as the G. I. Bill of Rights–supported students in the United States were. Whether consciously or not, the Formalists, like their later counterparts among the American New Critics, began to provide such approaches, relying upon the demonstrated descriptive power of linguistics to do so.[8]

A rhetorical analysis, attentive to matters of manipulation, effect, and power, would have been appropriate—though it remains to be seen to what extent the scope of rhetoric is limited to a single cultural sphere—but instead, in a gesture that was to be repeated in all the other instances, linguistics was called upon. What was it that linguistics could offer? Most prominently, a scientific aura: a set of respectable and verifiable procedures that did not depend upon the idiosyncratic qualities of their performer for their successful execution. In other words, linguistics bracketed away the subject of the linguistic enterprise to focus exclusively upon the object. There lies the vaunted objectivity of linguistics, which appealed so much to the literary scholars of the first decade of the Soviet Union, who were faced with an increasingly heterogeneous population of readers. To be sure, there were some voices, most notably those of the Bakhtin circle,[9] that were raised in opposition to such a reductionist move, but they were a minority. The very same process was to take place in French structuralism some forty years later.

The paradigmatic moment in the French case is the one in which Roland Barthes launched his highly successful revisionist version of Saussurean semiology. Ferdinand de Saussure, it will be recalled, was far too prudent to make inordinate territorial claims on behalf of the science of linguistics that he was then codifying. He therefore assigned to something that he called "semiology" all the questions of social functioning that would remain outside of linguistics. In effect, Saussure was making semiology the heir to the abandoned tradition of rhetoric, this being most evident in his summary definition of semiology as a branch of social psychology. However, whereas rhetoric was based upon the notion of the proper, in the dual sense of the appropriate and of that which characteristically belongs to something—that is, it was still beholden to a problematics of mimesis—semiology would be based upon notions of difference and displacement, thus disrupting the mimetic ordering,[10] and, as the modifier "social" in front of psychology suggests, it would be resolutely sociohistorical in its concerns. Barthes, as is well known, radically reversed this vision. Basing his views upon the empirical observation that, at the time of his writing, linguistics alone among the possible semiological enterprises seemed to have undergone any genuine development, Barthes claimed that henceforth all further semiological studies would have to conform to the linguistic model of inquiry.[11] This act of revision, seemingly dictated by the unequal development of semiological studies, appears innocent enough, and the immediate gain is quite obvious: the analytical procedures of linguistics, many of its terminological coinages, its notational conventions, and indeed some of its theoretical orientations were taken over wholesale, not only by semiology but by nonsemiological structuralist approaches, frequently with little consideration or even awareness of the problems that arise in connection with the transportation of terms and procedures generated within one field of inquiry to another. Linguistics did attempt to sound some warnings, but by and large they went unheeded, and, paradoxically enough, what was taken by many literary scholars as evidence of a great and fruitful rapprochement between linguistics and their own discipline was seen by many linguists as the confirmation of the existence of an unbridgeable chasm between these two disciplines.

Barthes's revisionism had greater consequences still. It well-nigh obliterated the sociopsychological dimension of semiology, since, in the reversal of determination between linguistics and semiology, the dimension of the sociopsychological lost its theoretical raison d'être. Given Barthes's personal social and psychological interests, and given the structure of the problematic thus occulted, this dimension would reemerge both in Barthes and in semiotics, but in a form that one is tempted to describe as pathological. The famous problematics of desire, pleasure, and the subject, which is so important to the later Barthes, could be seen as the return of this repressed dimension in a guise determined by its repression: the problematics of the individual subject without any social dimension.

It is, of course, precisely in this realm of the subject, of desire, of pleasure, and of language's centrality, that structuralism proved most vulnerable to the critiques of the various poststructuralists. Despite their considerable differences, the strictures of Derrida, Foucault, Lacan, de Man, Lyotard, and Deleuze, to cite only some of the most prominent, all display an extraordinary awareness of linguistic operations at a level that exceeds both the formal approaches of linguistics and the more hermeneutical practices of literary studies, and indeed their arguments rely heavily upon rhetorical operations in their own constitution. In the light of the devastating power of these critiques, there are many among literary scholars who have come to think that linguistics has little if any contribution to make to literary studies.[12] Such a view is just as wrongheaded, in my judgment, as the one that claimed linguistics as a model for literary studies. For one thing, it betrays more ignorance about what has been going on in linguistics than anyone who deals with verbal artifacts ought to be comfortable with.

The structuralist view of linguistics was surprisingly selective and far from up-to-date in its awareness of ongoing linguistic research. The references in structuralism to Saussure, Trubetzkoy, Jakobson, the Prague School, Hjelmslev, and Benveniste were striking in their omission of the work of Anglo-American linguists. In some respects, the situation paralleled a similar omission of Anglo-American philosophy. Although the emergence of structuralism is contemporaneous with the relatively short-lived hegemony of the Chomskyan version of transformational generative grammar, references to the latter are very rare in structuralist studies, and rarer still are attempts to use its procedures in literary analysis.[13] Not that I wish to urge the adoption of such a course presently. Rather, I wish to point out that the course of evolution in the field of linguistics since the heyday of, let us say, Chomsky's *Aspects of Syntax* shows some rather remarkable convergences with the evolution and present position of literary studies, in spite of rather different points of departure and orientation.

The chief difference between the structural linguistics upon which structuralism rested and the Anglo-American linguistics that gave rise to Chomskyan linguistics is to be found in their tackling of the question of where the linguistic operations described in their theories take place. Characteristically, the Continental tradition is silent upon this score, being content with the description of the operations,[14] and it thus progressively gives rise in its descriptions to a notion of language as an entity endowed with the ability to function as an autotelic agent. By contrast, the Anglo-American schools draw upon their own philosophical tradition and locate these operations in the mind—a philosopheme that, conceived of in the form of the Cartesian *cogito* and its subsequent avatars, has been subject to harrowing critique in Continental thought, but in its Anglo-American version continues to enjoy considerable status. My purpose is not to consider, let alone resolve, this curious happenstance of comparative cultural history, but to point out the consequences for linguistics and for theories of language.

A familiar argument for the existence of the mind is "that if you hear a bang and see a flash, you don't *hear* or *see* the simultaneity because you don't see the bang or hear the flash: so, it is argued, there must be something else, besides sight and hearing, that takes in the seeing and the hearing."[15] This something else is the mind. When Chomsky began to formulate his theory of language, he began by noting the extraordinary creative capacity that we, as humans, possess, which allows us to make up sentences that are understood by our interlocutors even though the e are sentences that neither we as speakers nor they as hearers may have ever heard uttered before. Imitation of a mechanical nature and conditioning could not provide the explanation for this ability, Chomsky concluded, and he proceeded to take this ability to create new but grammatical sentences as evidence of an innate linguistic competence.

This notion of competence has to be understood in relation to two other notions, not just one as is generally assumed. The one that is usually acknowledged, not least by Chomsky himself, even though he has proved unable so far to indicate its mode of articulation to competence, is the notion of performance, which designates the realm of the actual realizations of sentences. The second, which is more important for our concerns here, is the notion of general intelligence. Chomsky means competence to differ from a general intelligence by which we would acquire our linguistic ability. He argues that there is a specialized module of the mind—which itself consists, in this view, of a large set of such modules—that deals with language. Each module is quite distinct from the others, and there is no transfer from one module to another.[16] Hence the human linguistic capability must be innate and is not subject to learning, since learning would presuppose the mediation of an intermediate module. Such mediation is presupposed in the notion of general intelligence, which obviously accommodates itself better to theories of language acquisition.

The argument may seem abstruse, but much is at stake here, and it does not appear to admit of empirical resolution, given the highly idealized form that competence takes in Chomsky's descriptions of it. Yet the very program of linguistic inquiry is in fact at stake. As J. Margolis puts it in his very apposite discussion of these issues:

> In effect, if reference, speech act contexts, nonlinguistic factors of experience and behavior, social practices, and semantic and pragmatic aspects of linguistic use essentially affect the development of the grammar of a natural language—if the "surface" and "deep" features of a language cannot be systematically sorted to insure the independence of innate generative rules, or if the syntactic dimension of language cannot be insured as a measure of autonomy relative to aspects of language clearly dependent on contingent learning, or if the systems of competence and performance cannot be independently sorted—then, in Chomsky's view "language is a chaos." Of course, it would not be chaos, in the sense that it would remain subject to empirical analysis. But it would entail that the mind could not be a network of modular genetically programmed competences of the sort Chomsky envisages; it would entail the work of innate general intelligence—and hence, of the social contingencies of language acquisition.[17]

Margolis goes on to examine the consequences of such a finding. To begin with, reliance upon the mind as the locus of a "psychologically internalized system of generating *all* the cognitively pertinent behavior of human agents" is no longer possible. This would shatter the scientific aura of linguistics, for the notion of competence—and its antecedents in linguistics—had permitted the discipline to function as if it were the science specific to something that was akin to an organ of the body: the language-making mechanism. The abandonment of such a view would require a redefinition of linguistics and its status as a discipline.

First and foremost, linguistics would have to give up reliance upon notions of causality that it imported from the physical sciences when it saw itself as their counterpart, and, with such abandonment, it would have to give up its pretension to the discovery of laws. Linguistics would then rejoin the realm of the humanities, and recognize that the regularities that it uncovers are not amenable to elevation to the status of causal laws but that they constitute what Margolis felicitously calls "covering institutions":

> Institutions—practices, traditions, and the like—seem to have the peculiar property, first of all, that unlike causal laws they are themselves the result of causal forces; second, that they afford sufficient regularity, within given social and historical contexts, so that particular behavior and work can be causally explained by reference to them.[18]

What is remarkable about this view is that, although it originated in a radically different philosophical tradition and from a very different set of initial concerns, it corresponds to some of the most advanced views on language that have emerged in literary studies as a result of poststructuralist critiques. Indeed, Margolis's final summation about language is, if anything, more explicit than some of the poststructuralist statements on this subject:

> Language appears to be *sui generis;* essential to the actual aptitudes of human beings; irreducible to physical processes; inexplicable solely infrapsychologically; real only as embedded in the practices of an historical society; identifiable consensually or only in terms that presuppose consensual practices linking observer and observed; inseparable as far as meaning is concerned from the changing, novel, nonlinguistic experience of a people; incapable of being formulated as a closed system of rules; subject always to the need for improvisational interpretation and, therefore, subject also to the ineliminable psychological indeterminacies regarding intention and action.[19]

Within this perspective language is no longer an object, abstract to boot, that offers itself up passively for knowledge to the linguist, but is the complex interplay between institutionalized practices and individualized tactical decisions. It resembles far more the realm that the literary scholar has come to recognize as the field of his or her activity: a world of constituted discourses, whose institutionalization requires sociohistorical inquiry, and a set of practices that requires an inquiry into the realm of two complex and still little understood practices: writing and reading. In other words, for the emerging linguistics as well as for literary scholarship, the field of inquiry is praxical.

The dimension of the praxical poses many problems of analysis. No clear or unassailable claim has been made to its study. In the realm of language, it involves the interplay of discourses. But it is also in literary studies that one finds one of the oldest approaches to this realm: it is that part of poetics that Aristotle assigned to the study of the imitation of action, that is, to the representation of praxis that we call plot. A study of plot, such as the one that Thomas Pavel undertakes in *The Poetics of Plot*, is then doubly interesting: it addresses the problematic area that we have seen to emerge at the nexus of linguistics and literary studies, and it addresses that area in its most strategic location. If, from now on, linguistic phenomena, including literary ones, must be seen as practices that are deployed against a background of "covering institutions," then praxical approaches, among which studies of plot occupy a venerable place, can claim a certain degree of priority. The study of plot is then not only a relatively specialized subject matter within the sphere of poetics that is called "narratology," but is also that part of literary studies that is relevant to the understanding of praxis. Pavel's approach, which unites his interest in literary texts with his expertise in linguistic analysis, leads him to clarify these issues and to shed light on a historical phenomenon of importance: the fate of plot in literature.

II

Our attitude toward plot today is rather ambiguous: on the one hand, studies of plot enjoy a new status in literary scholarship and appear to increase in number and in degree of sophistication; on the other hand, as readers, and particularly as specialist readers, we tend to be wary of discussions of plot, and unless they are couched in the terminology devised by plot analysts, we dismiss them as paraphrase. This attitude is consistent with our evaluation of literary texts and films: we are more likely to valorize those that defy plot summation, and we associate the products of mass culture, best-sellers of the Robert Ludlum type, for example, or television crime shows, with plot development. The divide that Frederic Jameson found to be characteristic of modernist ideology[20] appears to operate here as well: little or no plot in the works of high culture, plot in those of mass culture, and the uneasy mediation of literary scholarship, which, though a decidedly high-culture activity, studies plot in both the artifacts of low culture and in those of *past* high culture, in the attempt to effect a reconciliation between the two poles of present Western culture.

In our value system, plot ranks low. We do recognize that it is important to the activity of reading, but at a relatively unsophisticated level: school children write plot summaries for their first book-report assignments, but, as they progress, we expect them to go beyond this elementary level of narrative and to consider the intricacies of characterization and point of view, as well as to engage in a rudimentary form of exegesis. In other words, we treat plot as too obvious for critical discussion, and we do so primarily because it seems to be the element of narrative that least contributes to art.

The apparent artlessness of plot may explain why literary criticism has tended to disdain it, as well as why those folklorists who view the object of their studies as artless tales value it. As is well known, it is among the folklorists that modern plot studies began. Since there exists a considerable literature on this subject,[21] there is no need to review the emergence and evolution of this field, save to note a few of its most salient features.

The decisive step in plot studies was taken when folklorists realized that their attempt to determine the provenance and the mode of transmission of the tales they studied could not be carried out by means of a simple characterization of the content of these tales; it required analysis of the structure of the tales, and such an analysis could be performed only if the basic unit of composition could be identified and specified. In a work whose Russian title, *Poetika sjuzetov*,[22] is similar to Pavel's, Aleksandr N. Veselovskij proposed that plot be considered as a structured series of motifs. The study of plot would then consist in determining the number and nature of motifs and the manner of their possible combination. Veselovskij further thought that there were certain types of plot that could be described as interrelating in more complex works.

Veselovskij's approach was fundamentally substantialist in that it was based upon actually occurring segments of narrative. Typically a motif may be: a dragon kidnaps the daughter of the czar; another motif may be: a witch steals a child. Vladimir Propp's well-known critique of this approach consisted in pointing out that such a conception of the fundamental unit remained much too beholden to the texts it immediately analyzed and that, as a result, it lacked any genuine power of generalization.[23] Propp recognized that Veselovskij's motifs could be understood in two complementary respects: they all represented an action and they all had to contribute to the completion of the tale, whereas their other features could be considered text-specific variants. Propp combined these two aspects in his definition of function, the name that he gave to the basic unit: "A Function in an action by some character or characters, defined from the point of view of its signification for the course of the action in the tale considered as a whole" (p. 19). In contrast to Veselovskij, Propp believed that his minimal units did not admit of free combination but that, within a given genre, they were limited in number and had to follow a rigorous order of appearance, determined by the teleology of the story.

Subsequent plot research has taken issue with this last stipulation, arguing, among other things, that Propp's morphological structure was really based upon a single tale, and urging a return to Aarne and Thompson type of motif analysis.[24] But this is to condemn the whole of the Proppian enterprise for the failure of one of its elements. The syntactic claims of Propp's theory ought not to blind us to the fact that by taking Veselovskij's substantialist notion of the motif and freeing it of its substance, he has given us access at a theoretical level to the notion of action. For Propp, it does not matter who performs an action, by what means, and for what reason; what matters is the action itself and the role that it plays in the story. Narratologists have not always separated these two aspects and have therefore concluded, too hastily, that shortcomings in one area affect the other. They have, as a result, encountered problems, chiefly with respect to the question of temporality in their models, the dimensions of which have not been apparent to them.

One of the areas in which we do not disparage plot quite as much as those that I discussed earlier is the area of experience. We acknowledge that plot, or, perhaps better, emplotment, is essential to the articulation of experience. Experience as a series of discrete events gains meaning and endows these events with signification only in the course of a reflection that relates these events through a "process of exclusion, stress, and subordination . . . carried out in the interest of constituting a story of a particular kind."[25] But while acknowledging the necessity of such emplotting, we distrust its results since, as Hayden White puts it, it does lead to a story of a particular kind; and we fear that the requirements of storytelling may prevail over what we would like to think of as the truth of the experience. It is disturbing enough to have a historian tell us that the accounts of the past produced by his colleagues are subject to a poetics of composition that may well determine their form without having to face the possibility that the same is true in everyday life. Yet that is precisely the step that Peter Brooks, and others in his wake, have taken in reading Freud's case histories as narratives. Narrative ordering, far from being secondary to the events that it supposedly orders, may in some instances be the very determinant of what constitutes an event.[26] Such a finding infinitely problematizes the relationship between the two dimensions of narrative that the Russian Formalists called *fabula* and *sjuzet,* that is, story and plot. This problem had led a distinguished narratologist like Gérard Genette to put the usefulness of the distinction into question and to call for a new sort of realism in discussions of narrative, one in which it will be acknowledged that actions do not exist independently of their representation.[27] Peter Brooks, on the other hand, less disturbed by the inability to maintain distinctions that motivates Genette than by the empirical observation that plot does matter, has sought to inquire into the psychological motivations of plot and has built a critical apparatus around the desire for plot.[28]

Brooks's approach produces very fruitful readings of important nineteenth- and twentieth-century texts, but at the same time it exemplifies the problematic position of plot studies and narratological research at present. In elevating desire to the central position of his narratological conception, Brooks attempts to resolve a problem that has hovered in the background of this discussion: what is it that propels plot and story forward? The failure to answer, and most frequently to consider, this question has been the greatest shortcoming of this branch of literary scholarship to date. Most of the models of narrative that have been proposed have turned out to be surprisingly static. A more interesting attempt has been the formulation of a model of options in the action, as in Claude Brémond's work.[29] Both types of models have not been praxical, however. To some extent this is part of the Proppian legacy, in which the perspective upon the plot was anchored in the locus of its completion, thus reducing everything to the timelessness of that moment. Brooks's great merit is to have drawn attention to this failure and to have attempted to resolve it. His solution, however, is not without problems. To rely upon desire is indeed to identify one of the great reservoirs of energy that twentieth-century theory has uncovered, but it is to project outside of plot and story the power of propulsion. The temporal perspective remains that of someone looking back, and even though Brooks's analyses follow the movement of the text, they do so from this perspective. A purely praxical approach requires a very strong conception of the immanence of decisions and of the interplay of the institutionalized with the possible. It requires a dialectical relationship between imposed patterns and optional ones.

Furthermore, Brooks's decision to locate the propulsion in a psychological category endows this entity with a form of a historicity that is belied by his selection of texts, something that Brooks does not entirely ignore. Unless one is to historicize desire—a distinct possibility, although presently a rather difficult undertaking—one has to explain why stories emphasizing plot thrive at some times and do not at others. The fragmentation of plot in the most recent fiction is a point in fact, and even though Brooks does show that it depends for its own forward movement upon the reader's knowledge of more traditional plot elements, it is nonetheless the case that plot recedes in this fiction to let such elements as the articulation of linguistic codes take over the task of forward propulsion.

What Brooks's exemplary gambit points to is what plot analysis and narratology in general have been all about—the problem of agency—and furthermore the problematic aspect of his approach makes clear that the problem of agency is a historical one. This is a matter of considerable philosophical and historical weight, and it pervades all of Western culture. It is therefore not surprising that it ought to manifest itself in plot analysis. In fact, as we saw earlier, this may be one of its strategic locations.

The problem of agency arises in modern times from the partial nature of the secularization that was carried out by Enlightenment philosophy. For the Scholastics, agency was one of the attributes of God; and the world, and everything in it, moved insofar as he exercised his divine will. Human will could rise in opposition to the divine will as part of its own freedom, but it did not have any agential power as such to determine the course of the affairs of the world. The Enlightenment encounters the problem of agency because the secularization that it carries out consists in bracketing away the divine instance and letting loose all that which had previously been an attribute of God. Although some of these attributes could function autonomously, others, and most notably agency, proved far more problematic. Diverse philosophical and, given the implications of this problem, political solutions were proposed, ranging from the consensus of free consciousnesses in Kant to the slave-master dialectic in Hegel, the class struggle in Marx, and the will to power in Nietzsche—to cite but the better known. The inability to identify a viable social agent of change haunts the thought of Adorno, and the search for a capable agent in the light of the apparent reluctance of the Western proletariats to fulfill that role has marshaled the forces of thinkers on the left, while the right has referred either to the mysterious, because apparently unknowable, laws of the market or to the even more mystical Invisible Hand. It is thus not only in the theory of plot that some sort of aporia has been reached.

The failure here has been one of historical analysis, both with respect to the emergence of the problematic philosopheme of agency and to the sociohistorical circumstances of its problematization. With respect to the first, we need to recognize that the Enlightenment gesture that loosened the philosophical problem of agency upon us was resolutely ahistorical in that it did not inquire into the attribution of agency to God in the first instance. A complete historical reconstruction is beyond the scope of this essay, but it would need to touch upon the role of Plotinus in the thought of the Fathers of the Church, and beyond, to the Aristotelian distinction between *dynamis, energeia,* and *entelecheia*. In Heidegger's summary definition, these must be understood as follows:

> Force, the capacity to be gathered in itself and prepared to work effects, to be in a position to do something, is what the Greeks (above all, Aristotle) denoted as *dynamis*. But power is every bit as much being empowered, in the sense of the process of dominance, the being-at-work of force, in Greek, *energeia*. Power is will as willing out beyond itself, precisely in that way to come to itself, to find and assert itself in the circumscribed simplicity of its essence, in Greek, *entelecheia*.[30]

But beyond these lies the unresolved problematics of being and change, in the doctrine of Heraclitus, for example. For our purposes here, what we need to retain is that the problem ought not to be put in terms of who or what is the agent of action or the purport of action, but, as Propp dimly recognized, that there is action inasmuch as there is change, whether this be located in a Heideggerian problematic of the nonidentity of being or some other philosophical framework.

Such a primacy of action justifies the attention that plot studies devote to their subject. By the same token, this very primacy ought to permit us to dispose of one of the problems that had agitated the field: the question of whether temporality or causality plays the determinant role in the articulation of actions. I would like to suggest that the ontological primacy of action renders this question moot, and that one has to turn it around and see whether the articulation of action is not what gives us both our sense of temporality and of causality. Some evidence of a linguistic nature could be adduced here: there are languages in which the representation of action is wholly mediated, in the absence of a tense system, through a system of aspectuals that distinguish stages of becoming in the accomplishment of an action without recourse to any notion of temporality or causality whatsoever. This suggests that immanent studies are called for, and that they ought to take the form of descriptive grammars.

This is precisely what Thomas Pavel has to offer us in *The Poetics of Plot*. Unlike his predecessors in this branch of poetics, he never loses sight of the action and of its transformative power. Adopting the conceptual apparatus and the notational conventions of transformational generative grammar, he makes *Move* the basic element of his grammar and proceeds to generate his terms from it, as well as to describe the modes of articulation of moves. His is a treatment that recognizes that plot is a covering institution in our culture and that it imposes, like any institution, restrictions on mobility. He repertories possible moves at a specific point in time and in a specific cultural milieu: the English Renaissance. The grammar that he puts forward in this book, the reader will rapidly discover, is accompanied by a praxical approach that determines its function in specific texts.

Pavel's selection of his texts serves to elucidate further the question of the historicity of plots and of their roles in the epistemes of their day. In one of the first texts that he analyzes, Pavel comes across the puzzling figure of Marlowe's Tamburlaine. Literary criticism has not been kind to this figure, whom it has contrasted with Faust. Whereas the latter's striving has been presented to us as an instance of the human existential predicament, Tamburlaine's apparent lust for power has been described in decidedly negative psychological and philosophical terms. But what if Tamburlaine were nothing but the rediscovery of agency as an autonomous force? His lack of a moral dimension would precisely correspond to the amorality of the world flux and be free of any pathos. Marlowe may well have represented at the beginning of our modernity the letting loose of what had until then been an attribute of God. It took philosophers some additional two hundred years before they came upon the problem, and by then the inquiry into agency in fiction had moved to the psychological sphere, save in the emergent popular literature of action and adventure. By starting with Tamburlaine, Pavel begins with his subject in its naked form.

6 The Time Machine

When Tzvetan Todorov coined the term "narratology" in 1969 to designate the study of narrative, he was responding to the then widespread belief that narrative was particularly amenable to being elevated to the status of an object of knowledge for a new science armed with its own concepts and analytical protocols. He was also responding to the hope, or perhaps more accurately, the desire, to lift all of literary and cultural studies to the dignity of science, a desire that strongly animated French structuralism. Todorov's programmatic enthusiasm seemed warranted then: whereas the previous half-century had been punctuated by occasional studies of the art of the novel, some rare analyses of point of view, and limited disquisitions on narrative organization, the sixties had seen colloquia and conferences, entire issues of journals, significant translations from the Russian and the Czech in addition to the more common European languages, as well as new publications appearing almost daily, all dealing with narrative. Twenty years later, the graduate student who ventures into this area is faced with an almost intractable bibliography, a wealth of specialized terms, and, in some instances, symbolic notations ranging from the linguistic to the mathematico-logical. For some time now, some of the best minds in the field, notably Gérard Genette and Wallace Martin, have called for a moment of reflection and assessment to determine where we are in relation to all of the theorizing that has passed for narratology, and there prevails a general sense of unease suggestive of unfulfilled expectations.

It is the type of situation that calls for the instinctive reactions of complete dismissal that one finds here and there, or for some project of redemption of a field that has gone astray. Didier Coste's *Narrative as Communication*[1] falls more into the latter mode, though redemption is quite foreign to its idiom. Coste refuses, however, to dismiss all that has been done in narrative theory simply because the expectations that were vested in it have not been fulfilled. They were, in any case, beyond fulfillment, since these expectations represented murky responses to the general situation of humanists in universities undergoing rapid expansion. Coste is far more interested in drawing up an inventory of the analytical tools and concepts that have been elaborated and showing that they constitute a workable overarching approach to the study of narrative, though not in the terms in which they were originally conceived. In other words, Coste proposes a new framework, that of a theory of communication, for the study of narrative, and he shows in his book that such an approach enables us to give narrative its due. At first sight, this claim may seem implausible. After all, in the eyes of most students of literature, communication theory is hardly in better shape than narrative theory, and it is therefore unlikely that the grafting of two lame legs on the same body would produce a smooth-running animal; yet that is the very challenge that Coste has taken up in *Narrative as Communication.*

The narratology that Todorov, and countless others in his wake, have sought to elaborate represented an extension of the very poetics that was being revived in the sixties as part of a larger if mostly unconscious societal project of establishing, and policing, a lasting order. Much of that impulse has remained with us, gaining strength rather than weakening from the various instances of sociopolitical, economic, and cultural disorder that have occurred since. The possibility of such an order presided over by the Hegelian figure of the state rests upon our ability to determine all possible actions, calculate their potential combinations, and analyze their outcome. Individual texts, such as the *Decameron,* can be treated as equivalent to languages whose action grammars are yet to be described. Once we had a large number of such individual descriptive grammars, we could determine the deep structures governing all actions, establish the felicity conditions for their accomplishment, and set a proper receptive framework for their interpretation. Even though it may have represented itself as politically progressive, such a narratology, as indeed all poetics, was in the service of a social engineering administered by an almighty state.

Roland Barthes is a case in point. In *S/Z*, his famous study of narrative in a Balzac short story, Barthes may have sought to separate himself from the hard structuralists by distinguishing between the classical readerly texts that are totalizable, decidable, continuous, and unified, and the writerly texts that are plural and open to the free play of signifiers and of difference, but his continued focus on the elementary action as the basic unit of narrative analysis firmly inscribes him within the narratological project. In his *Maupassant,* which resembles the *S/Z* a great deal, Greimas cuts the text up into "segments" that correspond to units of the narrative without explicitly taking up the logic of this segmentation. Barthes, who calls his segments "lexies" and "fragments," is far more conscious of the fact that these are artifices of reading, and indeed he seeks to recoup their artificiality in the service of his opposition between the writerly and the readerly. At stake is the very conception of action as denoted by discourse, for which Barthes invokes the Aristotelian term of *prohairesis.* Unlike Greimas, Barthes is not seeking to establish the existence of an all-encompassing and all-deciding structure for his text; nonetheless, he is forced to consider action in ways that are not much different from Greimas's conception of it. In borrowing the term *prohairesis* from Aristotle, who had invoked it in the context of deliberative discourse to denote the future projection of a course of action, Barthes simplifies its meaning to the rational determination of the result of an action. He recognizes, however, that nothing is more difficult than to arrive at such a determination unless one knows beforehand what the outcome of the entire sequence of actions is going to be. Armed with this knowledge, the analyst reads backwards as it were and discards those elements that will prove unproductive, keeping only those that will contribute to the general result. This procedure is tantamount to cheating and makes a mockery of the claim that the determination of the result is a rational one. In point of fact it is an interested determination based upon a form of privileged knowledge, applied ex post facto to a process that is supposed to be open-ended. Barthes acknowledges this by admitting that the prohairetic sequence is an artifice of reading, but he does not seem to notice what this entails.

He may well have thought of himself as arguing in favor of open-endedness, but in fact Barthes was operating with concepts that require closure. The workings of his prohairetic code project each sequence unto a closed continuum that determines both its identity, by means of the labels that the code bestows upon it, and its place in the narrative continuum. This continuum is thus ruled by a form of purposive necessity, not unlike Kant's nature, which ensures that whatever is left to punctual judgment at the level of the individual prohairetic sequence is ultimately recouped in the service of the whole. Barthes seems to be unaware of the fact that having started from premises inherent to poetics in which the purposiveness of form is a foundational postulate, he inevitably winds up with a teleological conception of the narrative process, even though the movement of the telos can be established only through the intervention of the reader.

This conception of action, in which the meaning of the action is determined by its place in the configuration of the whole, as assessed by a reader, lies at the center of all narrative theories. One is strongly tempted to say that it is no accident that this is so, but to yield to this temptation is to blind oneself to the very problem at hand, which is that of the commingling of story and history. The purposive necessity that binds the individual action or fact to the narrative whole finds its counterpart in the conception of history in which what Fredric Jameson calls "otherwise inert chronological and 'linear' data" are reorganized in the form of Necessity: "why what happened (at first received as 'empirical' fact) had to happen the way it did."[2] Narrative analysis has stressed this sense of an inexorable logic working itself out through the course of the narrative. Jameson understands this full well and draws out the consequences: for him, history becomes the experience of Necessity, that is, the experience of this inexorable logic. What we experience, however, is not this Necessity as the secret meaning of history, for that would reify history, but rather as a narrative category imposing an inexorable form upon events. In other words, Jameson attributes to history the capabilities of an agency on the basis of its narrative properties. This agency is not the traditional Aristotelian or Thomistic one of the first or ultimate cause of an action, but rather as the shaper of intelligibility.

We have seen that Barthes vests the possibility of this shaping in the reader, who "cheats" by bringing to bear upon the course of the text his privileged knowledge of the "outcome" of the text. Jameson knows that in order to make an equivalent claim in relation to history one would have to construct a transcendental position in relation to it, so that Barthes's almighty and immanent reader capable of traveling back and forth across the linearity of narrative time would find its counterpart in an almighty God, or in a principle of rationality, or in the all-powerful state armed with the laws of history. Jameson rejects this totalitarian possibility, the nefarious effects of which have been historically well attested, to posit instead the workings of an immanent principle: that of a form.

In Jameson's conception, history becomes not only the experience of necessity, but the experience of the fact that necessity is the form of history. We may well suspect at this stage that there has a been a transfer of properties from story to history, but the very impulse that led us to want to say earlier that this was no accident attests that it is not so, for Jameson's account rests on the solid Hegelian ground in which the transfer of properties goes from history to story and not the other way around. Narrative, in this conception, inevitably espouses the form of history and thus provides us with cognitive access to the latter's workings. In the formal terms that Jameson invokes, the transfer of properties from history to story is sublated, that is, the metaphor is annulled into its own catachresis, so that empirical readers need not play the role of transcendental readers and can still see the shaping of story by history. The catachresis itself is thus rendered necessary and indeed inscribed in the very process of history. The function of this process becomes apparent: to convert metaphor into catachresis, or, in less formal terms, to convert linguistic operations into "natural" agency. Narratology, for its part, must redouble this process by analyzing this "natural" agency back into linguistic operations and thus making the latter appear to be the result of the process of narratological analysis and not of a prior massive catachresis. In Marxian terms, one must posit the identity of the dialectics of nature and the dialectics of thought, the dialectics of history and of language.

The point of my retracing this ground is to help us recognize the underlying philosophical assumption of narratology: it is the Parmenidean postulate of Being's manifestation in language and its inverse reciprocal that language states Being. To be sure, this Parmenideanism is quite sophisticated now and does not expect that every statement corresponds to a state of being, an expectation that would have made fiction impossible; it now admits that the "stating" of Being takes place at a larger structural level, where story and history are indeed a way of stating or manifesting each other. Again, this should not surprise us inasmuch as this sort of Parmenideanism underlies all of poetics and subtends its dependence on mimesis. And if there is one thing that narratology has taken very seriously, it is the mimetic character of narrative representation, since it is this foundational belief in mimesis that has permitted the elaboration of the concept of minimal action in the first place. Even the Proppian notion of function partakes of this dependence: the mimetic correspondence is established at the level of the whole tale rather than that of each individual action.

This Parmenideanism manifests itself especially strongly in those studies of narrative that are concerned with the effect of narrative upon its recipients, and thus appear to be moving in the direction of the communicational approach that Coste takes in *Narrative as Communication*. Such studies typically deal with this problem under the name of identification and provide an account of the reading, or the viewing, process as one in which the narratee finds himself or herself interpellated by the narrative program of the work she or he is receiving, and thus reconstituted into the subject of this narrative program. The working of identification is premised on the catachresis of story and history: the reader reads the story and is shaped by history.

Identification is indeed the name of the operation by which catachresis takes place, since it transfers properties from one term to another and erases the memory of the transfer so that the two terms appear to be identical. In narratological studies of identification this operation is described in terms of cleaved consciousness and of the dilemma facing the reader, who is thus faced with two distinct temporal frames corresponding to the before and after of the reading. This dilemma, which corresponds to the modern predicament, has to do with the reader's ability both to remember and to forget the past, and to forget and remember the conditions under which he or she has come about in the present. It is no problem for a trope to hold both of these temporal frames within itself, since tropes do not inhabit phenomenological time, but as soon as human beings are expected to behave like tropes—especially as complicated a trope as catachresis, the description of which requires, after all, an anthropomorphized way of talking about language inasmuch as it is mediated through categories of remembrance and forgetting, that is, categories of human time—we are likely to be facing major difficulties. Identification narratology avoids these difficulties by focusing on the secondary issues of ideological manipulation, for it could not face the fact that it operates on the assumption that human beings are catachretic.

Identification narratology originates in, and subscribes to, the modern project of the Enlightenment. Its interest in narrative stems from the desire to discern between narratives of liberation and narratives of enslavement. It is committed, in other words, to promoting the autonomy of the reading subject. To understand such a subject as catachretic would be tantamount to admitting that this autonomy is heteronomous in origin, and that the function of the claim of autonomy is in fact to occult this constitutive heteronomy. Identification narratology takes such a heteronomy to be the operator of a deprivation of agency for the modern subject who has to be reinstated as capable agent.

Curiously enough, this agent then becomes capable of doing what history requires her or him to do—a strange definition of autonomy, though well-attested in Western, and especially Christian, thought.

Coste seeks to effect a break with this Parmenidean conception of the relation of language to Being and with the mimetic conception of action to which it has led. He is, however, fully cognizant of the fact that earlier attempts to break with Parmenideanism in Western thought have tended to privilege the imaginary and to cancel out the notion of agency. We need to bear in mind that Parmenidean doctrine establishes a set of identity equations between language and Being, that is, between language and reality. It ensures that language can and indeed does function referentially. Any tampering with these identity equations precipitates a crisis of referentiality. In modern times this problem has taken the form of a predicament in which we, as language-users and indeed as language-dependent beings, are forced to remember that language is a system of signs that is governed by its own internal economy and by the history of its past usages, while, at the same time, we must forget the artifactness of language to continue to be able to refer to reality. Modernity is haunted by this nondialectical conjunction of forgetting and remembering, and it has become increasingly aware of its dependence on language. This has proved extremely disturbing because one of the foundations of modernity has been the distinction between fact and fiction, a distinction that did not have the same preeminence in premodernity, where it was the distinction between sacred and profane that was paramount. To bear in mind that referentiality is mediated through the workings of language is to make fiction the mode of access to fact, a disturbing notion if one sees fact and fiction as polar opposites. It is this disturbance that catachretic approaches to story and history are meant to dispel, thereby preserving the underlying economy of modernity.

Within the framework of modernity it does appear that anything short of such a catachretic solution would result in the dissolving of another major axis of opposition: that between real and imaginary. Much of the aesthetic activity of the late nineteenth century and of the twentieth has recognized, and sought to accelerate, this dissolution. But this movement toward the imaginary, in modernity's topology, continues to be perceived as that of agential deprivation and thus elicits resistance and opposition, especially in view of the fact that this agential deprivation does not seem to strike at the major forces that shape our lives and our societies. This perception is incorrect, however, since it is grounded in modernity's conception of the imaginary, where the latter is opposed to the real and can thus offer nothing but a simulacrum or at best a representation of the real. It must be understood that the dissolution of the opposition between real and imaginary results in a commingling of what the two terms stand for as the ground of their differentiation. And therein lies a further consequence of note: the modern opposition between the real and the imaginary further mapped itself over the distinction between the collective and the individual, leading to the notion that all forms of collective imaginary were instances of ideological manipulation or illusion.

This is the new ground upon which Coste seeks to reconceptualize narratology. It is not a grammar of action but part and parcel of a theory of communication, where the latter is understood not as the exchange of messages but as the management of this collective imaginary charged with establishing and regulating the conditions of referentiality in the society that shares it. I should hasten to stress that I do mean referentiality and not reference or even referents, as is too often assumed to be the case. Coste is quite emphatic on this point himself.

What is the place of narrative in this conception? and the function of narratology? Since these are the questions that Coste addresses in *Narrative as Communication* I will limit myself to one aspect to which I have already alluded: *prohairesis*. As is well known, Aristotle considered narrative as part of the middle genre of rhetoric, that of deliberative discourse. The function of this genre is to prove to the assembled citizens of the city the need for, or indeed the necessity, of a particular course of action that one wishes to see them execute, or conversely, to dissuade them from a given course of action. Deliberative discourse, in other words, leads to action or to its abrogation. It is not, itself, a representation of an action, and is never meant to be a substitute for it. The best way of thinking about it is as enabling (or disabling) action. And this is where *prohairesis* comes in: we have seen earlier that Aristotle used this term to designate the future projection of a course of action. In other words, *prohairesis* has to do with time, with a special mode of representation called "projection," and with action considered as a course, that is, as a flow. The triggering mechanism for all of this is a decision, and decision is indeed the object of deliberative discourse. What we need to understand better is how decision relates to the constitutive features of *prohairesis*.

Aristotle and all subsequent narratologists have recognized that narrative has a special relationship to time. But they have all thought of time as infinite and homogeneous, analyzable in quantifiable moments of "objectively" equal value; such a time is linear, and ultimately absolute, experienced as a curse or at the very least as a predicament. Philosophy, which is oriented toward concepts, has sought a limitless time in which to define them, and thus has had little patience with decisions. Our habits of thought have been built up around concepts, the proper deployment of which requires the suspension of decisions, a deferral of any decision-making, since the latter, viewed from the perspective of the essence of the concept, can only mark the concept's submission to temporality's least attractive feature: its limitation of extension. Decisions are profoundly antithetical to philosophy in this respect. They "rush" time. What philosophical reflection seeks to defer indefinitely, a decision concentrates in a point, the moment, the time of decision. And this concentration has fatal consequences, from a philosophical perspective: it does not allow us to judge whether a statement is true, that is, whether it stands for a state of affairs, or whether a concept has found its proper embodiment. In the concentrated time of decision, the true is not separable from the state of affairs it purportedly stands for, and the concept is not distinguishable from the materiality which confronts us. Insofar as representation occurs in the time of decision, and it does, it is always representation for the other and not representation in itself. This is the fundamental reason why a communication approach to narrative has a chance to avoid the pitfalls of the philosophically sounder narratologies. To put it bluntly, we need to recognize that a decision entails that the elements it manages and affects exist in a temporal dimension that is incommensurable with the infinite extension of concepts inhabiting an infinite and homogeneous time.

It would be tempting to interpret this statement as Nietzsche's statements on perspective have been interpreted, that is, as calling for relativism and advocating a pluralism of worldviews. Such an interpretation runs counter to what is most important in a decision: its sense of urgency. When an assembly deliberates upon a course of action, it is precisely because its members have the sense that an inexorable logic is working its way and they perceive the end of this process as inimical to them. The function of the decision is not to calculate the end-product of the process but to figure out an escape from it. The decision is not meant to propose an alternate view or a new representation that will coexist peacefully with the older one, but to escape into a new temporal dimension free from as many of the constraints of the old one as possible.

To figure out how to escape involves a double catachresis: first the historical predicament has to be converted into story so that its full dimension can be apprehended. This involves the projection of a course of action. But this story is then treated as story so that history itself may be arrested: the time frame of the story is easily manipulated, and the function of the decision is to open up a different time, to produce more time where none was otherwise available, and this production of time permits the second catachresis, which does go from story to history, for the new time is one that can be lived. The function of the story, of its telling within the context of deliberative discourse, is thus to fracture philosophical time, to mobilize its rupture in the service of an alternative, one that will be marked by the sense of a beginning.

It is thus not accurate to say that decisions concentrate time; they produce it. Each such production entails a new mode of establishing referentiality, of organizing the time that has been produced by the decision, of inhabiting a time of our own making as opposed to the inhuman time of concepts. Narratology has been in the service of inhuman time; it has occulted the place of decision to concentrate on concepts of action, analyzed into minimal units, linked into inexorable logics attributed to inhuman forces. Such narratologies go hand in hand with a conception of a time ruled by forces beyond our control, and are indeed in the service of such forces. We have all noted at one time or another that the epoch of narratologies, the late 1960s to the mid-1980s, has been one of limited and uninspired narrative production in the industrialized world. The celebrated success of Latin American novels, and indeed of emergent literatures, has contrasted sharply with our Western orientation toward narratology, and frequently left the latter befuddled since this emergent writing refused to fit easily into its concepts. Such emergent writing has been putting into question narratology's methodological presupposition of an infinite and homogeneous time; better, it has been declaring itself incompatible and incommensurable with such a notion. Narratology's unconscious complicity in the assertion of a universal order, which would be that of "our" time, should not lead us however to jettison it altogether, for it is far from clear that a narratology that starts with different premises could not produce some time of its own. Such at least has been Didier Coste's courageous wager.

7 Paul de Man and the Perils of Intelligence

The three essays that follow this chapter are engaged with the work of Paul de Man. The first two were written while de Man was still alive, and the third shortly after his death; all three thus precede the revelations about de Man's wartime writings in a Belgian collaborationist newspaper. These revelations have caused some to denounce not only de Man as a private person but his work as well, forcing those who continue to find an engagement with de Man's thinking worthwhile to justify their opinion. The controversy that has ensued has spawned a multitude of writings, many of them intemperate among the defenders as well as among the attackers. Although this controversy is showing signs of abating, it is unlikely to wither away, for it does revolve around a point of central importance to de Man's thought: the extent to which we adhere to our opinions and even to our judgments.

The most serious and most thoughtful of de Man's detractors accuse him of having developed and propounded a doctrine of irresponsibility inasmuch as the deconstruction of the subject as a knowing, willing, and judging entity leaves these subjects unwilling to stand by their statements and actions and thus at the mercy of any drift. The best informed and most reflective of de Man's defenders reply that for de Man this is not a matter of will but of capacity: it is not that we lack the will to stand by our actions or statements but we cannot, and when we try to do so by the exercise of will, matters only get worse. Given the nature of this central bone of contention, it is inevitable that the person as well as the writings of de Man should be the object of the controversy.

Like many people, I read de Man before I met him. I read a few essays in the late sixties and found them confusing. The phenomenological cast of mind they betrayed was both oddly old-fashioned to someone who, having read a great deal of Merleau-Ponty within the distorting context of existentialism, was then very much taken with French structuralism and Tartu semiotics, and yet it was strangely attractive, for it seemed to be working against itself. It was precisely this impression of a thought in search of itself, so much at odds with the prevalent self-satisfaction of most traditional criticism and with the incipient dogmatism of the newer one, that determined my decision to accept a position at Yale when it was offered to me in 1973. De Man spent that year in Zurich, but his presence on the campus was already very strong, and it was apparent that few were left indifferent to it. Plots and counterplots were being hatched. Upon his return, de Man proved a most formidable though always affable academic infighter. Within a matter of months he had things under control both in the French department, of which he was the chairperson, and in Comparative Literature, where he was soon to be. Opponents were reduced to silence, or at most to muttering, and some were exiled to other universities. Some were put in a position where they had to give up prestigious name chairs so that younger colleagues would be kept on and new appointments made. All in all, it was a remarkable display of energy and drive. There was some anger and some bitterness—persisting to this day—but mostly there was puzzlement, for de Man did not evidence any of the characteristics of arrogance, bullheadedness, hunger for or enjoyment of power, that are commonly associated with individuals who embark on such a course. If anything, he appeared somewhat saddened and much burdened, as he undoubtedly was since he taught a full schedule, lectured widely, wrote some of his most important essays throughout this period, and directed scores of dissertations. He very much gave the impression of someone who did very well and very lucidly something to which he had no overriding personal commitment. The puzzlement was caused by this dual impression of seeing him succeed so well at something that he could have walked away from so easily. This impression, which is the strongest that I formed of de Man then and which has persisted, has led some to suspect him of hypocrisy, of wearing a mask.

If de Man was a hypocrite, though, it is only in the etymological sense of the term: he answered each person or each situation according to its needs. He responded to the fullest. It is this responsiveness, or response-ability to use a most serviceable Bakhtinian concept, that lies at the source of the unease felt by some and of the deep loyalty felt by others. In this instance, it is the loyal friends who are in error, I think. They assume an exclusiveness of concern or of response on de Man's part that he was not able to give. I once broached this matter with him, asking him how he managed to be so attentive to the needs of so many people and of so many situations. He started by denying that the number was that large to begin with, and then went on to say that most people were satisfied to give themselves over to one set of concerns. He agreed that this made for consistency and ease of management of one's energies, and was indeed a desirable and admirable virtue in friends and partners, but he wondered whether the responsibilities of intelligence were not to try to do what was possible in each situation even if it was to be at the expense of consistency. He quoted the familiar dictum about consistency as proof of the fact that popular wisdom expected more from intelligence.

When the revelations precipitated by Ortwin de Graef's discovery of de Man's wartime journalism, as his writings from this period have come to be known, began to circulate, I was more struck by the responses they evoked than by the writings themselves. It is only from the geographic and historical distances afforded by America that the actions of others are filtered through a prism of such moral clarity. Both of my parents have suffered at the hand of the Nazis; an uncle survived Auschwitz, much diminished; others died; my own health is forever affected by my having been conceived and born in a camp. But I know as a matter of historical fact that in the very same family that lost four lives to Nazi persecution others were far less loath to seek accommodation with the occupiers, and that although their acts have never been condoned there has always been a reluctance on the part of those who suffered to condemn them outright. It is not simply a matter of clan loyalty but a recognition that we are never in another person's shoes, no matter how close we may be to them, and we cannot tell whether we would do otherwise were we in their specific place, were we they.

This reluctance to leap to judgment is in strong contrast with the attitude displayed by many in academia and in the media. Focusing on the article of March 4, 1941, in which de Man asserts that the removal of European Jewry to a colony isolated from Europe would have "no deplorable consequences" for European literature, they evoke the horrors of the Holocaust to condemn him. There is no doubt in my mind that the article is wholly at home in antisemitic rhetoric and intent, and no sophistication of interpretation can dispel this impression. The very evocation of a "solution to the Jewish problem" does evoke for us the Holocaust, but it is anachronistic to say that it did for de Man. The Holocaust, and the discourses it has begotten, have made antisemitism untenable among thinking people since the war, even though it is quite obvious that the phenomenon not only persists but shows signs of resurgence in the United States as well as in many countries of both western and eastern Europe. Present-day Americans, and perhaps especially academics, tend to forget how pervasive antisemitism was in Europe, or indeed in the United States, before the war. It was no less pervasive in European culture than racism is in American culture. To be sure, the most virulent forms of it were left to fringe groups, but expressions of it were quite common, if modulated with slight irony, on the part of business people, intellectuals, and politicians. Much of this antisemitism was felt to be harmless by those who evinced it, just as the racism that is the common fare of country clubs is treated as anodyne by those who are steeped in it. Once legitimated by the power of the government, however illegitimate that government may have been, it could affirm itself without the decorum of shared deprecation. I doubt whether de Man was personally antisemitic—certainly nothing in his postwar life suggests it— but he certainly was culturally antisemitic during the war and probably before as well.

Some have argued that de Man's wartime writings do not amount to collaboration with the Nazis. For the most part they indeed deal with matters of literature, treated at a formal or thematic level alone, but what are we to make of a short text such as this one, dated April 12–14, 1941, which I translate in its entirety:[1]

The Literary Scene
Flemish Brochures on the Third Reich

Owing to long years of brainwashing by French and English propaganda, Belgian readers are ignorant of what has been done in Germany from a social and political viewpoint. They have been carefully left in the dark with respect to the intense effort of reconstruction that has been carried out in that country. This is why this collection of brochures published by Roskam in Amsterdam (and distributed in Flanders by Van Ditmar of Antwerp) brings forth valuable clarifications and important data on some current issues across the Rhine. The first booklet, by Hans Munster, is entitled, "Why German Workers Stand behind Adolf Hitler," and offers a global view of the accomplishments of the regime with respect to the well-being of the proletariat and the reabsorption of unemployment.

The second, written by Dr. H. Beute, deals with "German Land-holding Policy," one of the most revolutionary reforms in Nazi Policy.

The third, a global inquiry, stuffed with statistics and tables, on "What does the German Labor Service Do?", by H. Müller-Brandenburger, is invaluable for judging objectively this vast enterprise.

Finally, the last booklet brings us back to recent memories: "The Armistice 1918–1940," a comparative study, based on historical documents, of the conditions under which the two armistices were conceived. The study shows how the attitude of the victorious Germans was far more dignified, more just, and more humane than that of the French in 1918, who had won a far less clear victory.

Let us note that each of the booklets includes a bibliography that refers readers who want to deepen their knowledge of national-socialist doctrine to specialized works in German. Future installments in this series will deal with war finance, worker travels, and the marvels of the German chemical industry.

P.d.M.

There is no need to retroactively include Zyklon B among the wonders of German chemistry to admit that the tone and orientation of the piece are unabashedly propagandistic.

De Man's detractors take these articles as evidence of his guilt, and they adduce the fact that the mature scholar de Man never spoke or wrote about his wartime writings as further proof of the fact that he knew how damnable these writings were. Some scour his personal life, leaving literally no rug unturned to establish a pattern of mendacity and prevarication, which they then present as the hidden personal rationale for de Man's theoretical work on the gap between intention and action, thinking thus to cast discredit on all of his work. Many are troubled by de Man's silence, by his failure, as they see it, to have come forward and to confess what they are willing to concede may have been a youthful error. Defenders have relied primarily on psychological plausibility to question the possibility of such a course of action, but there is little doubt that de Man's silence has been as damaging as his overt actions, and perhaps even more so.

Should we then "burn de Man"? Obviously, I do not think so; otherwise I would not be reprinting the essays that follow or writing this one. Nor do I apply to him the familial behavior I described earlier of not condemning someone because one is not in that person's place and does not really know how one would have behaved if one had been, though I believe that argument to have considerable force. But I do not feel the need to invoke it, as I think we should continue to read de Man, and if anything, the controversy has given us even more reason to do so.

I stated earlier that the question at the heart of the controversy was the degree to which we can be said to stand by our actions and our statements. This question, which is central to the preoccupations of the mature de Man, is the question of modernity itself since the very fact of its being posed marks a distancing from the fundamental premise of modernity, which is that our actions and our statements have meaning insofar as we stand by them. Prior to modernity the problem did not arise, for there operated a set of identity equations, first drawn up by Parmenides, between being, the world, and language, so that the truth of the world was statable in language and was thus knowable; practical activity (ethical and political) was properly grounded. These identity equations failed to survive the onset of the moment that Heidegger has called "The Epoch of Worldviews" *(Die Zeit des Weltbildes)*—the arrival of modernity, which operates by means of "images of the world," that is, representations. These representations are discursive in nature and self-consciously provisional since they are legitimated not by the Parmenidean equations but by increasingly more elaborate procedures of verification. This process, which we associate with the progress of science, is familiar to us, but we tend to forget that it shatters the stability assured until then by the identity equations and makes legitimation a constant preoccupation of modernity, a preoccupation that must be addressed locally and specifically in each instance rather than globally as was the case in earlier times.

At the core of the new configuration of the economy of meaning lies the problem to which de Man devoted so much of his time: the relation of the subject to language. The provisional character of the worldviews elaborated within modernity draws attention to their constructed nature. This construction occurs on two levels: that of the worldview itself, which obeys all sorts of requirements but mostly that of being as accurate a rendition of the reality it tries to depict as possible, and also that of the discourse in which the worldview is stated, which must obey the rules of language. Modernity does not fail to subject language to its theorizing glance and thus to grant it the autonomy of a complex system in its own right. But in doing so, that is, in establishing that language is a conventional system of artificial signs governed by rules proper, and internal, to the system, it fractures the easy rapport that the subject had to the world when that relation was governed by the Parmenidean equations. The modern subject, living in the epoch of worldviews, constructs his or her cognitive apprehensions by means of language, and thus must bear in mind that to speak is to submit to the rules of language, to construct, to fictionalize, while at the same time telling the truth by establishing the referentiality of the world of the worldview. This is indeed the modern predicament that so fascinated de Man: the modern subject must both remember and forget the artifactness of language so as not to be a dupe of his or her own constructions and yet not renounce all pretensions to the cognition of the world and to the communication of this cognition.

The question we have seen to be at the heart of the de Man controversy is thus the question which preoccupied him most and is the issue of decisive importance for modernity: What is the relation of the modern subject to his or her utterances? What credibility are they to enjoy? Does the modern subject stand by (or under: *hypokeimenon*) his or her own utterances? Within the terms of consciousness that provide the central framework of modernity, the modern subject must bear in mind simultaneously that to speak is to construct, to falsify, and therefore to lie, and to tell the truth by instituting some referent. There is no self-evident solution to this problem, and modernity has worried this bone in a number of different ways, among which we may distinguish three principal ones.

The first corresponds to the moment of disillusion: the subject suddenly discovers that the truth he or she believed in is a verbal construct, a metaphor, a falsehood, and the subject recoils at this discovery. This moment, which is very much in evidence in Nietzsche when he asserts that a truth is simply a long-lasting falsehood, ushers in a form of radical nihilism that leaves the subject unable to stand by any utterance that he or she may make except those of a demystifying kind. This sort of nihilism is pervasive in de Man's writings of the late sixties and early seventies.

The second moment occurs after the initial shock has worn off and a process of partial recovery has begun to take place. The modern subject acknowledges that the statements he utters are not true in the sense of the older economy, but he feels that they provide nonetheless a basis for cognition and action. This is the moment of the *als ob*, of the *nonetheless*. The recovery draws upon the decisive experience of the modern subject, who has come to recognize the central role of language in relation to cognitive processes and has begun to come to terms with the fundamentally falsifying nature of language. The subject accepts as true the falseness of language, and makes this truth her own, thereby constructing a new equation in the form of a paradoxical proposition in which she opposes a local and punctual truth to a larger falsehood: I know that what I am saying is false in an absolute sense (that it will not stand up to examination once the constructed nature of language is brought into consideration) but it is nonetheless true in a punctual sense (and that is really all I need, for by the time the deeper examination will have been carried out, I will have moved on). This proposition admits of a variety of interpretations, but the most famous in modernity is that of the Pragmatists, who see in it the abandonment of the pretense to any sort of genuine finality and its replacement with a finality more suited to human finitude.

This proposition accepts the cleaving of the modern subject and forces him into the uncomfortable contortions of making himself stand by in a punctual way, that is, to think as true that which one knows full well not to be true. Modern consciousness is thus necessarily a consciousness of falsehood, but it has overcome in this moment its earlier pain at this discovery, for it no longer mourns the passing of Truth: it relies upon the modalizers of belief and precedes all of its statements by a tacit: "I believe that . . ." William James recognized a long time ago that belief is the means by which modern subjects make themselves stand by their utterances.

But this regime of tacit generalized belief speech acts is not bereft of problems, as de Man quickly saw in the seventies. What is the subject's relation to belief? Must it always be foregrounded and thus casting at least some doubt over the veracity of the proposition it modalizes? Or can it be forgotten, repressed, and invoked only when a challenge is raised? In the terms of the speech act theory that de Man explored then, the problem can be described as mapping the cleavage of the subject onto the distinction between the subject of the utterance and the subject of the enunciation. Formerly the two subjects were equated, as in the utterance: "de Man taught at Zurich in 1973," where the subject of the enunciation ("I state p" where p = "de Man taught at Zurich in 1973") is identical with the subject of the utterance. In the new economy of belief, the subject of the utterance is not equated to the subject of the enunciation but is subordinated to it: the value of the proposition p is determined not in and of itself but in relation to the authority or legitimacy of the "I" of "I believe p." What this means is that the sovereignty and the authority of the subject are at stake in every discursive act and are affirmed in them. This places a very heavy burden upon the subject, who reacts by raising the stakes: the subject must not only modulate the utterance with a tacit expression of belief but must also believe herself to be a legitimate and authoritative enunciator of this utterance. In other words, the subject must believe herself to be the legislator or the ruler, and achieve legitimation by a sort of *coup de force*.

In the third moment, the modern subject shies away from the violence presupposed by the regime of belief, and gives up belief itself. The abandonment of belief marks the passage into cynicism and the subject's acceptance of the fact of falsehood, and a decision to no longer stand by the possibility of thinking that a unique view of the world is necessary. At this time, the full possibilization of the possible takes place, and we enter the epoch of the modern imaginary in which arbitrariness reigns and the symbolic (as the instance of the Law) is neutralized. What does this entail? Modern consciousness knows itself to be a consciousness of falsehood and accepts this fact; it knows that this means that it cannot generate a narrative capable of totalizing the meaning of existence and of the world. This ultimate step in the demystification *(désenchantement, Entzäuberung)* of the world, accelerated by some historical catastrophes (Auschwitz, Hiroshima, the Gulag, to speak today's shorthand), leads the subject to give up truth (the Law) altogether and to accept the advent of the imaginary by instituting *fiction* as the way to constitute subjects and the world.

This new regime of generalized fiction, characteristic of a Nietzschean modernity, turns the imaginary into its own law and tolerates nothing but the imaginary, which is tantamount to a moralization of the imaginary—something that is very much in evidence in some strands of poststructuralism. This moralization of the imaginary is actually paradoxical since it affirms simultaneously the universal and subjective status of the law insofar as the new modern subject does not recognize any third instance such as God, Reason, or History as capable of grounding the law, while making of the law the act of self-positing *(selbst Setzung)* of the subject in his or her own name and that of all other subjects (the categorical imperative).

It should be clear then that the advent of the imaginary is not, as many people tend to think, the sublimated and subliminal locus of freedom where the subject is able to live in the mode of experimentation by anticipating, and then consuming, himself by scrolling the full repertory of possibilities in front of himself in an endless process of transgression of the law (as some interpreters of Bataille would have it). The law itself changes under this regime: it is now determined as a process of indeterminacy. We have here an antinomy that modernity does not know how to resolve: how does the modern subject legislate an interdiction to legislate, or legislate that no one should legislate for anyone else?

What is the status of such a law, whose kinship with Bateson's double bind is evident? It is the law that is in force when the subject assumes the memory of his own earlier forgetfulness, and what returns in this memory is the knowledge of the plasticity and the basic lability of the subject facing the real. What such a law accomplishes is a cognitive process in which the basic indeterminacy of the subject is overcome. This process itself takes the legalizing form of an institution and a constitution of the subject through the mediation of the linguistic sign. Thus, what the subject assumes in this act of recalling to memory of what had been forgotten, is, first of all, the fact that he acknowledges himself as the being of an institution (in the double sense of being instituted and of belonging to institutions), but, even more important, the subject acknowledges that language is the institution that is the condition of possibility for all institutions. This is the decisive proposition for modernity: *language is the originally instituting institution;* it provides the framework within which the practice of the subject will be that of a self-positing of the Self in language. From this point of view the modern subject, whom we saw earlier to be a consciousness of falsehood, becomes now the subject of inscription of Form, that is, the Artist.

This is the point to which de Man had come in his published writings, but it is not the point at which he meant to rest. In the conversations that led to the organization of his essays into the volumes that the University of Minnesota Press is bringing out, he had spoken repeatedly of the importance of the essays he meant to write on *The German Ideology* of Marx and Engels, and on Kenneth Burke. The logic of his inquiries into what was to him the central question of modernity was bringing him around to a far more direct challenge to modernity. Whether one took the atomistic notion of responsibility that I described earlier or the figure of the self-inscribing artist as one's point of departure, one could not help concluding that the logic of modernity uncovered by de Man led to perfectly legitimate and authoritative monads, each standing upon its conviction of personal legitimacy. But legitimacy is not an inherent trait; it must be conferred, and this conferral presupposes a social process. De Man had explored the predicament of modernity with his characteristic rigor and had arrived at the point that is at the root of modernity: the modern subject is an isolate who can only legislate for himself or for herself, and who can make no judgments about others or for others. Steadfastly opposed to any transcendental solution to this problem, for it would be only an attempt to reverse the thrust and the course of modernity, de Man was equally loath to relinquish any of the rigor of his analyses and posit some form of intersubjectivity as the corrective to the isolate subject. Intersubjectivity, far from reducing the problems he had come upon, only compounded them.

The most promising line of inquiry for him was the very one that had sustained his own approach. The rigor of his method was grounded in the forcing into the Procrustean bed of logic of all statements that purported to be true. It is this ambition of individual human reason to take itself for an instance of Transcendental Reason that he saw as the greatest danger, for it signals the existence of the persistent lure of certainty and of ultimate legitimation, whereas it is nothing more than ideology. Ideology is the arrogance of the finite subject who speaks as if he were the ultimate legislator, as if she had been appointed the final judge. The best prevention against the inveiglement of ideology is the practice of reading, in which the calculable well-formedness of various logics is constantly being fractured by a pervasive textuality.

De Man's challenge to modernity was to put forward a new mode of subject constitution, not one that relied upon the foundational operation of Cartesian radical doubt, but one that emerged in the act of reading itself, an act in which the subject, far from establishing his or her autonomy through the mastery of the text or the imposition of meaning on it, discovers the radical otherness of this text and his or her unredeemable indebtedness to it. The vaunted autonomy of the subject is, for de Man, but the forgetfulness of its foundational heteronomy.

De Man had succumbed to the allurements of ideology in the 1940s, and he knew their power. He had not tried to read the unfolding history but to proclaim its meaning from the podium that had been provided to him, and he had enslaved the very intelligence he was seeking to free. But he had also learned to fear the self-proclaimed finitude that undergirds liberalism, recognizing it as no more than the agnostic version of totalitarian ideology. By urging us to rethink our conceptions of the self and of the social on a linguistic basis, he was pushing us toward an overturning of modernity and toward forms of thought that would not succumb to the lures of ideology. He had learned that it was all too easy to stand by one's statements and one's actions; it was far more difficult to examine them critically. The revelations about his wartime writings should remind us of this concern. They should not lead us to denounce his failures, though we certainly should note them, but to ponder our own, and we are likely to discover that we need his mature writings for that task.

8   Caution! Reader at Work

Some time ago, Michael Riffaterre proposed that the verbal existence of objects is best apprehended through the notion of "descriptive system": rather than merely having names, objects are, linguistically speaking, the nexus between a number of nouns, epithets, motifs, narrative plots and situations, images, metaphors, oppositions, and so on, all of which can be summoned into print or consciousness directly or through one another's mediation.[1] The notion is a rich one and deserving of widespread application: for example, there is little doubt that a descriptive system comes into play as soon as Paul de Man's name appears. His preeminence in the field of literary theory is generally acknowledged, and his lectures at professional meetings and conferences attract large audiences of scholars and students. He is found to be lucid, trenchant ("surgical" is much more favored), uncompromisingly rigorous, austere, yet somehow affable, kind even. Although he deals with the leading critics and theoreticians of our day, his style is remarkably unpolemical. One listens to him as one witnesses a performance: one has the feeling beforehand that one knows what de Man will do, yet one still is awed by the elegance, precision, and economy of his performance; one has a reluctant but solid conviction that one could not duplicate it. De Man is thought to be highly original, yet, in a sense, he does exactly what we expect him to do. Therein lies the sense of our awe, but also of a certain malaise. If we are willing to concede that a certain degree of physical endowment enhanced by years of training does produce an exceptional athlete or star performer, we are most reluctant to extend such a concession to the realm of thought. Here feats must, indeed, be duplicated by others before they gain assent (philosophers of science call it verifiability) and cannot remain the prerogative of their inventor, lest charlatanism be suspected. Such is the critical temper of our times that lately a version of this charge has been leveled at Paul de Man: his is the criticism of performance; he is arbitrary; he is not the slayer of New Criticism but is its last faithful remnant, not a radical iconoclast but a pillar of the establishment. Questions are raised: What is the status of all discourses? Does de Man escape his blindness? If so, by virtue of what dispensation? If not, where is it located and why is it not fatal? Where does the authority of his discourse come from? Is there more to it than a rhetoric of mastery? In their contradiction, all of these assertions and questions do constitute a descriptive system, and it is one that presupposes that Paul de Man has been read. And here we run into a problem—not that de Man's books and articles have not been read, but rather because to claim to have read de Man presupposes that we know how to read. Yet if there is anything that de Man's work has been asserting with a quiet but insistent resolve, it is that we do not know what reading is. Thus, before making any determination on the accuracy of part or the whole of the de Manian descriptive system, we must learn to read, and learn to read the question of reading in de Man, starting with his first book, *Blindness and Insight*.[2]

I

Once upon a time, we all thought we knew how to read, and then came de Man . . . Even with its bathos alleviated by the fairy-tale motif and the Boileau citation, such a statement remains misleading, for it is far from certain that *we,* as literary scholars, knew how to read. The institutionalization of literary studies in European and American universities in the nineteenth century took place under the aegis of philology and literary history, ignoring, for the most part, the tradition of classical poetics and rhetoric. The first sought to establish texts, to make them as reliable as possible, so that the second could weave them into a satisfactory narrative of emergent national cultural achievment. It is not clear that texts were read, or, if they were, how.[3] To the trained scholarly gaze, they were made to yield a certain documentary information about the state of language, their authorship, their sources, the influences they had been subjected to,[4] and their place in a historical sequence or in some generic taxonomy. But alongside this function of information, texts had nothing to offer. It could in fact be suggested that, for the great age of literary history (roughly 1830–1939), literature had no cognitive value. The literary scholar in his or her capacity as historian certainly no longer felt authorized, let alone able, to state the truth, perhaps because the truth no longer wore the same cloak or rose from the same old well; it was much easier to write glosses upon the texts of those who, in a naiveté becoming their olden times, had dared utter it.

There arose then with respect to literature and other fields of inquiry, notably philosophy and history, a generic distinction between primary and secondary texts previously restricted to the relation of sacred text and commentary, the impact of which is still very much with us. It becomes clear in retrospect that it was constitutive of the disciplines themselves and, therefore, fundamental to the modern university. A division of labor results from this distinction: primary texts necessitated the development of techniques for the preservation and maintenance of their integrity and authenticity, while the writing of secondary texts posed problems of understanding and accuracy of account. Philology and textual criticism took care of the first (though not without encountering problems belonging to the realm of the second, as de Man rightly observes), while the second took the form of an insistent preoccupation with methodology.

Divorced from inquiry into truth, the secondary discourse is always in danger of falling into arbitrariness or divagation; only abeyance by rigorous methodological principles and investigatory protocols can ensure the verifiability and reproducibility of its assertions and results. The rise of the biological and physical sciences, with their clear distinction between object of knowledge as given *(datum)* and procedures of inquiry, served as a model for apprehending the relation of secondary discourse to primary text. Heidegger has been most persuasive on this score, drawing attention to the widespread assumption of a mode of thinking about things as a model for all forms of knowledge, and the specific elaboration of that model in Kant.[5] It is not surprising then to find a preoccupation with methodology in the works of the neo-Kantians and in that of Dilthey, who was most concerned with endowing the *Geisteswissenschaften,* or the humanities as we would call them, with what he saw as the rigor of scientific inquiry.

Modern literary studies, founded as they were upon the opposition of primary text and secondary discourse, did not escape the effect of this opposition; and the plethora of methodologies proposed in this century attests to this fact. Formalism, phenomenological criticism, the New Criticism, structuralism, most forms of semiotics, to name but a few of the more prominent, have in common a preoccupation with the development of the right approach to the study of literary texts, one that would provide the scholar, engaged in teaching as well as research, with a degree of validation in his or her practice. Literary critics, especially those of a theoretical bent, rightly devote their energy to the examination of these methodologies to assess their claims and ascertain their validity. Such is the stuff of contemporary polemics in literary studies, and quite proper it is.

Yet such is not the nature of de Man's own activity, although it bears some resemblance to it. If it were, de Man would be but a methodologist among others, for one can never mount a critique of an approach without at least implicitly holding some strong views on what the correct approach should be. Rather, his scrutiny of the critical practice of others—and that is what he does in the essays in *Blindness and Insight*—seeks to go beyond an inquiry into the validity, or to speak rapidly, into the success or failure of a given methodology, to an elucidation of the relationship of that methodology to its own necessity. That is, while de Man does not neglect to consider the capacity of a methology to abide by its own rules and to thus give us knowledge of the text it is applied to, such a consideration is, for him, secondary to the question of why the issue of methodology had to arise in the first place; and to the answer that the given methodology provides to that question, explicitly or not. For the practice of any methodological approach can be self-governing, whereas the question of the necessity of methodology raises the issue of what reading is.

II

It is a commonplace of undergraduate courses in literature to urge students to read a poem even though its opacity or denseness may initially rebuff them, for, it is held, there will suddenly occur a moment of illumination when everything will become clear, when they will understand; then, they will be able to reread the poem and see how what was opaque or dense was necessary to build up the triggering mechanism of the illumination. Leaving aside the pedagogical implications of such injunctions and promises,[6] let us consider the underlying assumptions of this description of the process of reading.

To begin with, it opposes the immediately apprehensible darkness of the sensible to the eventuality of the great clarity of the intelligible, yet makes the first the condition and the means of access to the second. It relies upon a well-known yet complex notion of expression in which the immediately perceptible materiality of the poem—its verbal component—is a means of access, yet a barrier, to the central core of meaning in the poem. The verbal component needs to be overcome to reach that core, but the overcoming itself is not easily described, for its achievement may depend more upon the qualities and the skills of the reader than, seemingly, upon any specific steps that can be taken to ensure its accomplishment. Moreover, it is not the case that the core of meaning is somehow held permanently imprisoned within that materiality, but rather that it becomes manifest in a flash of intuition that illuminates the whole and motivates its necessity.

There appear to be, then, two competing notions of expression at work here; the first is based upon the familiar model of the apparent and the hidden, where the hidden holds the key to the existential necessity of the apparent; whereas the second overcomes this model with an altogether different notion of the expression whose matrix is lightning. In opposition to the inside/outside dialectic of the first theory of expression, the model of lightning proposes a perfect congruence between the expression and that which is expressed. Lightning cannot be said to be hidden before its manifestation, but rather it expresses itself (if the word still applies) fully in the instant of its illumination. In fact, it suspends the difference between the manifest and the manifesting, producing in its instantaneity a moment of perfect presence. However, the punctual brevity of its flash is such as to displace its significance away from itself onto the surrounding darkness whose internal composition it reveals. Even if the eye were to train itself on the flash, and if it were able to predict the exact moment and place of its occurrence, it would remain unseeing, for it would be blinded by the force of the light; thus it is not lightning itself that we wish to see but what its flash reveals, the inner configuration of the surrounding landscape and the forces at play within it. The eye remains trained on the darkness, knowing it to hold a secret that the flash will disclose. The flash is not the secret but the occasion of the moment when all is in the light—the reward for peering into the dark.

Although quite different in their characterization of the mode of being of that which we presumably read for, the two theories of expression are far from incompatible. Indeed, a dialectical necessity unites them, for the patience in the practice of perception enjoined by the first would be far too aleatory without the guarantee of revelation provided by the second, while the latter needs the ascetic practice of the first to avoid falling into the trap of understanding by the predestination of the elect only. Each needs the other as well as a discipline, in the sense of Ignatius of Loyola: the first to ensure that lightning does strike; the second, even more formidably, that it strike repeatedly, at will, in the same place and with the same intensity. Such a desideratum reveals at once the limitations of the model of lightning—it is well known that in nature lightning tends to be rather mobile—and the inordinate ambition of these theories of expression underlying the most common practice of reading. Yet this limitation and its ambition are the two parameters of the question of methodology, for what is a method but a procedure designed to produce at will a certain result through the adoption of specific steps, treating the text as a given that can be made to yield its inner configuration?

This description of reading, based upon the practice of undergraduate courses, is admittedly crude; yet it differs only in degree from that to be found in the writings of leading theoreticians of literature. It is Paul de Man's burden to describe these differences and to question the persistence of this model. He does so through the now-familiar dialectic of blindness and insight that gives the volume its title, for it permits him to characterize various individuals' reading practices in terms of the necessary exclusion that their mode of reading implies, not simply as a form of neglect or ignorance but as the very originating locus of such insight as they achieve or illumination as they can provide.

Husserl states, or confirms, with great clarity that "philosophical knowledge can only come into being when it is turned back upon itself," but he does so only because he does not turn back upon his own statement that asserts as fundamental a crisis that is geographically and culturally localized. American New Criticism achieves its most productive insights when it describes the ironic play and the ambiguity of the texts that it began, and blindly continued, to consider as consisting of unitary form. Binswanger's inquiry into the ontology of the self and of art slides blindly, by its reliance upon the spatial metaphors that are the vehicles of conceptions of temporality, into an empirical moment, and in the process is forced, against its initial assumptions—never abandoned—to see the actual work of art in terms of self-mystification instead of self-actualization, a process of which it is a good instance. The very power of Georg Lukács's *Theory of the Novel* lies in its breakup of the organicist conception of the genre by means of the elevation of irony to the role of structural category; yet this very achievement should not permit the wide historical sweep of the book, since the latter is fully dependent upon a notion of temporality that is thoroughly organicist. Lukács is thus at once correct and wrong about the novel: correct insofar as he provides the ground for "a genuine hermeneutic of the novel," wrong in that he snatches his ground away just as it becomes manifest. He was able to reveal it, however, only because the very organicity that he denounces in the structure of the novel is still at play in his own story of the novel. Blanchot's deconstruction of the self proceeds by similarly bracketing away from the critic's knowing self the temporal dimension that allows him also to proceed in near-narrative fashion to describe the circular process of depersonalization, to, ultimately, have to confront the problem of temporality and of the self that it continued to preserve. Poulet's quest for the originating self of the literary act is forced, in its rigor, to confer upon the language it seeks to ground, the status of origin that it continues to refuse it in order to maintain the self. Thus, thoroughly grounded in presence, it inevitably ends with the non-presence of literature that it must refuse to recognize. Heidegger's insight that poetry is the attempt to name Being requires, in the logic of his thought, that such an attempt should actually occur successfully somewhere; yet Heidegger misreads Hölderlin by holding him up as the justifying example of this instance, whereas the latter thematizes the impossibility of such a naming. The methodological project of I. A. Richards and William Empson was meant to reduce the dispersion produced by reading, yet, unbeknown to itself, and most certainly against the very concept of form that is its starting ground, it winds up disclosing the ontological discontinuity of language just as it claims to have overcome its surface ruptures.[7]

The de Manian descriptive system is replete with laudatory characterizations of his readings of the critics and theoreticians just enumerated. It is rather laconic, though, concerning *how* de Man reads as opposed to what he reads. It may well be because this opposition of the how versus the what is very much put into question in de Man's readings. Even in the course of a superficial perusal of the essays in *Blindness and Insight,* one cannot fail to be struck by the relatively limited number of notions or concepts with which they deal: the self, temporality, the referential gap, ambiguity (as forerunner of undecidability), rhetoric, and so forth. This may explain why the suspicion has arisen that a rhetoric of mastery is deploying its own verbal armature over these texts and subjecting them to its domination. Such an assertion needs to be demonstrated, though, rather than just made. Is it not rather the case that the return of the same analytic concepts is motivated by the persistence of the same problematic under different guises? Whether such a persistence is structural or historically circumscribable and even determined, we shall have occasion to examine below.

I have suggested that the writings of the critics discussed by de Man differ in degree only, insofar as their theory of reading is concerned, from the model I described earlier. De Man's readings confirm this, but why should this be the case? The complementarity of what I called the two theories of expression articulates far more than just a theory of reading, although that may be its most strategic location; it constitutes, in its very contradictions, the way we have been thinking about meaning since the late eighteenth century at least. The complementary opposition of primary text and secondary discourse, although it may ostensibly eschew the saying of truth, remains very much in its orbit. It suggests that in the primary text the truth remains somehow burdened by its mode of representation, and it acts upon the belief that the truth can be attained and that indeed it can be given a better representation, of which the secondary text would be the very instantiation. In other words, the primary versus secondary opposition is predicated upon a prior opposition, which it locates in the primary text, between a truth or a meaning to be disclosed and the means of that disclosure. Although apparently granting the primary text the status of perfect presence that we saw in lightning, or, to use the discourse of poetics, that of a symbol where the relation of sign to referent or signifier to signified is fully motivated, the very practice of a secondary discourse is at least implicitly or unconsciously grounded in the belief that such a congruence has not been achieved, that it may not be achievable, or that it can be ruptured at will, since this practice proposes to substitute its own product—its text—as the vehicle for transporting the truth. Blindly, it sees itself as a better representation of the truth, whereas it is in fact engaged in an allegorical relation of mapping one sign with another, of sublating one sign by another.

The practice of a secondary discourse is thus founded on the premise that meaning, or the truth, is not "at home" in the langue of representation of the primary text, and that further, the secondary discourse can provide such a home. This claim is obviously tied to the ambition of methodology to have lightning strike at will, in the same place, and with the same intensity. In the dialectic of the two theories of expression, the role devolved upon the materiality of the text both before and after the bolt of lightning is that of the sensible appearance of that which can appear. The content of the apparent is therefore purified in the sense that it shows as superfluous its given trappings.

Givenness, we have seen earlier, is the attribute of nature in the so-called natural sciences, and therefore, insofar as the epistemological structure of primary and secondary instances models itself upon the structure of knowledge of these sciences, the object of the secondary instance is to free the content of the first from its natural trappings. The content of the apparent is therefore the existent freed from its naturalness. It is represented figurally by the apparent, but in such a way as to reduce the distance between its figuration and itself; meaning is congruent with its sign, hence the privileged status accorded to the primary text.

Yet, if this kind of free-standing appearance, to use Schiller's term,[8] does not reduce its content to existence, or better, states the truth of the existent as a sort of nullity, it is not itself a truth or that truth. Rather, it states it, but in its own mode, which, paradoxically with respect to truth but appropriately to itself, does not require its undoing, its disappearance, just because it has revealed its nullity. In the primary text, the immediate is indeed canceled, but this cancellation is carried out through immediate means; in other words, the cancellation is not a final act but part of a strategy of continuous canceling; it is a denial that goes on forever, and in that sense the apparent, revealing itself as apparent and therefore as the immediate trapping of truth, nonetheless does not free up that truth, but keeps on stating its inadequacy to hold it while holding it. In Hegelian terms—and this is, after all, a very Hegelian story—the idealization achieved in the dialectic of the two theories of expression is necessarily incomplete. The immediate is not reproduced, as some theories of mimesis would have it, but it is preserved; the materiality of the signs is essential to the aesthetic perspective. The superfluousness of the immediate can only be shown not as the truth but mediately through more (superfluous) immediacy. If the immediate were truly susceptible to elimination, then art would indeed disappear. In the meantime—and this form of temporal contingency would require a treatise unto itself[9]—the primary text is caught in a bind: it both announces the no longer mediate truth, yet blocks its advent through its own immediacy. It holds out the promise of the disappearance of the sensible and the manifestation of the perfect sign, yet it is powerless to achieve it, hence the awaiting of the bolt of lightning.

The bolt of lightning is, of course, meant to overcome the blocking action of the apparent, yet it is itself not wholly devoid of appearance; its mode of cancellation of the immediate, though, must be presumed to be more effective than the preserving cancellation of the apparent. In the latter, immediate being is negated; in fact it is there to be negated—idealized, in the Hegelian sense. But in the former, it is completely overcome, so that the truth can speak directly. The model of lightning implies this overcoming by suggesting that lightning is what it is in its very manifestation, that its manifestation is its being, that its appearance is its essence; in other words, that it is truth's own voice. By opposition, the apparent is then seen to have been caught in the gap between appearance and saying, and the primary text must be seen as laboring to maintain the materiality of the figural. Again, in Hegelian terms, art attempts to salvage the materiality of signs, and, in this manner, makes them into indices of idealization, whereas in lightning we get idealization itself. Such a formulation permits then the elaboration of the Hegelian project of studying the various forms and periods of art as differences in the degree of gap between appearance and saying—what de Man alludes to, in the essay on Richards and Empson, when he speaks of a genuine historical poetics. From after the lightning, meaning is shown to have been present in the apparent, but because the stress is on the showing of its presence, it cannot actually be claimed to be present. The structural gap of appearance and saying has thus a temporal dimension as well. For the theory of reading that we have been examining, a danger now arises, one that it has not fully exorcised though it attempts to bracket it away: namely, that truth is ineffable. The structural significance of the model of lightning in the dialectic of the two theories of expression lies in the exorcism of this possibility.

By positing a difference between aesthetic language and the language of inquiry governed by reason—what we have been calling so far the apparent and the order of manifestation of lightning—the oppositional theory of primary versus secondary status of text can describe the first instance of language (aesthetic language) as superfluous, as reductive of the presence of truth. A form of language trained upon reason—logical in the strong sense of the term (derived from the Logos) as well as in the technical one, that is, a methodological use of language—would no longer block access to meaning but would manifest it, no longer mediate it through figures but permit it to speak in its own voice. Such a mode of discursive practice is superior to intuition even, for the latter may gain access to truth but leave it ineffable, whereas the object of a methodological practice is to give truth or meaning a vehicle in which it can make itself manifest unmediated.

The methodological enterprise implies then not only that the language of representation is inadequate to the statement of the truth, but that any language that is not methodologically rigorous is going to be inadequate because it will remain within the orbit of representation. By constraining one's discourse to be answerable to the rules of reason— that is, by constructing a methodology—one frees it from the constraints of representation and makes it into an adequate instrument for the conveyance of truth.

Aesthetic appearence is thus disqualified, for it gave us but false presence; but is language, any form of language, up to playing the role of representational vehicle that the methodological enterprise requires of it? That is the question toward which de Man found himself increasingly propelled as he reflected upon the reading practice of his subjects. By virtue of what dispensation is methodological discourse free of the materiality that weighted aesthetic signs? Is this not an instance of the eye being blinded by the lightning upon which it is trained and claiming to have seen the truth? In methodological discourse, the materiality of the signifier is not simply abrogated because the discourse claims to be subjected to reason. Meaning continues to be mediate, mediated by signs. To return to our earlier formulation: meaning may not have been "at home" in aesthetic language, but it was not because it was aesthetic but because it was language. We may have shed the notion of the ineffable and thus the concept of an occulted meaning or truth, but we do not have immediate truth; we are still back in the figural but in a specific mode, and it is Paul de Man's most important contribution to have drawn our attention to it, to have inquired into and described that mode.

The realm of the apparent holds the truth hidden away, so that its only means of access are the figures of the apparent; yet these figures are not known to be figures, for they are the only mode of being that lends itself to knowledge, and, unless one wishes to invoke a Platonic theory of recollection, no conclusion concerning them is possible. During the brief reign of lightning, or in the (deluded) possibility of methodological absolutism, truth is meant to be visible in unmediated form, in and of itself, and especially free of figuration. In the realm that is ours, where we have shed any belief in the ineffable and know the impossibility of unmediated truth, we are indeed back in the figural, where the figural is known as figural. In other words, we are in the rhetorical, as de Man has been showing us all along.

Here we may aspire to the clarity of reason, but all we may achieve is the elucidation of the understanding that, not knowing truth, none-theless seeks to write its laws by reducing the numbing heterogeneity of the immediate to a set of apprehensible unities. The danger for this understanding is not so much the error of fact that methodologists are so concerned with, but the isolation of thoughts and ideas and their conversion into autonomous objects of knowledge independent of their productive ground; in other words, their reification. The un-derstanding is prey to ideology and to the familiar dichotomies of our thinking: thought becomes abstract, knowledge partial, and theory opposed to practice. Against this risk and this danger, de Man's theo-retical practice consists in pushing the understanding by a relentless questioning into its last redoubts where, in the moment of undecid-ability—the place of aporia—it is forced to surrender its claim to be-ing reason's lieutenant and to acknowledge that, unlike reason, it la-bors in the realm of representation and not in that of the concept, and that it must come to terms with the materiality of its object as well as acknowledge its own continuity with that object.

In its ideological moment, understanding opposes the literary to the real, framing the former in its form and valorizing the latter as that which is outside the frame—the referent. At that moment, what is within the frame is thought of as the representation of that which is outside of it, the sign of a referent. But under de Man's questioning, the understanding must abandon its pretensions, and, as we have seen earlier, it turns out that there is no difference of being between what is within and what is outside of the frame: they are both of representa-tion. The difference, for difference there is—and here one must be careful not to fall into Platonism—lies in the fact that what is within the frame is not the simulacrum of a simulacrum—which would, at best, lead back to the project of historical poetics—but the "simula-crity" of this simulacrum, and this constitutes a form of cognition of which the frame is probably the emblem.

In its determination of signifying value, reason can be presumed to be primarily semantic; the understanding relies upon syntax in its attempt to convert heterogeneity into unity, and de Man is well known for his persistent interrogation of grammar. Rhetoric knows itself as rhetoric, hence its superiority to other textual practices. Their failure comes from their fall into objectivity: they are discourses upon an ob-ject—what I have called, following Hegel, the ideological position. Only rhetoric carries within its scope its for-itself and its in-itself. One could say, if the words still had meaning, that it comprises even its blindness.

Rhetoric, as a mode of language, accommodates itself to human finitude, for, unlike other modes, it need not locate anything beyond its boundaries: it operates on the materiality of the text and achieves effects. Since it is internally cleaved between a collection of tropes and a technique of persuasion, it is itself sufficiently mobile to avoid falling into positional ideology. In this manner the how and the what of reading converge. Against Descartes's injunction to examine an assertion for its hidden falsehood, or Kant's recommendation that a statement be projected against its horizon of illusion, de Man's rhetorical inquiry consists in recognizing the finiteness of the text and in bringing out its rhetorical machine. At first, this seems like an abandonment of the "higher" questions of truth and falsehood, self and experience, meaning and significance, that texts are ostensibly read for. That would be the case if the figural mechanism that de Man investigates were just a simulacrum, but because it is much more than that, the inscription of the "simulacrity" of a simulacrum, it manages to achieve something that the "higher" pursuits do not. In their delusion, they believe that they have left the realm of representation and reside now in that of reason; de Man harbors no such illusion, but, having brought the understanding to a point of paralysis, and reached the point of the inscription of the "simulacrity" of the simulacrum, he stands at the very edge of human finitude. To some, this may not seem enough; they may wish to take refuge in forms of utopian thought or seek to impose an ideal. De Man proposes a more modest form of activity. It is neither heroic, because it is not transforming, nor fatalistic, because it does not submit or follow blindly, but it seeks to collaborate in an explicitation that is already at work and whose movement it attempts to espouse.

De Man does not read then to constitute his identity or that of the text, nor to reach some beyond of the text, by whatever name it may be called. He seeks to locate the blind spot of the text as the organizer of the space of the vision contained in the text, and the vision's concomitant blindness. This spot of blindness is the solar position that blinds yet regulates the revolution of the spheres around itself. The sun has no "revolutionary" history; or, rather, its history lies elsewhere, in another dimension. That is why any critique of de Man that concludes somewhat hastily on the basis of the chronological span of his readings that the predicament he locates and describes can be explained as a general condition of, let us say, post-Enlightenment thought, is ultimately off the mark. De Man has no quarrel with history provided its finitude is recognized. In fact, if anything his inquiry is an attempt to ask the historical question at the very edge of that finitude, for how are we to consider the activity that does the inscribing of the "simulacrity" of the simulacrum? That question, which begins to emerge only now, poses the very problem of history since it forces us to confront the question of what that activity is.

De Man's characteristic stance can be described in terms of Hegel's notion of *Bildung*: to be cultivated is to practice a form of ascesis, for it requires not so much the acquisition of information or even knowledge but a progressive renunciation of the representational. For Hegel, who believed in the Absolute, it meant that we needed to die to the immediate in all of its forms. De Man's thought is resolutely secular, or more precisely, sufficiently freed of the transcendental to be called finite; and thus living in the realm of representation, as we all do, he simply "sees fewer and fewer new things; the substantial content of most new things seems to such a man rather well known" (*Enzyklopädie* § 454). We may indeed know beforehand what de Man will do, but can we espouse his movement?

9　The Tiger on the Paper Mat

After the publication of *Allegories of Reading* in 1979, Paul de Man found himself constantly besieged by requests for articles, introductions, conference papers, and other forms of scholarly communication. Whereas some scholars live in a tragic mode, the disjunction between what they consider their proper intellectual pursuits and the demands made upon them by their profession, Paul de Man had come to think of this disjunction as the relation between the contingency of the historical and the necessity of coherent thought, with the former imposing a salutary heterogeneity upon the latter's inevitable drift toward single-minded totalization. Though he remained steadfast in his concerns, he framed them according to the demands of the moment in which they were ultimately written, and he drew a certain pleasure from the ironies that attended their publication.

The very number of calls made upon de Man in these years and his ability to write a great many major pieces in rapid succession eventually led him, in late 1981 and early 1982, to formulate a general plan for publishing in book form the essays that he had been writing and that he planned to write in the near future. *The Resistance to Theory*[1] was conceived as a unit of this general plan.

While he was properly suspicious of most forms of articulation, and particularly of those that claimed the ability to periodize, de Man did not fail to recognize their heuristic value, especially when it came to such mundane matters as publication. During the discussions that led to the formulation of the plan of publication, he put forward the following organization of his writings. His first essays—no reference was made to those now known as his wartime journalism—constitute the properly *critical* face of his activity. In them he considered authors as classical as Montaigne and as modern as Borges and wondered about the present possibilities of poetry or of the historical sense in America. The very practice of such criticism led him to question its validity, an interrogation soon exacerbated by the fact that he had entered the academic profession at a time when the New Criticism was extending its hegemony over the teaching of literature in American universities. He thus began to concern himself more with matters of methodology and to write about the works of other critics rather than those of poets or novelists. The results of this phase of his work are to be found in the revised edition of *Blindness and Insight.* It is in the essays gathered in that volume that Paul de Man articulated a stance that was properly *theoretical,* and while he was not alone to do so then, his adoption of such a stance proved to be very influential in American academic circles.

He did not entirely welcome this influence for a number of reasons, not the least of which had to do with his own misgivings with respect to the theoretical instance so enthusiastically embraced in some quarters and denounced with equal eagerness and passion in others. In the course of these theoretical essays de Man had come to delimit a problematic which was fundamental to him, but which until then had been mediated through categories of consciousness and temporality inherited from the Hegelian substratum of phenomenology: *the matter of reading.* Reading, as de Man began to conceive of it, is far more radical than any theoretical enterprise can admit. As we shall see later, reading disrupts the continuity between the theoretical and the phenomenal and thus forces a recognition of the incompatibility of language and intuition. Since the latter constitutes the foundational basis of cognition upon which perception, consciousness, experience, and the logic and the understanding, not to mention the aesthetics that are attendant to them, are constructed, there results a wholesale shakeout in the organization and conceptualization of knowledge, from which language, conceived as a double system of tropes and persuasion, that is, as a rhetorical entity, emerges as the unavoidable dimensionality of all cognition. This was the view first adumbrated in "The Rhetoric of Temporality" and developed in *Allegories of Reading.* There followed a number of essays, now collected in *The Rhetoric of Romanticism,* in which implications of this conception of reading were explored over a historically circumscribed corpus.

De Man realized that the conception of reading that he had uncovered in his own theoretical essays had to overcome two major obstacles: the first is posed by the theoretical enterprise itself, while the second has to do with the history of philosophical thought since the eighteenth century. He thus formulated two projects to deal with these problems, neither of which was finished at the time of his death in

December 1983, though both were far advanced toward completion. The second came to be entitled *The Aesthetic Ideology,* and it contains essays that focus on how the radical nature of Kant's conception of aesthetic judgment—which approximates de Man's own notion of the radicalness of reading—was given a more reassuring path in Schiller's interpretation and in its subsequent fate in the philosophical tradition. Aesthetic judgment came to be replaced or overlaid by an ideological construct of values, now commonly taken to be the aesthetic, even though, de Man insists, the underlying judgment will not support such an overlay but will actively work to dismantle it. Only an activity such as reading can come in touch with this process and experience the resistance of the material to the ideological overlay. The shape of the volume is apparent, though de Man did not live to write two essays that would have been of considerable interest: one on Kierkegaard as seen by Adorno, and the other on Marx's *The German Ideology.* This collection of essays thus represents, among other things, de Man's intervention in the current debates on modernity and postmodernity.

The essays gathered in *The Resistance to Theory* were meant to reexamine the work of other theorists, in a manner somewhat analogous to that found in *Blindness and Insight,* in order to determine what about the theoretical enterprise itself blinds it to the radicalness of reading and in order to disengage the principle of this blindness, which de Man came to conceive of as a "resistance" for reasons I shall attempt to explore later. This volume too is unfinished. From the outset *The Resistance to Theory* was meant to include three essays of which two appear here in preparatory form and one not at all: essays on Bakhtin and on Benjamin, for which the papers appearing in this volume were early versions still to be revised, and an essay on Kenneth Burke, which de Man had wanted very much to write for quite some time and which he considered the "social" counterpart to the more "formalist" essay on Riffaterre, though equally meant to arrive at a notion of inscription that would wreak havoc with the attempt to deal with history and the social only through its representational forms.

This brief outline gives a sense of the direction that Paul de Man felt his work was taking when he was struck down by illness. He labored hard to bring it to completion, taking advantage of every moment of remission, though quite aware that the task he had embarked upon would always remain incomplete. The texts he has left behind invite us to pursue his reflection, challenging us to read them in the radical way he had begun to formulate.

Again, the account I give here is not meant to be canonical, nor does it represent more than a punctual attempt to rationalize the publication in book form of essays written for the bewildering array of occasions that mobilize present-day scholarship. From a more thematic perspective, one could formulate different articulations of the de Man oeuvre, with pivotal roles going to essays such as "Heidegger's Exegeses of Hölderlin," "The Rhetoric of Temporality," and "Shelley Disfigured." But the articulation that I describe governs the publication of Paul de Man's essays and, as such, it is likely to play a role in the mode of their reading, even if it is to be no more but no less than a certain form of resistance.

II

All the essays in *The Resistance to Theory* engage the question of theory as it has come to dominate our literary scene, and since theory is primarily a concern of academically situated scholars, the essays also touch upon questions of pedagogy and institutional determination, although de Man did not feel that the latter was as important in the North American context as in the European one (see his interview in *The Resistance to Theory*, which was broadcast in part on the cultural service of RAI International, in which he usefully distinguishes between his attitude and that of Derrida in this respect). The title of the volume is borrowed from one of the essays which originally bore quite a different title, but whose retitling brings together all the questions of theory, pedagogy, and institutionalization that are among the principal themes of *The Resistance to Theory*, along with the figure of resistance which is attached to them here.

The essay "The Resistance to Theory" was originally entitled "Literary Theory: Aims and Methods." It was commissioned by the Committee on Research Activities of the Modern Language Association for its volume *Introduction to Scholarship in Modern Languages and Literatures*, where it was to figure as the section on literary theory. De Man found it difficult to write the pedagogical piece that was expected of him and instead wrote an essay in which he attempted to determine the nature of the resistance that theory poses to its own definition. The essay he submitted encountered a resistance of another kind: it was judged inappropriate for the volume the MLA was producing, and an altogether different essay was then commissioned from Paul Hernadi. De Man did not quarrel with this judgment; he simply retitled the essay for oral delivery at Amherst College in the spring of

1981 and determined soon thereafter that it should provide the title of the collection on theory that he was then contemplating.

The sequence of events in this little brouhaha ought to make clear that the term "resistance" refers only secondarily, and almost ironically, to the institutional forms of resistance to theory as they were experienced in the seventies and eighties in the United States. Although de Man did anticipate some form of such resistance to his essay, as the introductory paragraphs make clear, he used the term in the essay itself with a very different view in mind. As is almost always the case with his coinages, the figures he puts into motion in his texts have a technical meaning which it is useful to recall.

The term "resistance" names a property of matter recognized since antiquity: its perceptibility to touch and inertial opposition to muscular exertion. For Aristotle, *ta physika* are characterized by the resistance they oppose to us, and they thus become objects of our cognition: it is by virtue of this resistance that we know them to be outside of ourselves and not illusions fostered upon us by our unreliable sensory apparatus. Resistance is a property of the referent, we would say today, which allows this referent to become the object of knowledge of the subject that we are. Without this resistance, we would never be able to ascertain whether the phenomenal or the sensible is really "out there" and thus whether we have any knowledge of such an "out there." To the extent that theory has cognitive pretensions, resistance is very important to it as a precondition for the theory's cognitive reach into the phenomenal. This is a venerable problem not only of literary theory but of language philosophy, as the following passage in the essay seems to indicate in its recondite way:

> If a cat is called a tiger it can easily be dismissed as a paper tiger; the question remains however why one was so scared of the cat in the first place. The same tactic works in reverse: calling the cat a mouse and then deriding it for its pretense to be mighty. Rather than being drawn into this polemical whirlpool, it might be better to try to call the cat a cat and to document, however briefly, the contemporary version of the resistance to theory in this country. ("The Resistance to Theory," p. 5)

Passages such as this one are not at all rare in de Man's writings. One may think for example, of the justly famous play on Archie Bunker/ archè debunker in "Semiology and Rhetoric." As in that passage, we seem to have an instance of postmodern writing here with its borrowings of current political slogans ("paper tiger"), popular culture (Mighty Mouse of Saturday morning television cartoon fare), paronomasia ("deriding"), and so forth. And its cognitive dimension is to be found in what Riffaterre would call the conversion of a matrix: instead of "to call a spade a spade" we have "to call a cat a cat," an apparent reaffirmation of the feline code of the passage, but since the meaning of "to call a spade a spade" is that of the primacy of denomination over decorum, or in somewhat different terms, of denotation over connotation, we have a version of a famous conundrum of language philosophy and of the philosophy of mind: "the cat is on the mat." In other words, the problem is that of the cognitive dimension of language: how it apprehends the real. And in the play on the size of the cat and on its putative fearsomeness, de Man further alludes to his own discussion, and to Derrida's, of the famous passage on the "giant" in Rousseau in which the relation of figural language to denotation is explored. All of which are certified theoretical problems, indeed topoi of recent theory.

It may be useful at this juncture to recall what theory is. Presently we tend to use the term to mean a system of concepts that aims to give a global explanation to an area of knowledge, and we oppose it to praxis by virtue of the fact that it is a form of speculative knowledge. The term obviously has taken on this meaning after Kant, though it appears in most of the Western languages earlier, by way of Latin translations from the Greek (with a rather interesting swerve through Arabic that we need not concern ourselves with here). Etymologically, the term comes from the Greek verb *theorein,* to look at, to contemplate, to survey. And in Greek, it does not enter into an opposition with praxis—an opposition constructed in Idealist philosophy and eventually used to combat the latter—but rather with *aesthesis,* something that Ruskin recalls in his *Modern Painters:*

> The impressions of beauty . . . are neither sensual nor intellectual but moral, and for the faculty receiving them . . . no term can be more accurate . . . than that employed by the Greeks, "theoretic" which I pray permission to use and to call the operation of the faculty itself "Theoria." (II, iii, par. 1, and then again in paragraph 8): The mere animal consciousness of the pleasantness I call Aesthesis, but the exulting, reverent, and grateful perception of it I call Theoria.

Ruskin articulates the opposition between *aesthesis* and *theoria* around the matter-of-factness of the first and the jubilatory character of the second without inquiring into the provenance of this jubilation.

The latter is indeed well attested. It comes from the fact that the act of looking at, of surveying, designated by *theorein* does not designate a private act carried out by a cogitating philosopher but a very public one with important social consequences. The Greeks designated certain individuals, chosen on the basis of their probity and their general standing in the polity, to act as legates on certain formal occasions in other city-states or in matters of considerable political importance. These individuals bore the title of *theoros,* and collectively constituted a *theoria.* (It may be useful to bear in mind that the word is always a plural collective.) They were summoned on special occasions to attest the occurrence of some event, to witness its happenstance, and to then verbally certify its having taken place. (We may recall here the role of witnesses to the execution of death sentences in the American judicial system.) In other words, their function was one of see-and-tell. To be sure, other individuals in the city could see and tell, but their telling was no more than a *claim* that they had seen something, and it needed some authority to adjudicate the validity of such a claim. The city needed a more official and more ascertainable form of knowledge if it was not to lose itself in endless claims and counterclaims. The *theoria* provided such a bedrock of certainty: what it certified as having seen could become the object of public discourse. The individual citizen, indeed even women, slaves, and children, were capable of aesthesis, that is, perception, but these perceptions had no social standing. They were not sanctioned and thus could not form the basis of deliberation, judgment, and action in the polity. Only the theoretically attested event could be treated as a fact. The institutional nature of this certification ought not to escape us, as well as its social inscription. Indeed, it may be of more than theoretical interest, in our current sense of the term, to wonder how this social dimension of the certification of events, of the granting to something the discursive standing of "real," came to be occulted, though that would take us too far afield from our immediate concerns.

The structure of the functioning of the Greek *theoria* is as follows then: between the event and its entry into public discourse, there is a mediating instance invested with undeniable authority by the polity. This authority effects the passage from the seen to the told; it puts into socially acceptable and reliable language what it apprehends. This authority, the *theoria,* has to use language itself though, and its language is not yet covered by the guarantees it brings to the polity.

In fact, it must construct that guarantee within itself, although the *theoria* is alone socially recognized as capable of wielding such language. The structure of such a language must be of a nature to permit the following, admittedly awkward paraphrase: "We who now address you here, were there then and we witnessed there then what we are about to tell you here now in order that you here and we here may all talk here now and in the future about how what happened there then affects us here." In other words, such a language must be deictically articulated, something that did not escape Hegel as he embarked on his own theoretical project in *The Phenomenology of Mind* with a consideration of the "this." And it is the problematic in the background of "the cat is on the mat" discussion, the famous paper tiger of the philosophy of language and mind. One understands more readily why jubilation attended to the theoretical among the Greeks: they had solved the problem until philosophers came along and attempted to ground everything in sense perception, in aesthesis, with a theorizing of their own, appropriated from the *polis* in ways as yet little understood, as the sole mediation.

III

Deixis is the linguistic mechanism that permits the articulation of all of these distinctions between the here and the there, the now and the then, the we and the you. It establishes the existence of an "out there" that is not an "over here," and thus it is fundamental to the theoretical enterprise. It gives it its authority. "The cat is on the mat" problem is a problem of deixis: the sentence is true only insofar as the utterer refers to a given cat, that is, the cat is a cat that has been referred to or otherwise brought to the attention of the addressee. For all practical purposes, the sentence must be taken to mean something like: "this cat that you and I are aware of is now on this mat that you and I are aware of." Of course none of us speaks in this way, just as the *theoria* did not speak in the way that I indicated earlier, but the proper functioning of the discourse that we wield presupposes that sort of structural capacity to specify deixis. The history of languages is instructive in this regard: it is well known that the present-day articles of Romance languages are descendants of Latin demonstratives, and the medieval forms of these articles still had strong demonstrative capabilities and have to be translated as such. Many utterances can be evaluated in terms of their claims to truthfulness only when this deictic dimension is brought into consideration. Neither the logical nor the grammatical structure of a sentence suffices for these purposes; they may provide assurances of well-formedness, but they are helpless to determine whether the sentence is true with respect to a certain state of affairs.

Theories of language have been aware of this problem for a long time, and it is indeed the Stoics who came to give this problem the name of deixis. Modern linguistics has refined it, and the present canonical form of the problem is one articulated in rapid succession by Emile Benveniste and Roman Jakobson, who made explicit the role played by the act of uttering in the functioning of deixis. Benveniste in his "Formal Apparatus of Enunciation"[2] identifies the specificity of the deictics with the fact that they refer to the instance of discourse: they have no objective referents outside of the discourse; they actually make reference to what has no referent since their meaning is determinable only by means of the instance of discourse that they occur in. Benveniste then activates the Saussurean opposition of *langue* and *parole* to conclude that deictics are the verbal mechanism that permits language to become discourse, that is they effect the passage from the virtuality of *langue* to the actuality of *parole*. Jakobson's analysis of deictics, which he calls "shifters," is quite similar though it originates in, and indeed closely espouses, Peircian notions on the subject.

What is interesting about this theory of deixis is that it appears to run counter to what seemed to be the very core of the problem. On the one hand, the indicational capability of deixis, its ability to indicate a here and now, had been taken as the very bedrock of referentiality. This is where language encountered the *resistance* of what it talked about, and thus it had cognitive value; it apprehended the world. On the other hand, once the mechanism at work in deixis was investigated and described, it turned out that deictics do not refer to anything tangible, to anything that has any resistance, as is clear from the very instability of the terms themselves ("I" becomes "you" when you address me; "here" turns into "there," and so on). Deictics refer to the instance of discourse, Benveniste tells us, and this is a dismal finding for those who placed their hope in the referential capacity of language, for it is clear that deictics were the great hope of referentiality. But it would be too quick to conclude that, as a result, deictics lock us into language.

Deictics do refer; they refer to the fact that language has taken place and that it is something that takes place, even something that offers resistance. Benveniste's reliance upon the Saussurean terminology and its Aristotelian overtones ought not to blind us to the fact that deictics are the means by which language makes itself into *something that takes place and something that can be referred to,* and it is from this inaugural act of reference that all other forms of reference will flow. It is, in the terminology that de Man uses, the resistance of language to language that grounds all other forms of resistance. To language, all of the real is fungible but itself, and the resistance that language opposes to itself—which may take the form of troping—establishes the reality of language to language, which then constructs all other forms of reference upon this fundamental model. In terms of the opposition that Heidegger has reconstructed from antiquity, the taking place of language ("enunciation" in Benveniste's terminology) is its ontological dimension, whereas the type of reference that takes place within the space opened up by the inaugural act of language's taking place is the ontic.

The ontic comes to deploy itself in the space that the ontological has opened up for it. This inaugural act of opening up a space de Man formulates as *inscription,* and one can readily see that the very deployment of the ontic requires the effacement of the ontological, hence a dialectic, in the Kantian and not the Hegelian sense, of inscription and effacement, which in this book on theory comes to replace the earlier dialectic of blindness and insight characteristic of criticism.

The problematics of inscription, worked out in the essay on Riffaterre in *The Resistance to Theory,* rejoins an older preoccupation of de Man, namely history. It may be useful in this regard to compare briefly his itinerary with that of Hegel, against which much of this thinking takes place, an *against* that has to be taken to mean both "in opposition to" and in the sense of "resting against."

In his *Phenomenology of Spirit,* Hegel too analyzed deixis through the act of indication as he embarked upon his examination of the relationship of sense certainty to cognition. He came to the conclusion that to show something, that is, to apprehend its this-ness, necessitates a recognition of the fact that sense certainty is a dialectical process of negation and mediation. This process affects natural consciousness— Hegel's operative notion in this text—which puts itself forward as the unmediated and the immediate, but is shown in the analysis of showing not to be a given but a *Geschichte,* that is, a history. This type of history belongs to the ontic, since it is the result of mediation and is in the realm of representation. Paul de Man came early to understand that this articulation of history depended upon the central position of consciousness, and his own early preoccupation with this category, which has led some to believe that he was somehow affiliated with the Geneva school, was an attempt to dislodge consciousness from the central position it occupied in the Hegelian edifice. When de Man came into contact with the thought of Heidegger—almost contrapuntally in the French environment in which he li~ed then, since it was Hegel that the French were discovering as they were finally beginning to translate him—he recognized a preoccupation similar to his own, and in the distinction of the ontic and the ontological, the possibility of distinguishing a history that is caught up in representation and one that is not. And while such a possibility was present in Hegel's thought, it was under the sway of the dialectic, which effectively robbed it of its radicality.

In Heidegger, however, the distinction between *Historie* and *Geschichte,* which maps the two different conceptions of the historical dimension, lends itself somewhat easily to certain forms of recuperation, best exemplified by the success of Heideggerian ideas in theological circles. The historical dimension that presides over the constitution of the apparent and is itself not of the apparent, to speak the language of idealist philosophy, can far too rapidly be conceived as a form of transcendentalism that effectively removes history from human view.

The problematic status of praxis in contemporary thought derives in great part from this situation. Conceived of in relation to theory, praxis is subject to the latter, and when the latter runs into problems, praxis appears arbitrary or willful. Indeed willfulness, whether constructed immediately as such or conceived along the lines of desire, has figured prominently in recent thought as a way out of this predicament. Paul de Man seems to have adopted another strategy, one that led him to recognize that the mapping of the opposition/dependency of theory and praxis left aesthetics free-standing. In a first movement, he restores the ancient relation between *aesthesis* and *theoria* and problematizes their relation, and most of us have followed with considerable interest what he has done there. But we ought not to lose sight of the fact that de Man's remapping has liberated praxis from the hold that theory has had over it. It is incumbent upon us now to deal with praxis, though it becomes rapidly clear that our old ways of dealing with it, beholden as they were to the supremacy of theory and the autonomy of *aesthesis,* will not do. Praxis thus stands presently as a rather mysterious entity, the figure of the agency *(Handlung)* that we thought we had lost when we secularized but that now returns without the godhead that adorned it, as the figure of history.

The death of Paul de Man is thus a great loss since he was beginning to move into this phase of his thinking, which was going to become apparent in the essays on Burke, Kierkegaard, and Marx. But there is enough for us to *read* in *The Resistance to Theory*, and for quite a while.

10   The Domestication of Derrida

On July 17, 1976, H.M. Queen Elizabeth II rose from her seat, approached the microphone, and staring into the Canadian Broadcasting Company camera's eye, which retransmitted the event simultaneously to more than a hundred countries around the world, said, in heavily accented French: "Je déclare ouverts les dix-huitièmes Jeux Olympiques de l'ère moderne, que nous célébrons dans la ville de Montréal." [1] For the speech act theorist, even more than for the sports enthusiast, the moment was particularly savory: The most competent agent one could summon in all of one's examples, the Queen herself, speaking as the sovereign of Canada from the specially constructed podium in the Olympic Stadium at the appointed time and with full knowledge of her responsibilities, had just uttered the perfect illocutionary sentence, to be followed imminently by the release of balloons and doves and the start of the parade of the national teams, thereby confirming the perlocutionary force of the utterance. The event was indeed a classic illustration of J. L. Austin's theories. [2] But before anything happened, indeed before the throng assembled under the unfinished dome of the stadium had begun to roar, the Queen was speaking again, this time in her own English: "I declare open the Olympic Games of 1976, celebrating the 21st Olympiad of the modern era." [3] This time the crowd did roar and the released pigeons and balloons rose toward the gap in the roof of the stadium and the parade started. But for the speech act theorist, there was only shock: How could she do it? How could the Games be "opened" twice?

Here was a conundrum for the theory. Surely, it must be the case that the sentence in French "opened" the Games and that the English was merely a translation of it; yet all about the declaration in English, from its formal characteristics to its conditions of utterance, qualified it for the same sort of description as illocutionary act as the French, even more so perhaps since "it" was followed by activity actually characteristic of an "opening." But, if that was the case, then what was the status of the utterance in French? It too had qualified; nothing in its initial evaluation had been wrong. But between it and the realization of its (?)perlocutionary force stood the second utterance. And the two sentences were not symmetrical translations of each other: one spoke of the Games of the 21st Olympiad, accurately placing the event within the four-year-interval method of calculating time characteristic of Olympic chronometry since its revival in 1896, while the other numbered the actual games that had taken place since 1896, omitting the games canceled by war in 1916, 1940, and 1944. Both sentences then referred to the same thing, although this "thing" was yet to be, but they were not, strictly speaking, in a relation of translation with each other. A similar asymmetrical construction governed the verb to "to celebrate": for the French, "nous" (whether audience-inclusive or royal-exclusive) celebrate the Games in Montreal, whereas for the English it is the Games which celebrate the Olympiad. How could the Queen be so perverse? Surely, she meant to "open" the Games, if for no other reason than to see her daughter defend the colors of the United Kingdom in the equestrian competition. Yet the whole thing had been flubbed. Confound Canadian bilingualism! The only solace to be found was in the decision of twenty-three nations to boycott the Games because of the International Olympic Committee's refusal to bar New Zealand from participation because its national rugby team was touring South Africa in violation of the international sports boycott of that country—but perhaps just because they were as bemused as the speech act theorist about the actual status of the Montreal Games: Had they actually been opened? If so at what point?

The predicament of the speech act theorist in this example of alternating Capitolian height and Tarpeian depth could be treated as a local one and, depending upon one's predilections, it could be used either for the confirmation of a prior rejection of the theory or for the elaboration of a better apparatus that would somehow, if not quite extricate the theory from this impasse, at least gain the assent of others that it had done so. But to restrict the impact of this instance of royal double-talk to speech act theory, whether from complacency or defensiveness, is to blunt the seriousness of the occurrence. For what matters here is that in spite of the fact that they were not properly "opened," the Games did take place: athletes competed, records fell, and even closing ceremonies, of equally dubious status, were held. If speech act theory were a theory at all, if a theory was at work here, then the failure to produce a correct or, as some linguists like to say, a grammatical, utterance of the "opening" should clearly have resulted in no Games at all. To be sure, one could explain the problem away by pointing out that the declaration of opening is but a ritual and that in our secularized world the outer forms of ritual suffice for its efficacy, but this merely displaces the ground of the explanation and leaves intact the problem of speech act theory.[4]

The question is of some importance because speech act theory has come to represent in contemporary thought about language a rare bulwark against a formalism preoccupied with the internal structures and functioning of language and discourse, and against all instrumental views of language that posit it as being in a secondary relation to whatever is defined as the primary (the psychological, the social, or whatever). Speech act theory has attempted to think language in a continuum with other aspects of human activity, thus providing speculative room for, among others, ethico-political dimensions of linguistic experience. The predicament raised by the opening declaration(s) of the Montreal Olympics relegates it to the status of poetry or philosophy in Aristotle's *Poetics* (§9, 1451 a36–1451 b11), where these two discursive practices are defined, in opposition to history, by their separation from the world of actuality. For any theory of language that does not start out with formalistic assumptions, this is a deadly blow, for it makes language and its internal constituents the limits of its inquiry. Whether speech act theory can extricate itself from this predicament is a question best left to its practitioners;[5] what matters more to those of us concerned with the possibility of a practice of literary criticism is to understand both how such a predicament has come about and what it signifies for our own activity.

I

Followers of the recent critical scene in the United States will have no difficulty in identifying the paradigm of the predicament: Two equally well formed linguistic entities occur in juxtaposition in such a way that they are mutually contradictory and require an interpretive decision in favor of the one or the other, yet no possibility of making such a decision exists. This is the paradigm of aporia;[6] sometimes it is identified with deconstruction, but the appropriateness of that designation is very much open to question.[7] It ought to be stressed also, and this fact is generally forgotten in discussions of aporia, that the indecision is a readerly one only, for the text, just as the Olympics did in the previous example, simply proceeds along with nary a notice of the problem.

The most meticulous thinker of aporia has been Paul de Man, who, trained in techniques of close reading at Harvard and in philosophical inquiry in Europe, began to explore the possibility of a critical practice based upon its most fundamental act: reading. In a series of papers written during the sixties, de Man analyzed the reading practices of prominent critics and critical schools and, finally, upon encountering Jacques Derrida's *De la Grammatologie,* formulated the question of "the future possibility of literary criticism" (*Blindness and Insight,* p. 111; hereafter *BI*). To some, it has not always been apparent what the answer to that question has been; yet the very fact that de Man went on subsequently to write *Allegories of Reading* and to work on other projects ought to serve as a clue, and, given the persistence of the question, encourage those concerned to examine his handling of the issue. I shall follow then the emergence of the question of a critical practice grounded in reading to its full discussion in the crucial essay of *Blindness and Insight,* "The Rhetoric of Blindness: Jacques Derrida's Reading of Rousseau" (*BI*, pp. 102–141).

It is well known that in the essays devoted to American New Criticism, Binswanger, Lukács, Blanchot, and Poulet, which came to be published as a lengthy introduction to "The Rhetoric of Blindness," de Man applied his considerable exegetical powers to discern in every case a "flagrant contradiction" (*BI*, p. 27) between the central critical achievement of these critics and the means by which they had obtained it. A single example suffices: Examining the methodological claims of American New Criticism, de Man identifies the role played by "intentional fallacy" in the metapractical thought of these critics. Drawing upon his ample knowledge of phenomenology, he easily demonstrates that the concept of intentionality meant to be exorcised by the intentional fallacy is a thoroughly misunderstood one, although it plays a foundational role in establishing the poem as a thing, that is, as an autonomous entity possessing unity. Intentional fallacy is then further seen as the very device which allows the claim to autonomy of the poem to rest upon a Coleridgian notion of organic unity. But in Coleridge himself, de Man is quick to show, the notion of organic unity requires the concomitant notion of the will, which is nothing but a properly understood concept of intentionality. If, at this juncture in de Man's analysis, the New Critics appear to be in somewhat of a critical quagmire, having first misunderstood intention and then failed to grasp that organic unity required intentionality, they nevertheless go on, like the Olympic Games, to their major achievements: The application of the techniques of close reading to works assumed to be free-standing and unitary produces a plurality of significations and, against all expectations, makes the New Critics celebrants of irony and ambiguity.

Similar patterns of a movement in the thought of the critics he reads emerge from the other analyses: An initial claim resting upon a misunderstanding or a particularly repressed content is shown to have made possible, once its full force is unveiled by de Man, the very achievements of the critics. De Man is not content merely to follow this movement; he shows not only the originating error but also whence it came: for example, the New Critics mistook their own projection of the totalization characteristic of interpretation for a property of the text which they then had to see as unity. A more dramatic critic, and one more mindful of academic power games, might have used the acuity of his analyses to invalidate the claims of his predecessors and to disqualify them. But de Man, with commendable, and characteristic, restraint, refrained from any such course and chose instead to interrogate the very recurrence of a pattern in which the best critics of the day seemed "curiously doomed to say something quite different from what they meant to say" (*BI*, pp. 105–106).

Paul de Man had begun his meditation on the significance of this pattern in one of his early essays, reviewing Heidegger's reading of Hölderlin ("Heidegger's Exegeses of Hölderlin"; hereafter HEH). As is his wont, de Man is quick to show that Heidegger misreads Hölderlin, yet the misreading is productive: Heidegger claims that, in conformity with his own thinking about the relation of language to Being, Hölderlin's poetry successfully "names" Being through poetic naming; this claim is not borne out by Hölderlin's text, and in that sense Heidegger is quite wrong. What actually occurs in Hölderlin's poems is that the attempt to name Being is constantly thwarted, caught up in a series of intervening stages of mediation which not only postpone the naming of Being but deny its very possibility. Again, de Man's reading is so persuasive that his reader is a little taken aback when, in the concluding pages of the essay, de Man praises Heidegger: Heidegger may indeed have been wrong on the actual success or failure of Hölderlin's poetic project, but it is his great merit to have identified this project as the desire to name Being. And lest his reader attribute such a statement to an observance of the conventions of polite reviewing, de Man formulates this early view of the problem of reading and criticism: Error need not be fatal to the critic as long as his reading represents a grasp of the problematic at hand. Heidegger may stand at the opposite end of Hölderlin, and in that he is quite wrong; but he has gotten hold of the right vector to Hölderlin, and a second reader, in this instance de Man, can correct Heidegger's apprehension. "To say the opposite is still to be talking about the same thing" (HEH, p. 809): This statement sums up de Man's early view of the dialectically productive power of error.

What is striking, yet frequently unappreciated, about de Man's procedure is its almost obsessive preoccupation with truth. It is quite clear that in the Heidegger/Hölderlin essay, for example, de Man follows standard scientific procedure and, attempting to falsify, in the technical sense of the term, Heidegger's claims, immediately succeeds. Rigorously analyzing the scope of his falsification, he limits it to the specific evaluation of Hölderlin's project and thus shows that the discovery of the project remains as the valid part of Heidegger's claims. At this stage, de Man's conception of his own activity seems to be governed by almost Popperian concepts of truth and falsehood, and his notion of critical writing, a version of scientific theory building. Yet, as a phenomenologist rather than an analytical philosopher, de Man sees this slightly differently, or more precisely, focuses on the process rather than the result.

The granting of truth-value status to a proposition represents one's free agreement to that proposition, a free agreement which can be granted only after careful deliberation. It is the very freedom of the thinker which is implied in such a process, for to agree to a proposition under some form of coercion is to alienate oneself in the agreement. This free agreement to a proposition represents, then, the preservation of one's self, one's very own identity, at the crucial moment when that self is challenged by the unknown where thought is leading it. The mechanism of the agreement is then also a mechanism for the preservation of one's self as same, indeed for the reduction to sameness of all that which in its radical otherness would challenge the self and perhaps lead to its fragmentation or cleavage. Metacritical thought, if one is allowed this term to designate an activity, such as de Man's in the Heidegger/Hölderlin essay, thus seeks to establish truth-value testing as a means for the creation of an intellectual space in which certitude would obtain, where the self, in full grasp of the prop-

ositions to which it acquiesces, could deploy its thought freely. Metacritical thought, like philosophy, would, by reducing the other to the
same, eliminate obstacles to thought and thus render thought free.
Thought could then roam through the realm of being, and indeed invest more and more of it, in a process deployed in History. In this view
nothing happens to the Self: actions take place, events occur, time pas-
ses; yet the Self remains it-self, its very own Self, same unto itself. The
transitory is merely the dimension of its history.

For this type of thought, the autonomy provided by freedom is crucial.[8] The irruption of any new foreign datum is immediately perceived
as an obstacle to be overcome and integrated, and truth is the mechanism of this overcoming and integration. The potential violence of the
encounter with the external is deflected by turning the external into
evidentiary matter, which preserves the Self as knowing subject exer-
cising its cognitive ability freely. External realities may threaten this
freedom, but truth allows the Self to comprehend them and to contain
them. As Kierkegaard had observed, this notion of truth is totally removed from that of revealed truth or indeed from any revelation or
encounter with the divine. It deals only with the Socratic version of
the already known which merely needs to be discovered or found (invented) in the Self, which serves as the mold of any unknown. But a
phenomenological analysis of truth opens up yet another space, the
space of experience. Truth requires the thinker to enter into a relation
with a reality distinct from his own. We do not gain any experience
unless we are brought beyond our familiar horizons. The movement
of truth requires a transportation of the Self away from its intimate
surroundings, from the space of sameness, to a beyond. Truth implies
then not merely an exteriority which would serve as the (necessarily
temporary) boundary of the realm of the Same, but a genuine beyond,
that of transcendence, which would not be content merely to challenge the Self but would oppose to it its radical indifference, threaten
it with a capacity for unstoppable irruption. The transcendent remains foreign and maintains, like Hölderlin's Being, its singularity.[9]

A practice of literary criticism grounded in reading will have to have
recourse, in varying degree, to both modes of conceiving truth. Insofar
as the critic's own text seeks to account for a reading, or becomes the
space where a reading deploys itself, it must first command the critic's
assent to the propositions he or she formulates regarding the text read.
A more phenomenological criticism, such as that of Georges Poulet,
for instance, will attempt to capture the experience of a radical oth-

erness by opening itself up to the constitutive elements of the other's text. Any reflection upon the truth value of critical statements will eventually encounter these modalities singly and in combination.

De Man's early encounter with the problem in the Heidegger/Hölderlin essay was simple enough. Entirely circumscribed within the conception of truth as free agreement, he merely had to correct dialectically Heidegger's error by revising his assessment of Hölderlin's attempt to name Being. But in de Man's essays of the 1960s, correction through dialectics does not prove possible: the New Critics do not come to uncover ambiguity and irony in poetic texts by means of an error which can be reversed dialectically; rather, they do so by means of an "error" which must be maintained as such, whose truth they must not recognize in order to reach their judgments. With respect to the conceptual system which establishes the organic unity of the text, the discovery of textual polysemy takes on the form of an irruption which is unexplainable. De Man can explain it by showing that the exclusionary gesture of the intentional fallacy permits the occult return of intentionality as the guarantor of organic unity and, therefore, authorizes the application of techniques of close reading, which in turn lead to the overturning of unity by discovering textual ambiguity and irony. This final step does not lead to the affirmation of the intentional fallacy, for it remains quite unexamined and still shrouded in misprision, nor does it lead to its renewed rejection: the inaugural gesture of exclusion is too foundational to be repeated. De Man can describe and explain this sort of pattern as he unveils it in his readings of the other critics; yet the explanations remain conjunctural, accounting for the specific form in which the problem arose. Were it random, this would be the proper way of proceeding, but the very recurrence of the pattern suggests that a more powerful explanation is to be sought, one which would attempt to account for the nature of this mechanism. De Man came upon such an explanation in Jacques Derrida's *De la Grammatologie*,[10] but its very power required a number of precautions.

II

De La Grammatologie presents itself as a book in two parts: the first, roughly one-third of the total length, serves as a general theoretical introduction to the problematics of logocentrism, while the second is devoted to what appears to be a more historical approach to the epoch of logocentrism, centered upon Rousseau, a writer who also held con-

siderable interest for de Man, as part of his own project of a "historical reflection on Romanticism" (*Allegories of Reading*, p. ix). But this
apparent structure is misleading: the Rousseau section starts with a
lengthy discussion of Claude Lévi-Strauss and additional theoretical
considerations, the most important of which, for our purposes, occurs
at the very center of the book (*G*, 226–234; 157–164) under the sub-
heading: "The Exorbitant Question of Method." Anyone even mar-
ginally acquainted with Derrida's thought[11] will not fail to be struck
by the irony of having the question of method placed under the rubric
of the exorbitant, and then the compounded irony of the exorbitant
occurring at the very center of the book.

"The Exorbitant Question" is a meditation upon reading. In a book
ostensibly concerned with writing, the question of reading arises in
the context of a discussion of the mediations which mark the gap
between "total absence and the absolute plenitude of presence" (*G*,
226; 157). Rousseau himself rejects explicitly the recourse to mediations; instead, his impatience at not being able to locate himself in
either absence or plenitude seeks a derivative, what Derrida, following
Rousseau, calls a "supplement."[12] The supplement comes to hold the
middle between total absence and presence: "le supplément tient ici
le milieu entre l'absence et la présence totales" (*G*, 226; 157). External
to the given of the problem, the supplement is there first to appease
Rousseau's impatience and then, more important, to appease the concept of the intermediary: "La virulence de ce concept est ainsi apaisée
comme si on avait pu l'arraisonner, le domestiquer, l'apprivoiser" (*G*,
226). The translator renders this difficult sentence as: "The virulence
of this concept is thus appeased, as if one were able to arrest it, domes-
ticate it, tame it" (*G*, 157). Which is close enough except for the term
arraisonner, which does not mean "to arrest" but, rather, is a naval
term describing the action of boarding a suspect vessel and conducting
an inspection. But it is clear that beside this scheme of policing, Derrida sought to force the French language to yield a term which would
describe a mode of apprehension by reason *(raison)* similar in scope
and effect to the German philosophical *begreifen*, whose role in the
constitution of the concept *(Begriff)*, as a seizing by reason, is well
known. But, as language would have it, the term, of considerable antiquity,[13] is in its maritime context a catachresis: its earliest meaning
had little to do with order on the high seas though a great deal with
smuggling: it meant "to seek to persuade"[14] and designated the very
project of rhetoric.

The meditation upon reading, upon "our reading" as Derrida

writes (*G*, 226; 158), is thus marked from its inception by the problem
of mapping that gap which is marked by the absence of the text read
and its total presence. The reading, which is designed to serve as a
mediation to the text's solidary conjunction of absence and presence,
is itself caught between the ability to subject to scrutiny implied by
the inspection which follows the boarding and the displacement effected by the rhetorical project. What is the "task of reading" then?

> Reading must always aim at a certain relationship, unperceived by
> the writer, between what he commands and what he does not com-
> mand of the patterns of the language that he uses. This relationship
> is not a certain quantitative distribution of shadow and light, of
> weakness or of force, but a signifying structure that critical reading
> should produce. (*G*, 227; 158)

Derrida is acutely aware of the possible misprisions which the word
"produce" may engender and, therefore, attempts to foreclose them
through a *via negativa* in which he rejects the reproducing commentary as well as the so-called transgression of the text toward an external referent. This leads to the famous "il n'y a pas de hors-texte" (*G*,
227; 158). The reading must remain immanent; it must not let itself
slowly drift toward the uncovering of the presumed content, the transcendental signified: "Literary writing has . . . lent itself to this transcendent reading, in that search for the signified which we here put
into question, not to annul it but to understand it within a system to
which such a reading is blind" (*G*, 229; 160). The system of the writing which carries the assertory content of the writing is occulted in
this very content and may be, indeed generally is, at odds with it, for
it is caught within the closure of logocentrism. The task of reading,
insofar as it is a productive one, is to spell out the relationship between
the asserted and the system of the writing which asserts it: "what
Rousseau has said, as philosopher, or as psychologist, of writing in
general, cannot be separated from the system of his own writing" (*G*,
230; 160). Reading then occupies a locus which is both necessary for
the articulation of the asserted to writing, and yet whose explicit articulation ruptures that first articulation, deconstructing the totality of
logocentrism which guaranteed it. To the extent that such a reading
traces a path around that totality according to a logic which exceeds
the logic of logocentrism, it is by necessity exorbitant. In the reading
of Rousseau the path of the exorbitant is already traced by the supple-

ment, which also both occupies the locus of the mediation and exceeds the system of mediation.

The reading of Rousseau remains immanent to the text insofar as the text no longer constitutes a fixedness inhabited by a transcendental meaning to be divined, but, rather, marks the space of an operativity to which Derrida gives the name of textuality. But this operativity is not simple. By virtue of its exorbitant path, which carries it beyond the laws of logocentrism (such as identity, in this instance), the supplement does not remain stable but exploits "the virtualities of meaning" (*G*, 234; 163). This is a genuine production, Derrida insists, for it not only does not "duplicate what Rousseau thought of this relationship," but is rendered necessary by the fact that the relationship is never articulated in Rousseau's text:

> The concept of the supplement is a sort of blind spot [*tache aveugle*] in Rousseau's text, the not-seen that opens and limits visibility. But the production, if it attempts to make the not-seen accessible to sight, does not leave the text. Moreover, it is only by illusion that it has ever believed that it was doing so . . . What we call production is necessarily a text, the system of a writing and a reading about which we know a priori, but only now and only through a knowledge which is no longer knowledge, that they are ordered around their own blind spot. (*G*, 234; 164; translation modified)

I have followed Derrida's text at some length with a reproductive commentary because it is a section of *De La Grammatologie* which has escaped the attention it deserves; moreover, and more to the point of our project, de Man's relation to the exorbitant is far from simple, even upon first examination.

The movement of Derrida's argument is caught entirely in what could be described as a diacritical gesture: on page 227 the project is formulated of opening a space of reading under the name of "task of reading": *une tâche de lecture;* seven pages later, the project is brought to its conclusion and the space of reading is opened around its ordering principle: [*une*] *tache aveugle,* "a blind spot." The task of reading consists, then, in opening up a space which reveals a blind spot, just as the literal losing of a circumflex accent, shaped like an overhanging roof, turns the purposeful activity of imposing a tax on the text ("task" derives from "tax") into a blind spot. The irruption of blindness in reading is the result of Derrida's meditation, and de Man has no difficulty in recognizing in the complex interplay of blindness and insight the mechanism of the pattern which he has been encountering. Generally unaware of the close proximity of "The Exorbitant Question" and de Man's own rhetoric of "blindness and insight," most readings of "The Rhetoric of Blindess: Jacques Derrida's Reading of Rousseau" have tended to valorize the second part of de Man's essay, where, most brilliantly, he is seen as at once refuting Derrida's evaluation of Rousseau as blinded by/to his own textuality and asserting that this is but a ploy on Derrida's part to deconstruct the critical tradition of Rousseau by means of Rousseau himself. This last point is generally taken to be de Man's master stroke, for it is seen as advancing ironically a reading of Derrida to which Derrida can only assent. Such readings of the essay may not have heeded a Pascalian injunction which de Man adopts as the epigraph to *Allegories of Reading*: "Quand on lit trop vite ou trop doucement on n'entend rien."

At its most obvious, what needs to be remarked first is de Man's embrace of the logic of blindness and insight to describe the complex processes of meaning formation in the critics he studied.[15] The first ten pages of "The Rhetoric of Blindness" are devoted to a retrospective discussion of the previous essays from the vantage point of the new terminology, effectively turning them into an introduction to the essay on Derrida. Recognizing the dialectical potential of a concept such as blindness, de Man starts out with insight and formulates the nature of the mechanism that has been producing the pattern he has been encountering:

> Their [the critics he studies] critical stance . . . is defeated by their own critical results. A penetrating but difficult insight into the nature of literary language ensues. It seems, however, that this insight could only be gained because the critics were in the grip of this peculiar blindness: their language could grope toward a certain degree of insight only because their method remained oblivious to the perception of this insight. (*BI*, p. 106)

What is less obvious is that the adoption of the blindness and insight paradigm as descriptor of a structure and its operations does not imply a similar adoption of Derrida's entire theory of reading. This is particularly difficult to argue, let alone demonstrate, because Derrida's theory was already defined negatively, and de Man's treatment proceeds mainly by selective use of silence. These are not preciosities of style, but indications of the complexity of the matter.

De Man subjects to silence the guiding principle of Derrida's meditation upon reading: production. The last sentence of "The Exorbitant Question" bears a more careful examination:

> What we call production is necessarily a text, the system of a writing and of a reading about which we know a priori, but only now and only through a knowledge which is no longer knowledge, that they are ordered around their own blind spot. (*G*, 234; 164; translation mine)

Production was a term very much in vogue at the time Derrida wrote *De la Grammatologie,* most notably among his early boosters in the *Tel Quel* group, who used it in what they claimed was a Marxist sense. Textual production, as the origination of the text under analysis, was being defined as the project of a criticism which would move beyond the synchronic descriptive imperative of structuralism. Derrida writes of production otherwise: It is a text itself, and it alters knowledge to such an extent that it is knowable to a knowledge which is no longer knowledge. In other words, production opens up the question of knowledge and, through it, the question of truth. The classical structure of knowledge is articulated around a knowing subject who, in the act of knowing, takes possession of the object. Subject and object are both predetermined in their constitution and in their very relationship. The knowing subject encounters the object, takes hold of it through perception, formulates a proposition concerning the object, and then, in the act of judgment, freely assents to this proposition. We have seen this to be one of the modalities of truth. Derrida's critique of logocentrism deconstructs the solidary opposition of subject and object as well as the deliberative modality of truth. Rousseau's relation to the supplement is much more fluid than the subject/object relation allows, for neither "Rousseau" nor the "supplement" constitute stable entities but represent a lability capable of multiple configurations, in which the idea of one somehow seizing and possessing the other is hardly thinkable. Insofar as the operation of cognition is the experience of an otherness, it cannot be converted into a category whose recuperative movement would lead back to identity and identification. For the "knowing subject" there is no return to the point of departure. Textuality cannot be thought of as a form of energy which agitates a text but remains equal to itself.[16] Nor is it a technique for the reduction by means of a *via negativa* of the world of the Other to mine. Both of these conceptions continue logocentrism by affirming the sameness of being to itself and centering thought upon its own apprehension. The movement Derrida traced in the wake of the supplement is one which starts from the Identical in the direction of the Other but never returns to the Identical. To borrow a striking contrast: "to the myth of Ulysses returning to Ithaca, we would oppose the story of Abraham leaving forever the land of his fathers for a country still unknown, and forbidding his servant to ever bring back even his son to the point of departure."[17]

The cognition which occurs here is of a different order from that proposed by the classical structure of knowledge. Whereas the latter had always been governed by a certain *skopia,* a sight which seizes a totality in its interpreting glance, the former resembles more a blind groping of something radically unknown.[18] Such a palpation is not gratuitous or playful; it does result in a certain kind of cognition, sometimes even in knowledge when the thing is identified, when it becomes an object. Yet what happens is that, as in the case of any radical experience, we speak more of the experience as event, as epiphany of the other, than anything else. Production begins to take on the meaning of pro-duction, a bringing forth of the Other, of the transcendental. But the very deconstruction of logocentrism undertaken by Derrida has insisted on the solidarity of the concept of the transcendental with the other structural concepts of logocentrism, and thus it is not possible that Derrida meant by production the irruption of the transcendental, at least not the transcendental as logocentrism has known it. That is why, for Derrida, pro-duction is necessarily a text, that is, a mode of inscription of a transcendental, not ontological but grammatologic, which does not overhang the text in the way that, in its classical conception, the signified dominates the signifier, but rather is the disruptive operativity which, just at the moment when a hermeneutic and an exegesis have peeled away the cultural determinations of the text and begun to seize it as a totality, radically disrupts it by putting us in touch with the blind spot at its core.

Why is it that de Man does not assume, along with the blind spot, the discussion of the task of reading as production? As one might by now expect, the matter is not broached directly, but there is no lack of clues. To begin with, even though écriture as advanced by Derrida is not a phenomenal entity,[19] the recourse to production permits misreadings in that direction. For de Man "a literary text is not a phenomenal event that can be granted any form of positive existence, whether as a fact of nature or as an act of the mind. It leads to no transcendental perception, intuition or knowledge but merely solicits an understanding that has to remain immanent because it poses the problem of its intelligibility in its own terms" (*BI*, p. 107). In other words, a text is neither a production, in the sense of the manufacture of an artifact, nor a pro-duction. De Man means to exorcise the possibility of a return to the phenomenal: "However negative it may sound, deconstruction implies the possibility of rebuilding" (*BI*, p. 149). Not that he misunderstands deconstruction, which most emphatically does not imply, in the logical sense of the term, a rebuilding; but the dictionary term "deconstruction" inevitably suggests, by virtue of its semantic associations, the possibility of reconstruction and can, therefore, precipitate, as indeed it has, calls for a move "beyond deconstruction." It is precisely because he anticipates such calls that de Man means not to provide them with any ground for a toe-hold in his text. This raises a strategic question: how to attack logocentrism if a deconstruction can turn into a construction? Metaphysics, like a child's bounce-back dummy, is constantly being knocked down but just keeps standing up again, its fundamental ballast intact. How can one attempt to stand outside metaphysics when one remembers that the categorics of inside and outside are fundamental to, and governed by, metaphysics? De Man's reading of Derrida's theory of reading hinges on this strategic question.

Derrida's notion of production as pro-duction, and pro-duction as text, is, for all its precautions, still formulated within the orbit of the phenomenal and, therefore, risks leading back to it. It may, like Hölderlin's text which is incessantly traversed by the impossibility of naming Being, occasion a reading like Heidegger's which sees it as successfully achieving its goal. The movement of displacement which occurs in Derrida's text at the moment when the pro-duction of the transcendental undoes the transcendental and the phenomenal by stating that production is a text, is necessarily fraught with dangers for it could be read in the mode of loss, whereby the displacement would be categorized as an effect of the transcendental, which would leave the latter intact. As de Man reads it, what is required is a more explicit focusing on the question of knowledge. Thus, in the case of Rousseau, Derrida's "structurization of Rousseau's text in terms of a presence-absence system leaves the cognitive system of deliberate knowledge versus passive knowledge unresolved and distributes it evenly on both sides" (*BI*, p. 118)—which is in accordance with Derrida's general project, adds de Man, but may permit the kinds of misreadings we have been concerned with.

What de Man calls the "cognitive system," and I have been referring to as the two modalities of truth, has certain implications for the manner in which one conducts an argument, that is, one's textual strategy. Truth as manifestation, in Derrida's argument: as pro-duction, immediately before it is asserted that it is a text, presupposes the occurrence of instances of epiphany which can be recorded. It partakes of the characteristics of a sacred history in which the irruption or the manifestation of the divine marks moments of plenitude and articulated stages in a history which holds the promise of ultimate revelation. Derrida's text follows the structure of such a movement and, therefore, adopts narrative as its fundamental device. Of course, in the end, this movement is shown to lead to production as text, and, therefore, to have been proceeding in a certain blindness—not Derrida's, who knew that this is no end, that there is no end, but for the reader who is conditioned to expect ends for narratives, even if they have to take the form of interruption.

We have seen that the other modality of truth, in which thought invests the realm of being, is also dependent upon narrative: The progressive conquest of being by reason requires the chronicling of its expansion. History as science, what Heidegger calls *Historie,* is indeed born from the historicity of presence *(Geschichtlichkeit)* and, therefore, is located within logocentrism.[20] Derrida's dilemma is that to make logocentrism manifest, he must tell its history, or as de Man, eager to stress the dependence upon narrative form, puts it, its "story" *(BI,* p. 119). Derrida's double dependence upon narrative permits the contamination of his deconstruction by logocentrism. Already, in his essay on Blanchot, de Man had noted that at times narrative must be held in check *(BI,* p. 78), not that it is incapable of insight, but, rather, that the insight it provides is brought forth in blindness. To continue to speak though of "insight brought forth in blindness" is to continue being dependent upon narrative and redoubling the process, taking refuge in a structure of *mise-en-abyme* which in turn requires a reversal of polarities of height and depth for the illusory avoidance of new blindness. This is the path of endless repetition and regression.

De Man returns to the non-phenomenality of the text instead, for it provides not an outside to this problematic but rather a structurally indeterminate moment which is not a locus. Just as in the verb *arraisonner,* the moment of mastery by reason is profiled on the horizon, yet it has not occurred, one is in an in-between which is not a mediation, for it turns out that the bringing forth to reason, *a-raison-er,* does not obey the logic of reason but is the realm of rhetoric. Rhetoric, as hardly needs repeating, bears only a distant relationship to truth. As a technique based upon the study of causes insofar as they produce effects of persuasion, it permits the handling of words without concern for the handling of things or objects. It permits an autonomous functioning of discourse without depriving it of effectiveness. We have seen that *arraisonner*, in Derrida's text, marks the very moment when the supplement substitutes itself to the intermediary; in this metabola, it is mediation itself which is exceeded; a dimension which is no longer just an in-between is opened. The violence of the intermediary is contained, but through a violence of a different sort. Whereas the first endangered discourse, the latter preserves itself at the cost of nearly everything else. In the little allegory of the word, it is the operation of boarding the ship that smuggles in the contraband, with all the trappings of legitimacy at its disposal. It is precisely because all is confined to the discursive that it is already in the text; no irruption takes place, nor is there need to presuppose any outside. It is, at once and seamlessly, part of the discourse in which it finds itself and a subversion of that discourse, yet without any of the peripeteia or agonistics of narrative. *Arraisonner* is marked by what de Man calls its "rhetoricity": "any text that implicitly or explicitly signifies its own rhetorical mode and prefigures its own misunderstanding as the correlative of its rhetorical nature" (*BI*, p. 136). De Man will come to claim that such a rhetoricity is at work in both Rousseau's and Derrida's texts. Tactically, this resolution, if one can call it that, emerges with some difficulty, for de Man has to introduce the question of rhetoric in his own text via Derrida's assessment of Rousseau's statements on the figurality of language.[21] But the difficulty is worthwhile, for it avoids the pitfalls of production.

III

Nicht durch Zorn, sondern durch Lachen tödtet man.   *F. Nietzsche*

De Man is able to state that Derrida's "chapter on method, on literary interpretation as deconstruction, is flawless" (*BI*, p. 139) because he sees the rhetoricity of Derrida's own text as leading him to adopt the strategy of narrative deployment for his argument:

Throughout, Derrida uses Heidegger's and Nietzsche's fiction of metaphysics as a period in Western thought in order to dramatize, to give tension and suspense to the argument, exactly as Rousseau gave tension and suspense to the story of language and of society by making them pseudo-historical. Neither is Derrida taken in by the theatricality of his gesture or the fiction of his narrative. (*BI*, p. 137)

However, as de Man's "corrective" reading of Derrida's handling of figurality in Rousseau demonstrates, Derrida's procedure is not without risks. De Man may claim that the question of his own blindness is "one which he is by definition incompetent to ask" (*BI*, p. 106), yet we may assume that it has received his attention. An indication is provided in the only evaluative statement which does not praise Derrida in the essay: Rousseau harbors no hope that he could escape misunderstanding; "he cuts himself off once and forever from all future disciples. In this respect, Derrida's text is less radical, less mature than Rousseau's" (*BI*, p. 140). As the context of the discussion makes clear, it is the fact that Rousseau did not seek to "correct" those he polemicized with, but rather sought to indict language itself, which earns him the accolade refused to Derrida. Derrida's deconstructive enterprise, as radical as it may seem to us, is not radical enough for de Man, for it is still inscribed within the historical fiction of the epoch of metaphysics. To treat logocentrism as an epoch, in the wake of Heidegger and Nietzsche, is to still hold out for a possibility of undeceived language. From de Man's perspective, such a possibility is still maintained in Derrida's text, however much it may be barred by the deconstructive gesture, by the structural focus upon écriture, a focus with respect to which the question of reading is exorbitant.

Since écriture is not a concept, it is not amenable to dialectical "correction" through reading, which is not a concept either. Rather, since écriture requires the deployment of a narrative—the story of logocentrism, only a different story—the story of reading can be juxtaposed to it. But, as de Man reminds us, "unlike epistemological statements, stories do not cancel each other out" (*BI*, p. 119), and he chooses not to give us this story. Since, however, his reluctance has led many to attempt to write the story of a "beyond deconstruction," I shall have no such qualms, and fewer illusions.

Philosophical thought arises historically, but, from the moment of its emergence, it seeks to define itself as a form of cognition which would be based on a first principle understood as the foundation of

all forms of being and thought. Philosophical thought is thus in a
quandary from its inception: It must grant the status of philosophical
question to the very circumstances which gave rise to it while formulating the mode of philosophical questioning as independent of any
contingent considerations. In the *Phenomenology of Mind*, Hegel proposes to address this difficulty by starting with the recognition of contingent phenomenal knowledge and contingent natural consciousness,
and advancing the hypothesis that it is by the experience of thought
upon the totality of the contingent that we reach the universal. In this
manner the contingency of the historical is not an irreducible obstacle
but a necessary stage in the constitution of the universal. This solution
requires, however, the positioning or the importation of a first principle which will ground both knowledge and its object; otherwise
an endless dialogue will ensue. This principle is found in the transcendental possibility, that is, in the capacity of natural consciousness to
transcend phenomenal knowledge. In our tradition, and at least since
Descartes, the transcendental possibility has been conceived of as the
subject, which constitutes the locus from which the question can be
decided under the form of truth. We rejoin here the world of logocentrism, equally based upon the assumption of an identity of thought
and being.

But the identity of thought and being is not immediate; otherwise
the problem would not have arisen immediately, nor would philosophy have had any historical roots. As Hegel thinks of mediation, it is
based upon the recognition of the contingency of the contingent. The
mode of my being in the world translates itself through actions which
I undertake and by which I transform both the world and myself; but
what matters in such a formulation is that, in each case, the instrument of the action is mediated: I am the instrument of the transformation of the world, and it is through this externality that I transform
myself. Mediation is a structure of indirection. Thought proceeds in
similar fashion since consciousness apprehends itself only as consciousness of something else. In ordinary thinking, natural consciousness does not keep track of this mediation. It takes itself as immediate
consciousness of the external. It is only in a movement of return upon
itself that reflection, as mediated reflection upon itself apprehends this
movement. This leads to the reexamination of truth, for if, in the first
instance, truth was the adequation of thought to being, but thought
and being are mediations of each other, then the propositions of truth
are valid only insofar as we reproduce their conditions of emergence.

But—and here the paradox grows—this is nothing more than a primary utterance forgotten by simple reflection. The forgetfulness of simple reflection consists in the fact that it tends to lose itself in its object; it can regain its status as reflection only by means of a second reflection, one which can pretend to truth only insofar as it monitors its own condition of emergence. But this, in turn, implies that propositions have only locally determined meaning, so that all that is given up is the claim to totality, universality, and transcendence. Expectations are scaled down, but the basic mechanism is left intact. This possibility was already envisaged by Hegel, who recognized that the apparatus of the absolute remains absolute, and that it functions no less because its *deus* has become *absconditus*. Local mediations draw their power and are authorized by absolute mediation.

This moment, which takes the form of a structured opposition between the age of the symbol and that of allegory in Gadamer,[22] immediately suggesting a historical periodization, places us in the epoch which lives in the age of the ruin of the symbolic. What then are our options? One is the Marxian, which, refusing this periodicity, proceeds from the recognition that the totalization did not in fact occur and abandons description for prescription. The identity of ontological thought has never been realized; praxis and thought have not been united. Let us seek this identity and this unity, but in the meantime, recognize that the claim that it has occurred opens up the space of the ideological by occulting contradictory social reality.

Another avatar is the attempt through various neo-Kantianisms to reopen the epistemological question in such a way that the concept of identity becomes part of the very project of knowledge conceived of as the dimension of life (for example, Dilthey). This culminates in Heidegger's effort to describe understanding as the very mode of being in *Dasein,* a proposition upon which Gadamer would build his hermeneutics. In this instance, the hermeneutic moment coincides with the second reflection which redresses the structure of prejudgment *(Vorverständnis),* which has been carried out in predetermined form by language, texts, and tradition. An unresolvable dialogue, rendered endless by our finitude, ensues. But the moment that a form of prejudgment or prejudice is elevated to the rank of principle of comprehension, it permits forms of existential commitments which will require in turn a new form of enlightenment. And since the problem can now be reformulated within the framework of a communicational model that would ensure the formation of correct understanding through proper communicational procedures, then various forms of pragmatics, that is, sciences of speech in action, will come to the fore, for they alone can determine the conditions of successful communication, where success is measured by the realization of the identity of the speaking subject. Thus, in order not to return to the Queen of England who also sometimes speaks as the Sovereign of Canada, we may give exemplary status to Jürgen Habermas's attempt to determine, on the basis of a second reflection, the constitutive and regulative principle of all communication.[23] Truth is achieved by discursive consensus, and its validity is assured by the invocation of an ideal communication situation which relies on the operation of contrafactual falsification to detect shortcomings in its constitution. Once again, we have truth as adequation. Once again we are locked into perpetual discussion and infinite dialogue. Once more we are in logocentrism.

My narrative is sketchy, and it is built of propositions each of which would require voluminous demonstration. But it does lead us back, following the erection and simultaneous collapse of the Hegelian enterprise, to the inescapable conclusion that any history of philosophy is a philosophy of history and, therefore, also a theory of narrative. More discouragingly, it shows that the structure of logocentrism is at work more than ever in the discourse of philosophy after Rousseau, and that current attempts, including those on the so-called New Left, are mired in the same problematic, that is, the problematic of the same. One indeed cannot oppose a story which would cancel the story of logocentrism. De Man, therefore, does not write this story, nor does he seek to produce it. He reads instead, for there, in reading, is the space which renders such production unnecessary. A counter-story, an agonistics, only allows the terrible dialectic to work its wonders and to reduce to identity the seeming other. Reading, however, in the legitimate operation of boarding for inspection, smuggles in the contraband. But at what cost? it is now frequently asked. Derrida is domesticated by de Man's reading, tamed, and has lost his virulence. Yet it was not long ago that he asserted:

A deconstructive practice which would not bear upon "institutional apparatuses and historical processes" (to use your terms), which would remain content to operate upon philosophemes or conceptual signified, or discourses, etc., would not be deconstructive; whatever its originality, it would but reproduce the gesture of self-criticism in philosophy in its internal tradition. This was clear from the outset, from the minimal definition of deconstruction, which bore upon logocentrism, the last instance of meaning or of the "transcendental signified," the transcendental signifier, the last instance in general, etc.[24]

Is this Derrida tamed, domesticated? Only in the sense which those two terms can have in Derrida's text (G, p. 226), where they occur immediately after *arraisonner*. But that is another story.

11 The Semiotics of Semiotics

On September 28, 1982, there appeared in the *New York Times* an article on the subject of semiotics. This was a significant event, for it brought to the attention of the larger literate public a form of inquiry that is still far from having gained general acceptance in the academic world in which it is mostly practiced. But, to semioticians, the *Times*'s choice of location for the printing of the article was even more significant than the publication itself: it appeared within the pages of the Science supplement, appropriately called "Science Times." From its authoritative position, the *New York Times* appeared to have decided one of the longer-lasting controversies within the field: is semiotics a science? a discipline? or a mode of dealing with signification that cuts across disciplines? Since it is unlikely that the editor of "Science Times" was familiar with the intricacies of this debate, it may prove enlightening to inquire into the reasons that led him to include semiotics within the scope of science. For suddenly what is at stake here is no longer the status of claims made by semioticians about their own field, but rather the way in which that field is perceived and in which it makes sense to someone outside of it. In other words, what the *Times*'s report precipitated is the need for an inquiry into the semiotic status of semiotics.

The Crisis of Meaning and the Commodity

Boot Fetishism at the New York Times

The *Times* is a thorough newspaper: it knows what it wants and knows how to get it. The author of the article on semiotics, Maya Pines, spoke to many people calling themselves semioticians or so called by others. In every instance she asked them to define their field and to provide examples of what they did. She also asked them if they had anything "semiotic" to say about the fact that a number of erstwhile and affluent New Yorkers were wearing cowboy boots as part of their daily attire. In fact, the question is reproduced as the lead sentence of the article: "What does it mean when a man wears cowboy boots, even though he lives in a city?"[1]

It soon became apparent that this was far from an idle question. Pines and her editor had little patience with those explanations that related the wearing of cowboy boots in urban settings to machismo, American myths about the cowboy, or the desire for wide-open spaces. Such interpretations struck them as neither novel nor especially semiotic; they could have thought them up themselves, they argued, with a little help from scholars in American Studies or, more generally, from students of American culture. The semioticians interviewed were uneasy with the concentration on the boots, fearing that the example was too trivial, and offered instead to discuss matters more representative of semiotic inquiry, such as stop signs and their manufacture, table manners, or the conventions of landscape painting. But the *Times* was not to be deterred, and the matter was pursued until an explanation satisfactory to Pines and the editor was provided. Such doggedness in the pursuit of cowboy boots deserves some attention.

On Cowboy Boots

Before inquiring into the *Times*'s preoccupation and fascination with cowboy boots, it is necessary to restate, in a fuller version than was ultimately published, the explanation that satisfied "Science Times."

Cowboy boots, with their special cowhide, leather tooling, and design, have traditionally been part of the attire of the cowboy. Designed to be worn during lengthy sojourns on horseback, they had a specific use-value to the cowboy. Rapidly, together with other elements of the cowboy's dress (the hat, the belt, and the vest, in particular), they became emblematic of a certain mode of life and began to be adopted as the distinctive wear of certain regions of the United States: the West and the Southwest. In this guise, their value resided primarily in their signaling one's belonging to a larger community of individuals sharing a relation to the land and, presumably, some values; they were community-integrative.

In the 1970s, there opened up two additional avenues for the wearing of cowboy boots. The first was the relatively short-lived yet highly significant emergence of the long-distance trucker as a sort of cowboy of the highways. Depicted as a genuine working man, though in actual fact frequently self-employed or the equivalent, in the service sector, of a sharecropper, the trucker, as hero of country music and as the vehicle for the promotion of CB radios, was treated as a populist enemy of the system symbolized by the "bears" of the highway patrol, and of the regulatory power of government, most evident in the imposition of a lowered speed limit. As a wearer of cowboy boots he was, in the language of the article, "virile, self-reliant, and free to roam the open spaces" of America, like his mythical cowboy predecessor of Western romance and film. The myth of the trucker occulted the genuine crisis that was then shaking that sector of the economy: strikes, takeovers, and moves toward monopolization. Much of this resulted in violence in the mid-seventies, especially on the Pennsylvania Turnpike. But, of course, the largest crisis was due to the gasoline and diesel fuel shortages caused by the oil embargo and the ensuing imposition of controls over the supply of energy by the oil cartels. The cowboy boots were an ironic sign, since alongside their obvious reference to the overt features of the cowboy myth, they also seemed to allude to the less reassuring aspects of that myth by foretelling the obsolescence and eventual demise of the trucker, who may have had the desire to run (through) America but literally did not have the energy.

The second track was precisely the energy track. The boots, as part of the old Western gear, were inherited, and adopted, by the new oil and gas money-makers of the energy-producing states, to such an extent that not only the latter but those who, for professional reasons, came in contact with them began to wear cowboy boots, frequently of very expensive quality. Here another aspect of the boots—or, to speak the language of semiotics, another semic feature—was being reactivated: vitality, which, in the seventies and eighties, translated itself into the possession or the supplying of virtually limitless energy.

At this moment in time (1980–1981), then, cowboy boots constitute a rather complex and internally contradictory semiotic entity. They partake of all the following: the old American myth of the cowboy; the trucker's seemingly populist and semi-anarchic dream of unregulated wandering and enterprising; the *gemeinschaftlich* uniform of the West rising against Washington in the so-called "sagebrush rebellion"; and the new oil money effectively capturing the apparatus of the state with the election of a new President who, quite appropriately, ties these various strands together: he has played cowboys, comes from the West, owns a ranch, ran against the regulatory power of so-called "big government," was bankrolled by oil interests, and is frequently photographed wearing cowboy boots both functionally, in horseback riding, or socially, at Santa Barbara receptions.

It becomes clear that, with the final nudge into aesthetic conversion provided by John Travolta in *Urban Cowboy*, and with the sartorial extravagance authorized if not demanded by New York discotheques, a number of affluent New Yorkers who ordinarily cared and knew as much about cowboys as about cowpies could begin to adopt cowboy boots. As the article states quite accurately, "they, of course, do not want real cowboy boots, just the *idea* of cowboy boots. So they buy boots made of lizard and snake that serves as symbols or signs of cowboy boots, in which they can roam the city with a feeling of power, but which wouldn't be too much good for rounding up cattle." These boots, frequently costing over a thousand dollars a pair, serve then a phantasmatic integrative function that unites their wearers into some sort of brotherhood of mastery: those who handle the world masterfully. The New York wearer of boots is a latecomer to this amalgamation since his role was generally limited to *not* voting for Carter, thus permitting the election of Reagan in 1980. The purchase of the boots is his first affirmative act in this respect.

Crisis of Meaning

This answer was acceptable to Pines and to the "Science Times" editor, both in its own terms—it does explain the puzzling occurrence of expensive cowboy boots on some New Yorkers' feet—and as an example of semiotic analysis: scholars in American Studies could talk of the myth of the cowboy, psychologists, of the New Yorker's feeling of powerlessness, but the ability to weave complex historical and contemporary data with behavioral patterns, psychological motivations, political effects, and ideological resonances had to be the hallmark of a new science.

Semiotics had provided an answer to the question of what it means when a New Yorker wears cowboy boots in the city. But the question itself deserves scrutiny. Clearly, this sartorial development must have been very puzzling to "Science Times," since it was willing to grant its imprimatur to the explanatory and analytic system that accounted for it. I am going to suggest that this is because it was far more perceptive than many literary scholars, and indeed many semioticians, of something that has been going on around us without our being able or willing to recognize it, whereas "Science Times" not only did so but found its strategic location.

What has been going on is what the Germans have lately taken to calling a *Sinnkrise,* a crisis of meaning.[2] Its manifestations are multiform: the great explanatory systems of the West are felt to be inadequate, if not obsolete, whether they be of a social-democratic, Marxist, or bourgeois-liberal variety. The master narratives are dying for lack of credibility, as Jean-François Lyotard has argued in *The Postmodern Condition,*[3] and nothing is taking their place. Politics appear to take on more anarchic forms, or to adopt previously inconceivable dimensions. Here it will suffice to invoke the example of the emergence and rise of the Solidarity movement in Poland, a phenomenon that has proved to be beyond the explanatory powers or the conceptual scope of either the traditional Left or Right, and equally troublesome to both.

But a diagnosis formulated in such broad terms as the "crisis of meaning" does not lend itself to any sort of resolution, but, at best, a description of its etiology. What "Science Times" experienced was more specific, and therein lies its value: it felt the crisis as a crisis of a specific artifact, the cowboy boots, and we, in turn, can see this crisis as a more general, yet specific, crisis of the commodity. The *Times* could have seen it as a broad existential crisis, or as a mere fad, localized at that, or as a psychological condition affecting a restricted population, but it did not seek philosophical, sociological, group—or individual—psychological explanations. The mystery was *in* the boots, and the old reliable explanations of the behavior of commodities were inadequate to the mystery they posed. These boots were not part of that system of commodity behavior, and therefore a new explanatory regress had to arise to explain them. I belabor this point, for its significance can scarcely be exaggerated: such means as were available to "Science Times" for the uncovering, description, and analysis of the meaning of a certain commodity were unequal to the task. Given the role played by commodities, their production, distribution, and consumption, in our social life, such an inability was potentially catastrophic. Since these means (historico-cultural, economic, psychological, and so forth) had been developed in response to, and as an accompaniment to, the production of commodities, then their inadequacy in the instance of the cowboy boots logically suggested that these boots had gotten on New Yorkers' feet by means of a different mode of production, one that was unknown to "Science Times" as of yet, but which, the writer and editor correctly averred on the basis of their knowledge of the laws pertaining to modes of production, had also to have given rise to an explanatory system that could, among other things, explain the phenomenon they found so puzzling. And clearly, the descriptive and analytic regress of a mode of production deserves the name of *science*. The *New York Times* knows what it is doing.

We are led then at this juncture to the following set of considerations: if the "Science Times"'s intuition is correct, then we are presently dealing with a new mode of production; if we fail to describe it, then we shall certainly fail to understand what semiotics is all about. Thus the first task we face is an inquiry into, and a description of, this mode of production. It should be followed by an examination of the question whether semiotics is adequate to this mode of production, in the sense that it is its product as well.

This set of considerations has emerged as a complex configuration that necessarily poses itself historically. That gives rise to the further question as to whether semiotics is blind to its own historicity or, indeed, to all historicity, as some have claimed. Furthermore, we must also ask: what does the historical—which, if it is to be true to itself, must itself be historical and therefore must be considered, at least with some presumption, to be the product of an older mode of production—look like in semiotics if there is now a new mode of production in place?

A comprehensive answer to these questions cannot be given in these pages. I will limit myself to an examination of the following propositions: (1) that there is a shift in the mode of production; (2) that semiotics is somehow implicated in this shift; (3) that semiotics has its semiotic way of dealing with history. I would like to suggest at the outset, though, that, in my view, any practice of semiotics that fails to take the historical into consideration leads to scientistic, as opposed to scientific, semiotics and constitutes a misprision of its basis and scope.

The Mode of Production of Semiotics

Since my ultimate concerns are with literature, my discussion of the mode of production, though conducted in economic terms, will be aimed principally at the status of meaning in the mode of production. Such an approach is, in any case, further justified by the fact that it was in the form of a "crisis of meaning" that this mode of production disclosed itself to us in the first place.

Productive and Unproductive Labor

A discussion of the meaning of commodities must, in classical terms, invoke the value of commodities. The apparently self-evident notion that too high a price in relation to the use-value of a commodity inhibits its purchase is clearly challenged in the case of the cowboy boots New Yorkers wear to discotheques, theaters, and restaurants.

The discussion of value is best framed in terms of productivity. For classical economics, a product brings wealth if it increases the real salary of its recipient by making him or her more efficient. Strictly speaking, the degree of productivity is independent of the socioeconomic status of the producer, who may be an artisan, a salaried worker, or a mass production financier. For Marxist political economy, which starts from the point of departure of classical economics, value is produced only in the making of a material object by *salaried* individuals.

Such a formulation leads to a certain amount of conceptual difficulty when one attempts to think of the status of writers, composers, playwrights, and generally other producers of artistic artifacts as producers of market wealth. The difficulty lies in the applicability of the question of surplus-value to their productions: what kind of labor produces surplus value? This question in turn leads to the distinction between productive and unproductive labor, where the former is defined as labor that creates value and permits the accumulation of capital while the latter does not. In other words, productive labor leads to the growth of capital and the creation of surplus-value, while unproductive labor is of interest to the purchaser of labor only through the use-value of the product. For Marx, under capitalism only salaried individuals can be productive since, by selling their labor power, they create capital. As a result, and against the tenets of classical economics, unsalaried workers—those who receive royalties for example—or even salaried workers who create capital only implicitly, through the consumption implied in their activity, are not productive. They do create wealth within the capitalist mode of production, but it is a type of wealth that, properly speaking, is external to this mode. It is important to bear in mind that an activity that may promote consumption or production is not in itself productive of wealth in this analysis. (My subsequent discussion of the mode of production of repetition is indebted to Jacques Attali's reflections on the subject in connection with his theorizing on music.)[4]

Productive Unproductive Labor

A *locus classicus* of philosophy and political economy is the artisan who produces an artifact and proceeds to sell it. When I purchase a basket from a basket-weaver, I deal with him or her as a seller of merchandise and not as a seller of labor even though it is his or her labor that produced the basket. In this sense, an artisan is unproductive, although it would probably be better to say that the distinction between productive and unproductive labor is alien to this category of producers.

But what happens in the case of those producers we have identified as troublesome? Let us follow Attali's analysis of the musical composer who has written a song. Since she is paid by royalties, she is, technically, unproductive, yet her product is not fixed the way a basket is: it may be printed by salaried workers, sold to musicians, create surplus-value, and then a salaried musician may perform it, giving a formal representation of it. It is in fact in this performance that we feel that the song, as the composer's product, has truly come into its own. Yet, from the perspective that is ours here, the composer's status, and especially the status of her labor, leaves all of this quite perplexing with respect to the issue of productivity. Clearly the composer is at the origin of the process that leads to the performance; yet, just as clearly, since she sells her song against a part of the surplus-value obtained through the use-value of the song (the royalty on the performance), she is at once unproductive in the sense we have defined, yet a part of each performance. Her remuneration is paid in the form of a royalty. In a sense, she manages to keep ownership of her labor power. How is that possible? The explanation lies in her distinction from the basket-weaver. Unlike the latter, the composer does not really sell an artifact that is a finished commodity. Rather, she produces a program, in an almost cybernetic sense, for further investment of labor power. In fact, this program is taken over by capitalist production, which purchases labor power from salaried individuals to realize it. The composer is then not an artisan but what Attali calls a "designer," and she enjoys a status more akin to that of a *rentier* than that of an artisan, with whom she is frequently confused. Writers and composers are not the only ones in our society to enjoy such a status: anyone who designs programs for further production is a designer. Our economy is replete with such designers, many of them self-employed. Those who are salaried cannot, of course, be considered as enjoying *rentier*-like status.

The Marxian distinction between salaried and unsalaried is all-important here: the self-employed designer—the composer in our example—is not paid for her labor since what she is paid is independent of the quantity of labor that she will have furnished, whereas her salaried counterpart, whether paid by the hour or the year, is paid on that labor. The self-employed designer's income depends upon the quantity of demand that the product of her labor generates. It is in this sense that the designer creates a program that gives rise to and sustains an entire industry.

Though it permits us to apprehend the specific differential status of the designer, Marxian economics has paid scant attention to the role played by this individual, focusing rather upon those who sell their labor: the proletariat. Classical economics has been more concerned with investors and the accumulators or creators of capital, and in both frameworks for an analysis of capitalism, the designer seems to have escaped the attention s/he deserves. We shall see that the crisis of meaning and the crisis of the commodity have a great deal to do with this function.

The Production of Demand

If we return to the basket-weaver, we can observe that, as an artisan, he manufactures unique artifacts and sells them. No two of his baskets are quite alike. In fact, he is likely to vary the design somewhat with each object, even though he may be conforming to a general pattern of his own invention or to one prevalent in his community. The same situation obtains in early capitalism, though for somewhat different reasons: a design is used only once, primarily because the technical means for its reuse are not available. Under such circumstances, every object is, if not custom-made, at least of sufficient difference from other objects of the same class to permit easy identification and differentiation, and thus the establishment of a specific relationship with its owner. Attali calls this mode of production the "mode of representation," for here the product *represents* the labor that has gone into its production. If, however, the design is used over and over again, then we are dealing with the "mode of repetition." In this mode the product no longer stands in relation to the labor that has produced it.

In the market system, then, representation refers to that which results from a singular act, whereas repetition holds sway as soon as serial organization prevails. Books, records, designer clothes, and cans of tomato purée are all instances of repetition, while custom-built cabinets, a dress by a grand couturier, a painting, or a lecture are instances of representation.

Representation emerges with capitalism, but it does little to sustain the latter's appetite for profit. By contrast, repetition permits one to capitalize upon the designer's work by creating use-value out of her product over and over again. But the kind of use-value created here differs from the one created by the basket-weaver, for example. When I purchase a basket from the individual who wove it, I may be attracted by its shape or colors, or I may be in need of a basket in order to carry some groceries I have just purchased, or, perhaps, I intend to make a gift of it to someone. In any case I envisage some use of it as I acquire it, and generally I arrive at this notion by myself. The weaver has not taken any part of the surplus-value he has created and used it to stimulate my interest in the basket. A somewhat different situation arises in the case of serially produced artifacts. The integrity of the old use-value has to be broken up here since some of the surplus-value produced has to be used to pay a royalty to the designer, on the one hand, and an additional portion of the surplus-value—and it is an ever-increasing one—has to be devoted to giving meaning to the artifact, on the other. In a market situation, to give meaning to an artifact is to convince a potential buyer that the artifact has a use-value. For, indeed, the serially produced object does not evidence its use-value as readily as our basket.

Indeed, to deflect a part of the surplus-value in order to establish the existence of use-value, as is commonly done with advertising, is to acknowledge that the meaning of the commodity (that is, its use-value) is not necessarily obvious. Of course, this procedure is used in order to promote sales, that is, to increase or, properly speaking, to *produce demand*. But the logic of this mechanism is ultimately self-defeating: repetition requires that a substantial portion of the surplus-value obtained in the production of the supply be spent to produce demand; the production of demand requires that use-value be established; the establishment of use-value requires a further deflection of surplus-value, making less and less of it available for the production of the object and its actual use-value as opposed to the establishment of the latter. In other words, repetition is a mechanism for the progressive diversion of surplus-value away from investment in the production of additional use-value, and its rechanneling into the *establishment* of use-value or the production of demand.

Under the regime of repetition, then, use-value must be established for commodities; otherwise there is likely to occur loss of meaning. Labor is used to produce demand, and production proper becomes increasingly reproduction and payment of royalties. The production of demand, as establishment of use-value, thus becomes a wholesale production of meaning, carried out principally by the economic sphere itself, with the assistance of the public sphere when the state intervenes to further promote meaningfulness, that is, demand. For very rapidly here, one goes from producing demand to producing consumers.

But, Attali is quick to point out, the necessity of investing surplus-value in order to establish use-value takes on increasingly the appearance of disorder, the disorder that is inevitable in replication from a mold, where flaws occur with ever-greater force and frequency with each copy. The logic of repetition is such that the increasing difficulty of producing demand begins to put strains on the system's ability to produce supply. The state of the U.S. automobile industry is eloquent testimony to this fact. The mode of repetition is then faced with its breakdown: it produces artifacts whose use-value cannot be easily (read: cheaply) established, and which therefore remain unsold; it then uses up surplus-value in the attempt to sell them, that is, in the attempt to make them meaningful to buyers; and thus it begins to use up capital that otherwise would have been invested in the production of commodities. In the mode of production of repetition, the system feeds upon itself: it is forced to use profit in unproductive ways. Paying royalties to designers and paying for the establishment of the meaning of its productions, it fails to accumulate the capital necessary for further production. One recourse is to establish an internal designing unit and thus remove the designers from the unproductive, in our sense, system of royalty payments to the productive one of salaried labor. This is done more and more often. Nonetheless, the dangers are sufficiently great that the very codes of production are endangered.

This, in fact, is what seems to be happening—to such an extent that whole modes of analysis based upon the existence of these codes and the existence of these processes of production (the classical as well as the Marxist) are being rendered obsolescent, since they are suddenly left without any object upon which to train their analytic power.

The Production of Semiotics

It is in this context that semiotics is produced. The effect of the mode of production of repetition is an increase in disorder and an endangering, and a diminution, of use-value, which is thematized as an endangering and a loss of meaning. Under such circumstances, the uncovering, localization, and preservation of meaning acquire urgency. Yet these are tasks to which analytical instruments, concepts, and explanatory regresses derived from the mode of production of representation are, by definition as well as a matter of empirical fact, unequal. They cannot be altogether jettisoned, of course, for we do have many artifacts around dating from representation, but they do need to be reterritorialized so that they can be recycled under repetition. The relationship of "American (cultural) Studies" to semiotics in the case of the cowboy boots is a good instance of such a remapping, one that, it should now be obvious, does not derive from some will to power or imperial imperative of semiotics, but is a systemic necessity under repetition.

The question that presently arises is whether semiotics, or more specifically, semioticians, are aware of the historical role they are called upon to play. What is at stake here is not the frequently invoked distribution between a materialist and an idealist semiotics. Such a distinction is, in any case, dependent upon, and concerned with, two concepts that are concepts of the mode of representation and thus of antiquarian interest within the mode of repetition that has given rise to semiotics. Rather, what is at stake is whether semiotics, as a product of the mode of repetition, is to serve that mode by providing it with its alibi—an alibi to be construed quite literally since it would consist in claiming that meaning, though not immediately apprehensible, is nonetheless localizable and therefore recoverable—or whether semiotics will be the science through which we will know that mode and be able to overcome it, that is, whether semiotics can be a critical practice.

The prospects for the latter option do not appear too promising at first. For repetition does not let itself be known as such, that is, as repetition, but rather, because it offers itself through its artifacts and not its process, and because of its insistence upon the production of demand as the establishment of meaning, it gives itself in the guise of representation. A semiotics that would serve repetition would be then a semiotics of representation, blind to its inscription within repetition. Such, unfortunately, appears to be the case with the bulk of semiotics being practiced today. It is a semiotics of representation *for* repetition.

The possibility of a critical practice of semiotics hinges on the ability of semiotics to remap semiotically the historical, and it is to this that we need to turn.

II

Semiotics and History

It is generally held, by its promoters and detractors alike, that semiotics is not a form of historical thought, although it is acknowledged that, through the distinction between diachrony and synchrony, it provides conceptual and operational room for history. Such a tenet requires examination for at least two reasons: (1) if semiotics is indeed a theory of signification, then history must be signified in it not only under such guises as it had previously but in some specifically semiotic ways; (2) for the sake of its self-constitution, semiotics must examine its own system of inclusions and exclusions.

In both cases, the apparent neglect of history should constitute one of the privileged modes of access to semiotics, since it would also permit us to determine whether semiotics can be a critical practice. It should be borne in mind that Saussure himself, far from being ignorant of or oblivious to history, was, before inventing modern linguistics and semiotics, a brilliant student of Indo-European comparative linguistics; indeed, it is upon the work he had done in that most historical of fields that the reputation he enjoyed in his lifetime rested. Yet most contemporary semioticians ignore Saussure's early work, and in fact act as if the opposition diachrony versus synchrony were not just a systemic one but the operator of a periodization in Saussure's own career, neatly separating his diachronic comparative linguistics from his synchronic theoretical work in structural linguistics. It will be my contention that this *parti-pris* unnecessarily impoverishes our understanding of semiotics and prevents the latter from achieving the status that Saussure envisaged for it: that of a form of *social psychology*.

Substance and Substance-Effect

Comparative linguistics, one of the nineteenth century's great historical sciences, came into being to reconstruct Indo-European, the lost parent language of most European languages. In common with the procedures of most other historical endeavors, it relied heavily upon substantive evidence, in this case the occurrence of, and patterns of repetition in, some sounds in the same words in the descendent languages. By way of illustration, let us consider the following example (I follow here the excellent discussion of Saussure's achievement in the *Mémoire* in an article by William Diver):[5]

Sanskrit	mata
Doric	mater
Latin	mater
English	mother

Trying to reconstruct the word for "mother," we find that every descendent language that retains that word has an *m* initial position. We can proceed then to reconstruct the *m* as the initial sound in the parent language in the word for "mother." Such reasoning is based entirely upon the evidence we observe, and, more specifically, upon the fact that we observe the recurrence of the same substance (the sound *m*) in the same position. The comparative method, which consists in the reconstruction of the elements of the parent language on the basis of a comparison of the features of the descendent languages, does not rely upon arguments from substance alone, for, if it did, it would rapidly run into unresolvable situations caused by anything from an unwanted proliferation of forms in the descendent languages to a paucity of evidence. But, as in all the other historical disciplines, the evidence provided by substance was considered the most telling one because irrefutable.

Yet, inevitably, as in other fields of historical inquiry, some of the evidentiary substance would be missing or prove contradictory, thus impeding the reconstruction of the parent language. The co-occurrence in similar environments of two distinct phonemes (the term is of course a later coinage, which I use here for ease of discussion), the middle consonants *d* and *t* in the words *Bruder* and *fater,* for example, would either necessitate the positing of both in the same location in the parent language—a step that would destroy the functionality of that language, since it would then have to contain all the sounds to be found in all of the descendent languages—or it would require the formulation of a rule that would account for such a co-occurrence. It is, of course, the latter procedure that was followed, and, indeed, all the great achievements of historical linguistics lie in this domain.

The formulation of such explanatory rules, or laws as they became known in the field (Grimm's law, Werner's law, and so on), represented an accommodation to discontinuity in the chain of substantive evidence, whether the latter was due to divergent evolution or to the outright loss of some forms. In other words, the reconstruction of substance in the parent language could not proceed on the basis of substance alone, but had to rely upon the introduction of the complementary notion of "significant difference" or "value." Prior to Saussure's contribution to this field, all work in this field, all work in Indo-European reconstruction involved a greater or lesser mix of substance and difference in the reconstruction of the original language. Yet there occurred problems that seemed beyond solution, no matter how ingenious a mix of substance and difference was concocted. It is to one of these problems that Saussure devoted his *Mémoire sur le système primitif des voyelles dans les langues indo-européennes* of 1879. In order to appreciate Saussure's boldness of thought—*Denkgestus*—which, I will argue, led him to invent semiotics, it is useful to follow William Diver's description of Saussure's solution to the problem of semi-consonants.

Apparently, in the course of the evolution of the parent language, some consonants were lost during the pre-historic period of every descendent language. What makes the problem of their reconstruction arduous is the fact that they left very clear traces but that these traces took on the appearance of an almost entirely regular correspondence of long vowels, which suggested the possibility of formulating a law that would explain their occurrence.

In Greek, for example, there are a number of morphological irregularities such as the following:

leipo	lipemen	loipos	"leave"
theka	themen	thomos	"put"
doka	domen	doron	"give"

In each instance we have a singular verb form, a plural verbal form, and a verbal noun. The irregularity we shall consider is the variation in appearance of the vowel of the first syllable, where we observe dipthongs such as *ei, oi;* short vowels and long vowels. Saussure took this data and looked at it somewhat differently:

leip-o	the-ka	do-ka
loip-os	tho-mos	do-ron
lip-emen	the-men	do-men

Saussure then argued as follows: in the first column, we observe the alternation *e, o,* and 0. Perhaps the variations in the second and third columns are disguised versions of what occurs in the first, namely that the *e* and the *o* of the bottom words of these columns (*themen* and *domen*) are not the usual *e* and *o,* but are part of the root remaining after the real vowel had dropped out, leaving in actual fact nothing, which we mark, as in the first column, by 0. These *e* and *o,* if we are to compare them to the sounds of the first column, are not equivalent to the *e* and *o* of the two top forms (*leipo* and *loipos*), but to the *i* of the bottom form, *lipemen.* The *e* and *o* would thus be the vestiges of a consonant that was lost prehistorically in all known languages. We should rewrite our data then as follows:

leip-o	theE-ka	de0-ka
loip-os	thoE-mos	do0-ron
l ip-emen	th E-men	d 0-men

where the capital letter is used to indicate a lost element. Now all three columns present the same form as far as the vowels are concerned: an *e* in the top form, an *o* in the middle one, and 0 in the bottom one. In the bottom forms, what is left has to take over the function of the vowel.

In the first column, then, the *i* is part of the root in all three forms, while the *e* and the *o* are part of the morphology. The *E* and the 0 in the other two columns are part of the root as well, but they have been lost in the evolution of the languages. They subsist in the form of a lengthening of that verbal element which had to take over their vowel function as they disappeared, or become the vowel itself in the bottom forms. What was confusing about this problem was that the kind of correspondences which then appeared on the surface resembled vowel variations that had been studied in the nineteenth century. These correspondences had been called *Ablaut,* and they had been collected wherever they occurred.

What Saussure did was to cut the Gordian knot of this problem by positing the existence of a single relation, a "common value" as Diver accurately dubs it, among all the various types of *Ablaut*. This was tantamount to asserting that all the variation of substance could be explained by a single relationship of value. Saussure did start from the contradictory nature of the substantive evidence, but, unlike his predecessors or his contemporaries, instead of arriving at a significant difference that would apportion the substance into two or more meaningful ensembles, he derived sets of differences that, he claimed, were possible only if some substance, the lost semi-consonant whose properties he described, had been present initially and then had been lost. In other words, Saussure did not reconstruct substance by looking at substance or by mixing substance and difference, but by turning his back on substance altogether. He brought to bear upon each other columns or chains of differences, and he set them up so that they would lead to further chains of differences, finally claiming that at the intersection of the latter there had to have been substance.

Linguists of Saussure's day, though impressed with the elegance of his solution, and not a little swayed by the power of his reasoning, nonetheless rejected it because they could not accept its radical departure from substance. Quite correctly, they perceived the incompatibility of the procedure followed by Saussure with the very project of historical linguistics, which was so dependent upon substance. The story does have a happy ending in that Saussure was ultimately vindicated: in 1903, there were discovered some inscriptions which, when deciphered by the Polish linguist Kurylowicz some twenty-seven years later—long after Saussure's death—proved to be in the then undescribed Indo-European language Hittite, and contained substantive evidence that the semi-consonant postulated by Saussure did exist. It was then duly reconstructed into the Indo-European parent language.

I have discussed this early work of Saussure at length because it provides evidence of his preoccupation with historical data and also because the solution he proposed to the problem was to prove determinant not only to his rethinking of linguistics and to his invention of semiotics, but also to the specifically semiotic way of envisaging the historical. We ourselves lack the evidentiary chain from the *Mémoire* to the lectures that would ultimately become the *Cours de linguistique générale,* and the explanation proposed here will have none of Saussure's elegance nor its probative value. It is not meant to be conclusive in respect of the historical question of Saussure's own evolution, but rather to draw attention to the link between the two periods in his career, and through them to the relationship of historical linguistics to semiotics.

The Substance-Effect and Its Locus

There is no doubt that what comparative linguists could not accept was but the point of departure for further thought on Saussure's part. If he could reason his way to the reconstruction of a specific substance on the basis of differential chains of difference alone, what was the necessity of substance in the first place? He had been able to assert the absence of the lost substance because he had been able to *read* the effect of the latter in the differential organization of the chains of differences. But to reason thus was still to reason historically, that is, from substance. If substance were not to be invoked at all, Saussure would be truer to his actual procedure, which consisted in reasoning from sets of differences. To restate then the reasoning, but by taking difference and not substance as one's point of view, one would assert that *at the intersection of two or more differential chains of structured difference there would be produced an effect equal to that produced by the occurrence of substance at that point.* The historical perspective of the *Mémoire* required the assertion of an attestable (that is, reconstruable) substance, whereas a differentialist one would be content with the notation of the substance-effect.

It is far from clear that the significance of this paradigmatic shift, in Kuhn's terms, has been fully appreciated until quite recently, when Umberto Eco, in his *Theory of Semiotics,* proceeding purely deductively, reformulated the description of the sign as the intersection of two codes, which he had previously described as chains of structured differences.[6]

What I have called the substance-effect takes place then in the very locus that will be occupied by the sign. It would be tempting to conflate sign and substance-effect on the basis of this positional commonality, but to do so would be to blind ourselves to the specifically semiotic mode of historical inscription.

Substance-effect is a differentialist concept that marks the location where an inscription can take place. To be sure, it imposes restrictions on the sort of inscription that it can be; nonetheless, it retains the important possibility that no inscription will occur. The sign, on the other hand, is always some materiality, some substance. It is insofar as it is a substance that, in the act that summons it forth into the locus of the substance-effect, it can become inscription, an inscription that both fulfills the positional substance-effect requirements of the differential chains of structured differences, and exceeds them. It exceeds them because the very substantiality of the sign is, strictly speaking, not required by the purely structural determination of the substance-effect. Yet the substance of the sign, its materiality, is necessary to mark the inscription, but it does so by operating a swerve: the materiality of the sign not only serves to mark the inscription of the substance-effect, it also marks the sign's appurtenance to an order other than that of pure signification. The materiality of the sign is already charged with the previous history of that sign, the history of its previous placements, and that history is sufficiently strong to obscure the play of pure semiosis that the substance-effect was to mark. Instead of having the exact and determinate structural position of signification, we get the latter overlaid with a materiality that brings with it the history of its past instantiations. And, of course, such a process is not limited to one locus in the production of the utterance, but pervades it through and through, indeed becomes its law.

In other words, the distinction between substance-effect and sign— a distinction that semiotics has so far failed to make, for, quite rightly, it may have feared that it would wreak havoc with one of the features of semiotics that has proved very appealing to many, namely its susceptibility to formalization—and there distinction between position and substance, permit us to think both the syntactico-logical requirements of semiosis and the historical excedent of semiosis that the materiality of the sign brings into the process. The substantiality of the sign marks the fact that a substance-effect is all that semiosis requires, but that the inscription of the position of this substance-effect, because it can be only inscribed by a substance, displays a substance in that locus in a swerve that necessarily draws in areas of semiosis other than those involved in the production of meaning at that point, thereby producing the paradoxical effect of a simultaneous incompleteness of meaning (positionally) and a proliferation of meaning (substantially). The ex-cedence of the sign brings into play other considerations than those of the pure semiosis; its externality to the semiotic process under way marks the introduction of other interests and of a temporality that recasts the semiosis by inscribing it within history, but a history that must first be understood as operating in the gap between the determination of the substance-effect and the inscription of a substance into that locus.

By introducing a distinction between the locus of the substance-effect, defined as the space of the inscription of the sign to come, and that inscription, semiotics opens up a whole new way of considering such problems as the historical process, freedom, determination, and so forth. This is not the place to inquire into them, even though they constitute the semiotic re-inscription of the historical, but I would like to underscore the link between this conception of semiosis and Saussure's description of semiology as a branch of social psychology,[7] a statement often remarked upon, yet still considered obscure. One of the most unfortunate consequences of the occultation of semiotics' handling of history has been the development of a purely static conception of the semiotic, with, until recently, little attention paid to the actual production of signs. Yet, if the social realm is to be treated as a social text, that is, as the locus of semiotization, it is the very process at work in the gap between the substance-effect and the inscription of substance into its locus that is most deserving of inquiry.

III

Fredric Jameson, in an article on the sixties,[8] proceeds to derive both semiotics and poststructuralism from high structuralism, of which they would be the "break-down products." Semiotics, in his scheme, is a "reduction to a kind of scientism, sheer method and analytic technique," while poststructuralism is "the transformation of structuralist approaches into active ideologies in which ethical, political and historical consequences are drawn from the hitherto more relatively epistemological 'structuralist' positions." We have seen earlier that a certain kind of semiotics is indeed a scientism, but we have also seen that that form of semiotics does not exhaust the potentiality of semiotics, and in fact is at variance with the determinate scope of semiotics. Indeed, to see semiotics and poststructuralism as just the breakdown products of structuralism is to endow the past, and a limited area of it in fact, with far more power of determination than seems either prudent or warranted.

The Place of Semiotics

If we remain true to the conception of the semiotic elaboration of substance-effect and sign that was worked out in the previous section of this essay, and connect it with the analysis of the mode of production of repetition developed in the first section, we obtain the following: at the systemic level, the mode of production of repetition so taxes the surplus value of the commodity, in order, it will be recalled, to produce demand by establishing meaningfulness, that it grinds up its own productive codes and resources, and produces greater disorder and less meaning. Systematically, then, a convergence of codes, in Eco's conception of sign-formation, is produced in such a way as to achieve the locus of a substance-effect that, ideally within a logic of repetition, should be occupied by a meaning-localizing, preserving, and indexing entity. Now, following our own analysis of Saussure's distinction between the locus of the substance-effect and the sign that comes to occupy that locus, we see that the locus of this substance-effect is historically occupied by the entity called semiotics. The Saussurean analysis requires that we recognize, and indeed inquire into, the provenance of this materiality which, though it occupies the locus of the substance-effect, is not fully coincident with it and may either exceed it or come short of its requirements, but, in any case, by its own inscription in that locus, establishes links to other realms and thus lays the ground for the eventual skewing of the system into which it has just been inscribed, in such a way as to produce its demise, or more precisely, its passing into another system. In other words, I am only making explicit now what I have been doing all along in this essay, which is treating semiotics as a sign in a manner consonant with my interpretation of the problematics of the sign and substance-effect in Saussure. I am claiming, then, to have been doing semiotics and not merely to have been writing about it.

Some of this is in some sense startling. The logic of my inquiry, which started with the question of the status of semiotics as science in the *New York Times*, forces me to recognize that semiotics must have existed before the mode of production of repetition in order to be available for the occupation of the locus of the substance-effect defined in that system. To switch semiotic patron saints, and go from Saussure to Peirce, I am semiotically justified for such a lateral inquiry into the provenance of semiotics because, as Peirce reminds us, a sign is always in relation to another sign and not just in relation to the system in which it is inscribed, as Saussure stressed.

This is not the place to trace the historical roots of semiotics, but it needs to be stressed that it is an area of semiotic inquiry that practitioners of this field may ignore only at considerable peril to the understanding of their endeavor. For our purposes, it will suffice to mark one important historical antecedent.

The Simulacrum

Semiotics is the historical heir to the notion of *simulacrum* as Gilles Deleuze defines it in his distinction between copy and simulacrum in Plato.[9] Plato's thought revolves around the ability to make this distinction, but the distinction itself depends upon the prior placement of the Ideas or Forms into a transcendental position. As Deleuze points out, the copy must resemble the Idea, whereas the simulacrum is under no such injunction. Plato's thought is indeed not concerned with the specification of the concept as much as it is with the establishment of legitimacy. A copy is legitimated through its resemblance to the model *(mimesis);* it stands for the model, it is its representation. The simulacrum, on the other hand, is entirely constructed upon a disparity, a dissimilarity, and implies a perversion of a phantasmatic order, Deleuze further argues. And Plato views his task as the prevention of a general infiltration by simulacra. We must bear in mind that the resemblance of the copy is not that of a thing to another, but that of an object to the Idea, since it is only in the Idea that the relations and constitutive proportions of the internal essence are to be found. The simulacrum is not a copy of a copy; rather it is a thing that no longer resembles a model; it only resembles other simulacra, and it enters into unholy alliances with them. It may produce an effect of resemblance, but this effect is external to it and the result of means specifically mobilized to produce that effect. It is not, in any way, the result of its internal properties. The links between the copy and the simulacrum with the commodity under representation and under repetition become apparent.

The copy proceeds from a form of knowledge, a knowledge of the Idea in which image it is constructed, but there is no such knowledge at work in the simulacrum. It is, as Deleuze puts it, an encounter. The simulacrum lets us infer vast dimensions, depths, and distances that the observer can scarcely be expected to master. And it is because he or she does master them that the impression of a resemblance arises. The simulacrum includes within itself the differential viewpoint.

In this respect, the second part of Jameson's assertion concerning the transformation of poststructuralism into active ideologies must also be challenged. Insofar as poststructuralism pursues either a genealogical strategy (Foucault) or a rhetorical one (deconstruction), it remains beholden to representation and to the copy, for genealogy may indeed denounce the false claim of a present construct but can do so only by relying upon a prior belief in authenticity, while rhetoric must always begin by posing the relation of property, of appropriateness, in order to dislodge the claims to transparence or naturalness of a discourse. In both instances, even though the system of representation is denounced, it is denounced in the name of its own values. Hence the logical superiority of deconstruction over genealogy, since it recognizes, and acknowledges, its own aporetic position.

But these are not the only possibilities. The simulacrum, or, within the mode of production of repetition, the production of demand that is its correlative, releases the repressed and thus releases the power of the phantasm. To the representational relation of copy to model, commodity to program, substance-effect to system, it counterposes the relation of simulacrum to simulacrum, materiality to materiality, sign to sign. It destroys copies and models, and marks the advent of a creative chaos. But one must be careful not to succumb here to another temptation, one into which some forms of semiotics have indeed fallen: the destruction of some models and some representations may be nothing more than a strategy for the conservation and the perpetuation of the established order of representations and models. It is what I called earlier repetition in the service of representation. It masquerades as the semiotics of playfulness and of the pleasure of the signifier.

The other destruction leads to a creative chaos that puts simulacra in motion. Here the relation of sign to sign is not that of the subordination demanded by the system, nor that of domination or submission, not even that of monadic autonomy, but that of a congruence that I shall describe, owing to a certain contagious effect, by the word *solidarity*.

In summary, then: the mode of production that put cowboy boots on the feet of New Yorkers feeds upon itself and produces meaninglessness. In the systemic place for the ideological remedy of this signifying disorder, we find semiotics, which, as an unreflected practice, may indeed present itself as a scientism capable of safeguarding such meaning as this mode of production allows. But semiotics is the heir to the tradition of the lateral dimension, the simulacrum, the medieval jacquerie, against the hierarchy of the vertical dimension. Rather than helping to preserve the remnants of representation within the mode of repetition that is ours, semiotics can accelerate the demise of both.

12   From Eye to Ear: The Paths of Allegory in Philo

Philo's role as allegorist is well-known, and there is no lack of studies on the subject.[1] However, most of them are written from a doctrinal perspective and thus seek to reconstruct a Philonian dogma or to determine the sources of his allegories rather than to elucidate their nature. The allegorical method plays a fundamental and necessary role in Philo's thought. It proceeds from a reflection upon language: unlike Greek allegory, which was practiced mostly upon Homeric texts and had as its goal the elimination of the ethical contradictions present in these texts, and their ordering into a whole that could be used for moral instruction, Philo's allegory deals with a text that is irrevocably double, the Bible, of divine inspiration and human expression. My purpose here is to retrace some of the elements of this reflection by following its development in two texts: the *De confusione linguarum*,[2] a commentary upon the verses of chapter 11 of Genesis, which tell the story of the Tower of Babel, and the *De migratione Abrahami*,[3] which comments upon the first verses of chapter 12 of Genesis, in which the beginnings of Abraham's story are told.

Both texts begin by staging a migration. Abraham leaves his native Chaldea upon receiving God's call, and he heads for the places where the destiny of his lineage is to be revealed. The Builders of the Tower of Babel migrate as well, and, like Abraham, they head from east to west, but Philo presents these two migratory movements as opposed to each other though dependent upon each other. Since the migration of the Builders of the Tower comes first, both textually and logically, I shall begin with it.

The biblical text that is commented upon in this treatise reads as follows in the translation of the Septuagint cited by Philo:

And all the earth was one lip and there was one voice to all. And it came to pass as they moved from the east, they found a plain in the land of Shinar and dwelt there. And a man said to his neighbour, "Come, let us make bricks and bake them with fire." And the brick became as stone to them and the clay was asphalt to them. And they said, "Come, let us build for ourselves a city and a tower, whose head shall be unto heaven, and let us make our name before we are scattered abroad, on the face of all the earth." And the Lord came down to see the city and the tower which the sons of men built. And the Lord said, "Behold, they have all one race and one lip, and they have begun to do this, and now nothing shall fail from them of all that they attempt to do. Come and let us go down and confuse their tongue there, that they may not understand each the voice of his neighbour." And the Lord scattered them abroad thence on the face of all the earth, and they ceased building the city and the tower. Therefore the name of the city was called 'Confusion,' because the Lord confounded there the lips of the whole earth, and the Lord scattered them thence over the face of the whole earth. [Gen. xi. 1–9] (*De confusione* 1)

Philo precedes his commentary by a warning: in no way must this text be thought similar to any pagan myths dealing with the origin of tongues, and least of all to those with which it shares some formal characteristics. The object of this argument is twofold, polemical and exegetical: on the one hand, it is a standard feature of Philo's apologetics that never deviates from emphasizing the unique character of Judaism, no element of which can ever be traced to a common mythical trove shared with pagan religions;[4] on the other hand, it seeks to establish the validity of his reading method in opposition to others. This treatise is the only one in which Philo insists upon the original and individual nature of the reading he puts forward, a gesture that is quite rare in the Jewish exegetical tradition according to commentators.[5]

This argument ends in a paragraph that has challenged editors and translators. Here is its literal translation, with the sole addition of the two words in brackets supplying a lacuna in the manuscripts:

And so the authors of these bad faith explanations will see themselves already refuted on their own ground by those [who use] explanations ready at hand, and who are content to look for the apparent meaning of the laws only, without deliberate polemics, without reverse sophistication, but by following docilely the logic of the text, a way which avoids the traps.[6]

No translator holds this version as satisfactory or even possible. Editors, translators, and commentators are troubled by the fact that Philo, who, in their view, should be expounding his allegorical method here, says very clearly, if the manuscripts are to be believed, that the apparent sense of the text to be glossed suffices to put into question interpretations that are themselves obviously based upon the apparent sense. Some suppose that Philo is mounting quite exceptionally a defense of the literal method of reading, but then face the difficult task of explaining what such a defense is doing at the beginning of an allegorical commentary. Others have recourse to a proven trick-of-the-trade of philologists faced with lack of understanding: they "restore" the words, phrases, or even the sentences that are "missing" from a "corrupt" text until they obtain a sense that conforms to what is believed to be Philo's intended meaning. The text of the manuscripts simply urges that "the logic of the text" be followed. According to this logic, the apparent sense or the letter of the sacred text allows an interpretation as well as the refutation of this interpretation. The literal level of the text is thus contradictory inasmuch as it permits contradictory interpretations: it can be called illegible.

To enter into the game of interpretations, then, leads to error and confusion. What Philo proposes to do is not to let himself be ensnared in the illegibility of the text[7] but, on the contrary, to interrogate this illegibility by means of the allegorical method, which alone acknowledges that the text summons forth contradictory, unacceptable, and yet solidary interpretations. Inasmuch as the text is illegible, its illegibility is already allegorized; Philo's method of reading will try to delimit and to question it.

The theme of migration will be the first object of the commentary. It too is preceded by a relatively long excursus which serves both as a preparation for it and as an explanation. The text of the LXX used by Philo follows the Hebrew very closely in this instance, and the first sentence is somewhat curious: "And all the earth was one lip [*kheilos*, a word quite rare in Greek for 'language'] and there was one *phonē* to all." This union of lip and sound is dealt with by Philo in a double register, ethical and musical, so that the state of affairs that precedes the migration of the Builders is presented as a symphony of perversions. *Symphony* must be understood here as a discordant concert, graceless and lacking harmony (*De confusione* 15), that is, a symphony without harmony, orchestrated around a savage rhythm. In Philo's musical code, the opposition rhythm versus harmony is a mapped upon the ethical polarity good versus evil. The morally reprehensible character of the mode of existence of the Builders of the Tower—and Philo immediately reminds us that it is a verbal mode of existence—stems from its submission to a rhythm that excludes harmony by definition.

Perversion must be taken in the precise sense that Philo gives it: turning an object away from its proper function. The Builders thus find themselves in a state from which harmony is absent and where everything is turned away from its proper function to the sways of a rhythmic flux that surges up to the lip, which is manifest, in other words, in language. The word *kheilos* allows Philo to speak of language (which at this stage could certainly not be *logos,* either human or divine) in the terms of a flux, since the word *kheilos* designates river banks as well (cf. *De confusione* 29). More than another word for language, *glotta* (tongue), *kheilos* permits him to suggest that the language that is in question here stands at the edge of this flux, regulating its course while being both washed and beaten by it. To avoid giving the impression that such a condition necessarily leads to paralysis or impotence, Philo invokes the example of an Egyptian hydraulic machine thanks to which a peasant can irrigate his field in spite of the perversion of the functions of hands and feet in the operation of the machine (which requires that hands "walk" while feet grip) and the state of permanent falling that it engenders. This obvious image of productive labor makes it clear that rhythmic perversion need not result in sterility (*De confusione* 38).

When the migration does finally take place, the future Builders settle in Shinar, which Philo renders by the Greek *Ektinagmos,* meaning "shaking out." This name suits perfectly the locale chosen by these people because "all the life of the fools is torn and hustled and shaken, ever in chaos and disturbance, and keeping no trace of genuine good treasured within it" (*De confusione* 69). This migration, which is thus not a genuine one, merely ratifies the state of affairs that prevailed before it was undertaken. The Builders-to-be, already caught up in cacophonic perversion, are now settling in it.

This entire passage can certainly be read on a doctrinal level as a warning against the dangers that the soul will encounter when it leaves its native ground (although one is left with the vexing problem of explaining what is the perverted rhythm in which it already finds itself) and proceeds to settle in the agitated world of the senses and of passions. But this structure is also the allegory of the movement that leads away from the proper and toward the appropriation of that which cannot be proper. Philo counterposes the attitude of the person embued with wisdom, conceived along Platonic lines as being cast adrift in a strange land, which is thus tantamount to an alienation without the counterpart of an appropriation: "To alienate himself from it [the body], never to count it as his own, is, he holds, to give it its due" (*De confusione* 82). Linguistically, the migration to Shinar is the perversion of language because it limits itself to the expressive function, and its content is limited to the rhythm that agitates the body. The play of instincts invoked here by Philo resembles that which Kristeva called the "semiotic."[8]

Settling in Shinar is thus alienation in perversion, and the project of building the Tower will be taken by Philo as evidence of the desire to make this alienation permanent. According to the Bible, the Tower is built with bricks of clay held together by asphalt. These two materials are the object of a long commentary by Philo, who sees in them a generalization of perversion: brittle clay is supposed to take on the hardness of stone, whereas asphalt, which is supposed to represent stable security, is converted by a play upon the Greek *sphallo* (to glide) into viscous mortar.

Bricks are an art of the fake: they result from the conversion of the continuous into the discrete, which may be defensible, but this operation requires the destruction of the homogeneous character of the continuous, since water must be added to the clay:

> When the workman has taken the two substances of earth and water, one solid and the other liquid, but both in the process of dissolution or destruction, and by mixing them has produced a third on the boundary line between the two, called clay, he divides it up into portions and without interruption gives each of the sections its proper shape . . . This process is copied by the naturally depraved, when they first mix the unreasoning and exuberant impulses of passion with the gravest vices, and then divide the mixture into its kinds, sense into sight and hearing, and again into taste and smell and touch; passion into pleasure and lust, and fear and grief; vices in general into folly, profligacy, cowardice, injustice, and the other members of that fraternity and family. (*De confusione* 89–90)

The fashioning of the brick may well present the advantage of the production of the concept as a discrete unit carved from a continuum, but it condemns it to be vitiated from the start because it corrupts the homogeneity of this continuum, all the while presenting the concept as an authentic and pure sample of it. Asphalt, which was meant to be used as a protective coating and hardened shell,[9] liquefies so that concepts are no longer held together by the syntagmatic armor it is meant to provide.

The construction of the Tower thus proceeds in its logic of generalized rhythmic perversion. It is accompanied by an exchange of functions in which a synesthesia of the senses manifests itself in language. The stage of development represented by the Tower is that of settling in the improper, signified by the elaboration of concepts that, owing to the absence of partitioning between sense and language, are necessarily mixed, that is figural, metaphorical, and improper. The syntagmatic ordering of these concepts, far from receiving the stable and reassuring shell of asphalt, that is, reasoning, takes the form of a syntax agitated by the savage rhythm of the flux. If the situation prevailing prior to the construction of the Tower could be described by means of Kristeva's semiotic, then the construction itself represents an attempt to elaborate a symbolic that would not effect a break with this semiotic—a gesture that has been recently revived in some theoretical quarters. Philo sees that such an attempt is not without interest, provided that it takes the form of harmonizing what he called the discordant concert. He hastens to show that the conception of the symbolic implied in the construction of the Tower is nothing more than the generalization of this type of concert and that this is a feature of all moves toward appropriation: "Their vocal organ, though every note is entirely tuneless and highly unmelodious, is supremely harmonized to produce disharmony, with a consonance which it turns to mere dissonance" (*De confusione* 150).

This is precisely the object of God's intervention. Philo returns to his starting point to remind us that the Babel narrative in the Bible has nothing to do with the creation of the some seventy languages and dialects that the Alexandrian philologists had inventoried around the world. He rests his case on negative evidence: had that been the case, the Bible would have spoken of "separation" and not "confusion." And "confusion" is a technical term of the chemistry of his day, where it refers to "not juxtaposition, but the mutual coextension and complete interpenetration of dissimilar parts, though their various qualities can still be distinguished by artificial means" (*De confusione* 187). God's intervention is thus meant to put an end to what had been called perversion earlier; it was never God's intent to put the various parts of the living being in mutual interpenetration and exchange of functions:

> Observe that he who fashioned the living being, brought none of its
> parts into fellowship with any other. The eyes cannot hear, nor the
> ears see; the palatal juices cannot smell, nor the nostrils taste; nor
> again can speech have any of the sensations which the senses pro-
> duce, just as on the other hand the senses have no power of utter-
> ance. For the the great Contriver knew that it was well for them that
> none should hear the voice of his neighbour. (*De confusione*
> 194–195)

In this discourse of castration it is indeed a matter of the freeze
brought on by the symbolic. It is effected by the divine Logos defined
as the image of God. In fact, had there not existed a God, whom Philo
has kept off the stage until this moment of his text, all of the linguistic
activity would have unfolded in a sort of normalcy: the cacophonic
concert to the beat of the passions and of the senses, and the symbolic
of the "Shaking out" that grows out of it, work; they function; they
even aim at achieving a "great name" even though they stem from
evil. The language that precedes confusion, in its two stages of development, the semiotic and the symbolic, is always already an allegory
of the language that various contemporary theoretical enterprises seek
to unveil from under a linguistic theory that is accused of having occulted its true nature. Philo's commentary preempts this sort of reappropriation.

The allegory requires the intervention of God here and his location
in a transcendental position (God *comes down* to look at the Tower).
The cacophonic concert and the symbolic of the Shaking out are indeed possible only in the absence of transcendental meaning—the
only meaning possible, according to Philo. Once the existence of the
latter is unveiled or asserted, the order of the past is condemned:
the migration was no migration at all; it was a journey within the
Same. It is then time to distinguish between inside and outside, and,
once that is done, all the familiar dichotomies of metaphysics are precipitated. The intervention of meaning, or rather the unveiling of its
location, results in an impermeable partitioning between the various
parts of the living being and in their harmonization within language.
This language can no longer be described as a bank washed and
beaten by the flux: the word *kheilos* is banished; even *glotta*, tongue,
does not sufficiently express the interiorization that has just been ef-

fected. The punishment of Babel thus consists in the revelation of the location of meaning, a location that lies beyond access, and thus in castration. In the language of the allegory that unfolds in the text, the punishment takes the form of making humans deaf and dumb, to others and to ourselves, by abolishing the symphony of perversions (*De confusione* 189). In the sudden silence that replaces the cacophony, we are now ready to receive the fullness of a word that is *logos*. This is the major theme of the *De migratione Abrahami,* one of Philo's most complex treatises.

At first sight, Philo's commentary upon the beginnings of Abraham's story is a set of doctrinal considerations grouped around the theme of conversion. The problematics of language that we had followed in the *De confusione* appears explicitly in only one part of the treatise (*De migratione* 46–85). It seems to me, however, to be responsible for the curious organization of the treatise as a whole, and especially of the sequence of the events that it relates. The mutual dependence of a certain theory of language and a certain conception of time; their interplay; the strategies that this imposes to veri-diction—these are some of the problems that Philo addresses in his commentary. These problems require the allegorical method, the foundations of which had been laid in the *De confusione*. I will confine my comments to the explicit part of this problematics.

Philo looks upon the confusion effected by God at Babel as rehearsing the gesture of exile from earthly paradise, but in an interiorized mode this time: after the humans' initial fault, God separates himself from them; then at Babel, God separates them from themselves, he brings separation within themselves. This second sundering, which is but the insistant repetition of the first, is necessary in the onto-theological economy of Philo's reasoning: the interiorization of exile, because it carries the separation within us, allows the isolation, and thus the eventual liberation, of that which will be able to take, and to trace, the road of return. Before Babel, evil, as a somatic flux that negated theological functionalism, ruled over the being of humans; henceforth, by making us deaf and dumb to the instincts that agitate the body, the symbolic becomes available for an exit out of what we had first to acknowledge as an inside: the body, Egypt, evil (these three terms are always equivalent in Philo) toward an outside that constitutes this opposition: meaning.

The necessity of effecting silence within ourselves is a frequent theme in Philo's writings. In the *De ebrietate* it is presented in the terms of the Stoics' opposition between proffered speech (*logos prophorikos*) and interior speech (*logos endiathetos*):

> And we shall put to death "the one who is closest to us." And what is closest to thought is proffered speech (*o kata prophoran esti logon*): through verisimilitudes, probabilities, and specious reasoning, it fills us with false opinions for the ruin of our most precious good, truth. [71] Why not punish then this impure sophisticate by condemning it to the death that is appropriate to it: silence? For silence is indeed the death of speech. Only then will the spirit be safe from its crafty insinuations, and so, completely liberated from the pleasures of its "brother," the body, and from the bewitching of the senses, its immediate "neighbors," as well as from the sophisms of the language that "is closest" to it, it will be able, free and sole master of itself, to devote itself to all the matters of the intellect. (*De ebrietate* 70–71; translation mine)

The insistence upon the need to kill or to castrate the speech of the lip seeks to create conditions of receptivity.

Receptivity means indirection. The blow that fell at Babel puts an end to all problematics of textual production, as far as Philo is concerned, since linguistic activity, now based upon interior silence, can henceforth only take the form of a second-order activity: the apprehension of a meaning constituted as such elsewhere, and of its effectuation in language or retransmission, a procedure that only raises questions of noise management, as they say in information theory. In more familiar terms, it brings to the fore problems of interpretation and of faithfulness of reproduction (*mimesis*) that had not arisen until now. Receptivity presupposes the abandonment of a generative model and the elaboration of a communicational apparatus.

The central problem of this apparatus is human beings, since humans must be both the recipients of the meaning that issues from God and the senders of a signifying language. In a treatise dedicated to the figure of Abraham, it is Moses who will be invoked to demonstrate the workings of the machine. He is the ideal figure for this task: both privileged recipient of divine meaning and authorized re-transmitter of it. And yet, in Philo's texts, the figure of Moses is never exempt from a persistent ambiguity; like Joseph, who is also tied to Egypt, the figure of Moses, precisely because it is a figure, is marked with an ambiguity that Philo never discusses but that he exploits. The choice of Moses turns out to be surprising here, in spite of the overdetermination just mentioned, for in the biblical texts that Philo will invoke Moses is represented as speechless, first in front of God, which is in the logic of things, then in front of Pharaoh, which is more curious. In fact Moses feels so inadequate with respect to elocution that he calls upon God to help, who tells him to take Aaron, his brother, along. It is the workings of this text that Philo will use as material for his model of communication.

Moses is the wise man who knows how to produce silence within himself. He is thus in a state of receptivity, and it is not long before God opens communications with him. But when it is his turn to transmit forward God's message, Moses is not up to it. This is due, in Philo's view, to Moses' Egyptian side. For indeed the person whom the Jewish tradition calls the Scribe, and whom it has at times represented as a stutterer, initially recalls, in his relation to the word of God, Memnon, son of Dawn, worshipped by the Egyptians in the guise of an enormous statue built so that it would resound under the effect of the rays of the rising sun. Jacques Derrida has recently reminded us of Hegel's interest in this phenomenon, which he placed halfway between hieroglyphics and the plenitude of Greek speech.[10] Similarly, Moses begins by being nothing more than a *Klangstatue*: in relation to God all he need do is resound upon reception of the divine impulses and keep himself in the readiness that God expects from him. This state of readiness is the receptivity that was the stake of the blow struck by God at Babel.

The model of the statue of Memnon (which is not openly acknowledged by Philo) provides Philo with the two terms that were still missing for the mounting of his model of communication. He already knew that God was the source of the communication, that the Logos was the sender, that meaning or truth was the content of the message, and that the human intellect was the destination, but he still had to establish what was the medium of the transmission of the signal and what was the recipient. The model of the statue of Memnon not only brings the expected answer: light and the eye, but also, in its capacity as *Klangstatue*, it offers the paradigm of the passage from light to sound, from the eye to the ear, and thus allows the completion of Philo's double communicational diagram, which articulates the reception of divine meaning by humans with its retransmission among them:

God	Logos	wisdom	light	rays	eye	truth	intellect
SOURCE →	SENDER →	SIGNAL →	MEDIUM →	SIGNAL →	RECIPIENT →	MESSAGE →	DESTINATION
intellect	mouth	rhythm	air	sounds	ear	articulated sounds	intellect

The model of the *Klangstatue* is not adopted as such. For unlike the Hegelian *Klang,* which merely gives in another medium the stimulus that has been received from light, and thus has nothing to do with appropriation, Philo's *Klang* involves the entire economy of the anthropophotological metaphor.[11] Moses does not merely receive God's light; he sees it, or, more precisely, he takes hold of it by means of his eye, that is, he experiences its presence, which is the only mode of knowledge:

> All the same Moses applies the phrase "came down and saw" to Him, who in His prescience had comprehended all things, not only after but before they came to pass, and he did so to admonish and instruct us, that *the absent, who are at a long distance from the facts,* should never form conclusions hastily or rely on *precarious conjectures,* but should *come to close quarters with things,* inspect them one by one and carefully envisage them. (*De confusione* 140; emphasis added)

Taking hold of things by means of sight takes the sense of the Heideggerian *erblicken* here: as a mode of true knowledge, it is penetration by the gaze of that which, in the thing observed, orients the gaze properly toward us, that is, in what it properly is.[12] "Now the thing shewn is the thing worthy to be seen, contemplated, loved, the perfect good . . ." (*De migratione* 36).

This mode of knowledge, characteristic of contemplation, structured by, and structuring in turn, the oppositions interior-exterior, presence-absence, immediacy-distance, and totalization-fragmentation, depends in its workings upon the anthropophotological metaphor: the light must come from the outside; it must be seen; but it must also dazzle and blind once it is seen, thus taking hold of the seer in order to turn him or her into a new refracting source. Light, the trope of wisdom, or wisdom, the trope of light, sees itself, and in this act of taking hold of itself, it becomes the other tropological term:

> But wisdom is not only, after the manner of light, an instrument of light *(sophia de ou monon photos tropon organon tou oran estin),* but is able to see its own self besides. (*De migratione* 40)

Light, in the instant of its refraction against the ground of silence, constitutes this ground as such: possessing itself, light-wisdom constitutes itself as the possession of a being that has just been constituted by virtue of the fact that he possesses it (light/wisdom). As possession it marks the appropriation of meaning by the wise, and of the wise by meaning: the possibility of this operation of commutation marks the advent of exchange, the stage of the process of communication that the statue of Memnon could not cross since it failed to appropriate the rays of the sun.

> God's speech is pure, and the medium it uses is both pure and fast: but the Divine is an organ of pure and unalloyed speech, too subtle for the hearing to catch it, but visible to the soul which is single in virtue of its keenness of sight. (*De migratione* 52)

It should be noted that Philo invokes negatively the terms he had previously used in the *De confusione:* "pure and unalloyed." For human speech, by opposition and in spite of the Babel blow, is condemned to impurity and mixture: "ours [speech] mingles with air and betakes itself to the place akin to it, the ears" (ibid.); and to rhythm: "an impact on air made by the organs of mouth and tongue" (*De migratione* 47).

The relationship of meaning to language, where the latter is still taken in its pre-Babel physiology, is thus likely to remain difficult and subject to unpredictable variation (*De migratione* 34–35). Such uncertainty in the relation of meaning to language is unacceptable for Philo, and he launches his effort to redress the fate of language, an effort that leads him to allegory.

Meaning may be self-sufficient, but it remains without effect in the human world until it attaches itself to language:

> For the sake of this he was enjoined to call to his aid Aaron, the logos in utterance *(ton prophorikon logon)* . . . For the logical nature being the one mother of them both, its offspring are of course brothers. (*De migratione* 78)

Here it is language that is separated in turn from the body, from somatic nature, to be handed over to rational nature; this transfer is made possible by the double value of the word *logos:* speech and reason. The intellect, "unable to express the thoughts stored in it, employs speech which stands hard by as an interpreter, for the making known of its experiences" (ibid.). This very bystander who, once it was objectified, had to be killed by silence in the moment of contradiction, so that it could be first interiorized and then appropriated, is now being idealized by becoming the brother of the intellect and its interpreter. The move toward its liberation takes place in a subtle passage that is rich in consequences, where language ceases to appear in the guise of *phonē* to become stamp, imprint, and writing:

> For it is indeed a fact that language meeting the mind's conceptions, and wedding the parts of speech to them, mints them like uncoined gold, and gives the stamp of expression to what was unstamped and unexpressed before. (*De migratione* 79)[13]

The striking of the stamp, as the inscribing of the concept, gives *phonē* the value exchange it needed. Henceforth the efficacy of language is assured. It becomes trace, sacred text. The redressing and sublation of language are completed: for Philo, the possibility of writing, and a writing before the letter, is enough to guarantee proffered speech.

The rest of the passage is devoted to the demonstration of Aaron's oratorical superiority over the sophistic enchanters of Egypt:

> How would it have been possible for Moses to encounter these men, had he not in readiness speech the interpreter of thought, who is called Aaron? In this place Aaron or speech is spoken of as a "mouth"; further on he will also bear the name of "prophet," when the mind too is inspired and entitled "God." For He says "I give thee as God to Pharaoh, and Aaron thy brother shall be thy prophet." (*De migratione* 84)

The raising of language to the status of "prophet," that is, of a speech capable of plenitude since the prophet's foretellings are followed by fulfillment, consecrates its raising from the depths it had fallen to at Babel, its sublation.

The mechanism of the sublation *(Aufhebung)* of language that we have followed is that of a proportional process that plays itself out by means of presence and re-presentation: the occupant of the lowest position accedes to the median one in the second stage of the process:

STAGE I:	God	$\rightarrow$ Moses	$\rightarrow$ Aaron
STAGE II:	Moses	$\rightarrow$ Aaron	$\rightarrow$ Pharaoh

First, Moses, to whom God has made himself present, represents God to Aaron, who then, in Moses' presence, represents Moses to Pharaoh.

The structure of this process requires a displacement in which the recipient of the representation becomes a sender of it in turn, to finally become presence. Pharaoh could have inserted himself into this process, which could then have expanded *ad infinitum,* had he not cut himself off from Moses and Aaron by chasing them away. This play of a structure that achieves its perpetuation is too familiar to us today to need further remarking. Philo's text, however, unfolds this structure in such a way as to reveal that it is only a simulacrum of itself, and that it is devoid of any efficacy: Pharaoh *could not* enter into the structural game since his entry would have expelled both God and Moses from it, and Moses alone has experienced divine presence. Aaron knows the divine word only by echo (*De migratione* 80). Between Moses and Aaron there is, despite the fact of their brotherhood, a change of medium, from light to sound, that allows Philo to exploit thematically Pharaoh's lack of vision, which results in his blindness with respect to what is unfolding in front of him. The perception of the sublation of language as a proportional process is thus characteristic of Pharaonic blindness; it sees two stages where in point of fact there is continuity:

$$\text{God} \quad \rightarrow \text{Moses} \quad \rightarrow \text{Aaron} \quad \rightarrow \text{Pharaoh}$$

It is Pharaoh who, blind to God, takes Moses for God and Aaron as his prophet.[14] Any form of thought that limits itself to two terms will seek to build two-stage processes that will admit of reiteration, in the hope of ensuring its self-promotion, but this is a hope that is not to be fulfilled, and a lesson that allegory will remember.

If the passage from God to Moses is clear (in the light), that from Moses to Aaron remains mysterious (by echo). Philo does not appear to be able to extricate himself from his starting point, the passage from the eye to the ear. This passage, insofar as it is not yet of the ear, cannot be stated in articulated human language; insofar as it is no longer of the eye, it is not in the light and is thus too obscure to be apprehended by the intellect. There results thus an aporia that suddenly endangers the entire sublation of language and, by extension, threatens the very validity of the Sacred Text and the salvational project that depends on it. Philo is thus constrained to launch a salvage operation. In order to do so, he returns to writing, the possibility of which had made the communicational model operational. Writing, he now avers, does not exist at the level of possibility only but has actually "taken place" : "for holy writ, speaking of the tables on which the oracles were engraved, says that they were written by the Finger of God" (*De migratione* 85).

If we recall that the concept originates in an inscription, we may note then that the process described by Philo takes the form of a circle that starts with this originary writing, goes through an oracular speech act, its reception and engraving, and, finally, finds its confirmation in the scriptural tracings of God who, in effect, guarantees at this juncture the conformity of the copy to his initial writing. The three moments of writing are thus as follows: the writing of the concept, which makes its circulation in *phonē* possible; the notation of voice as authoritative text; the confirmation of the authority of this last text by the establishment of a relationship of equivalence with the originary writing. I speak of "equivalence" here rather than identity because there still obtains the irreducible difference of medium between the two, even though the scriptural act remains the same.

For Philo, then, writing designates an operation of fixation, first of the concept in language, and then of voice in a more stable medium. But the third writing, whose function is to fix meaning in the second, is caught in the Pharaonic moment we have just analyzed: by affirming the conformity of the second to the first, it affirms mostly that the second conforms to the writing that has preceded its own engraving.

The relationship thematized by means of the three writings is that of Philo's allegorical method, which stages the relationship between meaning, the biblical text, and Philo's allegory. The function of this allegory is to show that the sacred text, apprehensible in articulate human speech, conforms to the divine meaning, but all it can show is that the literal level of the biblical text constitutes its own conceptual level, that this literal level is the conceptual writing of which the allegory is the engraving.[15] In Philo's approach this moment is necessary so that allegory, conceptualized from the engraving of oracular speech, can recover, in the future and by refraction, the meaning that presided over the conceptual writing that made the oracular speech possible.[16] Allegory can thus pretend to the status of a discourse upon truth, but, inasmuch as its engraving does not receive the stamp of meaning, the truth it puts forward remains without efficacy. It is a rhetorical truth, devoid of the power of assertion.

Allegory, faced with the literality of the text that constitutes it, constitutes this literality as such by promoting it to the position of its own conceptual writing, so that it constitutes retroactively the first conceptual writing. This writing, which is the object of the transit from eye to ear, is deferred. Because it appears later, it must have been present: if Aaron is a prophet, we may conclude with Pharaoh that Moses is God, or, forewarned by Philo against such a gross blindness, we may conclude from Aaron's presence that there must be a God at the origin of the process that has placed him in front of us.

Pharaoh, as we know, concluded otherwise. He saw a historical and a political threat, that is, something altogether different from what Philo's terms suggest. In our archaeology, through the persistence of the problematics of signification, we may conclude that at the origin there must be a signifying process of the sign, or, like Pharaoh, we may see a threat. Let us remember however that it is in attempting to reduce this threat, that is, in attempting to appropriate fleeing speech, that Pharaoh perished. This truth is both archaeological and allegorical.

13 Religion, the State, and Post(al) Modernism

For some time now increasingly frequent, and strident, predictions of the end of theory have been made. These have been greeted, predictably, with glee among those who saw the theoretical onslaught of recent years as one more plague that a merciless god was visiting upon them. They drew solace from what may well be the manifesto of this tendency, Walter Benn Michaels and Steven Knapp's tract "Against Theory,"[1] in which a call for "an end to theory" was issued and theoreticians lambasted for being at best no more than apologists for their own practices and at worst power-hungry academics posing as adjudicators of the claims made by others while studiously avoiding the production of any work that could be used to indict their own views. The anti-theorists, as they have become known, are particularly virulent against what they view as the social and political disengagement of much recent theory, by which, it generally turns out, they mean deconstruction. They are not alone in this denunciation: even defenders of the theoretical enterprise, indeed of the very necessity of theory, such as Frank Lentricchia, view this as the gravest shortcoming of deconstruction, and one that, by implication, has given all theory the bad name it is presently being affixed with:

> In what goes by the name of deconstruction, he [William E. Cain, author of "English in America Reconsidered: Theory, Criticism, Marxism, and Social Change," published in the same volume as Lentricchia's response to it] sees a political cop-out—an elaborate theory which tries to undercut any and all justification of political choice, including the choice to work against "cruelty, suffering, and exploitation." As a theory, deconstruction (in effect, if not in explicit intention) works on behalf of quietism and political enervation . . . These are points that I would not quarrel with, since in *Criticism and Social Change* I make them myself.[2]

These charges are not new, nor do they appear subject to modification even in the face of such empirical evidence as the remarkable consistency of Derrida's political position during France's rightward swing or his personal and intellectual involvement in the anti-apartheid movement, where he has been joined by precious few of those who thunder against deconstruction's apoliticism. One may well wonder at the reasons behind this attitude, especially since it does not seem to be the preserve of the foes of deconstruction. Even well-disposed students of deconstruction, such as Jonathan Culler, while acknowledging the political potential of its stances, pay scant attention to the work in which this potential is being realized.

A case in point is Samuel Weber's earlier work, in particular his first English-language book, *Unwrapping Balzac*.[3] To be sure, Weber would be more aptly described as a theoretician of deconstructionist bent than a strict, undo-or-die deconstructionist—if there are any such outside of the imagination of deconstruction's enemies. He trained with Paul de Man, became sufficiently well acquainted with Adorno to be entrusted with the task of co-translating, with Sheree Weber, the essays in the collection *Prisms,* held the position of assistant at the University of Berlin under the philologist and hermeneuticist Peter Szondi, translated, and introduced to readers of German, the work of Jacques Lacan, and took part in the Western discovery of the Bakhtin Circle, before turning his attention to the theoretical and critical scene in the United States. The Balzac book, derived from his Cornell University dissertation, is remarkable in several respects. To begin with, it is one of the earliest instances of the poststructuralist study of literature. Weber challenges Roland Barthes's famous opposition between Balzac and Flaubert—the opposition upon which Barthes was attempting to construct his periodizing concept of the modern by distinguishing between readerly and writerly practices of literature. Using a mode of reading in text segments, which Barthes was to adopt and make famous some time later when he revised his earlier view of Balzac in *S/Z,* Weber brings out the complex interplay of elements that constitutes not only the economy of Balzac's *La Peau de Chagrin* but a broader semiotic, social, and literary economy as well. Nor does Weber's work give any comfort to those anti-theorists who assert that all theory is but the disguise of a will to power. In his work on Freud, originally in German and then in his own revision of the text into English, Weber examines this particular conception of theory and shows that the notion of theory as mastery, over the world or over texts, is untenable; it is rather a reading practice that relies on the polemical for the articulation of its stances, thus putting forward what are, in the language of this book, ultimately assumptions. To read Weber then is a challenge, one that would not permit some of the facile generalizations about either deconstruction or the end of theory currently being broadcast. It is also, inevitably, to enter in a polemic with him.

Paul de Man, reflecting upon the critical practice of a number of eminent thinkers, from literary critics like Georges Poulet to philosophers like Martin Heidegger, saw a curious interplay of blindness and insight in the production of these thinkers' most important critical ideas: the blindness, far from being disabling, was constitutive of the insight yet nonetheless remained a blindness to the person affected with it. It was this predicament of critical activity that led de Man to formulate a more properly theoretical stance as one in which the mechanism of blindness and insight would be understood without being disabled, or at least not in such a way as to render further insights impossible. De Man's solicitude in the preservation of the mechanism had something profoundly disquieting about it, if not downright scandalous. Our impulse, bred in the bone by several centuries of education, is to correct error when we come across it. De Man's willingness to let it be marked a profound break with a major component of the Western cognitive tradition, one that is the motor of the disciplines, and especially the scientific ones. And it was all the more puzzling since de Man did not shy away from polemics in which he did reprove others for making mistakes, of reasoning, of reading, or even of fact. Yet, in spite of the apparent arbitrariness in the willingness to countenance a blindness while correcting a mistake, de Man was highly consistent, if not clear to impatient readers. A blindness constitutive of an insight was far more interesting than the result of its correction would be: at best, the latter would smooth out the argumentative path through which the insight was obtained; at worst, it would erase the traces of the functioning of a cognitive mechanism that forced anyone examining it into wondering about the provenance of insight, and thus of the workings of cognition in general. Correcting errors sets the record straight, eliminates impediments to thought; reflecting upon blindness, on the other hand, forces thought into a reflective judgment about its own tortuous and discontinuous path, the very blindness of which consists in the fact that it has no guide to warn against its vagaries.

In *Institution and Interpretation*,[4] Samuel Weber distinguishes between these two modes by means of the category of institution, within which he differentiates between institutional functioning on the one hand, which corresponds to error-correction in de Man's formulation, and instituting on the other, which is precisely what thought is engaged in when it proceeds blindly, in de Man's sense, to cut a path where none has been traced before. Weber then properly links this problematic to the organization of knowledge and the constitution of the disciplines that are its building blocks. Since, as he had already shown in his *Unwrapping Balzac*, the organization of knowledge is far from indifferent to the organization of society, this concern with the instituting function of institutions is a gateway to the rich field of social and political reflection, the absence of which in deconstruction we saw being deplored, if not vilified, earlier. Yet even here one ought to be wary, and continue using the distinction between institutionalized functioning and instituting acts that Weber has drawn. Far too often, what is meant by the political, and even the social, among literary critics and theorists falls under the former—not that there is no value to this sort of politics or social thought, but its localization within the demarcation of the institution should make clear that its political program can only consist in a change of personnel in dominant positions, while its social one can only have a reformist outcome if it is ever implemented once the political project is carried out.

We tend to think of institutions as apparatuses, that is, as constituted bodies with their internal procedures and delimited field of intervention. But an institution is first and foremost a guiding idea, the idea of some determined goal to be reached for the common weal; it is this goal that is sought according to prescribed behavior and by the application of set procedures. The idea itself is adopted by a group of individuals who become its public possessors and implementers. This group then becomes the institution as a result of the combining of the guiding idea with the set procedures. The members of the group are shaped by the guiding idea they seek to implement and the procedures they apply; they adopt common behavior, develop similar attitudes, all of which tend to unify them into a determinate and identifiable group and give the institution its distinct unity. An institution then is a social crucible, and it may be something as traditional as a church or as contemporary as a mode of watching television. The role of the guiding idea is all-important, however, for without it we have forms of social behavior like all others rather an institution. The guiding idea is precisely what seeks to avoid the blind path-taking that so interested de Man in the arrival at insight. In short, the insightful path is turned into a beaten one, with the subsequent development of procedures within and by the institution being akin to road-improvement. The trail-blazing, or in Weber's terminology, the instituting, becomes a moment of odd standing in the now constituted institution. Its necessity is acknowledged, for without it the institution would not exist, but it no longer really matters except insofar as the marking out of the line that brought point of departure and point of arrival together is concerned. In other words, the instituting moment, which endows the entire institution with signification and meaning, is held within the institution as both proper to it and yet alien: it is its other, valued to be sure yet curiously irrelevant to immediate concerns.

In its day-to-day functioning, the institution manages to ignore this constitutive otherness within itself, and yet it cannot forget it since it stands as its foundational moment. Instituting and institution are not, then, two facets of the same entity, as some structurally-minded sociologists would have it. A particular relationship conjoins them, which defines not only the institution as a social phenomenon but the social itself. Institutions are fundamentally instruments of reproduction, not in the simple mechanical sense, but rather in that they ensure that regulative processes take place so as to contain what otherwise could threaten to turn into anarchic proliferation. The accomplishment of this task is far from mechanical; it requires a specific form of intellectual activity which consists in the reconduction of what appears particular through the paths of the general, or more precisely through that instituting insightful path which is no longer treated as particular but as general now that it has been widened, had culverts laid in, bridges thrown, and generally been turned more and more into a reliable and safe all-weather thoroughfare. This specific form of intellectual activity we have long known under the name of interpretation, and Weber is particularly keen on showing the role that it plays in institutions. Yet he also shows that this role is not confined to reproduction in the sense that I have been using, however.

Interpretation, when it is carried out with the rigor that it demands, inevitably goes beyond the procedural ground of the institution to encounter that of its instituting. Inasmuch as interpretation is itself a process of "meaning-discovery," it has to venture onto the ground where such meaning as is available within the institution that regulates it has been constituted. This is the second relationship of institution to instituting that Weber explores in *Institution and Interpretation,* striking out himself into territory that has hardly been explored. Interpretation, beholden as it is to the institutional framework that both authorizes and empowers it, finds itself indebted to the instituting act that enables it. It is this recurrent theme of debt that I find most interesting in the essays that constitute Weber's book.

Paul de Man's complex of blindness and insight, developed in relation to the critical propositions of individuals, has now been reworked in the context of the delimitation of disciplines as institutions, into another complex whereby meaning is located outside of the institution, or discipline in the academic context, that manages it on behalf of the society. De Man had noted that there was a gap between the blindness and the insight and that, furthermore, there was little prospect of their overcoming it on their own since it was constitutive not only of their respective positions but of their cognitive efficacy; as a result, he sought to delimit a theoretical space within which the mutual relations of the blindness to the insight could be described. Weber, on the other hand, already functioning in that theoretical space, takes the relationship to be one not of mutual ignorance but of active denial, generating guilt and indebtedness. At this stage of the reflection, we find that, in the institutional framework, meaning is not only sufficiently remote to warrant the elaboration of specific discovery procedures, but it is other, and an other to which we are indebted.

In the chapter entitled "The Debts of Deconstruction," which provides the most elaborated exposition of this problematic, Weber makes explicit the link between what may at first appear to be an obscure point in epistemology and the sociopolitical concerns that were our point of departure. He does so by means of Nietzsche's own heuristic myth on the origins of the gods. It will be recalled that Nietzsche views this as a sociopsychological process whereby all that we have today is attributed to the inventiveness of ancestors, who, as they recede into the past, must grow in stature so that they may indeed be viewed as the originators of all that has been developed since. Though Nietzsche himself makes no claim of veracity on behalf of this myth, it contains features that have found independent support in ethnographic materials. For example, one of the most vexing questions in the study of the relationship between thought and material conditions has been the lack of any traces left by the invention of agriculture, surely a major conceptual and material accomplishment with considerable consequences for the very survival of the species and its mode of acculturation. Yet all ethnographic inquiries come up short: agriculture goes back to time immemorial, the very same as the rest of the culture's materials, and its invention is attributed either to the founding ancestors or to a gift from the gods. We do seem to have here the sort of denial and indebtedness that Weber theorizes on the basis of Nietzsche's indications.

What is perhaps even more important about Nietzsche's myth is its methodological rigor: if the gods are truly human creations, as he believes, then one should not appeal to some other transcendental category, such as "natural" necessity, to account for their constitution. And since it is precisely the status of the transcendental that is at issue in this invention, one can hardly proceed in an ontological way either, even if one were so inclined, which Nietzsche definitely was not. Thus the only recourse left is the sociopsychological realm. This methodological rigor is important, for it locates the realm of the constitution of the gods as the social—thereby rejoining Durkheim's own conclusions in the matter before *his* lack of rigor pushed him to transcendentalize necessity—in such a way as to raise the question to which Weber is implicitly seeking to provide an answer in the essays of *Institution and Interpretation:* what is the social stake of constituting meaning as other and as external to society? The last part of the question does not represent an unwarranted extension of the earlier discussion on the externality of meaning to institutions: modern society has long been defined as a society of institutions; the externality of the meaning to them must then be seen as constitutive of this society itself.

What indeed is the stake? This is the question that haunts anyone who begins to reflect upon the social function of religion and wishes to go beyond the purely psychological reasons for the maintenance of religion as an institution to inquire into its instituting. We must begin by observing that if there is a social decision—whatever the actual nature of that decision-making mechanism may be—to attribute the origin, the mode of organization, the self-understanding, and the culture accomplishments of a society of whatever magnitude, be it a small tribe or a large state, to gods conceived of as inhabiting a distinct ontological realm, then this decision represents a desire and a determination to split the society from its first causes in such a way as to make the latter inaccessible to human intervention or tampering, as the many tales of woe befallen to those humans who have tried attest. As a result, the principles that preside over the organization of society and animate its rules are beyond its ken. They may be precious and are indeed highly valued, but they are inaccessible in precisely the same way that meaning is inaccessible to institutions in Weber's description, the scope of which is becoming apparent. What this means is that no one within the society—the status of strangers is much more problematic, as the reception of Cortés has shown—may claim the legitimacy of these principles as his or her own, and even less so to speak from the society's foundational locus, since the latter is beyond the reach of any human member of that society. What this means is that no one can occupy the seat of meaning, and therefore that of power, since, as we saw earlier, meaning is empowering. Again, anthropologists have long remarked upon the ambiguous status of the traditional tribal chief who claims no authority for himself and generally is hardly better off than his compatriots.[5] Both Nietzsche's myth and the reflection on religion point to the fact that society is constituted through the operation of exclusion whereby the foundational principles are set in a realm that transcends the society. A number of consequences derive from this: Since this realm is beyond the society, it is impossible for the society as a whole, or for anyone within it, to be in a position to reflect upon the society and its organization, hence the sense that the existing order is the only possible one and should be left alone. Furthermore, the organization of the society is meaningless to human cognitive powers: since meaning resides outside the society, it is not at all surprising that any effort to uncover it within should end with the conviction that arbitrariness or senselessness prevails, although a more appropriate and self-reflective conclusion would admit instead to the inadequacy of human powers for such a task. The third consequence is implicit in the earlier two: a society has no capacity to act upon itself; it cannot change itself, and least of all by acts of institutional or collective will. If change is to come, either it must have been programmed in the foundational principles, or it is the result of an intervention from this other realm.

The mechanism at work in these three consequences is twofold: first the acknowledgment of a separation, and then the attribution of value to that which is now cut off from society. The thread common to all three is power (to know, to endow with meaning, to alter). It is easy to see that what is involved here is the separation of power from the rest of human society and then the proclamation of its inaccessibility to the society. It would be even easier to be cynical about this and remark upon who profits from a conception in which power is not denied but access to it is. Such cynicism is very much exterior to a society ruled by this conception, however, and would beg the question by virtue of its location. Rather we need to observe that from within the society an important result obtains: if power resides eminently outside the society, there is no power for anyone inside the society to hold, and thus no one can hold power; all are equally powerless—as far as these three social facets of power are concerned. Indeed the sharing of this powerlessness is what constitutes the people's commonality and establishes them as the members of that society. This has always been the strongest point of religious thought, one that is necessarily lost in the institutional forms through which we know religion: all humans are equal with respect to the true powers of the universe because they are barred from power.

But it is also a very fragile one since it acknowledges the reality, and the experience, of power, and therefore its immediacy, only to proclaim its unattainable remoteness. The precarious balancing act between the two propositions calls for a safety net, that provided by a mediating instance. The individual, or group of individuals, who occupy this new position will represent themselves as the bridge between the powerless and the realm of power. As mediators, they are *of* the powerless but partake in the power whose effects they propose to channel. Perhaps even more important, they now span the gap between the two realms: they have made themselves, at least partially, other in order to ensure continued communication with the realm of the other. Mythological thought is well acquainted with these demigods who empower humans, are hated by the gods in whose realm they trespass and from whom they steal such things as fire or the secret of knowledge, and are both admired and dreaded by the humans. The separation between same and other has grown more complex, and since it is the mediators that one deals with in everyday experience, it is their otherness that comes more and more into view. The rulers, or more simply the state since this is the mediating instance I am speaking about, are no longer on the side of the powerless: they have access to knowledge, to meaning, and the power to change the society, and they have the authority of their mediating status to do so. The constitutive split whereby society came into being as the collection of all those who lived by certain principles forever beyond them is appropriated by the state, which represents itself as, literally, the interpreter of these principles. The instituting of society (by the split from its foundational principles) is now institutionalized and becomes highly irrelevant as all sorts of new questions emerge: who is fit to be a mediator-ruler? how is continuity in this position to be ensured? are there taboo domains or is all of the social realm open to state intervention? and so on. If religious thought is, in relation to power, an acknowledgment of its existence and then its neutralization by its expulsion from the realm of human attributes, the state is its complementary acknowledgment and appropriation by some humans. It both reverses religion and upholds it. Power continues to be felt immediately though it is mediated, but it is no longer remote. Mediation has made it more pervasive, and with this pervasiveness has come the breakdown of equality: there are now those who know, mean, and alter, and those who can only submit. Social division and the inequality that results from it find their justification here.

The principal difference between a society that submits to what I will call, for lack of a better term, a religious order and one that submits to a state-organized one lies in their attitude to otherness. It is immediately apparent that the first type makes the other an absolute other, whereas the second turns it into an inner component of the same. Yet it is not enough to remark upon the position of the other in both systems; we must also note that they differ in the way in which they believe that the other came to be. Nietzsche's account makes clear that the gods are the products of the society, and one can therefore speak of the social production of this otherness even though the form it takes is not a pro- but an ex-duction. And since this act of production of the other is at the same time the production of the society, we have a collective determination of the boundaries of the social and of the other. By contrast, in a state-organized society, the determination of otherness no longer directly affects the constitution of the social since those who hold state power first co-opt individuals, thereby making them other with respect to the rest of the society, and then let the state as an apparatus of power determine the configuration of the social. Thus neither the production of the other nor that of the social is collective; indeed in such an order there will be strong prohibitions on this type of production, as we shall shortly see, since it is the prerogative of the state. We are then in the following situation: for a society to constitute itself it must know where its legitimacy lies; furthermore it must have a sense that its order is neither anarchic nor nonsensical but must be, in some ways that may well be beyond our ken, the realization of a true order; although its intelligibility is a challenge to our limited cognitive means, it must possess it in principle. If all these conditions obtain, order and change are both possible and the society is assured of continuity. But for that to occur, the foundational principles cannot be found in the society at large but must be located in a space of otherness that ensures that they remain beyond the reach of human desire and temptation. This space of otherness is either absolute or mediated through the institutions of the state. In other words, as Nietzsche had already seen and Weber reminds us, the society carries a heavy burden of debt to this space of otherness: it owes its meaning, its organization, its capacity to act upon itself, and thus its ability to manage order and change. This is the foundational debt of meaning that pervades all institutions, including the academic disciplines that Weber is concerned with.

It is in relation to this state of affairs that the social dimension of deconstruction becomes more apparent. Institutions behave as if they did not carry this debt, as if the meaning they dispense was the result of their own activity or that of recognized meaning producers such as authors and critics as far as the institution of literary studies is concerned. When antitheorists claim that individual preferences or orientations determine the critical bent of literary judgments, they reaffirm this institutional conception with which they identify unbeknownst to themselves. To pursue the financial metaphor, institutions do not acknowledge the debt as their own but collect the interest on it, thereby fostering the formation and the maintenance in dominant position of a privileged class. This is the target of deconstructive practice, which aims at nothing less than, in a first stage, the restoration of a universal indebtedness since this appears to be the only ground on which equality, as a social fact, can be thought of. In this connection, it is worth observing that the privileging of the epistemological model in recent theory derives from the fact that the ethical model no longer had the capacity to produce equality and, again, those who are presently advocating a return to the ethical, and who frequently justify this return by their distaste for theory, are choosing a ground that cannot but result in inequality since it is always located in a postinstituting moment. The epistemological ground favored by deconstruction permits the assertion of an equality between all human beings by virtue of their dispossession from the domain of meaning. The insistence on aporia, undecidability, the fact of the dependence of our thought processes upon language and its tropological games, all convey the same sort of human powerlessness that obtained within religious thought, without any of the latter's transcendental dimension. Samuel Weber gives the best exposition of this conception when he describes the exemplary constitution of psychoanalysis as both an acknowledgment and a repudiation of debt. The model of assumption that he then disengages is precisely the one by which all disciplinary and institutional thought authorizes itself in such a way that it appears to be legitimate and yet beholden to no one for this legitimacy.

As a deconstructionist, Weber then has to describe that which constitutes the equality we all have and which institutions destroy. He does so by means of Derrida's reliance upon a communicational model that is autonomous from those who are its "users" in *La Carte Postale*. It is a giant Postal Service that uses us as the relays for the impulses it sends along its circuits, impulses that we insist on taking for messages from the relay that immediately precedes us. What matters here is not so much the accuracy of this description—something we do not have any standards for in any case—but rather its originating impulse: against the inequality fostered by the state we have the assertion of a fundamental equality; against the inequality-producing and distorting claims of empowerment of modernity, the dispossessing equality of postmodernity, or perhaps more accurately—since it is clearly directed against the state and its institutions and therefore still functions within the parameters of modernity—a postal modernity, which, as everyone knows, is characterized by the nonaccessibility of sender and receiver. The failure of the Postal Service deconstructs far more than any other enterprise the claims of legitimacy of the state because it shows that it cannot play the role of mediator which is its ground. If it cannot ensure the transmission of messages from same to same, what is the likelihood that it can do so with those that have to travel from other to same?

Yet in order to challenge the state in this way, deconstruction must hypostasize a postal system that is autonomous and beyond the ken of human powers. One may well wonder whether this is the best way of challenging the state and whether it is not more vulnerable elsewhere. The state itself has always shown an inordinate fear of the literary. One need only recall Plato's expulsion of the poets from his ideal state, the reluctance of Puritans on this score, and the difficulty that Philip Sidney found in mounting a defense of them. Plato's reasons are the most telling. Prior to the *Republic* his concerns are epistemological: we learn and we know that we do not know. In the *Repub-*

lic this cognitive concern moves to the issue of knowing that which is, that which truly is, a question that forces him to consider how we know that we know and brings him to the Form or Idea. What is to be known, then, is Being as determined by the Idea and as Idea. Knowing is essentially theoretical. It is in this context that Plato turns to a consideration of mimesis. Mimesis will be considered in the relation of theater to truth, and this relation is taken to be a theoretical one. Plato will indeed treat it at the theoretical level but on a political ground, somewhat in the fashion that the arguments in this essay have unraveled.

Plato begins to inquire into art and theater from a political perspective, that is, he evaluates art in relation to its position in the state, according to the essence of the state and the latter's foundation in relation to truth. Plato knows that poetry has the capacity to alter, to transform, and it must therefore be kept under surveillance. When he turns to the theater he is already suspicious, and this suspicion colors his reflection. What is the poet up to in drama? The poet provides the diegesis of events that may be past, present, or future and thus plays the role of witness. But the poet also engages in mimesis, that is, he or she utters speeches under the name of someone else, of another, speeches to which one then conforms. This other is created by the poet: mimesis creates otherness.

Mimesis does not take place, then, against a backdrop of some reality that one copies. It is neither the imitation nor the representation of a reality. To consider it in such terms is to take Plato in terms of the *adequatio* that Weber identifies as an obstacle to modern scientific thought in his introduction. For Plato, mimesis is far more worrisome than is generally suspected: through mimesis one can create otherness, and through it the distinction between real and apparent melts into air. Mimesis gives being to that which does not have it; it is a labor of presentation such that something other comes into being, which would not have existed without this labor. We experience mimesis as a mode of rendering, one in which the distinction between real and unreal is undecidable. Poets are dangerous, then, because they give being to that which does not have it; they produce otherness instead of placing themselves, and therefore all of us, in its debt. They serve as constant reminders of the fact that otherness, constitutive or otherwise, is a human production, and thus they empower us to think, to know, to give meaning, and to act upon our society. It is for this reason that poets must themselves be expelled into otherness and that their "messages" must be processed, like certain cheeses, through institutions. The persistent concern with epistemology and the literary in deconstruction derives from a social concern rather than representing a turning away from it, as the accusers pretend.

14   In-Quest of Modernity

Michael Nerlich's *Ideology of Adventure*[1] is a most unusual book. At first sight it appears to be a straightforward narrative explanation of a major question in intellectual history: what accounts for the distinct mode of development of Western civilization, a mode that led it to turn its back upon traditional values and to systematically explore and exploit that which was unknown to it. This question, which is none other than the question of how modernity came to be, receives an original answer in this book: a particular ideological orientation was forged under specific historical circumstances and progressively took on the form of what *Annales* historians have been calling a *mentalité*, a mindset.

Nerlich makes a very persuasive case for the existence of this mindset, which he calls the ideology of adventure. He traces its beginnings in the high Middle Ages and follows its mutations and transformations into the middle of the eighteenth century, that is, into the period where most traditional accounts of modernity set the beginning of this stage of development of civilization. Most such accounts do so on the basis of the conjunction of the rise of the industrial revolution with the well-known intellectual achievements of the Enlightenment. They face then the very vexing, and still unresolved, problem of the co-occurrence in time and space of both of these phenomena. Nerlich's approach avoids this pitfall since it does not seek to account for the occurrence of great individual works—often the staple of intellectual history—whose relation to anything else that occurs in the same time-frame is most problematic. Instead he pursues doggedly the constitution of the ideological orientation that makes such works possible. As a result, he *can* turn to major works and offer readings remarkable for their comprehensiveness and elucidation of major critical conundrums. An extraordinary example of the success of his approach is provided by the analysis of *The Merchant of Venice*,[2] which, among other things, provides the best discussion to date of the stubborn problem of antisemitism in the play.

To characterize Nerlich's project in this way is to suggest that it is itself a modern one, for indeed, what is more modern than the quest for the origins of modernity? A number of additional features appear to support such a judgment. Nerlich embraces the narrative mode of history without any misgivings, in fact with an enthusiasm all too rare these days; he pursues his inquiry within the discourse and the analytical framework of Marxist scholarship, again without any visible discomfort, indeed going so far in his apparent orthodoxy as to ritually begin his chapters with authoritative quotations from Engels; he evidences an obvious enthusiasm for his subject matter, indicating repeatedly that it sheds new light upon what he himself has called "the unknown history of our modernity,"[3] that is, it enlightens us with respect to modernity, thus fulfilling one of modernity's most abiding concerns.

Modernity has indeed been characterized—not least by Heidegger—as dominated by the idea that thought progresses from enlightenment to enlightenment in history; it does so by reexamining critically the very ground of its origin so that this ground becomes ever more secure. As a result, the history of this thought consists in ever more insistent claims of ground recovery, renewal, renascence, returns, and the like, all in the name of ever-greater forward motion. The key to this conception is the notion of an overcoming of the present by means of a critical return to the past. In this way, the new is immediately made valuable, becomes a value in itself, because it is constituted by means of a reappropriation of the original ground. This mechanism of modern thought is most powerful: any critique that is mounted against it will seek to anchor itself in some ground that it will have to claim to be more originary than the ground of the thought it criticizes, thereby repeating the very *Denkgestus*—movement of thought—that it critiques; so that, at best, it will take that thought's place but leave the operating mechanism of modernity intact. The recognition of the power of such a mechanism has led some—Adorno comes readily to mind—to believe that there is no overcoming of modernity and that we had better hunker down for the long haul.

Nerlich seems to be oblivious to Adorno's pessimism. For one thing, his conception of *mentalité* does not allow him to imagine a privileged locus into which one could retreat from the pervasiveness of modernity in order to hibernate until it is overcome. For another, it is not at all clear that such an overcoming will obtain in time, that is in the very dimension of history that modernity has fostered upon us. Here, Nerlich's insistence upon the fact that it is the history of *our* modernity, unknown or otherwise, that he is concerned with should have tipped us off. The historical mode of modernity would have been satisfied by the phrase "the unknown history of modernity." Such a characterization would have been consonant with the world-historical nature of the construct "modernity," which can then take its place in the development of thought alongside such other periodizing concepts as antiquity and the Middle Ages, all of which function within a distinctly modern conception of history, a conception which is the secular successor to the Christian notion of history as salvation. To insert the modifier "our" in front of history in such a context in order to designate Western European experience is to radically alter the scope and the locus of inscription of the term "history," and to distance oneself from modernity as well. Modernity is no longer cast as a necessary stage in the progress of thought (or in the *Entwicklung* of the Spirit, as Hegel had it), but as a contingent historical construct in relation to ourselves, who are equally contingent. Both of us partake of evenmentiality, and we are thus doubly historicized: we in relation to modernity, and modernity in relation to us. Modernity is not something that happens to us; we, such as we are, are constituted by it. But modernity is itself something that we set into motion and have been carrying out as a project, to use Habermas's phrase.

This double historicization and mutual dependence are of considerable theoretical import. The concept of history operative in modernity, and indeed characteristic of the latter inasmuch as historical narrative has been its chief mode of account, was formulated in order to deal with the ever-greater production of the new in modernity, and thus to unmoor us from any stable and permanent foundation which could hinder the search for the new, which, as we have seen, came to be viewed as the supreme value of modernity. At the same time, such an unmooring from stable foundations could not be radical nor final, for it would result in the inability to establish any certainty. Modernity's conception of history voids this problem by introducing the concept of development, which permits the foundational ground, be it the subject, the Spirit in Hegel's sense, or indeed anything, to evolve in such a way that it provides stability for certainty, and thus defines history as a set of master narratives, in Jean-François Lyotard's formulation.

Nerlich adopts one of these master narratives, the Marxist one, as his framework, but in focusing on ideology he comes upon a foundational ground that is both productive and produced; furthermore, adventure turns out to involve a form of uncertainty, and even of chance, that is not recoverable within any model of development as *Entwicklung*, hence the double historicization that he then effects. This double historicization effectively takes Nerlich outside of modernity, though not through any willful action of his own. On the contrary, he remains far too faithful to the mode of modernity to evince any desire to overcome it. If anything, the features of his mode of arguing and telling the story of modernity through that ideology of adventure are so much in the mold of modernity that they appear to be parodistic of it. Trying to make explicit what is implied in the Marxist analysis of modernity, Nerlich does not seek to be new or to provide something new, and that is how, in spite of the fact that he remains faithful to modernity in every other respect, he is not a modern. He effects a swerve around modernity, a swerve that deserves some examination.

The story of the unknown history of our modernity that he tells remains unfinished as history. In the Preface to *Ideology of Adventure* Nerlich tells the story of how he came to write this book, why it stops when it does, and states that he is presently working on an *aesthetics* of adventure, both as successor to, and completion of, the present, and more historical, book. It is this movement from the historical to the aesthetic, a movement already adumbrated in *Ideology of Adventure*, that lies at the heart of Nerlich's swerve.

It is not quite correct to say that Nerlich's history of our modernity remains unfinished as history. To be sure, the story he tells in his book stops in the middle of the eighteenth century, but this interruption is neither gratuitous nor fortuitous. I would like to suggest that it marks an end, not that of our modernity nor of its history, but of the historical mode in relation to modernity. The story Nerlich has told until then is that of an emergent and a rising modernity; it is an epic of modernity. Like all epics, it has its heroic figures and high deeds, but like them it is followed by the establishment of an increasingly bureaucratic state that reveres its past heroes only to ensure that their example is permanently confined to a safe because irretrievable past. As soon as modernity overcomes opposition residual of older civilizational formations, it changes its relationship to history: no longer *telos, eschaton,* or the dimension of emergence and conquest, it is now a structure of legitimation, one that projects the future as the authentic fulfillment of a foundational past. The organization of knowledge in the nineteenth century under the aegis of history is part and parcel of this process. To be sure, Marxism and other oppositional movements will continue to seek the mantle of a heroic history for their undertakings, but the battle they wage is successful only when the opponent subscribes to the same conception of heroic history, that is, when the opponent is itself an adept of modernity. Such was the case in Russia, in China, and in a number of so-called Third World countries. But as soon as the opponent is modern such movements falter, for they wage their struggle in a dimension that no longer has any genuine existence and therefore cannot sustain their effort.

We have thus two different conceptions of history, both of which pertain to modernity: one which I will continue calling for the sake of convenience heroic history, and which corresponds to the ascendant mode of modernity, and the second, history as the structure of legitimation, once modernity triumphs. Nerlich tells the first kind of history since he is pursuing the constitution and workings of the ideology that, according to his persuasive account, made our modernity what it has been. But he inevitably has to tell this history in the second mode, the legitimating mode, since neither the telling nor the reading of such a history can be itself heroic, and, in any case, it must be part of modernity's self-accounting. In this respect, Nerlich's "uncovering" of the ideology of adventure as the secret propulsion of modernity qualifies as novel, but its novelty is immediately undercut by the built-in claim that this ideology is the newly established and critically vetted foundational ground of modernity itself. What is new, then, is the self-consciousness that we as moderns can have of this hitherto unknown ground. So far the movement of Nerlich's work seems to conform to the requirements of what one could call the signifying economy of modernity: both conceptions of history are in play; the position of the new is not only preserved but properly extended from the realm of things to that of consciousness; a new and presumably more stable ground is uncovered and critically vouched for; modernity, once again, will have overcome itself and thus consolidated its hegemony. Nerlich would thus once again appear to be an irretrievable modern, overcoming modernity by its own rule and thus ultimately not at all able to overcome it and lead us to some putative postmodernity.

Nerlich knows better, however, than to seek to overcome modernity on its own ground. Since his enterprise is inscribed in the dual historical discourse of modernity, any overcoming in the form of a subsequent development he would propose would necessarily turn into one more figure in the phenomenology of modernity—a fate that seems to have befallen quite a few of the recent claims of postmodern status. Instead he focuses on one aspect of the dual historical discourse of modernity: the actual temporal status of history as a structure of legitimation. In the heroic notion of history, temporality is relatively unproblematic since it can be accounted for through the articulation of actions, causes, effects, and catastrophes, however complex this articulation may be in its own right. In history as a structure of legitimation, temporality is far more problematic. The conception of foundational ground that is central to this view of history requires that such a ground be conceived as an originary one, but this requirement does not proceed from the notion of foundational ground itself, which is, properly speaking, an ontological notion, but from the fact that this ontological notion is itself inscribed within a historical discourse that is only beginning to disengage itself from the heroic mode of history. In other words, in history as a structure of legitimation the ontological and the temporal are so intertwined as to be subject to confusion. This confusion is precisely what makes possible the claim that a foundational ground that is originary is recovered at some ulterior point in time.[4]

The ordinary way in which the ontological and the temporal dimensions of this second conception of history are dealt with in the critical discourse of modernity is to establish the nature and identity of the foundational ground through a critical examination and then to proceed to either claim or establish that this ground is originary in time as well. Nerlich does not follow this procedure; he appears to be oblivious to this order of precedence based upon the unacknowledged yet central dialectic of the ontological and the temporal, or Being and Time as Heidegger had it for short. Such a disregard is far from idiosyncratic to Nerlich; it is part and parcel of the constitutive field of modernity. Because he focuses his analysis of modernity on its constitutive ideology, Nerlich is able to escape the confusion between the ontological and the temporal that is to be found at the core of modernity's ideology, and it is in accordance with the signifying economy of modernity that he is in the process of uncovering, as opposed to its ideology, that he acts as if the originary, or rather the merely earlier in time, had foundational power.

At first this may seem to be an inconsequential move. After all, it appears to make precedence in time the rule by which one shall establish right of dominion, and we certainly have enough examples of the prevalence of such a rule, especially in the legal domain, to find it nearly self-evident. But a closer examination reveals its profoundly unsettling nature. To begin with, there is nothing modern about such a rule: it is characteristic of custom-based societies, and these take tradition as their supreme value and not the new. If this is a rule of modernity, it is one that robs it of its distinctiveness. This is indeed what happens in Nerlich's analysis.

Nerlich's analysis of the ideology of adventure leads him to place the beginnings of modernity in what is, for most scholars, the high Middle Ages. In fact, in one of his most recent publications, he goes so far as to identify a generally neglected, and certainly misunderstood, text of the Old French writer Chrétien de Troyes, the *Guillaume d'Angleterre* (dated in the last third of the twelfth century), as the locus in which the distinctly modern conception of adventure is first articulated.[5] The effect of such a placement is startling: what is generally known as modernity is not new with respect to what Nerlich identifies as modernity. In and of itself, this should not be surprising, given the alteration of the time frames. Yet it is startling all the same because, first of all, the very highest value of modernity, that is, the new, is not respected by modernity itself, and second, because the consequences of such a move produce effects, within what we have traditionally known as modernity, that we have been associating with postmodernity. Again, such an early occurrence of these effects may be explained away by the intimation that they are the result of Nerlich's general move to advance the dates for modernity, but this would beg the issue. If such effects can move at will, they occur independently of their relation to specific temporal markers, and appear instead to be triggered by the playing out of a given sequence; they are then structural rather than historical. Furthermore, what is true of the effects must also obtain for the causes. The category of the historical, as understood within modernity and as central to it, begins to dissolve.

This dissolution is not to be confused with the very modern notion of an end of history—whatever form one may give to this end. Nor should it lead us to invoke another very modern distinction: that between history as some sort of objective process in which we are all caught and history as our mode of relating to such a process. This distinction allows modern thinkers to sacrifice the history of consciousness—by definition always partial and unequal to its object—to real or effective history, which grows more unknowable, if not mystical, with each such sacrifice. Rather, it is meant to bring us to recognize that the very reality that we have fashioned as part of the project of our modernity is characterized by a remarkable degree of immobility, and this in spite, or perhaps because, of the accelerating rate of change and introduction of ever new things and ideas. Lyotard is very much on the mark when he asserts that it is the state that is fond of order—and therefore of history, which chronicles the fluctuations of order—and not capitalism, which stands as one of the names by which modernity goes.[6] But capitalism or modernity cannot be studied only through the effects it produces, nor through a notion like that of the aesthetics of the sublime; these are but ways of suggesting that modernity or capitalism can only be figured but ultimately is unknowable. Modernity is unknowable only from the perspective of history which, after all, is its very own instrument of legitimation, and, as such, cannot be expected to be anything but opaque in relation to modernity. But it has an economy which is both a political and a signifying one, and this economy is cognitively accessible.

When, writing in the historical mode, Nerlich reaches the point where progress becomes routine, he recognizes that this very historical mode becomes obsolete as an analytical tool and can only serve ends of legitimation. Routine is always meant to produce uniformity and to prevent upheavals; it is the very opposite of the new. When the new is routinized, as is the case presently, novelty is but an instrument to ensure a greater uniformization in the rates of progress, so that ultimately a form of immobilism takes hold under conditions of controlled and uniform forward motion. Progress obtains, but it is no longer the progress of the Enlightenment or of the heroic conception of history. It is a form of progress that is a vestige of the very idea of progress. It certainly forecloses the notion of adventure, except as a consumer good (adventure cruises up the Amazon are currently being offered by a travel company).

What is the nature of the immobility we have been speaking about? Can one properly speak of an immobility in an environment given over to change? From a sociological point of view, one could answer by pointing out that the changes in material conditions that are fostered upon us through advertising and other less subtle means do not entail any changes in relations of power or domination, far from it. It may be more useful, however, to address this issue, albeit very briefly, from a philosophical perspective. The apparent paradox of an ever-changing environment and a resultant immobility has been analyzed by Heidegger as the very essence of *tekhnē* which, for him, has been the dominant orientation of Western civilization since the post-Socratics. It is the essense of *tekhnē* to gain mastery not only over the natural environment by first objectifying it to ourselves as knowing subjects, but to put into place an all-encompassing mechanism of mastery that would objectify all of reality, including human beings in order to submit it to its operations. The all-encompassing ambition of this mechanism Heidegger saw at the root of what for him were the three great totalitarian ventures of the twentieth century: fascism, communism, and Americanism, and there was little doubt that he considered the last most likely to succeed where the first two had failed, not least because it had gone far further than they had in abandoning any notion of heroic history.

Heidegger sought to characterize the nature of the mastering mechanism. The task proved very arduous since one could never be quite sure that one's very own inquiry was not part and parcel of the mechanism's reach over hitherto freestanding areas. Since this mechanism, which he called the *Ge-stell,* achieved its initial hold over that which it sought to control by turning it into an object of knowledge, by objectifying it, it became progressively clear to Heidegger that any resistance to it would have to work itself through nonobjectifying modes of knowledge, the aesthetic being foremost among these.

The particular intertwining of the logical and the historical discursive modes that we saw earlier inevitably falls into the form of an argumentative narrative in which the developmental logic internal to some entity is forced to vie with competing logics, acts of will, or catastrophes. The focus, at all times, is on an object, either as it is or as it is becoming. The aesthetic mode, by contrast, is an economic one: cognitively, it is far more concerned (if one can speak of concern in this context) with the interaction between all of the constitutive elements of a given happenstance in time and place—what is generally referred to as aesthetic experience. In short, it is far more process-oriented than output-directed, to speak the language of economics that is adequate to it. The outputs may vary, and indeed be "new," but the productive mechanism remains remarkably stable even when it "improves" itself. This is as true of the political economy as it is of the signifying one, which is what the aesthetic is concerned with.

In *Ideology of Adventure* Nerlich has studiously avoided aesthetic discussions, for the story he had to tell was still amenable to telling in the mode of history. But as he brings his story to the point where modernity becomes triumphant, it becomes clearer to him that the historical mode will become less and less cognitively rewarding, and that, to maintain the sharpness and the rigor of the analyses he has carried out so far, he needs to take up a different cognitive mode, that of the aesthetic. In this respect he breaks with the discursive mold of modernity that he had faithfully espoused, but he breaks it only because he has pushed it to its limit.

It should be noted, however, that this is a break the fault line of which was already traced in modernity. Nerlich studies the ideology of adventure; his conception of ideology leads to view rather unproblematically the means by which such an ideology was vehicled. These means were stories, plays, novels, and other cultural artifacts. Nothing could be further from an actual adventure, with its dangers, risks, and high feats, than reading about an adventure in the coziness of one's home. To be sure, one can take a psychosocial tack and speak of vicarious enjoyment and ego-building functions; nonetheless, reading, even of adventure stories, is far closer to the older *otium studiosum* than to the new *negotium*. The older *otium studiosum* had as its aim the understanding of what made the world run, the agency that was at work within it, be it God, nature, or human will. *Negotium* has as its aim to be that agency, and for quite a while it was thought that human will, if bold and resolute enough, could indeed be such an agency. But as the human itself came within its purview it became less and less clear that will was enough, and a growing suspicion that something like Heidegger's *Ge-stell* was at work began to take hold. The *otium studiosum* of reading has once again regained its right to be. The ideology of adventure may have incited us to become willful agents; the literature of adventure invites us to meditate upon agency, and Michael Nerlich, to reflect upon their articulation.

15 The Further Possibility of Knowledge

Michel de Certeau is the author of nearly a score of books that range in subject matter from theology and history of religions to anthropology and that include theoretical reflections on the writing of history as well as contributions to contemporary cultural criticism, literary theory, and the analysis of everyday life. In his case, this is not merely an indication of a profusion of intellectual interests but rather the proper and legitimate exercise of certifiably acquired knowledge: he has received advanced training in theology, history, the study of comparative religions, psychoanalysis, and anthropology. He has taught in all these fields at major universities in France and in the Americas, dividing his time between the University of California at Los Angeles, where he taught literature, and Paris, where, in addition to his teaching and research duties, he was active in a number of collective endeavors, not the least of which was the journal *Traverses,* a very stimulating pluridisciplinary publication of the design center at Beaubourg.

Certeau's book *Heterologies*[1] provides ample evidence of this wide range of activity, and its title, though perhaps not altogether euphonious in English, is further indication that the author not only is aware of this but intends it. "Heterology" is a term that has come to designate a philosophical countertradition that, in shorthand, could be described as being deeply suspicious of the Parmenidean principle of the identity of thought and being. Although Certeau does not make overt reference to the themes and motifs of this tradition, his choice of title, significantly pluralized, places him among those who have reacted against the modern forms of this prejudice, that is, against the mainstream of speculative philosophy which finds the Parmenidean principle embodied in the inexorable workings of the Hegelian dialectic as it paves the way for the Spirit's conquest of the world. Certeau's line of attack upon this problem is of interest to all who are concerned with the present state, and the further possibilities, of knowledge, for it is the very organization of knowledge, in its present dependence (albeit a generally unconscious one) upon the Hegelian model, that figures at the center of his preoccupations.

I

Most members of the countervailing tradition—Nietzsche, Heidegger, Bataille, Blanchot, Derrida—have been mainly concerned with either the ontological or the epistemological questions that any critique of the Hegelian position inevitably raises. Certeau tends to stay away from these aspects of the matter in order to explore other, seemingly less momentous, features, primarily of a discursive order. In the process he shows quite conclusively how pervasive, and nefarious, the Parmenidean model is across what we like to call the disciplines, and by what means we may work around it. In contrast, then, to the tradition of which he is a part, Certeau has clear practical aims. There is thus something very atheoretical about his endeavor, not because of any opposition to theory as such, but because the old construction of the opposition of theory and practice is part of the speculative edifice that Certeau no longer finds hospitable or, perhaps more accurately, affordable. It exacts too high a price for the amenities that it provides. But this atheoretical stance does not make for an absence of theory in what he writes, as the reader will quickly discover. It simply makes for a different positioning of the theoretical, one that strikes me as quite novel.

Certeau relegates to the background the epistemological questions that have recently figured so prominently in our discussions as he conducts his reflection on the present organization of knowledge. This reflection leads him to pay special attention to the question of the Other, a question that figures as a leitmotif in many of the current discussions of knowledge, whether they originate in epistemological concerns or not. This is not the place for an exhaustive historical analysis of the emergence of this issue in contemporary reflections, but it may be useful to recall two somewhat different areas in which it has imposed itself on our consciousness far beyond any theoretical concern that we may have: the conception of the subject as the organizer and sense-maker of lived experience, and the challenge posed to forms of Western thought by the liberation movements of the past forty years. Both of these have contributed to a sense of fragmentation that is widespread in our culture and that has been diversely theorized in recent years.

II

The first may be usefully approached through the process of social abstraction, of which Certeau, in his multifarious guises, would appear to be a prime example. This process, whose nature was recognized in the Enlightenment—the period during which it achieved nearly universal extension in the industrializing countries—cleaves the subject and disrupts other entities, such as the family, in order to tailor it to the needs of production. There results an internal division of the subject between the kind of self that one needs to be in certain situations, generally linked to one's means of livelihood, and the kind of self that one is in other settings. The individual no longer feels his or her self to be a whole, but rather a series of diverse zones, subject to differing constraints, frequently of an irreconcilable sort. The paradigmatic, though extreme, example here is of the Nazi executioner who carries out his orders cold-bloodedly (if he is not the one who gives them) but sheds tears of most exquisite sensitivity at the performance of a Beethoven quartet. The results of this process of social abstraction have been thematized in literature, with varying degrees of pathos, as the fragmentation of the self; they have also constituted the psychological ground of French existentialism. Most contemporary theory, save for those strands of it that retain some connection to Marxist perspectives, has generally accepted this fragmentation and has sought to ground it either ontologically or psychologically. In fact, it has tended to focus its efforts on bringing theories of the subject in line with this experience. And, since the fundamental effect of this experience is to create a sense of powerlessness with respect to one's ability to direct or control larger historical processes, history as a dimension of human practice has borne the brunt of these efforts. Notions of desire or even of the aleatory have been put forward in its stead.

It would be tempting to see Michel de Certeau's rather large range of pursuits as an instance of this process of social abstraction in the intellectual field. This field does not so readily admit of this process, however. Our present organization of knowledge may very well share with other forms of the division of labor a commitment to the efficiency of performance, but, rightly or wrongly, it conceives itself more properly as an allocation of competences that are appropriate to their object, an object that is no longer defined as a given of the world but that is a construct of the theoretical and methodological traditions of each discipline. The disciplinary outlook, in other words, permits each discipline to function as if the problem of fragmentation did not arise since the concepts that it mobilizes and the operations it performs are adequate, if not isomorphic, to its object—an elegant variant of the Parmenidean principle of the identity of thought and being. This may well account for the blindness of the disciplinary perspective to the problem of fragmentation: it is constitutive of that perspective.

In such a context, the reach of Certeau's activities is bound to be seen as excessive, and his attitude as extravagant, unless it can be construed as one of the reminders that the disciplines do not really constitute wholly autonomous domains but are part of a larger whole. To be sure, there have been ample periodic reminders of the fact that the disciplines do not, and properly cannot, close up upon themselves, but these very reminders serve more as boundary markers than as attempts to open up the disciplines. The same may be said of the persistent yet unfruitful efforts to establish interdisciplinary approaches over the past thirty years. And, of course, there have been claims of primacy of position made on behalf of certain disciplines or specific approaches, most significantly the Husserlian one for phenomenology, and, more recently, the rather widespread one for the more scholastic conceptions of semiotics. But Certeau's approach seeks neither to affirm some evanescent unity nor to play the role of the protector of the integrity of the present configuration of knowledge. His attitude is more scandalous in that he seeks to exacerbate the fragmentation by deliberately uncovering the ways in which the various disciplinary enterprises rely upon models and paradigms borrowed from one another, and never less so than when they proclaim their independence, so that the mutual relation of the disciplines is never one of autonomy or of heteronomy, but some sort of complicated set of textual relations that needs to be unraveled in each instance—a task that Certeau accomplishes with maestria in several of the chapters of *Heterologies*. His is a challenge to the present organization of knowledge, a challenge that is attentive to the dimension of crisis throughout this area.

III

In retrospect, it should have been obvious at the time that the great sociopolitical upheavals of the late 1950s and 1960s, especially those regrouped under the names of decolonization and liberation movements, would have a major impact on the ways of knowledge. This impact, though it began to occur almost immediately, has not, for the most part, been recognized for a variety of reasons, the strongest of which is the imperviousness of the branches of knowledge—as an organic conception of the disciplines likes to call them—to phenomena that "fall" outside their predefined scope and, at a more general level, our reluctance to see a relationship so global in reach—between the epistemology of knowledge and the liberation of people—a relationship that we are not properly able to theorize. Yet there is no need for a belief in the totalizability of social phenomena, nor is it necessary to have a fully articulated theory of the cross-determinations of economic, social, political, psychological, and epistemological phenomena, to take note of such an impact. In what follows, I will try to sketch briefly the main lines of the evolving form of impact.

Decolonization, as we know, has been a multifaceted process that does not lend itself to facile generalization. Yet it may be apprehended at the discursive level as a tense interaction of the older liberal discourse (gnawed from within by its reliance upon late eighteenth-century conceptions of the role of nations as both agents of history and containers of lower forms of agency) and the Marxist one, an interaction particularly visible in the cultural movement called French existentialism. The ideology of universalism common to the two discourses can be the means of enslavement—instrumental reason in the service of rapacity unrestrained in the laissez-faire market of liberalism or the even greater omnipotence of the hypostasized state—or it can be emancipatory. This is the famous dialectic of the Enlightenment that requires the vigilance of intellectuals to ensure that the positive project of modernism prevails over its less savory alter ego, in Habermas's self-assumed historical task, so noble yet so difficult to carry out. For a Sartre, for example, the struggles of the colonized were just and deserved the support of all individuals of conscience because of the legitimacy of their claim to universal rights. A similar attitude prevailed in liberal circles in the American civil rights movement. But when the latter evolved in the direction of Black Power, that is, toward the rejection of the ideology of universalism, and began to put forth a claim of particularism, liberal support vanished, and indeed changed into outright hostility, since the universalism that constituted the core of its ideological stance presupposes the eradication of particularisms.

Be that as it may, decolonization was followed by a reterritorialization that became rapidly conceptualized through notions of core and periphery, in which the former colonial powers together with other economically dominant nations constitute the core whereas the former colonies form the periphery. The latter admits of measurement in relation to the core as an index of its degree of development, where it is of course implicit that the core's own development is normative and somehow "natural." Such an approach requires that one distinguish circles, if not outright peripheries, within the core as well and that ultimately some center be located, even if it means that national and regional boundaries must be ignored. Part of the present broader economic crisis certainly seems to have to do with the determination of such a new center.

Again, in retrospect, it is apparent that, of all the poststructuralism, deconstruction is the one that has reacted critically to this development—what we know as neocolonialism—by doggedly revealing the fact that there never is anything "natural" or "inevitable" or to be taken for granted in the setting up of center and periphery. It is always the result of specific and discernible operations: rhetorical ones in texts, power ones in the broader social area; though there may well be a gain in describing the latter in terms of the subtle analytics of textual operations. This would explain, among other things, the difficult relationship of deconstruction to the previous forms of emancipatory discourses, especially the institutionalized Marxist one: the neocolonialism of center and periphery is practiced as much if not more by the Soviet Union as it is by the Western powers, whether the old colonial empires or the new neocolonial ones.

Structuralism, for its part, shared in the operative conceptualization of neocolonialism by elevating the notion of function, or, more precisely, of efficiency, to the highest. It is more efficient to structure in terms of center and periphery. In Gramscian terms, structuralism, by which I mean the international movement called French Structuralism, thus would correspond to the position of the organic intellectual formation, whereas the poststructuralisms would represent an emancipatory response to the hegemony of neocolonialism. The relation of deconstruction to structuralism becomes clearer in the process.

There is another movement that challenges our thought even further: the wars of liberation against neocolonialism that differ from the earlier colonialist ones in that they are not waged from a position of nation—something that is understandable to liberalism—or of class—as Marxism would prefer it—but from settings or entities that have not been thought out within the framework of Western tradition. Such will remain the enduring significance of the Cuban revolution, which can be usefully contrasted in this respect to the Algerian war of national independence. Such are the characteristics of the complex struggles being waged in parts of Africa and in Central America, though they differ markedly from one another. Whatever views one may hold with respect to these struggles, one must acknowledge that they are part of a series of challenges to the dominant forms and organizations of knowledge among us. The response to these new liberation struggles is telling. There is relatively little attempt to understand them in their specificity; it is easier to impose upon them the bipolarity that is so constitutive a part of structuralism: there will not be one center with its periphery but two antagonistic centers with their own peripheries, with flashpoints at the boundaries.

As in the case of the fragmented subject, the historical dimension is again ignored: historical forces are taken to be no more than acts of willfulness, perhaps of an irrational form, which it is then easy to attribute to "terrorists." Not only does such a reformulation ignore the specificity of the political movements at hand, but, as Certeau shows in the case of the struggles of the autochthonous peoples of the Americas, it deprives them of a ground from which to make their claims. But, as daily headlines make clear, such a ground is being found, though we tend to experience the resulting claims as disruptions to our patterns of perception, and we find ourselves in a position of bewilderment that makes us easy prey to manipulations of all sorts. We do not know, often enough, what the values that we hold require of us in the face of phenomena that strike us as other.

IV

Western thought has always thematized the other as a threat to be reduced, as a potential same-to-be, a yet-not-same. The paradigmatic conception here is that of the quest in romances of chivalry in which the adventurous knight leaves Arthur's court—the realm of the known—to encounter some form of otherness, a domain in which the courtly values of the Arthurian world do not prevail. The quest is brought to an end when this alien domain is brought within the hegemonic sway of the Arthurian world: the other has been reduced to (more of) the same. The quest has shown that the other is amenable to being reduced to the status of the same. And, in those few instances where the errant knight—Lohengrin, for example—does find a form of otherness that he prefers to the realm of the same from which he came, this otherness is interpreted—by contemporary critics as much as by medieval writers—as the realm of the dead, for it is ideologically inconceivable that there should exist an otherness of the same ontological status as the same, without there being immediately mounted an effort at its appropriation.

Again, we may be unable to provide a satisfactory theorization of the link between epistemology and broader forms of social practice, but it is clear that the hegemonic impulse thematized in the chivalric quest was a fact of culture and that its failure in the political realm—witness the case of the wars upon Islam (the Crusades)—in no way invalidated its hold in other areas, especially in the practice of knowledge, as Edward Said has convincingly shown. Politically, the West may have had to grudgingly accept the existence of the Islamic otherness, but in the realm of knowledge it acknowledged no such possibility.

This hegemonic tendency of the cognitive realm is not the exclusive purview of traditional disciplines. It permeates the writings of even the most theoretically daring thinkers, as is evident in the case of Michel Foucalt. Foucalt conceived of himself as the surveyor of these very hegemonic modes of cognition, so someone who would describe their systematicity and their hold. Though he labeled his enterprise an archaeology, he paid scant attention to the ways in which these hegemonic modes of cognition did establish themselves and to the means by which they managed to maintain their grasp. In fact, his own concern with the hegemonic forced him to discard with a ruthlessness equal to that of what he was describing any practices, discursive or otherwise, that sought to maintain any autonomy with respect to these hegemonic behemoths. This led to the famous problem of his inability to articulate the movement, or the shift, from one hegemonic mode of cognition to another. Certeau, by contrast, is attentive to precisely this constitutive moment, even in Foucault's own case, to the interplay of "emergent" and "residual" forces as Raymond Williams usefully calls them, that is, to the impulses, the enabling conditions, for living in relation to these hegemonic forces. That is why he is always concerned with practices and discourses—and the distinction between these two is not ontological as far as he is concerned—that are either on the wane or in the making, or that even do not quite manage to constitute themselves. Foucault's descriptions present a

vast machinery of power; Certeau's pit individual or small-group efforts against this machinery as a mode of interaction that constitutes
the lived experience of these people. He is, therefore, more attentive
to the actual working of power as well as to the tactics, strategies, and
ruses that the neutralization of such vast power requires.

V

We have seen, however, that not all forms of otherness allow themselves to be subsumed into sameness, and indeed, there has been growing recognition of this fact within Western thought itself. One discipline that has been existentially concerned with this realization is
anthropology, especially among its American practitioners. The
wrenching experience of the Vietnam war, in which anthropologists
saw the findings of their fieldwork mobilized to accomplish the destruction of the cultures, if not the annihilation of the peoples, whom
they had studied, has led anthropologists to question their role, and
by extension, that of knowledge, in the spread of hegemony. The debates at the annual meetings of the American Anthropological Association during the late sixties and seventies failed to produce a solution,
for the problem far exceeds the conjunctural dimension in which it
was generally considered.

Significantly, though, the proposed solutions sought to correct the
perceived vulnerability of the epistemological with an injection of the
ethical. Otherness, thematized as cultural diversity, not only calls for
the respect that the anthropoligist is expected to grant it, but, in a self-
reflexive gesture, is further expected to relativize the position of the
anthropologist. As Clifford Geertz succinctly puts it:

> To see ourselves as others see us can be eye-opening. To see others
> as sharing a nature with ourselves is the merest decency. But it is
> from the far more difficult achievement of seeing ourselves amongst
> others, as a local example of the forms human life has locally taken,
> a case among cases, a world among worlds, that the largeness of
> mind, without which objectivity is self-congratulation and tolerance
> a sham, comes. If interpretive anthropology has any general office in
> the world it is to keep reteaching this fugitive truth.

In this rather remarkable concluding paragraph to the introduction of
his *Local Knowledge,* Geertz articulates the main tenets of a newly
emerging conception of knowledge, a conception that one finds work-

ing its way into some of the theses of Jean-François Lyotard's *The Postmodern Condition* as well. Knowledge must surrender its global pretensions. Its reach is always limited to its loci and condition of emergence, what Geertz calls the local and Lyotard, the pagan (from the Latin *pagus,* enclosed field). It must not serve as an instrument of domination; in fact, it must renounce mastery as such. Its relations with others must be governed, for Geertz at least, by ethical considerations. The language of tolerance, objectivity, sham, and fugitive truth here is a subtle mixture of religious discourse and Enlightenment rationalism.

This "fugitive truth" is a bitter pill to swallow for the rationalism that is, properly speaking, the heir to gnosticism, because it puts into question the latter's progressive legitimation against a notion of truth that is somehow beyond the immediate purview of reason. Against the notion that salvation originates in faith *(pistis),* gnosticism has always held that it is the result of knowledge *(gnosis)* and that error or false knowledge are the causes of perdition. Yet gnosticism did not stand alone but rather as a rationalist instrument of support of revealed truth, and this is in Judaism, Christianity, and later in Islam. But its support was qualified and limited to the extent that the gnostic held that reason was sufficient to reach the truths of religion. In the Christian West, a giant step toward the acceptance of the gnostic position was made in Aquinas's famous assertion that nothing in faith is contrary to reason, and its corollary that reason is a proper avenue to the realm of the truths of faith—a significant extension of the Anselmian *fides quaerens intellectum* position. The gnostic viewpoint was given legitimacy. It achieved supremacy with the Cartesian reversal of the relationship of faith and reason in relation to truth: henceforth the belief in God and the truths that he dispenses would be subject to the prior operations of reason. And this reason, it turns out, can be quite constraining: I discover the truth through the free exercise of my own reason; therefore I cannot refuse this truth; I must adopt it, as must all who are equally rational. The gnostic viewpoint far surpasses the uncertainties of faith because it rests on the certitudes of rationality. The reason of the Enlightenment is fundamentally gnostic, and, since it seeks to replace the vagaries of faith with the certitudes of rationality, it is logical that it should attempt to assert its hegemony. To sin against faith is to sin against a God whose designs are at best tortuous or visible "in a glass darkly," but, in any case, in need of mediation. But to sin against reason is a matter of easy demonstration and therefore calls for immediate correction in all the meanings of this term. If the shift in our conception of knowledge, articulated by Geertz, does represent more than a passing aberration, we may well come to see modernity as the period when the gnostic claim to be able to account rationally for all truths has held sway and the period that is currently beginning as one that seeks to distance itself from this gnostic domination.

The most consistent denouncer of the gnostic position in our day has been the French philosopher and Talmudic scholar Emmanuel Lévinas, who, in a work that spans nearly fifty years, has rigorously argued for a notion of truth that is at considerable odds with the dominant rationalist one, a notion that relies upon the category—or, more accurately within the Lévinasian framework, upon the lived experience—of the other. Against a notion of the truth as the instrument of a mastery being exercised by the knower over areas of the unknown as he or she brings them within the fold of the same, Lévinas argues that there is a form of truth that is totally alien to me, that I do not discover within myself, but that calls on me from beyond me, and it requires me to leave the realms of the known and of the same in order to settle in a land that is under its rule. Here the knower sets out on an adventure of uncertain outcome, and the instruments that he or she brings may well be inappropriate to the tasks that will arise. Reason will play a role, but it will be a secondary one; it can only come into play once the primary fact of the irruption of the other has been experienced. And this other is not a threat to be reduced or an object that I give myself to know in my capacity as knowing subject, but that which constitutes me as an ethical being: in my originary encounter I discover my responsibility for the existence of this other, a responsibility that will lie at the root of all my subsequent ethical decisions. Knowledge and its operations are subordinated to this initial ethical moment, for the responsibility that I then experience is the very ground of my response-ability, that is, my capacity to communicate with others and with myself in noncoercive ways. Reason can now deploy itself in the field that has been opened up by the relation I have to the other. It is a reason chastised, not likely to seek hegemonic control, for were it to do so it would have to do violence to my self as the self that is in this relation of response-ability to the other.

VI

Lévinas's position provides philosophical and theoretical underpinnings for a more epistemologically oriented position such as that of

Geertz. It is significant that there is currently quite a vogue of interest in his work and that it is beginning to reshape the attitudes and positions of established critics. Tzvetan Todorov, for example, reads the encounter between the Europeans and the autochthonous inhabitants of the New World through Lévinasian lenses, and he interprets Bakhtin's notion of dialogue similarly. Yet this position, and the uses to which it is being put in literary criticism, raise considerable questions perhaps best formulated by Edward Said in his *The World, the Text, and the Critic.*

Said is concerned with the emergence of this new conception of knowledge, for it signals to him the abandonment of the secular position of the intellectual and a return to what he sees as religious criticism practiced by clerics who are not capable of, or even really interested in, maintaining a truly critical position. The reliance upon an almighty form of reason provided a solution to the human need for certainty, and in Kant's famous phrase, it gave rise to the Idea of a consensus of all free and rational consciousnesses, thus establishing a sense of group solidarity and of communal belonging—features that Said believes to constitute fundamental human needs. But he finds that increasingly these needs are being addressed through the religious dimension rather than through the secular one, and he takes the present concern with the other as an instance of this phenomenon. In the conclusion to his book, he sees the return of relation in the theories and practices of criticism that put forward notions of unthinkability, undecidability, and paradox, as well as in those that make direct appeal to "magic, divine ordinance, or sacred texts." Further, he sees evidence of it even in those theoretical approaches that one would presume to be immune, such as Marxism, feminism, and psychoanalysis, for in much of their current practice, these "stress the private and hermetic over the public and social."

For the organization and the practice of knowledge, the results are "unpleasant to contemplate. There is an increase in the number of fixed special languages, many of them impenetrable, deliberately obscure, willfully illogical. . . . Instead of discrimination and evaluation, we have an intensified division of intellectual labor." The critical dimension of criticism is rapidly eroding as the critic, evincing the same sort of belief as the neoconservative in the mystical workings of the marketplace, renounces the responsibilities of the intellectual in order to "become a cleric in the worst sense of the word."

These are serious charges, and they deserve a much more detailed examination than I can give them here. As my own earlier character-ization of the problematic condition of the practice and organization of knowledge ought to indicate, I share Said's concerns and accept large parts of his diagnosis. I am struck, however, by the fact that Said is unable to overcome, or to reinscribe, the problem that he so ably describes, and must content himself with a general appeal for a more secular criticism. His predicament, it seems to me, comes from the fact that he has not sufficiently examined the ground of the present return to religion, a ground that I shall attempt to make more explicit by returning to my earlier assertion about the Hegelian form of our present organization of knowledge. I will also claim that Michel de Certeau's handling of these issues may well get us out of Said's predic-ament.

Said's stated preference for a form of criticism that openly assumes a social and political responsibility as well as his distaste for certain forms of philosophical theorizing lead him to construe the problem of the organization of knowledge in sociological terms that, to me, already partake of the problem he seeks to address. Quite rightly, Said brings to the fore of his considerations the role that the institutional-ization of knowledge has played. Describing this institutionalization through the passage of filiation to affiliation, he is able to show how forms of authority are instituted and used to create a sense of caste among those who are so affiliated. Curiously enough, though, Said does not seem to recognize in this pattern the accomplishment of a project that is properly Hegelian in origin, a project that already fore-sees all the other features of the present situation. Of course, it has become commonplace to assert that this project has failed and thus to suggest that it no longer need concern us, yet a closer examination of the organization of knowledge may well lead us to reconsider this widespread belief.

It will be recalled that Hegel proposed a global interpretation of history that focuses on the status of knowledge. Roughly speaking, this interpretation runs as follows: history is over because knowledge has become absolute. Rationality is the absolute becoming of the spirit in history, the stages of history marking the progressive develop-ment of the spirit as it invests ever more of the world. It is generally forgotten, however, that this development and the manner of its in-vestment proceed through institutionalized forms, so that another way of describing history is to record the progressive institutionalization of rationality until it becomes absolute in the ultimate institution, the

Hegelian State, at which point history comes to an end. It was Hegel's ambition to thematize the entire narrative of Western rationality, a project that has been widely discussed and generally rejected. But it was as much his ambition to announce its ultimate accomplishment in history, that is, in the institutions through which rationality would henceforth exercise its hold over all of reality and the modes of cognition we bring to bear upon it. And this second aspect of the project has received less attention, since it must have seemed that the ascertained failure of the first would take care of the second, and since Hegel himself devoted more attention to the first, which he considered a historical precondition of the second. Yet the very multiplication of disciplines, their autonomization, the rise of the specialized languages that Said rightly deplores, the shunting away of the historical dimension toward ever more remote corners—all of these provide ample evidence of the fact that the present organization of knowledge has aligned itself upon the Hegelian conception, though mostly without any direct knowledge of it. Perhaps the best index of that alignment is the suspicion, if not the outright hostility, with which any questioning of the fundamental mechanism of this organization, namely the Hegelian dialectic identified for all practical purposes with rationality itself—though never under its proper name—is greeted within the boundaries of these institutionalized forms of knowledge.

This is where the heterological countertradition comes in. It has focused, as I indicated earlier, on the epistemological dimension of the problem. But the strategies available to it are limited: either it must deconstruct the epistemology from within, a rather arduous task that constantly runs the risk of becoming one more specialized language on the verge of institutionalization or, as the fate of deconstruction in American universities demonstrates, a new system of affiliation, in Said's terms; or it must critique this epistemology from the outside, and then it runs the risk of relying upon the ethical and the figure of the other and its possible religious overtones. In other words, the two strategies require that one position oneself with respect to the central Hegelian claim of the end of history. The second strategy relies directly upon the consensual perception that history has not come to an end, and seeks to anchor the epistemological in something other than the spirit's own deployment. History is thus retained, and one remains agnostic with respect to the outcome of the Hegelian prediction, but at a cost that Said is right to see as unbearable since it reestablishes the dominance of the religious over the rational which Hegel himself found to prevail prior to the advent of absolute knowledge.

It is against the discomforts of this "solution," as much as against the problem itself, that the first, and more properly heterological, strategy has evolved. It begins by granting, for the sake of the argument as it were, the Hegelian thesis on the end of history; then it proceeds to unravel the institutional claims of rationality, showing that the institutionalization that presently prevails does not correspond to the Hegelian principle of the deployment of the spirit that alone could properly justify it. But this strategy does not seek to establish in an oblique way what the other strategy already takes for granted, namely that history has not come to an end; rather it seeks to show that indeed a certain kind of history may well have come to an end but that this ending does not exhaust history. If anything, this strategy, as pursued in some of Derrida's, and especially Paul de Man's, writings, may allow us to finally come to grips with history.

In his rightful anguish, Said allows himself to be caught on a ground that fails to distinguish between these two strategies. He desires the historical dimension but not at the price that the second strategy exacts, for its construct of the historical as sacred or transcendent is precisely the kind of history that he seeks to avoid; yet he cannot accept the tortuous way in which the first strategy proceeds to the historical, drawing justification from the fact that indeed it does not seem to attain it.

But in Michel de Certeau's work, it is attained. The heterological counter-tradition has shown that the particular vulnerability of the Hegelian claims lies in their inability to articulate the dependence of knowledge upon language. Although Hegel took great pains, in the narrative part of his project, to show that the progressive development of the spirit, and the concomitant rise of absolute knowledge, consisted primarily in their liberation from material forms (hence the appropriateness of the Idealist label), he was blind to the materiality of language, going so far as to state that the language of poetry had achieved such a liberation. The heterological tradition, focusing upon epistemological issues, has sought in the ontological dimension the reasons for this particular resistance of language, frequently granting a privileged status to literature as the linguistic practice in which this resistance is most easily apparent in the form of a complex nondialectical interplay of the representational and the nonrepresentational.

Certeau, for his part, has preferred to avoid a ground that is rather uncertain since literature is first and foremost an institutional determination, and thus to seek to ground it ontologically may well amount to no more than shoring up the institution at the very moment when its vulnerability becomes apparent. The quality that is recognized in literature, he seems to think, does not come from the fact that it is a special mode of language, but rather from the fact that it is a part of language, a mode of language use, that is, a discourse. Unlike language, which, as an object of knowledge, is a construct of philosophers and linguists, discourses constitute forms of actual social interaction and practice. As such, they are not irrational, but they are subject to the pulls and pressures of the situations in which they are used as well as to the weights of their own tradition. They must always handle the complex interplay of that which is of the order of representation and the nonrepresentable part which is just as much constitutive of them, their own other. And because of this dual nature, they are not really disciplines—these operate within the realm of representation which is thematized by Hegel as the investment of the real by the spirit; they are logics, that is, they have a coherence *sui generis,* one that needs to be rigorously and thoroughly described in each instance. For Certeau, the most important role in the constitution of that logic is reserved for the complex, and properly textual, play of the other with the more overt, representational part of the discourse, hence his designation of his project as *heterologies.* This other, which forces discourses to take the meandering appearance that they have, is not a magical or a transcendental entity; it is the discourse's mode of relation to its own historicity in the moment of its utterance.

In my earlier reference to the gnostic conception of rationality, I indicated the moral power of this rationality, which could claim hegemonic domination because of the universalism of its assertions. Such a claim is inherent in the Hegelian conception of rationality, of course, to the extent that it represents the development of the spirit. But it is also inherent, though less overtly explicit, in the institutions of rationality, including the disciplines—though the emergence of the expert as a major figure of authority in our culture shows that such claims are societally acknowledged and even receive legal sanction. This gnostic conception of rationality, and its Hegelian institutional implementation, remove human beings from the sphere of history as practice, since history is conceived of then as the inexorable process of rationality's own rational development. Here are to be found further causes of the sense of loss of historical agency that accompanies the fragmentation of the self characteristic of social abstraction, and reasons for the bewilderment that marks our inability to comprehend historical processes that exceed those of our institutionalized knowledge. Certeau's conception of discourse, so different from Foucault's hegemonic one, recovers an agential dimension for us inasmuch as it recognizes that discursive activity is a form of social activity, an activity in which we attempt to apply the roles of the discourses that we assume. These may not be heroic roles, but they place us much more squarely in front of our responsibility as historical actors.

16 Emergent Literature and the Field of Comparative Literature

It is in the nature of knowledge to be unstable: on one hand, it must ensure its continuance by the preservation of the achievements of the past; on the other, it must not let them stand in the way of new advances and discoveries. The precarious equilibrium and the resulting tensions between the reproduction of existing knowledge and the production of new knowledge are not allowed to propagate their instability in society at large; they are contained within the apparatus of knowledge and especially in its institutional forms, which, in our day, means the academic disciplines. Any crisis that may affect these disciplines should thus be limited in scope, or at least in impact, and should not threaten either the edifice of knowledge or society itself; at worst, a discipline may collapse—a most unlikely happenstance given the power of endurance provided by its institutional setting—necessitating a realignment in the division of intellectual labor. Since the logic of modern societies requires ever greater specialization, that is, division of labor, it is more likely that a discipline in some form of trouble will in fact be subdivided into two or more new ones, as, for instance, seems to be happening to biology recently under the stress of its own development. Disciplines are generally quite resilient, though, as befits the institutions they are. Were one to threaten implosion—as opposed to subdivision—the resources of the entire apparatus of knowledge could be counted upon to be mobilized in a rescue, for the collapse of any discipline poses a threat to the entire organization of knowledge, not least by disclosing its constructed and malleable character.

Under what circumstances is a discipline at risk? There appears to be scant literature on the subject. It is acknowledged that various disciplines have, at different times, undergone rather profound changes, but such changes, having been internally negotiated and contained, are seen as part of the normal instability of the entire enterprise of knowledge. Four conditions, it seems to me, must obtain in order to put a discipline in jeopardy. These four conditions derive from the four basic constitutive elements of a discipline: (1) a normative object of study; (2) a defined field within which this object obtains or is constituted; (3) a determinate set of theories and methodological procedures that are applied to the object in the field (these theories and methodologies need not be at all unified or even dovetail with each other, though there must be a sense that they are limited in number); (4) a set of individuals who are recognized and identify themselves as practitioners of the discipline and some of whom are engaged in, among other things, the training of those who will succeed them in this practice.

Comparative Literature is doing very well as far as the fourth element is concerned, at least in North America. The number of programs and departments has grown considerably in recent years, and there is a sense that comparatists, alongside feminists and scholars of ethnic studies, represent what is most progressive and most interesting in the teaching of literature. Some disagreement still obtains as to who is a properly trained and qualified comparatist, but it tends to be obscured in the relative success of the enterprise at large.

In recent years, it is the third element that has received the most attention. When even such mass-media instruments as the *New York Times* and *Newsweek* begin to write about the theoretical and methodological disputes that have agitated our domain, it is clear that this agitation must have reached a threshold beyond which a more direct societal interest begins to assert itself. We have all been involved in these disputes, frequently shifting ground as the issues became defined and redefined. As yet, however, we have little understanding of what precipitated the whole brouhaha in the first place. And in the absence of such understanding, there proliferate two unreflecting reactions: one that seems characteristic of the times, namely a recourse to some version of conspiracy theory, with its heavy-handed insistence on foreign importation and then concentration in unlikely loci of subversion (Johns Hopkins! Yale!), the other more in keeping with a predominant mode of comparative inquiry (though not entirely incompatible with the first), the search for influence, with its explanations by means of locating the *origin* of some theory or methodology. It matters little that everything that originates somewhere does not exert an influence and that if the notion of influence is to have any value at all it must not only identify the original material but must also account for the receptiveness it encounters in its new setting. In any case we must acknowledge that we do not presently have any consensual view for the success of Russian formalism, French structuralism, deconstruction, semiotics, reception aesthetics, the work of the Bakhtin group, or the current vogue of what some have taken to calling the new historicism; thus, we have left ourselves open to the charge that we are given to faddish fluctuations and have no standards by which to evaluate our theories and methods.

We may not have much understanding of what lies behind the theoretical agitation of recent years, but we know what some of its consequences have been. Indeed, these have figured prominently in the controversies. One of the foremost has been the sudden uncertainty surrounding the very object of our study. Until quite recently it was the work, and the work was taken to be a given of our discipline. But disciplines do not have givens; as constitutive parts of the apparatus of knowledge, they have objects that are constructed by and for them. Students of literature discovered slowly that the work, by which we frequently meant the masterpiece, was a notion located at the intersection of a periodizing concept with a generic one and defined by literary history. Even the retheorization of the work as text, while attentive to dimensions explicitly excluded by the notion of work, remained beholden to literary history for the production of the texts to be studied. However removed they may have been from its assumptions, theoreticians of diverse stripe found themselves governed by the parameters of a literary history that they mistakenly assumed to be either obsolete or so discredited as no longer to warrant any examination.[1] As they found themselves forced to focus their attention upon it, they discovered that the very definition of the object of the entire discipline had to be rethought. In the present division of labor, academic departments that deal with "national" literatures hold on to previously elaborated canons of texts that must be taught if for no other reason than to maintain the institutional identity of their department. To be sure, these canons are challenged, especially by feminist critics, but it is interesting to observe that this challenge takes place within previously defined national boundaries, somehow intimating that, whatever the status of gender, it either comes after nationhood—an eighteenth-century concept—or is significantly altered by it.[2] Comparatists have never had any such canon, as even a conservative conception of the discipline made clear.[3] Instead, we have either maintained the definitions of object that obtain in the "national" literatures or have attempted to develop our own on the basis of some specific theoretical and methodological orientation. Those who are inclined to pursue the project of a general poetics thus focus on general processes that are presumed to obtain in literary works, regardless of period or national origin; others, more inclined to the elucidation of cognitive or epistemological problems, look at literary texts as privileged examples for the staging of such problems; still others bring a social dimension to bear upon their studies. But all view the material support of their object rather unproblematically: it is a text that has been defined somewhere as literary. It is precisely this privilege of the literary text that is challenged in some of the most promising methodological approaches today, which, for the sake of convenience, we could label discourse analysis.

Here the object is defined in a completely novel way, one that partakes of the preoccupation of the poetician, the epistemologist, the sociologist of literature, and indeed many others. For the discourse analyst there is, strictly speaking, no literary discourse. There are only multiform discourses that together are the warp and woof of the prevalent social discourse, of which literature is a socially defined use. It is at this juncture that the discourse analyst encounters the greatest difficulty: having redefined the object of inquiry in such a way that it would not be tainted by any of the social privileges granted to literature, discourse analysis finds it very difficult to reconnect with the literary phenomenon. It can deal with discourse *about* literature but is stymied when it comes to the discourse *of* literature. Some practitioners in this area ultimately give up on literature altogether. It must be noted, however, that in spite of its global pretensions, discourse analysis accepts the dominant framework of the nation-state as its geographical boundary and generally follows the periodizatioons set in literary history.[4]

The reasons for the difficulties of discourse analysis are instructive: having set its sights on the whole of the universe of discourses, discourse analysis cannot internally generate the differentiations it needs in order to specify an entity like literature. The recourse to pragmatics, which is the preferred strategy under circumstances, does not solve the problem, which is one of *field*. Objects must have fields in which they are either found or constituted, and fields cannot be conceived of as the totality of the phenomena construable under the object if the approach is to have any success in analytic differentiation. The predicament is not unique to discourse analysis; far from it. It is inherent to the problem of literary study today. Yet the problem of field is the one that has received the least attention, even among comparatists, for whom it is absolutely central.

To comparatists the problem of field presents itself as a challenge to the historical construction of the discipline. It was constituted to compensate for the orientation of literary studies along national lines, but, we must acknowledge, from the outset we have privileged certain literatures, notably the German, French, and English. We have granted very limited status to such others as the Italian, Russian, or Spanish, and except in the newly developing area of East-West studies, we have remained firmly Eurocentric, even when dealing with texts from the Americas.[5] Even in East-West studies, that is, in the area where developments in Chinese, Japanese, and, less frequently, Indian, or even Arabic, literatures are studied by comparison with those in European literatures, it is always the latter that have provided the terms of reference, so that we have had considerations of symbolism in Chinese poetry, in which, for example, the Chinese phenomena were described in terms of their congruence, or divergence, from French and German ones.

What we are dealing with here is a long-standing pretension and implicit assumption of Comparative Literature: despite the diversity and multifariousness of literary phenomena, it is possible to hold a unified discourse about them. This pretension is the heir to the old project of a general poetics which was challenged and ultimately brought to a standstill by the European turn to nationalism in the eighteenth and nineteenth centuries. Comparative Literature is the haven in which the idea of this project has been preserved. The challenge posed by the establishment of distinct French, German, and English literatures is nothing, however, in comparison with that which issues today from the emergence of all sorts of new literatures: in Africa, Asia, Latin America, Canada (with its two "national" literatures), Australia, as well as black literature in the United States, women's literature in many parts of the world, native people's literature in the New World, and so on.[6] The project of a general poetics could move in the general direction of the complementary study of ethnopoetics on one hand and of universals of literature on the other, incidentally recapturing Herder's conception of literary study,[7] and thus could institutionalize the division of labor between Comparative Literature and the "national" literatures along lines often suggested in the debates during our period of theoretical development: theory in Comparative Literature and analysis and criticism in the "national" literatures.

Such a division of labor is ultimately untenable, whatever appeal it may have had or may still hold. There is no atheoretical approach to literature; there are only more or less consciously held theoretical tenets. The present "decline" of theory in Comparative Literature is due in great part to the fact that many of the theoretical developments of the past twenty years have become part and parcel of literary analysis. When a certain theoretical hegemony—that of New Criticism in North America—was challenged, Comparative Literature provided an institutional setting from which this challenge could be mounted. Today we have a much more heightened theoretical awareness in all areas of literary scholarship, and one cannot draw an institutional separation by means of theory, even if one wants to. And there are excellent reasons for not wanting to, not the least of which is the implied autonomization of theory.

One of the criticisms most frequently addressed to those working in the area of theory is precisely their tendency to detach themselves from the study of literary works and to operate exclusively in the world of concepts. This criticism cuts across political lines: conservatives, such as Denis Donoghue, interpret this detachment as arrogance and a turning of one's back upon the tradition, which for him clearly means the institution of literary studies; progressives, like Edward Said, see it as a refusal to carry out the critical function of the intellectual in the social world, as a retreat into a form of religiosity. This is not the place to rehearse the controversies surrounding these arguments, but it must be acknowledged that a speculative tendency was very much in evidence in the theoretical enterprise, propelling it toward ever greater autonomization.

It is important to understand the nature of this propulsion, for it is doubly articulated. To begin with, the theoretical impulse originated in an operation of demystification: it sought to bring back to light the constructed and institutionally determined character of the objects of literary study, something that the institution of literature, like all the other institutions within the apparatus of knowledge, prefers to gloss over, though, in all fairness, without denying its factuality. Institutionalized knowledge practices—another name for disciplines—have rules and protocols for the determination of their objects; once some entity is constituted as such an object, its constructed character is left out of consideration, and it functions for all practical purposes as a given. It is precisely the function of methodological and theoretical debates to delimit the parameters of object construction. Such debates serve, then, as reminders that what a particular discipline takes to be a given is actually a construct. Furthermore, the debate over the redefinition of object-construction parameters accentuates the constructed character of the discipline as a whole and therefore its autonomy from any external object, from any givenness. To put it more simply: the entire apparatus of knowledge—and, *a fortiori*, the disciplines—functions on the premise that objects are available to or given for the cognitive operations specified within the apparatus; at the same time, this apparatus constructs these objects, that is, determines conditions of givenness. The two parts of this operation are not incompatible, but they do not admit of simultaneous consideration: one must be carried out before the other. The discomfort caused by theory stems from its attempts to maintain both aspects of the cognitive operation at the same time. The result is that theory appears to be at a further remove from the object—in this instance, the work—than the atheoretical approaches practiced within the institution, and thus it tends to be perceived as functioning autonomously.

The second part of this doubly articulated propulsion toward autonomy is to be found in the very relation of the cognitive to the given, constitutive of the prevailing apparatus of knowledge. In terms borrowed from the history of philosophy, one could describe it as the permanent temptation of Hegelianism within Kantianism, that is, the passage from the realm of the empirical to that of the conceptual. The cognitive model constructed by Kant acknowledges the given but grants it the status of an otherness, that is, as both constitutive of and a challenge to the knowing instance.[8] This model places all knowledge in a painful predicament: it ultimately depends upon something that it does not control but must accept as it finds it. The predicament is a historical one, however: it affects only the conception of knowledge that we find underpinning modernity. The ancients, notably Aristotle, accepted this initial givenness through theories of being; modernity rests upon the forgetfulness of being, as Heidegger reminds us, and it cannot readily accept anything the provenance of which it can neither control nor account for. In Heidegger's terminology, the totalizing and all-embracing pretension is a characteristic of *tekhnē*, by which he means the specific cognitive orientation of modernity, in which the knowable must be reduced to the status of an object upon which a knowing subject can perform specified cognitive operations.[9] From the outset of modernity, givenness is a problem, since for modernity everything must be brought within the orbit of the subject, and yet givenness cannot be accounted for by the sustaining role (in the sense of the Greek *hypokeimenon*) of the subject; on the contrary, it is precisely that which escapes the subject; the object is but a poor substitute for it. Hegel's solution was to hold out the hope, to be fulfilled in the fullness of time, of all givenness being invested by the Spirit—his designation for the knowing instance—so that ultimately given and known would coincide in Absolute Knowledge. It is this drive toward the reduction of the distance between given and known that constitutes the second element of the double articulation we have been examining.

Combined with the first, it leads to a heightened sense of the importance of the constructed in all knowledge and to a powerful urge to turn one's back upon all givenness. Givenness appears to be superfluous, since, at best, it is but a purport for the constructs with which one really works. Furthermore, since all the models for implementing *tekhnē* require the sort of internal coherence that can be made answerable to logic or to mathematical variations of it, the forgetfulness, or rather the deliberate pushing aside, of the given does away with its logically irreducible character in favor of constructs conceived along logically acceptable lines. The theoretical enterprise is thus both structurally and historically propelled toward greater autonomy: knowledge becomes more conceptual in modernity, and theory, in a first stage, partakes of its movement.

There is a second movement as well, however, which is also staged in Kant, though hardly in Kantianism if by that one means the body of doctrine extracted from Kant's writings. In the first two *Critiques*, Kant indeed provided the underpinnings of the model of knowledge that prevails in modernity, but thorough thinker that he was, he did not turn his back on the problem of givenness; he returned to it in the *Critique of Judgment*, where the long analytics of the beautiful, and especially of the sublime, constitutes, among other things, a lengthy reflection upon the given as the other of knowledge. Here it suffices to note that this otherness, which challenges and defies our cognitive ability, is precisely what forces Kant to conceive of aesthetic judgment as contentless and as beyond the purview of either reason or the understanding: in the aesthetic experience, that which offers itself to our sensory apparatus neither possesses the form characteristic of reason's object nor grants a hold to the law-making of the understanding; it merely, but irreducibly, is.[10] Incidentally, this is the phenomenon that Paul de Man sought to apprehend by the phrase "the resistance to theory."[11]

It has often been remarked that the third *Critique* entertains a strange relationship to the previous two; it starts as a continuation of their effort to provide a solid ground for the operations of knowledge, but in the process of argumentation it snatches that ground from under them in order to claim as foundational the results of the reflections it undertook on their basis, thus casting some doubt upon the notions of ground, primacy, base, and upon the entire architechtonics of the three *Critiques*. We are at one such juncture in the argument here. What is revealed as mere being (in the sense of existing) in the operation of aesthetic judgment cannot be collapsed back into some new-fangled ontology, given the thrust of the previous *Critiques*. To begin with, it gives itself in the sphere of experience and thus cannot be reduced to any of the transcendental instances previously examined. To say that it is in the sphere of experience is to acknowledge that it exists in time and space, yet given the treatment of these two categories in the first *Critique,* one must go farther and recognize that this givenness, inaccessible to either reason or the understanding, conveys no other content but the fact of its being in space and time. This givenness is what Paul de Man came to call inscription.[12] It corresponds to the formal definition of the chronotope in Mikhail Bakhtin's reflection on this subject.[13] What is thus given to experience is what the first *Critique* established as the very condition of experience, experientiality itself. And since experientiality defines subjecthood, the experience of experientiality constitutes subjects.

Thus, whereas the first two *Critiques* appear to derive their propulsion from the sovereign position of the subject, the third addresses the constitution of the subject itself and rests on that which resists the cognitive ("theoretical," in Kant's terminology) pretensions of the subject and eventually leads the subject to recognize itself as a historical being, that is, as a being that counterposes its own activity in space and time to the givenness it encounters. This activity and its products constitute the realm of culture, although the provenance of culture cannot be accounted for in the terms I have put forward so far, since culture is never an individual project but a collective one.

It will be recalled that when he speaks of aesthetic judgment Kant is very insistent that the maker of this judgment must intimately feel that others would make the same judgment were they in her or his place. Insofar as this insistence has received attention, it has been interpreted in the light of the categorical imperative of the *Critique of Practical Reason* as reaffirming human universality. If we take it that, among other things, the third *Critique* is concerned with the constitution of the subject, then this reading has to be modified in the light of earlier findings. Faced with the givenness that constitutes it as subject in a punctual moment of space and time, the subject, insists Kant, feels very strongly that others would make the same judgment were they in his or her place. Since the subject has just experienced experientiality and has come to see itself as subject, Kant's insistence means that the subject acknowledges that the encounter with givenness will equally constitute others as subjects.

This notion has far-reaching consequences, one of which is of immediate interest to me here: for the newly constituted subject to make this step, it is necessary that she or he not only imagine that others locate themselves in the very site she or he is occupying—tantamount to the reduction of others to same—but that this new subject occupy, in principle if not empirically, a number of different loci in space and time which others may occupy and that the subject experience experientiality there, that is, verify that subjects are constituted there. This is not some sort of conversion of same to other, as one might wish to conclude, but rather the delimitation of a field of experientiality—that is, of subject constitution—which is not reductive to sameness since, it will be recalled, all of this is contentless and formless. In other words, what takes place in the aesthetic judgment is not a singular event—as seems to be the case in Gadamer's reconstruction of hermeneutics on a Heideggerian ground—but the demarcating of a field within which subjects are constituted as entities inhabiting a given set of spatiotemporal conditions, in such a way that these conditions define their commonality or, as Heidegger would put it, their destiny. It is in a concretely delimited field that both community and society are elaborated, the first by establishing a relation between all who are constituted into subjects in and by the field, and the second by means of the relations that are established with respect to the givenness that gave rise to the field.[14]

Defined in this way, the notion of field takes priority over the notions of cognitive object and subject, let alone theory. It is an enabling condition for the elaboration of these notions, which then interact to form the cognitive dimension of the culture delimited by the field. It is within this culture that the apparatus of knowledge is constructed and the disciplines are assigned their roles. We saw earlier that the notion of "field" is one of the four elements of a discipline, but the term "field" was used in a different sense from the one that I have just elicited from Kant. In relation to disciplines, "field" refers to a parcel of the culturally constructed domain of knowledge as it is subject to the operations of the apparatus of knowledge, whereas field (without quotation marks) is the enabling condition of cultural elaboration. At this juncture, I would like to put forward the following claim: the "field" of Comparative Literature is field. In other words, I take it that, within the prevalent organization of knowledge, it is incumbent upon comparatists to inquire into the relationship of culture to givenness, to its other.

If a culture is formed by the cognitive operations performed within a field, its internal economy stands in a particular relationship to the givenness that led to the constitution of the field in the first instance. This givenness is not part of the culture, since it precedes it, yet it pervades the culture, since it could be said to animate it inasmuch as it determines not only the conditions of its emergence but the dimensions of the field within which it evolves. It is thus an active principle rather than a passive one, as the term *givenness* may have connoted. It should be clear that it does not manifest itself as such within the culture, for culture is a construct in response to it. If it has any existence within the culture, it is figural, although it may be better to view it as the operator of certain effects. The following example provides a good instance of such effect production and may help us in understanding this operator.

Ezekiel Mphahlele is a contemporary black South African writer who has been very much concerned with problems of cultural identity in both his fictional and his critical writings. It does not take a great effort of the imagination to see that the lived experience of any South African, let alone that of a black writer forced into exile and banned both personally and in his writings and yet eventually returned to his land, will require reflection upon issues of cultural inclusion and exclusion, identity and empowerment, that is, a theory of culture. Mphahlele's work marks the various stages in the elaboration of such a theory, from his early autobiographical writings to the two versions of his first collection of essays and to the later critical writings.[15] For our immediate purposes, one strand in this ongoing reflection bears closer examination.

The young Zeke Mphahlele, having been raised in the slums of Pretoria, suddenly got the opportunity to receive a Western education that would eventually take him to England. Like many other Africans before him, indeed, like anyone who did not belong to the class whose culture was set as the norm of Western education, Mphahlele felt doubly alienated: from his milieu, which could not provide him with the nurturing support he needed in—and which was presupposed by—the education he was receiving, and from the culture he was assimilating in the course of this education. After having made an attempt to assimilate this culture, notably in his senior thesis devoted to English romantic poetry, Mphahlele turns his attention to the question of cultural assimilation itself and, for his master's thesis, studies the representation of blacks in Western literature. Predictably, he finds such representations far from perfect, but he is not content with remarking their distortion; he is far more concerned with the claim of universality and totalization that he finds in Western knowledge, which trips upon the problem of blackness. Taking it as an ideological problem, he turns his attention to *négritude,* which he rejects for its elitist and attentivist orientation, and determines to rethink the problem, which, for him, is an existential one in the personal dimension and a political one as far as the collectivity of black South Africans is concerned.[16]

It is not surprising, then, that his initial formulation should follow Sartrean lines or, more accurately, Franz Fanon's version of Sartre's existential psychology,[17] though in terms of inside versus outside. Because of his education, his language, his frame of literary reference, Mphahlele is white inside while on the outside he is black—and this outside can never be forgotten in the land of apartheid. Mphahlele could have followed the Sartrean path at this juncture, but his distrust of individualism and his commitment to a nonelitist stand took him in a slightly different direction that has far less to do with the personal dimension of Sartrean psychology. He discovers, and therefore knows, that he is white inside, but this knowledge does not bring him any closer to whites, not because of his external blackness but rather because whites, even in South Africa, know that they are white only in a casual way. It is the way in which he knows that he is white on the inside that differentiates Mphahlele from whites. At this juncture he is tempted to conclude that it is the knowing instance, namely his consciousness, that makes for this difference, that is, that his consciousness of being white is different from the fact that is so known and that this consciousness is precisely where his blackness resides. Conjuncturally, this conclusion translates itself into the impetus animating the Black Consciousness movement of the sixties and seventies, which Mphahlele provides. Mphahlele is nothing if not rigorous however, and he quickly realizes that to establish such a divergence between the knowing and the known would make it impossible to bring being black within the sphere of the known and thus to make such knowledge casual knowledge. The result would be that he would know that he is black casually, the way whites know they are whites, and therefore would confirm his being white by the mode of this knowledge, characteristic of whites. At this juncture, Mphahlele is struggling with the mechanism of the dialectic into which he has been drawn and which seems to drag him inevitably through all the stages of the Hegelian master-slave interplay. There is no turning back once one is drawn in, and Mphahlele understands that the dialectic must be played out till it overcomes itself. In other words, whites must learn to know that they are whites in a noncasual way. The Black Consciousness movement, like the Black Power movement in the United States or in the Caribbean, had attempted to do just that, but it had done so from the position of blackness, thus choosing as a ground the very instability upon which the dialectic was being played. Mphahlele understands the dangers of such positioning—he had already seen it in *négritude*—and distinguishes between the fact that whites must be challenged to know that they are white in a noncasual way and to associate this challenge, and knowledge, with blackness, on one side, and the fact that the consciousness of sameness and therefore of difference is not only consciousness but a locus from which a reinscribing of black-and-white relations can be launched. This locus is experienced as consciousness by the individual but is not thereby either contained or defined by consciousness.[18] Mphahlele attempts to address this through the notion of a double stream of consciousness, which is a way of acknowledging that consciousness is not the producer but the product of an operativity that remains unknowable, since there is no consciousness to know it.

Mphahlele's reflection brings us to the same point we had reached in reflecting upon givenness, with this difference: we must understand givenness not as a passive (or a resultative, in the linguistic sense of the term) but as an active principle. Givenness is agency. As such it never gives itself but is figured in that which is given, and it is knowable only through its figurations: God, nature, history, consciousness, the state, language are some of those that have historically been proposed. Yet it is accessible, as Mphahlele's working out of a noncasual way for whites to know that they are whites demonstrates. In dialectical terms, this new knowledge that whites have should be called black knowledge in opposition to the casual white knowledge, but what matters beyond the dialectic here is that this knowledge is not produced through a play of negativity and sublation; it is not because one negates the casual that one reaches what, for lack of a better term, I have been calling the noncasual, nor is it because of a dialectic of self and nonself in which the latter is positioned as other. The casualness of white knowledge is the result of its univocity, of its reliance upon a stable and fixed positionality. When, under Mphahlele's questioning, it is thrust to the ground of its production, it comes upon the fact that this ground is not a position but a field that determines positionality. Mphahlele was no longer interested in playing the positional games that are still to be found in the writings of even such antiapartheid writers as Nadine Gordimer, André Brink, or Molefe Pheto.[19] His commitment to a social and revolutionary role for the writer required an understanding of the rules of this positional game, of how they control moves, and of the interest of the game itself.

The question of the "field" of Comparative Literature can be asked again, but it cannot be answered in the theoretical or methodological way in which it was reached, since the field we have uncovered is the ground upon which the theoretical gaze is formed and is thus conditioned by it. We must attempt to address this field by means of the givenness that animates it. The work of another writer, also from austral Africa, may prove of some help. It is a short story written in Portuguese, titled "O Relógio" ("The Watch"), by the Angolan writer Manuel Rui.[20] This short story contains a double narrative: the story of a watch and the story of the telling of the story of the watch, a structure that makes any paraphrase or summary perilous. In an area under the control of the Movimento Popular para a Liberação do Angola (MPLA) prior to its final victory over the Portuguese, there lives a veteran *comandante* of the rebel forces. Having lost a leg on a Portuguese mine, he is now retired and spends much of his time with children. A ritual has developed whereby the story of the watch is recounted every Sunday. The children are by now quite familiar with the plot of the story, yet they continue to coax it out of the *comandante*, who thus functions as traditional storyteller and priest substitute in this Sunday ritual. The storytelling is far from straightforward. The children interrupt with questions, remind the *comandante* of details he gave previously, seek new precision, and store in their memory the new elements as they are being elaborated. In fact, the story provides one of the best descriptions of the collective labor involved in the production of an oral tale. At first, only the *comandante* is aware of what is going on. Progressively, the children become emboldened and grow more secure in their role as coauthors of this story, so much so that the particular telling that is the focus of the written tale has them elaborate a new ending to the story. This complex creative process, at once traditional and revolutionary—in all senses of the term—is constantly redefining the boundaries of the historical and the fictional, with an attention to aesthetic, cognitive, and political significance.

The story of the watch is itself quite simple. The beginning gives a flavor of the whole:

> O Comandante abria sempre da mesma maneira: —O relógio foi fabricado na Suiça e a marca era Omega. —E onde está a Suiça? — Muito longe. Não é uma pessoa. E um país, muito longe, na Europa e là faz muito frío. Era o costume. A garotada interrompía. (p. 22)

> The Captain always began in the same way: "The watch was Swiss-made and its brand was Omega." "And where is this Swiss?" "Very far. I don't mean a person. It's a country, very far, in Europe, and it's very cold there." That is the way it went. The kids would break in.

Through the give-and-take between the *comandante* and the children, we learn that this Swiss watch was sold to a Portuguese dealer, who shipped it to the capital of Angola, Luanda, where it was sold in a shop called Paris Jewellers. This telling takes quite some time because the children want to know why watches are not made in Angola (which provides raw materials) or even in Portugal and what are the advantages of naming a jewelry store after the capital of France. Eventually the story progresses to the point where a major in the Portuguese expeditionary forces sent to put down the MPLA purchases the watch. This very major is sent in pursuit of the *comandante* and his troop and is killed in an ambush they set. One of the rebels makes the *comandante* a gift of the plundered watch. In the subsequent pursuit by the Portuguese seeking to avenge the ambush, the *comandante* and his squad are forced to cross into neighboring Zaire, where they have to use the watch to ransom themselves from a corrupt Zairois police official about to turn them over to their pursuers. This is the basic story told by the *comandante* every Sunday. The account purports to be historical, though subject to the embellishment and the greater precision demanded by the children. But on this particular Sunday one of the children suggests the story need not end there. Let the

Zairois assist an anti-MPLA (and United States and South African–supported) group and enter Luanda and establish a base, then let the watch be recovered by daring MPLA pioneers who seize the Zairois prisoner. Finally, let the watch be returned to the children of the Portuguese major with an account of its peregrinations in the form of a song sung by the children and carried to Portugal in a conch. Such is the story. Although it calls for a full analysis, a few remarks may suffice for our purposes.

It would be tempting to read the story as an allegory of one sort or another: temporality is clearly one of the stakes; the brand name of the watch suggests an ending, if not the end, of Western domination; and new epoch is foreshadowed both in the return of the watch to Europe and in the collective elaboration of the tale, which renews ties with traditional modes of African storytelling that presumably were endangered by colonization. Such a reading, or variations thereof, would depend on the treatment of the watch as either a symbol or the objective correlative of one. The story lays such stress on the material aspect of the watch, its provenance, its process of fabrication, and its circuitous deambulations, as to intimate a resistance to this type of reading. The watch does not stand for anything; it is, and by just being, it forces readerly reactions in the direction of symbolic interpretation.[21] It brings the various protagonists within the measure of the time that it marks. The distant Swiss watchmaker, the Portuguese import-export agent, the colonial shopkeeper with dreams of grandeur, the imperialist military agent, the revolutionary, the neocolonial stooge, the rising generations of liberated Africans and postimperialist metropolitans—all are brought within its orbit; all share the same chronotope, the measure of which it punctuates in accordance with the workings of its inner mechanism. It organizes a discursive space, the very space that an interpretive reading will attempt to fill, the dimensions of which are already adumbrated in the children's relentless questioning. This interdiscursive space is its field, and it must be the "field" of Comparative Literature, in the sense not so much that we must fill it as that we must be attentive to the mode of its constitution and indeed must participate in it as do the children of the story, who eventually wrest away the *comandante*'s command over the story in order to send it in a circulation that is not necessarily different from that of the watch, though with a rather different set of themes attached to it.[22]

It is not irrelevant to a consideration of this story to note that Manuel Rui's book was not actually printed in Angola, even though Luanda is given as its place of publication, and that no date of publication appears. The book was in fact printed in Portugal by Edições 70 for the Union of Angolan Writers at a time when such printing presses as could operate in Angola were still fully mobilized in the revolutionary effort that followed independence. Manuel Rui's manuscript had traveled to Lisbon, where, following the April revolution, it was printed on postimperial Portugal's presses and then returned to Angola, thereby adding a further twist to the production of the story and preventing anyone from determining its temporal end. This is far more than a critical conceit, as a quick return to the story shows.

At one juncture, the *comandante* compares his own stainless-steel utilitarian watch with the watch of the story and characterizes the latter as a "relógio de burguês"—a bourgeois watch. The insistence on the process of fabrication and, even more so, on the various trades the watch was subject to takes on additional meaning. The circulation of this bourgeois commodity reveals the existence of a world economic system that recognizes national boundaries only when it finds it suitable to its own ends. So pervasive is such a system that even a war of national liberation begins to look dubious: the nation-state it will result in is likely to become but one more relay in the circulation of commodities. To this world order built on the relationship to the commodity and punctuated by the limits of nation-states and the rhythms of linear time, the story counterposes a field of discursive creativity that is repetitive, endless, and articulated around the relationship among those who are engaged with the givenness within it. To a world socioeconomic order of commodity production and circulation across national boundaries, it opposes the dialogic community of the *comandante*—the children, the Portuguese major's children, Angolan writers, Portuguese publishers, North American readers and critics, and so on.

This may appear to be a binary opposition, but only because a third term is occulted. Much is made in the story of the children's slow determination to send the watch, and its story, back to Portugal. The crippled *comandante,* firmly committed to a realistic mode of storytelling, following perhaps the ideological and aesthetic orientations of his chief, Augustinho Neto, head of the MPLA and eventually president of Angola as well as an internationally renowned poet, had never imagined this eventuality. Like Neto, he was involved in building the nation and attempting to endow it with a literature worthy of it, an

Angolan literature. The children see other boundaries than those of the state and seem wary of the state's institutions. Their form of creative realism recognizes that state institutions, if not the state itself, are at best inadequate protection from and perhaps willing accomplices of the world system, and that the discursive creativity they employ must not be contained within obsolete structures. For their story they want the agential power presently harnessed on behalf of the commodity in late capitalism against the petrified and monumentalizing approach of national literature.

It is my claim that it is precisely this hegemonic and monumentalizing view of literature which is challenged by emergent literature. "Emergent literatures" are not to be understood then as literatures that are in a state of development that is somehow inferior to that of fully developed, or "emerged," literatures—our own disciplinary version of "underdevelopment" or "developing" literatures, if you wish, with attendant "Third-Worldist" ideologies—but rather as those literatures that cannot be readily comprehended within the hegemonic view of literature that has been dominant in our discipline. In his view, emergent literatures will include writings by racial and ethnic minorities in countries such as the United States; literature by women in, let us say, Italy, France, or Australia; and much of the new writing from Africa, Asia, and Latin America, including the Caribbean.

Emergent literatures represent a different conception of field and of object from that represented by the often used expression "emerging literatures." The latter reflects a Hegelian conceptualization according to which the new literatures are viewed as representing less mature stages of canonical literatures, which we as theoreticians and analysts of literature should have little difficulty in understanding—so little, perhaps, that they may not warrant the commitment of our time and may well be left to others, such as students writing dissertations. It is not difficult to see that this attitude seeks to perpetuate existing theoretical hegemonies. If my notion of emergent literatures as literatures that challenge these hegemonies is to be retained, we could readily conceive that a contemporary writer from a Third World country could write in a nonemergent way. And in fact this happens even in the career of a single individual. Witness the case of V. S. Naipaul. His early novels, such as *A House for Mr. Biswas,* are good examples of emergent literature, with their attempt to record the discourse of everyday life in colonial Trinidad and especially the features of what

Mervyne Alleyne has called "post-creole English."[23] But the later novels—such as *The Guerrillas,* which is also set in Trinidad—with their standardized diction and their representation of different speech as alienatingly distant from the norm implicitly shared by a North Atlantic reader and writer, are not emergent literature. It is no accident that at this juncture Naipaul should become the favorite Third World writer of the *Times Literary Supplement* and the *New York Review of Books* and that a powerful lobby should seek the Nobel Prize for him. And yet even then Naipaul remains problematic. Where will the institution of literature as presently constituted put him? Doesn't part of the exceptional treatment being accorded him go beyond ideological convergence and mark the fact that he must be treated exceptionally if the prevalent division of labor in literary studies is to be preserved? Otherwise, where will we teach him? in British literature? in West Indian or East Indian literature? His very prominence occults these questions, and yet it indelibly inscribes them and the problems they represent within the field of Comparative Literature.

Notes

Credits

Index

Notes

1. Reading for Culture

1. Jauss, *Literaturgeschichte als Provokation* (Frankfurt: Suhrkamp Verlag, 1970); English translation by Timothy Bahti, *Towards an Aesthetics of Reception,* Introduction by Paul de Man (Minneapolis: University of Minnesota Press, 1982), p. 7.
2. It was delivered on April 13, 1967, under the title "What Is Meant by Literary History and to What End Is Its Study?" This is obviously an ironic allusion to Schiller's "Was heiβt und zu welchem Ende studiert man Universalgeschichte?" Feeling perhaps that too few in his audience had noticed the nature of the provocation intended, Jauss altered the title by labeling his project a provocation. The inaugural lecture was therefore published as "Literaturgeschichte als Provokation der Literaturwissenschaft" (1967) and was eventually foreshortened to *Literaturgeschichte als Provokation.*
3. Harald Weinrich, "Thirty Years after Ernst Robert Curtius' Book *Europäische Literatur und lateinisches Mittelalter* (1948)," *Romanic Review* 69.4 (1978), 262.
4. Ibid.
5. Jauss, *Zeit und Erinnerung in Marcel Proust's "A la Recherche du Temps Perdu"* (1955; Frankfurt: Suhrkamp, 1986).
6. Jurij Tynjanov and Roman Jakobson, "Problemi izucenija literaturi i jazika," *Texte der Russichen Formalisten,* vol. II, ed. Wolf Dieter Stempel (Munich: Fink Verlag, 1972).
7. Gadamer, *Warheit und Methode* (1960; 4th ed., Tübingen: Mohr, 1975; English translation *Truth and Method* (New York: Seabury Press, 1974).
8. Adorno's seminar had been disrupted throughout the academic year 1968–69 with the distribution of leaflets, name calling ("Teddy," to remind him of his American sojourn), and so on. Students finally occupied Jürgen Habermas's office. Adorno opposed their forceful removal. Yet when it took place on January 31, 1969, at the instigation of the rector of the university, Adorno was photographed shaking hands with the po-

lice officer leading the raiding party. The gesture of courteous leave-taking was represented as evidence of Adorno's "treachery."

9. Theodor W. Adorno, *Kierkegaard: Konstruktion des Ästhetischen, G.S.,* vol. 2 (Frankfurt: Suhrkamp Verlag, 1979), pp. 60–69; English translation by Robert Hullot-Kentor, *Kierkegaard: Construction of the Aesthetic* (Minneapolis: University of Minnesota Press, 1989).

10. Geoffrey Hartman, *Criticism in the Wilderness* (New Haven and London: Yale University Press, 1980).

11. F. R. Leavis, *The Living Principle: "English" as a Discipline of Thought* (New York: Oxford University Press, 1980).

12. Collected in *Beyond Culture,* uniform edition (New York: Harcourt Brace Jovanovich, 1965), pp. 55–76.

2. The Changing Face of History

1. Arnaldo Momigliano, "History in an Age of Ideologies," *The American Scholar* (Autumn 1982), 495–507.

2. Ibn Khaldun, *The Muqaddimah: An Introduction to History,* 2nd ed., translated from Arabic by Franz Rosenthal (Princeton, 1967).

3. Immanuel Kant, "The Idea of Universal History from a Cosmopolitical Point of View," in *On History,* ed. Lewis White Beck (Indianapolis, 1963), pp. 11–26.

4. Mandrou, *De la culture populaire au XVIIe et au XVIIIe siècles* (Paris, 1964); *Magistrats et sorciers en France au XVIIe siècle* (Paris, 1968).

5. Duby, *Les trois ordres ou l'imaginaire du féodalisme* (Paris, 1978; English ed.: *The Three Orders: Feudal Society Imagined,* trans. T. N. Bisson [Chicago, 1980]) and numerous other works.

6. Ariès, *Essais sur l'historie de la mort en Occident* (Paris, 1975; English ed.: *Western Attitudes towards Death from the Middle Ages to the Present,* trans. Patricia M. Ranum [Baltimore, 1974]); Vovelle, *La mort et l'Occident de 1300 à nos jours* (Paris, 1982).

7. Carlo Ginzburg, *Il formaggio e i vermi: Il cosmo di un mugnaio del '500* (Turin, 1976; English ed.: *The Cheese and the Worms: The Cosmos of a Sixteenth-Century Miller,* trans. John Tedeschi and Anne Tedeschi [Baltimore, 1980]).

8. Francisco de Quevedo, "La España defendida," in *Obras completas: Prosa,* ed. F. Buendía (Madrid, 1961), pp. 488–526.

9. J. N. Hillgarth, *The Spanish Kingdoms, 1250–1516* (Oxford, 1976–1978).

10. Sánchez-Albornoz, *España, un enigma histórico* (Buenos Aires, 1956).

11. Translated by Edmund King (Princeton, 1954).

12. See especially Eugenio Asensio, *La España imaginada de Américo Castro* (Barcelona, 1976), pp. 34–40; and Sánchez-Albornoz, *España.*

13. Asunción Domenech, "Entrevista a José Antonio Maravall," *Historia 16* (December 1980), 109–114.

14. *Poder, honor y élites en el siglo XVII* (Madrid, 1979).

15. Maravall, "From the Renaissance to the Baroque: The Diphasic Schema of a Social Crisis," trans. Terry Cochran, in *Literature among Discourses: The Spanish Golden Age*, ed. Wlad Godzich and Nicholas Spadaccini (Minneapolis, 1986), pp. 3–40.

16. *The Structure of Spanish History*, p. 41.

17. See Heinrich Wölfflin, *Renaissance und Barock* (1888); Werner Weisbach, *Der Barok als Kunst der Gegenreformation* (Berlin, 1921); and Frank Warnke, *Versions of Baroque: European Literature in the Seventeenth Century* (New Haven, 1972). For an overview of the literature in this area see Gerald Gillespie, "Renaissance, Mannerism, Baroque," in *German Baroque Literature*, ed. Gerhart Hoffmeister (New York, 1983), pp. 3–24.

18. J. A. Maravall, *Culture of the Baroque* (Minneapolis: University of Minnesota Press, 1986), p. xxxiii.

19. Cf. Maravall, "La cultura de crisis barroca," *Historia 16*, extra 12 (December 1979), 80–90.

20. Ibid., p. 82.

21. Ibid., p. 89.

22. Cf. Maravall, "Seminario sobre la cultura del barroco," *Actas del II° Coloquio del Grupo de Estudios Sobre Teatro Español* (GESTE), Toulouse, November 16–17, 1978, pp. 21–22.

23. See Nicholas Spadaccini, "Cervantes' Aesthetic of Reception in the *Entremeses*," in *Critical Essays on Cervantes*, ed. Ruth E. Saffar (Boston, 1987).

24. Maravall, *Honor, poder y élites*, pp. 14 15.

3. Popular Culture and Spanish Literary History

1. Peter Burke, "Oblique Approaches to the History of Popular Culture," in *Approaches to Popular Culture*, ed. C. W. E. Bigsby (Bowling Green, 1977), pp. 69–106.

2. Marc Fumaroli, *L'Age de l'éloquence: rhétorique et "res literaria," de la Renaissance au seuil de l'époque classique* (Paris, 1980), p. 31.

3. José Antonio Maravall, *La cultura del Barroco* (Barcelona, 1975).

4. Walter Benjamin, *Ursprung der deutschen Trauerspiels* (Berlin, 1928).

5. For a discussion of these collections, see Colin Smith, Introduction to *Spanish Ballads* (Oxford, 1964), esp. pp. 8–12.

6. Elizabeth Eisenstein, *The Printing Press as an Agent of Change*, 2 vols. (Cambridge, 1979). Henceforth this book is cited in the text by volume and page number.

7. Luiz Costa Lima, *Dispersa demanda: ensaios sobre literatura e teoria* (Rio de Janeiro, 1981), pp. 16ff. See also Eric Havelock, *A Preface to Plato* (Cambridge, 1963).

8. Michel de Certeau, *L'invention du quotidien, I: Arts de faire* (Paris, 1980).

9. D. W. Cruickshank, "Literature and the Book Trade in Golden-Age Spain," *Modern Language Review* 73 (1978), 800.

10. Ramón Menéndez Pidal, *Romancer hispánico. Teoriá e historia* (Madrid, 1953), vol. 2, pp. 66–67.

11. Cruickshank, "Literature and the Book Trade," p. 806. See also Augustin González de Amezúa y Mayo, *Opúsculos históricas-literarios*, 3 vols. (Madrid, 1951–53), vol. 1, pp. 371–373.

12. José Ignacio Tellecha, "Bible et théologie en 'langue vulgaire.' Discussion à propos du Catéchisme de Carranza," in *L'Humanisme dans les lettres espagnoles,* ed. Augustin Redondo (Paris, 1979), p. 230.

13. Fray Luís de León, *De los nombres de Cristo,* ed. Cristóbal Cuevas (Madrid, 1977), p. 140.

14. Antonio Márquez, *Literatura e inquisición en España, 1478–1834* (Madrid, 1980), p. 148.

15. Bartolomé Bennassar, *Un Siècle d'Or espagnol, vers 1525–vers 1648* (Paris, 1982), p. 260.

16. Peter Burke, *Popular Culture in Early Modern Europe* (New York, 1978), p. 63.

17. Maria Corti, *An Introduction to Literary Semiotics,* trans. Margherita Bogat and Allen Mandelbaum (Bloomington, 1978), p. 152, n. 20.

18. Antonio Rodríguez Moñino, *Construcción crítica y realidad histórica en la poesía española de los siglos XVI y XVII* (Madrid, 1968), p. 14. Subsequent references to this book are cited in the text by page number.

19. See Rodríguez Moñino, ibid.; E. M. Wilson, *Some Aspects of Spanish Literary History* (Oxford, 1967); F. J. Norton and E. M. Wilson, *Two Spanish Verse Chapbooks, A Facsimile Edition with Bibliographical and Textual Studies* (Cambridge, 1969); María Cruz García de Enterría, *Sociedad y poesía de cordel en el Barroco* (Madrid, 1973). Subsequent references to these works are cited in the text by page number.

20. Giuseppe Di Stefano, "*I pliegos sueltos* della Biblioteca Colombina nel Cinquecento. Note a un inventario," *Romance Philology* 34 (1980), 79–80, 91.

21. Cristóbal de Castillejo, "Represión contra los poetas españoles que escriben en verso italiano," in *Obras de amores. Obras de conversación y pasatiempo,* ed. Jesús Domínguez Bordona (Madrid, 1926), Clásicos Castellanos, vol. 79, pp. 233–234.

22. Juan Luis Alborg, *Historia de la literatura española, I: Edad media y renacimiento,* 2nd ed. (Madrid, 1970), pp. 665–666.

23. Burke, *Popular Culture in Early Modern Europe,* p. 23.

24. Maxime Chevalier, *Lectura y lectores en la España de los siglos XVI* (Madrid, 1976), p. 99.

25. María Cruz García de Enterría, *Literaturas marginadas* (Madrid, 1983), p. 33.

26. Mercedes Agulló y Cobo, *Relaciones de sucesos* (Madrid, 1966). See also Cruickshank, "Literature and the Book Trade," p. 816.

27. María Cruz García de Enterría, "Un Memorial, casi desconocido, de Lope de Vega," *Boletín de la Real Academia Española* 51 (1971), 139–160; reprinted in *Sociedad,* pp. 88–89.

4. After the Storyteller

1. For this argument, see Tzvetan Todorov, *La Grammaire du Decaméron* (The Hague: Mouton, 1969).

2. *Morphology of the Folktale* (Bloomington: Indiana Research Center in Anthropology, 1958); Russian original published in 1928. For a discussion of the problematic relation of the French structuralists, especially Lévi-Strauss, to Propp's work, see Anatoly Liberman, Introduction to Vladimir Propp, *Theory and History of Folklore* (Minneapolis: University of Minnesota Press, 1983).

3. *Einfache Formen* (Tubingen, 1968); original published in 1929.

4. Victor Shklovsky, "Parodijnyj roman. *Tristram Shandy* Sterne," in *Texte der russischen Formalisten,* vol. I, ed. Jurij Striedter (Munich: Wilhelm Fink Verlag, 1969), pp. 245–300.

5. "Story and Discourse in the Analysis of Narrative," in Jonathan Culler, *The Pursuit of Signs: Semiotics, Literature, Deconstruction* (Ithaca: Cornell University Press, 1981), p. 169–170.

6. Ibid., p. 187. Culler provides several examples of such analytic dilemmas. One that deserves consultation in its own right is Cynthia Chase's "The Decomposition of Elephants: Double-Reading *Daniel Deronda,*" *PMLA* 93:2 (March 1978), 215–227.

7. Friedrich Nietzsche, *Werke,* ed. K. Schlechta, vol. 3 (Munich: Hanser, 1966), p. 804.

8. Culler, *The Pursuit of Signs,* p. 183.

9. *La Condition post-moderne* (Paris: Minuit, 1979); in English, *The Postmodern Condition,* trans. Geoffrey Bennington and Brian Massumi (Minneapolis: University of Minnesota Press, 1984).

10. An equation that is not meant to state that history as the temporal dimension of human existence is a narrative. Rather, since history has been knowable only through the kind of narratives that we call history, it is properly unknowable unless its dependence upon narrative form can be broken. Obviously, this is far too complex a subject to be treated in a

note. One would need to differentiate at least between the positions of Foucault and Derrida, who debated the issue among themselves. Derrida's arguments can be found in: "Cogito et histoire de la folie," *Revue de Métaphysique et de Morale* 68 (1963), 460–494; in English translation in *Writing and Difference,* trans. Alan Bass (Chicago: University of Chicago Press, 1978), 31–63, and in "A propos de 'Cogito et histoire de la folie,'" *Revue de Métaphysique et de Morale* 69 (1964), 116–119. Derrida's essays were occasioned by the publication of Michel Foucault, *Folie et déraison: Histoire de la folie à l'age classique* (Paris: Plon, 1961); partially translated as *Madness and Civilization: A History of Insanity in the Age of Reason* (New York: Pantheon, 1965). Foucault's reply to Derrida is contained in the expanded version of the book published under the title *Histoire de la folie* (Paris: Gallimard, 1972).

11. *Story and Situation: Narrative Seduction and the Power of Fiction* (Minneapolis: University of Minnesota Press, 1984).

12. "Der Erzähler. Betrachtungen zum Werk Nikolai Lesskows," *Gesammelte Schriften,* II. 2, Werkausgabe vol. 5 (Frankfurt: Suhrkamp, 1980), pp. 438–465; in English, "The Storyteller: Reflections on the Works of Nikolai Leskov," in *Illuminations,* trans. Harry Zohn (New York: Schocken Books, 1969), pp. 83–109. For the sake of convenience, references will be to the English version.

13. "Die politische Entstellung des Post-Strukturalismus," in *Hefte für kritische Literaturwissenschaft 5,* ed. Jochen Schulte-Sasse (Frankfurt: Suhrkamp, 1984).

14. Chambers is aware of the work of Jean Baudrillard on seduction (*De la Séduction* [Paris: Galilée, 1979]), though not of the more recent but closer in tone essay on strategies (*Les Stratégies fatales* [Paris: Grasset, 1983]). In any case, Chambers differentiates between strategy, which he defines as the "practice of those who are masters of the terrain," and tactica, defined as the practice of those who are not in control of the situation (see the last chapter of *Story and Situation*). Chambers takes seduction to be a tactic even though it leads to a mastery of the situation. It is also obvious that the critic cannot resort to strategy—hence Chambers's cautiousness vis-à-vis theory—but must rely on tactics.

15. Henry James, *The Novels and Tales of Henry James: The New York Edition,* vol. 15 (New York: A. M. Kelley, 1970), p. 230.

16. I owe this observation to Samuel Weber, whose reading of the tale converges with, and nicely supplements, that of Chambers. See the third chapter of his forthcoming *Institution and Interpretation* (Minneapolis: University of Minnesota Press).

17. The choice of the art-tale for this study strikes me as being, in Chambers's own terms, strategic. The presumption of completion and finition that is so important a part of the argument for the commodification of the art-

tale makes it a privileged object of study. By contrast, the novel calls for the kind of inquiry we associate with Mikhail Bakhtin. This may also account for the fact that all narratologists, dependent on the subject-object model, choose to write about short stories, their protestation that this is for pedagogical reasons notwithstanding. Chambers's forthrightness is refreshing. It remains to be seen whether the critical option of a return to narrative is possible in the case of longer prose, or whether the latter forces us into the meantime between the two storytellers.

5. Where the Action Is

1. Thomas Pavel, *The Poetics of Plot: The Case of English Renaissance Drama* (Minneapolis: University of Minnesota Press, 1985).
2. *Le Miroir persan* (Paris: Denoël, 1978).
3. *Inflexions de voix* (Montréal: Les Presses le l'Université de Montréal, 1976).
4. Most notably, *La Syntaxe narrative des tragédies de Corneille* (Paris: Klincksieck, 1976).
5. This account excludes such nonhistorical endeavors as the *Grammaire* of Port-Royal.
6. For a remarkable recent study, see Marc Fumaroli, *L'Age de l'éloquence: Rhétorique et "res literaria" de la Renaissance au seuil de l'époque classique* (Geneva: Droz, 1980).
7. Such a tendency becomes particularly marked in the histories of literature of nations on the periphery of cultural power. For a parodistic treatment of these tendencies, see Witold Gombrowicz, *Dziennik* (Paris: Institut Littéraire, 1956).
8. I am not trying to suggest a cause-and-effect relation between these demographic phenomena and the developments in literary theory, but to draw attention to the background of these phenomena. The history of literary theory will have to take into account the changes in patterns and scope of literacy.
9. Most notably V. N. Voloshinov, *Marxism and the Philosophy of Language* (New York: Seminar Press, 1973).
10. Cf. my "Semiotics of Semiotics," Chapter 11 in this volume.
11. Roland Barthes, *Elements de Sémiologie,* in *Le Degré zéro de l'écriture* followed by *Eléments de sémiologie* (Paris: Gonthier, 1965).
12. This discussion excludes those concerned with speech-art theory and with text-linguistics. It also leaves aside the important work of the scholars of the Porter Institute of Poetics.
13. Among the exceptions stand the work of Nicolas Ruwet and that of Gerald Prince.

14. The exception here is the unjustly neglected work of Guillaume on the psychomechanics of language. See Gustave Guillaume, *Langage et science du langage* (Quebec: Presses de l'Université Laval, 1964).

15. G. E. M. Anscombe, *Metaphysics and the Philosophy of Mind* (Minneapolis: University of Minnesota Press, 1981), p. 57.

16. Noam Chomsky, *Language and Mind* (New York: Harcourt, Brace and World, 1968).

17. J. Margolis, *Philosophy of Psychology* (Englewood Cliffs, N.J.: Prentice-Hall, 1984), pp. 84–85.

18. Ibid., p. 88.

19. Ibid., p. 88.

20. Frederic Jameson, "Reification and Utopia in Mass Culture," *Social Text* 1 (1979), 130–148.

21. See Mieke Bal, *Narratologie* (Paris: Klincksieck, 1977); Seymour Chatman, *Story and Discourse* (Ithaca: Cornell University Press, 1978); Shlomith Rimmon-Kenan, *Narrative Fiction* (London: Methuen, 1983).

22. Aleksandr N. Veselovskij, *Poetika sjuzetov*, in *Sobranie socinenij*, series 1, vol. 2, first part (Saint Petersburg: Akademija Nauk, 1913).

23. *Morfologija skazki* (Leningrad: Akademija, 1928). For a thorough discussion of Propp's contribution to this area and to the misunderstandings that have attended his work, see Anatoly Liberman, Introduction to Vladimir Propp, *Theory and History of Folklore* (Minneapolis: University of Minnesota Press, 1984), pp. ix–lxxxi.

24. Claude Brémond and Jean Verrier, "Afanassiev et Propp," *Littérature* 45 (1981), 61–78.

25. Hayden White, *Metahistory: The Historical Imagination in Nineteenth-Century Europe* (Baltimore: Johns Hopkins University Press, 1973), p. 6, n. 5.

26. Peter Brooks, "Fictions of the Wolfman," *Diacritics* 9:1 (Spring 1979), 72–86. See also his "Freud's Masterplot: Questions of Narrative," *Yale French Studies* 55/56 (1977), 280–300.

27. Gérard Genette, *Nouveau Discours du récit* (Paris: Seuil, 1983).

28. Peter Brooks, *Reading for the Plot* (New York: Knopf, 1984).

29. Claude Brémond, *Logique du récit* (Paris: Seuil, 1973).

30. Martin Heidegger, *Nietzsche,* trans. D. F. Krell (San Francisco: Harper and Row, 1979), p. 64. The German original is to be found in *Nietzsche,* vol. 1 (Pfullingen: Neske, 1961), pp. 76–77.

6. The Time Machine

1. Didier Coste, *Narrative as Communication* (Minneapolis: University of Minnesota Press, 1989).

2. Fredric Jameson, *The Political Unconscious* (Ithaca: Cornell University Press, 1981), p. 101.

7. Paul de Man and the Perils of Intelligence

1. Paul de Man, *Wartime Journalism, 1939–1943,* ed. Werner Hamacher, Neil Hertz, and Thomas Kenan (Lincoln: University of Nebraska Press, 1988), p. 66.

8. Caution! Reader at Work

1. Michael Riffaterre, "Le Poème comme représentation," *Poétique* 4 (1970), 417–418.
2. Paul de Man, *Blindness and Insight: Essays in the Rhetoric of Contemporary Criticism,* 2nd ed., rev. (Minneapolis: University of Minnesota Press, 1983).
3. It is the specific merit of Hans Robert Jauss to have undertaken studies, theoretical and empirical, into past modes of reading. See his *Toward an Aesthetic of Reception,* trans. Timothy Bahti, with an introduction by Paul de Man (Minneapolis: University of Minnesota Press, 1982); and *Aesthetic Experience and Literary Hermeneutics,* trans. Michael Shaw, with an introduction by Wlad Godzich (Minneapolis: University of Minnesota Press, 1982).
4. The astrological origin of "concept" of influence is a telling index of the credibility of these claims endowed with "scientificity."
5. Martin Heidegger, *Die Frage nach dem Ding* (Tübingen: Max Niemayer Verlag, 1962); in English, *What Is a Thing?* trans. W. B. Barton, Jr., and Vera Deutsch, with an analysis by Eugene T. Gendlin (Chicago: Henry Regnery, 1967).
6. One of the more insidious ones has been the separation of students into two different groups on the basis of their success or failure in achieving illumination.
7. The case of Derrida in the important essay "The Rhetoric of Blindness" is somewhat different. I discuss it at length in *The Yale Critics: Deconstruction in America,* ed. J. Arac, W. Godzich, and W. Martin (Minneapolis: University of Minnesota Press, 1983).
8. Johann Christoph Friedrich von Schiller, *Über die ästhetische Erziehung des Menschen* (1795), 26th letter. I shall use the words "the apparent" in this sense. This is meant to be the English equivalent of the German "Schein" or the French "le paraître" (in opposition to "l'être"). My later "simulacrity of the simulacrum" is thus "Schein des Scheinens" or "l'apparence de l'apparaître."

9. It receives some attention in W. Godzich and J. Kittay, *The Emergence of Prose: An Essay in Prosaics* (Minneapolis: University of Minnesota Press, 1987).

9. The Tiger on the Paper Mat

1. Paul de Man, *The Resistance to Theory* (Minneapolis: University of Minnesota Press, 1986).
2. In *Problèmes de linguistique générale* (Paris, 1966).

10. The Domestication of Derrida

1. *Le Devoir,* July 19, 1976, p. 1.
2. *How to Do Things with Words* (Cambridge, Mass.: Harvard University Press, 1962).
3. *Washington Post,* July 18, 1976, p. A12.
4. Deconstructionists and their allies ought to ponder the power of the speech act theorists' lobby, which, intent upon preventing a repetition of the Montreal fiasco, managed to block any broadcasting of the 1980 "Opening" ceremonies from the Moscow games. This must have been the meaning of the much-used phrase "the symbolic significance of the Olympic boycott."
5. One may anticipate some of their reaction in John Searle's refusal to understand Derrida, who placed Searle in front of a similar instance of duplicitous duplication in "Limited Inc.," *Glyph* 2 (1974), 162–254.
6. From the Greek *poros,* "passage," with preceding privitive a-, meaning: without passage, blocking the flux, undecidable. Aporia has come to mean undecidability.
7. See Rodolphe Gasché, "Deconstruction as Criticism," *Glyph* 6 (1979), 177–215.
8. A more detailed analysis, which is out of place here, would show that this concept of freedom is necessarily auto-telic and must be axiomatic, independent of any justification.
9. This opposition of truth as manifestation vs. truth as adequation is well known since Heidegger's *Sein and Zeit* (1972).
10. Paris: Editions de Minuit, 1967; English version: *Of Grammatology,* translated and with a preface by Gayatri Chakravorty Spivak (Baltimore: Johns Hopkins University Press, 1976). This work will be cited in the text as *G,* followed by page number to both versions, French first.
11. Such as the standard text by which he had been known in his country for a long time before the more recent translations: "Structure, Sign, and Play in the Discourse of the Human Sciences," in *The Structuralist Controversy: The Language of Criticism and The Sciences of Man,* ed. Rich-

ard Macksey and Eugenio Donato (Baltimore: Johns Hopkins University Press, 1970), pp. 247–265.

12. But which Gayatri Spivak curiously chooses to translate as "substitute." Cf. *G*, 226: "Je trouvais dans Thérèse le supplément dont j'avais besoin," vs. *G*, 157: "I have found in Thérèse the substitute that I needed." Since the discussion which follows is concerned with the "supplement," and, indeed, the chapter is entitled "Ce dangereux supplément . . . ," this is a strange oversight.

13. The oldest attested occurrence in French dates to 1080.

14. "Comme si on avait pu l'arraisonner" should be rendered then as "as if it could have been brought to reason," which retains the sense of control as well as that of movement which "arrest" loses without forgoing the investment of a vehicle by reason.

15. I am not arguing from the perspective of a study of influences, and even less one of sources. I am more interested in bringing out the effects of a specific encounter.

16. Psychoanalytic versions of textuality need particularly to be examined on this point. Far too often the displacement they follow and inscribe is a surface one, caused by a cathexis which, remarkably, remains equal to itself, or at most "spends" itself, and then is unable to preserve its identity but remains within its orb.

17. Emmanuel Lévinas, *En Découvrant l'existence avec Husserl et Heidegger*, expanded edition (Paris: Vrin, 1967), p. 191. My translation.

18. The blindness is marked here somatically in the straining of the eyes leaving their sockets in an attempt to see, as in cartoons: ex-orbitant.

19. This point is brought out with considerable vigor and precision by Rodolphe Gasché's "Deconstruction as Criticism," which is fundamental for any discussion of this issue.

20. *Sein und Zeit*, pp. 394–395. Heidegger's argument is more complex since it is articulated around the notion of *Dasein* as possibility. History is organized around the possibility of an existence which has taken place, and it is in the name of such a project that it seeks out "data." It is not a recording of what has been, but the inquiry into the possibility of that which has taken place.

21. This is the best-known part of the essay, and there is no need to rehearse its arguments. Suffice it to note that the matter of this argument is not as central as it is generally believed. De Man is uncharacteristically assertive in his reading of the passage on metaphor in Rousseau, which, interestingly enough, is read somewhat differently in *Allegories of Reading*. Within "The Rhetoric of Blindness" essay, the matter is of tactical interest, tracing an approach to the strategically more important question of reading.

22. Hans-Georg Gadamer, *Warheit und Methode*, 4th ed. (Tübingen: Mohr, 1975).

23. *Der Universalitätsanspruch der Hermeneutik* (Frankfurt: Suhrkamp Verlag, 1971). Also "Was hei;gbt Universalpragmatik?" in *Sprachpragmatik und Philosophie,* ed. K. O. Apel and J. Habermas (Frankfurt: Suhrkamp Verlag, 1976), pp. 174–272.
24. "Ja, ou le faux-bond," *Digraphe* 11 (April 1977), 83–121, p. 117. My translation.

11. The Semiotics of Semiotics

1. Maya Pines, *New York Times,* September 28, 1982, p. 36.
2. See Manfred Frank, *Der Kommende Gott* (Frankfurt: Suhrkamp, 1982).
3. Jean-François Lyotard, *The Postmodern Condition,* trans. Geoffrey Bennington and Brian Massumi (Minneapolis: University of Minnesota Press, 1983).
4. See Jacques Attali, *Bruits: Essai sur l'économie politique de la musique* (Paris: Presses Universitaires de France, 1977).
5. William Diver, "Substance and Value in Linguistic Analysis," *Semiotexte* 1.2 (1974), 11–30.
6. Umberto Eco, *A Theory of Semiotics* (Bloomington and London: Indiana University Press, 1976), pp. 36–37.
7. Ferdinand de Saussure, *Course in General Linguistics,* trans. Wade Baskin (New York: McGraw-Hill, 1966), p. 16.
8. Fredric Jameson, "Periodizing the Sixties," in *The Ideologies of Theory* (Minneapolis: University of Minnesota Press, 1988), vol. 2, pp. 178–208.
9. Gilles Deleuze, *Logique du sens* (Paris: Minuit, 1968).

12. From Eye to Ear

1. See also the excellent introduction to the first volume of *Les Oeuvres de Philon d'Alexandrie,* ed. Roger Arnaldez et al. (Paris: Cerf, 1961).
2. In Philo, *Philo.* IV, ed. with an English translation by F. H. Colson and G. H. Whitaker, Loeb Classical Library (Cambridge, Mass.: Harvard University Press, 1985). This volume contains both the *De confusione* and the *De migratione.* References to Philo's text are to this edition and are cited by title and paragraph number.
3. Ibid.
4. Philo is most pleased to point out that the ordinary interpretation of these myths, which is also that of the story of Babel, is doubly erroneous: it is either contrary to the rules of the universe (a tower could never reach the heavens), or it is absurd in its argument (if the division of a single language into various tongues was meant to punish evildoers and promote goodness, it must be confessed that it is a very inefficient way to achieve this goal, and that result would cast doubt upon divine intelligence).

5. See also *De confusione* CXC and ff.
6. I follow the Greek with the help of J. G. Kahn, author of the Introduction to the French critical edition of this text, *Les Oeuvres de Philon,* vol. 13 (Paris: Cerf, 1963) p. 158. Kahn provides a literal translation in a note only to reject it.
7. The stakes here are to make of the biblical text either a Jewish version of a pagan myth, a move that Philo says can be made only in bad faith, in the literal sense of the term, or to portray God as incapable of choosing efficient means for the achievement of his goals.
8. Julia Kristeva, *La Révolution du langage poétique* (Paris: Seuil, 1974), pp. 17–100.
9. In the Bible of the LXX followed by Philo, Noah coats the architecture with asphalt.
10. Jacques Derrida, *Glas* (Paris: Galilée, 1974), p. 281.
11. Derrida's term in *Glas,* p. 110.
12. Martin Heidegger, *Der Satz vom Grund* (Pfüllingen: G. Neske, 1957), p. 85.
13. Philo is actually playing here on *asemos* and *episemos,* which allows him to suggest both the opposition of uncoined and coined money, and of that which is unclear and obvious.
14. Philo ignores or leaves aside the entire question of Moses' political dimension.
15. We now understand why Philo defended the literal level of the text, in spite of the fact that it sustains contradictory readings and thus appeared illegible. This very illegibility signals the play of the double writing and summons forth the allegorical reading which restores the legibility, not by helping us determine which of the interpretations is correct, but by re-marking upon the economy of the illegibility, that is, by ensuring that we understand the wherefor of the illegibility. Philo's allegory is most emphatically not an interpretation but a staging of the play of meaning in language, and we should bear in mind that this involves the relationship of *divine* meaning to *human* language. The function of the staging is to show how the finiteness of human language is made to cope in the biblical text with the difficulty of conveying that divine meaning and ensuring that we have access to it.
16. It is beyond the scope of this essay to develop the all-important problematics of temporality that is part and parcel of allegory. In the *De migratione* this problematics is figured by Isaac.

13. Religion, the State, and Post(al) Modernism

1. *Critical Inquiry,* Summer 1982.
2. "On Behalf of Theory," in *Criticism in the University,* ed. Gerald Graff and Reginald Gibbons (Evanston, Ill., 1985), pp. 105–106.

3. Toronto, 1979.
4. Minneapolis, 1987.
5. See Pierre Clastres, *Societies against the State* (New York, 1980).

14. In-Quest of Modernity

1. Michael Nerlich, *Ideology of Adventure,* Studies in Modern Consciousness 1100–1750, 2 vols. (Minneapolis: University of Minnesota Press, 1987).
2. The success of this analysis must have proved irresistible to Klaus Reichert, since he adopts it as his own in his recent book *Fortuna oder die Beständigkeit des Wechsels* (Frankfurt: Suhrkamp, 1985). There has been an unfortunate tendency on the part of some West German scholars not to acknowledge their debt to publications appearing in East Germany—perhaps in retaliation against similar practices there. Michael Nerlich teaches at the Technical University of West Berlin, but the German original of *The Ideology of Adventure* was published in East Berlin.
3. Michael Nerlich, *The Secret History of our Modernity,* CHS Occasional Papers, no. 3 (Minneapolis: University of Minnesota Center for Humanistic Studies, 1986).
4. This confusion leads to a number of aporias that are then elevated to central philosophical problems in modernity, such as the opposition of chance and necessity, where necessity represents the notion of a foundational essence disclosing itself in time, while chance marks the selection for the moments of such disclosure. This opposition then leads to such further philosophemes as the inexorable laws of history, the Hidden Hand, or the idea that human will, guided by reason, determines the course of history. These philosophemes are then sustained by the appropriate master narratives.
5. Michael Nerlich, "Der Kaufmann von Galvaïde, oder di Sünden des Chrestien-Forschung. Ein Essay über die Ursprünge der Moderne-Mentalität in der literarischen Gestaltung," *Lendemains* 45 (1987), 12–39. Once again, this is an extraordinarily persuasive essay that proceeds by showing *critically* the shortcomings of traditional scholarship on the subject, and then makes a case for its own reading of the text.
6. Jean-François Lyotard, "Rules and Paradoxes and Svelte Appendix," *Cultural Critique* 5 (Winter 1986–87), 215.

15. The Further Possibility of Knowledge

1. *Heterologies: Discourse on the Other,* trans. Brian Massumi (Minneapolis: University of Minnesota Press, 1986).

16. Emergent Literature and Comparative Literature

1. See Wlad Godzich and Nicholas Spadaccini, eds., *Literature among Discourses: The Spanish Golden Age* (Minneapolis: University of Minnesota Press, 1986).
2. I raise this matter not in order to point to a contradiction within current feminist concerns but rather to wonder at the wisdom of a strategy that takes the route of canon revision. Were this strategy to be successful, one of its consequences would be the reinforcement of national boundaries inasmuch as these would be further legitimated by women writers. One needs to ask oneself, though, what is the wisdom, if not the validity, of a selection that seeks to fit women writers within a canon previously defined on the basis of masculinist traits.
3. Werner P. Friederich, with the collaboration of David Henry Malone, *Outline of Comparative Literature from Dante Alighieri to Eugene O'Neill* (Chapel Hill: University of North Carolina Press, 1954).
4. See the writings of Pierre Bourdieu as a telling example of these problems.
5. For a discussion of these issues in the constitution of Comparative Literature, see Claudio Guillén, *Entre lo uno y lo diverso: Introducción a la literatura comparada* (Barcelona: Editorial Crítica, 1985), especially the first 121 pages.
6. Blacks, women, Chicanos, and native people have been writing for quite some time, of course, but the notion that their writings constitute distinctive traditions and bodies of literature is recent. It is in the name of this notion that the older writings are being reclaimed either from a forgotten past or from other constructs to which they seemed to belong.
7. Johann Gottfried von Herder, *Journal meiner Reise im Jahr 1769,* in his *Gesammelte Werke,* ed. B. Suphan (Berlin, 1807).
8. Martin Heidegger, "Die Zeit des Weltbildes," in *Holzwege* (Frankfurt: Vittorio Klostermann, 1950), pp. 69–104.
9. There is an attempt to recuperate this free-standingness by means of the purposiveness of nature, but a careful reading of the text shows that it is not accomplished. Such a reading cannot be attempted here. For a discussion of the third *Critique* along the lines suggested here, though with different objectives in view, see Samuel Weber's "The Foundering of Aesthetics: Thoughts on the Current State of Comparative Literature," in *The Comparative Perspective on Literature,* ed. Clayton Koelb and Susan Noakes (Ithaca: Cornell University Press, 1988), pp. 57–72.
10. This is not an ontological assertion, but it could lead to an inquiry along ontological lines, although this is not the course that will be followed here. The ontological line would have to come upon the discursive through the category of *deixis,* which cannot be touched upon here. See

Wlad Godzich and Jeffrey Kittay, *The Emergence of the Prose* (Minneapolis: University of Minnesota Press, 1987).

11. For a discussion of this notion, see Chapter 9 of this volume.

12. Ibid., pp. 27–53.

13. "Forms of Time and of the Chronotope in the Novel: Notes toward a Historical Poetics," in his *The Dialogic Imagination* (Austin: University of Texas Press, 1981), p. 85, n. 2.

14. I elaborate upon the relationship of society to givenness in Chapter 13 of this volume.

15. Ezekiel Mphahlele, *The African Image* (London: Faber and Faber, 1st ed., 1962; 2nd ed., 1974); *Voices in the Whirlwind* (London: Macmillan, 1972). I have profited from M. Chabani Manganyi, *Exiles and Homecomings: A Biography of Es'kia Mphahlele* (Johannesburg: Raven Press, 1983).

16. I follow South African antiapartheid usage in calling all nonwhite South Africans black, rejecting the apartheid-dictated distinction between "blacks," "coloreds," and "Indians."

17. Franz Fanon, *Peau noire, masques blancs* (1954, rpt. Paris: Maspéro, 1969).

18. White South African writers have struggled to the first part of this realization. In *July's People* (London: Jonathan Cape, 1981), Nadine Gordimer has her white heroine understand the black July only at the end of the novelette when he addresses her in his own language, which she does not understand. Similarly, André Brink in his earlier *A Dry White Season* (London: H. Allen, 1979) has his white hero understand that his effort to identify with Gordon Ngubene was scandalous to all blacks and that he must see himself as they see him in order to espouse their cause, as he wishes to do. Mphahlele comes upon this problem through a consideration of the modern African writer's relationship to tradition. He seeks to describe this relationship through temporal, structural, and eventually political terms (see *Voices in the Whirlwind*, esp. p. 144). The terminological lability points toward a discursive dimension that Mphahlele alludes to but does not develop in his critical writings, though it is very much in evidence in his fiction. For a superb thematization of this terminological mortality that ends in the identification of the discursive as a battleground, see the extraordinary novel by the Zairois writer M. a M. Ngal, *Giambatista Viko; ou, Le Viol du discours africain* (Lubumbashi: Alpha-Oméga, 1975).

19. Molefe Pheto, *And Night Fell* (London: Allison and Busby, 1983). Pheto is a good representative of the Black Consciousness movement.

20. Manuel Rui, "O Relógio," in *Sim Camarada!* (Luanda: União dos Escritores Angolanos, n.d.), pp. 19–55, but see the text for a discussion of publication data. The translation is mine.

21. There is reference to another watch in the story. It appears on the wrist of one of the two famous young heroes of the Angolan war of national liberation, as depicted in a revolutionary poster. The poster is clearly symbolic of revolutionary struggle, and the watch depicted therein overtly partakes of the symbolism. The *comandante* is reticent with respect to it; he begins by describing a watch not depicted on the poster, which belongs to the other hero, and ends by cutting the children's questions short. There is also a reference to his own watch, which is described in purely functional terms. The watch of the story is neither functional nor symbolic, that is, it is there neither to tell time nor to appeal to an immediately identifiable set of explanatory referents or signifieds. Its function is to force a textual circulation, the economy of which requires re-marking in the form of a critical discourse.

22. I use the term *interdiscursive* in the sense given to it by Jurgen Link, *Elementare Literatur und generative Diskursanalyse* (Munich: Wilhelm Fink, 1983), esp. pp. 48–72. Link analyzes a mode of social existence granted to semiotic objects in which they animate a number of diverse and frequently divergent discourses to constitute a space of interdiscursivity within which these objects are granted reality.

23. "A Linguistic Perspective on the Caribbean," in *Caribbean Contours,* ed. Sidney W. Mintz and Sally Price (Baltimore: Johns Hopkins University Press, 1985), pp. 155–179.

Credits

Introduction Part of this essay also appears in *The Materialities of Communication,* ed. Hans Ulrich Gumbrecht and Ludwig Pfeiffer (Stanford: Stanford University Press, forthcoming), reprinted by permission.

Chapter 1 Originally published as the Introduction to H. R. Jauss, *Aesthetic Experience and Literary Hermeneutics* (Minneapolis: University of Minnesota Press, 1982).

Chapter 2 Originally published as the Foreword to J. A. Maravall, *The Culture of the Baroque* (Minneapolis: University of Minnesota Press, 1986).

Chapter 3 Originally published in *Literature among Discourses,* ed. Wlad Godzich and Nicholas Spadaccini (Minneapolis: University of Minnesota Press, 1986).

Chapter 4 Originally published in Ross Chambers, *Story and Situation: Narrative Seduction and the Power of Fiction* (Minneapolis: University of Minnesota Press, 1984).

Chapter 5 Originally published in Thomas Pavel, *The Poetics of Plot: The Case of English Renaissance Drama* (Minneapolis: University of Minnesota Press, 1985).

Chapter 6 Originally published in Didier Coste, *Narrative as Communication* (Minneapolis: University of Minnesota Press, 1989).

Chapter 8 Originally published in Paul de Man, *Blindness and Insight: Essays in the Rhetoric of Contemporary Criticism,* 2nd ed., rev. (Minneapolis: University of Minnesota Press, 1983).

Chapter 9 Originally published as the Foreword to Paul de Man, *The Resistance to Theory* (Minneapolis: University of Minnesota Press, 1986).

Chapter 10 Originally published in Jonathan Arac, Wlad Godzich, and Wallace Martin, *The Yale Critics* (Minneapolis: University of Minnesota Press, 1983).

Chapter 11 Originally published in *On Signs,* ed. Marshall Blonsky (Baltimore: The Johns Hopkins University Press, 1985).

Chapter 12 Originally published in *Archéologie du Signe,* ed. Eugene Vance and Lucie Brind'Amour (Toronto: Pontifical Institute of Mediaeval Studies, 1983), pp. 45–61. Copyright 1983 by the Pontifical Institute of Mediaeval Studies, Toronto; reprinted by permission of the publisher.

Index